CLASSIC HARLEY BIG TWINS

CLASSIC HARLEY BIG TWINS
KNUCKLEHEAD, PANHEAD, SHOVELHEAD

BY GREG FIELD AND TOM MURPHY

This edition published in 2002 by MBI Publishing Company, Galtier Plaza, Suite 200, 380 Jackson Street, St. Paul, MN 55101-3885 USA

Harley-Davidson Knuckleheads © Greg Field, 1997
Harley-Davidson Panheads © Greg Field, 1995
Harley-Davidson Shovelhead © Tom Murphy, 1996

All rights reserved. With the exception of quoting brief passages for the purposes of review, no part of this publication may be reproduced without prior written permission from the Publisher.

The information in this book is true and complete to the best of our knowledge. All recommendations are made without any guarantee on the part of the author or Publisher, who also disclaim any liability incurred in connection with the use of this data or specific details.

We recognize that some words, model names and designations, for example, mentioned herein are the property of the trademark holder. We use them for identification purposes only. This is not an official publication.

MBI Publishing Company books are also available at discounts in bulk quantity for industrial or sales-promotional use. For details write to Special Sales Manager at Motorbooks International Wholesalers & Distributors, Galtier Plaza, Suite 200, 380 Jackson Street, St. Paul, MN 55101-3885 USA.

Library of Congress Cataloging-in-Publication Data Available

ISBN 0-7603-1356-3

Printed in China

On the front cover: The classic big twin engine appeared on Harley-Davidson motorcycles for decades, from the Flatheads of the late 1920s through the Shovelheads of the 1980s. *Jeff Hackett*

On the title page: The Superglide, introduced in 1971, brought a new look to Harley-Davidson big twins. *Jeff Hackett*

On the back cover, clockwise from top:
1939 EL Knucklehead *(Greg Field)*; 1969 FLH Electra Glide Shovelhead *(Jeff Hackett)*; 1950 Hydra-Glide Panhead *(Greg Field)*

On page 6: The instrument panel, shifter gate, and new tank emblem on a 1947 Knucklehead. *Greg Field*

On page 7: A 1939 EL, owned and restored by Eldon Brown. *Greg Field*

On page 8-9: The beginning and the end of the Knucklehead: Carmen Brown's 1936 EL and 1947 EL. *Greg Field*

On page 132: The handlebars and front end of a 1965 Electra-Glide. *Greg Field*

On page 133: Rob Carlson's 1950 Hydra-Glide. *Greg Field*

On page 134-135: The last of the spring-fork Panheads—Dave Monahan's 1949 FLP *(right)*—with the last of the Hydra-Glides—Dan Olberg's 1957 FLH *(left)*. *Greg Field*

On page 258: The original Shovelhead engine. *Harley-Davidson*

On page 259: The 1969 FLH Electra Glide, the last year of the "generator" motor. *Jeff Hackett*

CONTENTS

KNUCKLEHEADS

	ACKNOWLEDGMENTS	11
CHAPTER 1	1936: THE FIRST KNUCKLEHEAD	13
CHAPTER 2	1937–1939: THE KNUCKLEHEAD TAKES OVER	53
CHAPTER 3	1940–1946: THE BIG-PORT ENGINE	87
CHAPTER 4	1947: THE LAST KNUCKLEHEAD	119

PANHEADS

	ACKNOWLEDGMENTS	136
	INTRODUCTION	137
CHAPTER 1	1948: SPRINGER PANHEADS	140
CHAPTER 2	1949–1957: THE HYDRA-GLIDE	166
CHAPTER 3	1958–1964: THE DUO-GLIDE	210
CHAPTER 4	1965: THE ELECTRA-GLIDE	242
APPENDIX	1948–1965: HARLEY-DAVIDSON BIG TWIN OPTIONS GROUP	253

SHOVELHEADS

	ACKNOWLEDGMENTS	260
	INTRODUCTION	261
PART 1	THE 1966–1984 FL SERIES	272
	ELECTRA GLIDE	
	TOUR GLIDE	
PART 2	THE 1971–1984 FX SERIES	336
	SUPER GLIDE	
	LOW RIDER	
	FAT BOB	
	WIDE GLIDE	
	STURGIS	
	DISC GLIDE	
	FXR AND FXRS	
	SPORT GLIDE	
INDEX		382

KNUCKLEHEADS

BY GREG FIELD

Acknowledgments

I never could have imagined what a monumental project this book turned out to be. Without the help and encouragement of dozens of individuals, it would still be just a bunch of disorganized rantings on my computer's hard drive, so I offer my thanks to the following:

First, to the foremost scholars of the 1936 Knucklehead, who were so helpful in my Quixotic quest to tabulate the zillion-and-one changes made to the Knucklehead that first year. Because of the effort of these men, Chapter 1 of the Knucklehead saga is much more complete: Jerry Hatfield, Chris Haynes, Casey Hoekstra, Doug Leikala, and Gerry Lyons.

For letting me photograph their fine Knuckleheads: Dave Banks, Carman Brown, Eldon Brown, Rob Carlson, and Gary Strom of Kokesh Motorcycles (Spring Lake Park, Minnesota), Jeff Coffman of Jeff's American Classics (Dundee, Oregon), Jim "Aard" Conklin, Dave DeMartini of Northwest Custom Cycle (Snoqualmie, Washington), Valentino "Vick" Domowicz, Elmer Ehnes, Larry Engesether, Farmer Fred, Mike Golembiewski, Ron Lacey, Dave Monahan, Adolph Ogar, and Wayne Pierce, Sr. and Wayne Pierce, Jr., of Pierce's Harley-Davidson in DeKalb, Illinois.

For sharing their knowledge, time, photographs, or for helping me to find motorcycles to photograph: Rick Connor, Peter Eagan, George "Geo" Edwards of St. Paul Harley-Davidson (St. Paul, Minnesota), Brian Holden of the Deeley Motorcycle Museum (Vancouver, British Columbia), Rick "Chintzy" Krajewski of Competition Cycle (Milwaukee, Wisconsin), Dave Minerva, Gary Nelson, Bruce Palmer, Jerry Renner, and Steve Schlessinger at Jerry's House of Harley (Milwaukee, Wisconsin), Scott Rowinski, Carmen Tom of Downtown Harley-Davidson (Seattle, Washington), and Herbert Wagner.

For helping me with research material and photographs, the Harley-Davidson Motor Company, and in particular, Dr. Martin Jack Rosenblum and Susan Fariss in the archives and Ray Schlee in the restoration shop. Black-and-white photographs are courtesy of the Harley-Davidson Motor Company archives. All rights reserved.

For long-term encouragement and support to my parents, Laurie and Larry, my brothers and sisters, Scot, Shawn, Dawn, and Heather, and my good friends Owen Herman, Tim Lien, Tom Samuelsen, John Scharf, and Joe Sova.

For putting me up and putting up with me while in Milwaukee: Annie and Tobie Golembiewski; Ray, Carol, Becky, Katie, Tracy, Vicky, and Nicole Karshna; Ed and Jean Kwiecinski; and Jeff and Jackie Ciardo.

For tangible and intangible support to Keith, Jerry, Peter, Dustin, and Steve at the fabulous, motorcycle-friendly Buckaroo in Seattle.

For tolerating my "fluid" deadlines, editor Zack Miller and the rest of the staff of Motorbooks International.

Finally, to Jeni, who put up with so much obsessive behavior and gave up so much so that I had time to finish this manuscript.

If I have forgotten anyone, I hope they will forgive the oversight.

Knuckleheads at play. Three or four Knuckles are usually ridden in each show by the famous Seattle Cossacks precision motorcycle drill team. Yes, they really can hold the pyramid through a turn to reverse direction within the width of a street, and yes, that Cossack at the very back is doing a handstand between the bikes.

CHAPTER ONE

1936

The First Knucklehead

History is not often made in a ballroom, but it was on November 25, 1935. On that day, at the annual dealers' convention—after years of rumors and sporadic sightings—the assembled throng of Harley-Davidson dealers was treated to a vision of their future, the company's future. When the curtains parted, there stood parked upon the stage of the Green Room in Milwaukee's Shroeder Hotel a new motorcycle so different, so right, so inspired that the "eager, anxious crowd [leapt] to its feet and burst into prolonged cheers," according to the account in the January 1936 issue of *The Enthusiast*. Standing beside the new "61 OHV," chief engineer William S. Harley and "Hap" Jameson soaked up the adulation for their new baby. It was the day the legend began.

Dave Banks' EL, the 374th built, has the round tin covers on the rocker-shaft ends. Sometime during the production run, these covers were replaced by large chrome-plated hex nuts. Also during the production run, an air fitting was added to the front rocker housing that allowed the rider to clear clogged oil return lines from the valve-spring covers by applying air pressure to the nipple. Banks' bike was never retrofitted with the nipple. His bike also has the "notched" gear case cover used on early machines. Note the hole in the surface of the gear case, just aft of the brake pedal. Shown in the hole is one of the two rivets used to attach the breather baffle to the inside of the case. The holes for these rivets were sometimes leaded over. Years of engine vibration sometimes makes the lead plugs pop out, as these have.

After impatiently enduring the presentation of the whole 1936 line-up, the dealers rushed the stage to get a closer look at the new flagship of the line, Harley's new "little Big Twin." The machine before them was a masterpiece from any angle, a bold fusion of art deco and streamlining that looked both fast and mannered. More important, it looked like a *motorcycle*, as if it had been created that way, rather than—having slowly evolved from the first motorized bicycles that H-D had built. In fact, the only throwback to that heritage seemed to be the bicycle pedal on the kickstarter. The more the dealers looked, the more they appreciated it.

Symmetry defined the new machine. Twin gas tanks straddled the frame's backbone tube, each with its own chrome-plated filler cap and petcock. Bridging the gap between the tanks was the new instrument panel with a large, integral, 100-mile-per-hour speedometer (placed front and center, right where it would be easiest to read), an ammeter, an oil-pressure indicator, and the ignition switch. Twin downtubes swept down and back from the steering head to the rear axle clips. The sweeping V of the cylinders, highlighted on the right side by the gleaming pushrod covers, framed the dramatically slash-cut chrome-plated air-intake horn. And those cylinders were topped by polished aluminum rocker housings, each with two round, chrome-plated covers over the ends of the rocker shafts. It was everything the rumors said—and everything the dealers had hoped it would be. As far as the dealers were concerned, this was the Eighth Day, and creation was complete.

Enthusiasm for the new model spilled over to the banquet that evening, and after soaking up copious amounts of the famous Milwaukee "suds," some of the dealers got a little out of

An early-1936 61 owned and restored by Carman Brown of British Columbia. The 1936 61 introduced the most enduring aesthetics of any motorcycle. From end to end, it was a masterpiece, and elements of its style are evident on all the Harley-Davidson Big Twins that followed. This was no beefed-up motorized bicycle. This, at last, was a motorcycle. The only throwback to its older siblings was the bicycle-style kickstarter pedal.

control. During the turkey dinner, "two-gun 'Cactus Bill' Kennedy, a tough hombre from Phoenix, Arizona, [got] so excited . . . he [drew] a bead on the crystal chandelier, let out a blood-curdling yip-eee . . . and emptie[d] his six-gun . . . some of the more sedate dealers pass[ed] out . . . and the turkey on Bill's plate actually turn[ed] pale," according to *The Enthusiast*.

In the following days, the dealers toured the factory and attended sales seminars. History has not recorded whether H-D gave their dealers any further information on when the new model would be ready, but a curious thing happened after the curtain was drawn closed on the Green Room's stage: The most exciting new American motorcycle in over a decade disappeared as completely as if it had never been there at all. When Harley's 1936 models were announced to the public in the January 1936 issue of *The Enthusiast*, the new model—a machine that was truly innovative enough to warrant a good bit of hype—was not shown or mentioned at all. In fact, the only clue to its existence was in a small photograph of the assembled dealers at the November convention. Way in the background of the photo, appearing so small that you'd have to know it was there to make it out, was the new machine. But the caption for the photo made no mention of it, nor did the magazine's coverage of the convention. And so it would go, far into the machine's first year of production.

To the Harley-Davidson Motor Company, the enthusiasm of its dealers was welcome, but it also presented a quandary. After more than four years of spending heavily to develop the OHV, Harley was eager to begin recouping its costs, but knew well what would happen if the new model was released before it was ready. Still smarting from the disastrous introduction of its last new Big Twin, the company decided on a more cautious approach this time.

Roots of the 61

The company's past had been built on the foundation of its early intake-over-exhaust, or F-head, engines that gave it such success from 1903 to 1929. The company's present was being built on the newer side-valve, or flathead, engines that were introduced in 1929 (45-ci Series D) and 1930 (74-ci Series V), but these models proved to be disappointing in many ways. Initially, both proved to be trouble-prone, especially the V series, which had so many problems that the production line was shut down to fix them after a flood of dealer complaints gave H-D no other choice. To its credit, the company stood by its product, redesigning many parts to fix the problems on the production line and sending free kits to fix those bikes already on the streets. But the initial blunder had eroded confidence among the company's dealers and customers. They had to wonder: was it an honest mistake, or was Harley-Davidson inept and past its prime?

By 1931, most of the inadequacies of the first V-series machines had been fixed. Still, Harley's side-valve models were somewhat disappointing because they were not that much better than the old F-heads they replaced. Worse yet, they suffered in performance compared to the equivalent Indian models. In short, the Harley side-valves were decent motorcycles, but they weren't exciting motorcycles, certainly not exciting enough to win new customers—especially when times were so hard for so many. The company needed something radically new on which to build its future.

The Great Depression Begins

Motorcycle sales had been up and down for many years, but the trend was definitely down in 1931. In contrast, the trend had been up during the boom years of 1927–1929 when the side-valves were introduced. In 1929, H-D sold 23,989 machines, the largest number sold since 1918, when sales of military bikes inflated annual sales to 26,708. Then came "Black Thursday," October 24, 1929, when the stock market collapse began. On October 29, "Black Tuesday," the real crash came. Stock prices went into a death spin. In one week, $16 billion evaporated.

Reverberations from the crash spread slowly across America in 1930. In the early part of the year, the stock market began to recover. And those with wealth remained optimistic. Henry Ford, who had sold his one-millionth Model A the year before, opined that, "These really are good times but

This photo shows what may be the actual machine that met with such enthusiasm at the dealers' meeting at the Schroeder Hotel in Milwaukee, Wisconsin, on November 25, 1935—serial number 35E1002. This machine and the others like it (there were at least three, and there were thought to be as many as a dozen) are commonly referred to as the "pre-production" 1936 61s. It is not known when they were built, but certainly before October 17, 1935, when this photo was processed. Because it wears a 1935 serial number, it may in fact be a demonstrator model built when the bike was still slated for a late-1935 introduction. The valve springs are visible behind the oil fittings on the rocker housings, denoting the absence of valve-spring covers on the preproduction machines. A photo of oil-drenched 35E1003 that follows graphically shows how necessary the valve-spring covers were. Note the stamping "Burgess Battery Co." on the side of the muffler. This name is not commonly seen on the sides of production mufflers, but was sometimes stamped on the underside of the muffler, in much smaller letters. Also note the round, chrome-plated covers over the ends of the rocker-arm shafts on the aluminum rocker housings. *Copyright Harley-Davidson Michigan, Inc.*

only a few know it." Men of more modest means really did know better, and they were not in a spending mood, especially for something as frivolous as a motorcycle. Then came the final nail in the economic coffin: Congress passed the Smoot-Hawley Act in June, which sharply raised tariffs. In retaliation, other countries raised theirs. Unemployment rose further, and H-D's export sales, which had been as much as 40 percent of the company's business during the 1920s, dropped off sharply. When the results were tallied at the end of the fiscal year, Harley-Davidson's overall sales for the year dropped by nearly 25 percent, to 18,036. The Great Depression had begun.

Bill Harley's "Sump Oiler"

Which brings us back to 1931, a desperate and historic year. As alluded to earlier, the trend was down in 1931. Way down. Sales fell to 10,407, slightly more than half the number sold the previous year and the lowest total since the 3,853 sold in 1912! Clearly, the company was in trouble. Salaries had been cut, and hours had been slashed for nonsalaried workers. But despite the gloom, William S. Harley never gave up. Instead, in a flash of inspiration worthy of the great Thomas Edison, he proposed development of the motorcycle that would ultimately save the company—an OHV twin with a recirculating oil system, referred to as the "sump oiler." The board of directors gave its approval, and work began on what would ultimately be the 61 OHV. And here's where our story really begins.

If 1931 was a year of hardship—and it was—1932 was worse. The Dow dropped below 50. Over two million Americans wandered the country as vagrants. Unemployment rose to 24 percent overall, but reached 50 percent in some cities. Along with it, the suicide rate rose 30 percent.

Hard times grew worse in Milwaukee, too. Harley-Davidson workers were laid off, and the company's four founders imposed on themselves a 50 percent pay cut. Production fell to 7,218, a reduction of 30 percent compared to the previous year. But a new source of income was in the offing. The board of directors was approached by its Japanese importer and the Sankyo industrial firm with an offer to purchase a

Preproduction machine 35E1003 partially disassembled to show the new top end that made the 61 so exciting—and so troublesome. This preproduction machine was probably one of the unmarked road-test machines, as implied by the lack of tank decals. The cylinder heads lack provision for valve-spring covers, accounting for the oil-spattered appearance of the machine. The head on the right shows raised casting numbers on the bottom fin (casting numbers were usually recessed on production heads). The oil tank shows evidence that an earlier version of the oil tank had fittings farther out to the side. Note the welded-in plug on the side of the tank (there is another on the other side of the tank). Tanks with these plugs made it onto some production 1936 61s. The plug was leaded smooth before painting to hide the repair. Note the "notched" gear-case cover, a feature that also made it onto the early production machines. Note also the two pinstripes on the fenders. Finally, note the slash-cut, single-butted joint on the frame downtubes and the lack of sidecar lugs. This photo was processed on November 14, 1935, just over a week before the 61's debut at the dealers' convention. *Copyright Harley-Davidson Michigan, Inc.*

license to manufacture H-D motorcycles in Japan—an offer that was ultimately accepted. As bad as things got, however, work continued on the OHV.

Things really bottomed out in Milwaukee in 1933. Harley sales fell by almost half again, to just 3,703 machines. But things also began looking up. Prototype parts for the new 61 were cast and assembled into working engines. Bench tests were promising, so the board agreed to continue development and scheduled the OHV to be their lead model for 1935. The board also approved the sale of a manufacturing license to the Sankyo firm in Japan. Sankyo began setting up to produce the Harley-Davidson VL under the trade name Rikuo.

The Depression slowly began to ease its grip on the economy in 1934. The Dow rose only slightly, but the gross national product (GNP) rose 17 percent (versus shrinking by 4 percent in 1933). Harley sales nearly tripled for 1934, to 11,212 units—aided by the late introduction of 1935 models, which occurred in December, rather than in September. Unfortunately, development of the 61 OHV had fallen behind schedule, so when the 1935 models were announced, the 61 OHV was not among them. The first rideable machine had been assembled and tested in the spring and summer of 1934, but nagging problems with oil leaks prevented finalization of the design in time for 1935 production. The board of directors delayed introduction of the new model until 1936.

The United States' recovery accelerated somewhat in 1935. The Dow rose to a high of 144. The GNP grew 9 percent, and unemployment declined to near 20 percent.

In Milwaukee, Harley-Davidson's OHV was nearing completion in the summer of 1935. According to board of directors minutes unearthed by author Jerry Hatfield and presented in his book, *Inside Harley-Davidson*, there was even discussion of building 200 61s in the summer of 1935 but the sales department was opposed to the idea because it feared release of the 61 would adversely affect sales of the remaining 1935 side-valve Big Twins.

At the May meeting, the board discussed releasing the 61 in September 1935 or January 1936, even though continuing problems with chain and brake-lining wear caused some members of the board to suggest that the 61 project be stopped entirely. Company president Walter Davidson suggested that a different combination of sprockets might reduce chain wear. Davidson's suggestions apparently resulted in changing the transmission sprocket from 19 teeth to 22 teeth and the rear sprocket from 45 teeth to 51 teeth (based on data in the book *1930 to 1949 Models: Operation, Maintenance, and Specifications*, published by Harley-Davidson), which resulted in enough of an improvement that the board resolved that it would "probably go ahead with the job" at its June meeting. Although it is not recorded in the minutes, continuing difficulties with the 61 may have resulted in the decision to push back the new-model introduction into the winter for the second year in a row.

Oil Control

The big problem that remained to be solved was control of oil to and from the rocker arms and valves. On the prototype 61s, the valves, valve springs, and rocker arms were left uncovered. Many other OHV machines of the day also had uncovered mechanisms, but the rockers on those machines were typically lubricated by grease that was periodically resupplied through a grease fitting. Not so on the 61 engine; its signature feature, the OHV system, was lubricated by oil bled off from the engine's other great, new feature, its recirculating oil system. I say "bled off" because any lubricating oil supplied to lubricate the rockers, valves, and springs eventually ended up on the outside of the engine. And once the oil escaped the valve mechanism, the slipstream quickly carried it back to splatter all over rider and machine.

Approval for Production

As summer turned to fall, the solution to the oiling problem apparently proved elusive. Unfortunately, the new-model introduction date was fast approaching, and having already delayed the 61 OHV's introduction by a year, the company's managers were loathe to delay it any longer. At the October board meeting, the 61 was officially added to the line-up for 1936, and production was set for 1,600 units. No one knows whether approval came as a result of a long-sought solution to the oil-control problem or whether was made the decision with crossed fingers, trusting that luck and Bill Harley's design acumen would reveal a solution to the problem before full-scale production began. Evidence suggests the latter because photographs that were developed as late as December show no evidence of valve-spring enclosures on the 61.

Preproduction 61 OHVs

Consensus among many 1936 61 aficianados is that Harley-Davidson built a dozen or so preproduction machines for continued testing, for presentation at the convention and

Front and center on the skull-face instrument panel is a Stewart-Warner speedometer with a 100-mile-per-hour face, which was used only for 1936 on the 61. For 1937, the speedometer was calibrated up to 120 miles per hour because a well-tuned EL could come very close to outrunning the 100-mile-per-hour speedometer. The dice gearshift knob was included in the Deluxe Solo Group or was available for 60 cents at the time the bike was ordered.

for photography. No records exist to tell how many were built or when they were built, but we can conclude a few things from existing photographs: at least two 61s were built with 1935 serial numbers; at least one of these was extensively road-tested; and the road-test machine leaked a lot of oil because it still lacked covers for the rockers and valves.

The first conclusion is based on photos that show the motorcycles serial numbered 35E1002 and 35E1003. The second conclusion is supported by the engine-teardown photo of 35E1003, which shows the bike coated in grime and oil, and its kickstarter pedal shows wear from use and damage from a light spill or tip-over. The same photo supports the third conclusion, clearly showing that no valve-spring covers were used on these machines.

These photos also provide the only reliable time reference that is available to date the preproduction bikes. The photos of 35E1002 were processed October 17, 1935. The photos of the oil-soaked 35E1003 were processed on November 14, 1935, and were described as "motor close-ups for Joe Ryan." (Joe Ryan was H-D's service manager.) From this we can conclude that these preproduction machines had been completed no later than mid-October, more than a month before the 61's introduction at the convention.

The 61s serialed 35E1002 and 35E1003 are considered preproduction machines rather than experimental prototypes because their serial numbers are in the form of production serial numbers, rather than the form of experimental serial numbers (EX 3, for example). The serial numbers on these machines could also be taken as further proof that the 61 had been originally planned for the 1935 model line. The 61 OHV displayed at the November dealers' convention was likely one of these preproduction machines. Ultimately, these machines were probably scrapped.

Another British Columbian 1936 61, this one owned by Dave Banks. The Venetian Blue and Croydon Cream paint scheme shown was probably the most popular of its day, and it still is today, judging by the high percentage of machines that are restored to these colors.

Stealth Introduction

In the first dealer news bulletin following the dealers' convention—dated December 2, 1935—Harley-Davidson issued its first printed words about the 61 to make it clear to all that the new model was not yet ready and that it might not be for some time:

> For several years rumors have been current all over the country about a new twin that Harley-Davidson was developing and would have on the market any day. The most incredulous and many times positively amusing fabrications have been spread about this model. True, our engineering staff has been working for a long time on a model of new and original design and their efforts have finally reached the stage where such a motorcycle, a 61 cubic inch overhead, was shown to dealers in attendance at the National Dealers' Convention. However, production on this model will necessarily be extremely limited and we are therefore in no position to make a public announcement at this time.... Under no circumstances should this model be ordered as a demonstrator!

But as we shall soon see, even as the company was admonishing its dealers not to order OHV demonstrators, the assembly line was being readied for their production. Moreover, the new model had already been listed in a specification sheet for standard and special equipment groups dated December 1, 1935.

Pilot Production

Clearly, the company remained uneasy about the 61 despite dealer enthusiasm. One of the things that made them uneasy was undoubtedly the lack of an effective means to return oil from the valve-gear to the engine. Despite their unease—according to Hatfield's *Inside Harley-Davidson*, based on the minutes of the December 16, 1935, board of directors meeting—company managers had earlier made the decision to press on, building "10 or 15" pilot production bikes by mid-December to "check the flow of parts through the various buildup levels." The famous photo of the four company founders with what was reputed to be the first production 61 OHV was developed on December 12, 1935, and shows the founders with one of these pilot production bikes. No documentation exists to prove when the top-end oil-control problem was solved—which it eventually was, through introduction of cup-type valve-spring covers with oil return lines—but it was after the build date of the pilot production 61 pictured with the company founders because that machine definitely does not have the valve-spring covers.

A view inside the gear case showing how the cams, breather valve, and ignition circuit breaker are timed and how engine power is routed to power the oil pump and generator. *Copyright Harley-Davidson Michigan, Inc.*

The disassembled clutch on 35E1003, showing the major parts: splined drum, splined hub, pressure-plate/drive-plate assembly with springs, fiber discs with splines on their outside diameter, and steel discs with splines on their inside diameter. On production 1936 clutches, a "humped" steel disc was fitted in place of one of the flat steel discs in an effort to reduce rattle when the clutch was disengaged. This style of clutch was used through 1940. This early-style inner primary cover lacks the oil drain fitted to later covers because the oil drain is in the outer cover on early machines. *Copyright Harley-Davidson Michigan, Inc.*

After assembly, the first pilot-production machines were then turned over to the engineering department for road-testing. Apparently, problems were experienced with the motors because, "Most of these first production 61 OHVs were returned to the motor assembly section for reworking," according to Hatfield. The early production-line problems were apparently resolved by the December 16 date of the board meeting because, continued Hatfield, "Most reworking was by this time sufficiently infrequent and minor to be accomplished on the assembly line."

Unfortunately, we don't know what happened to the "10 or 15" pilot production machines. It is possible, as other authors have speculated, that some were sent to favored dealers for independent road-testing. If so, these bikes may have been the source of the much-repeated stories of "laps full of oil" after even a short test ride, since the pilot production machines almost certainly did not have the valve-spring covers. We know that these bikes were built in calendar-year 1935, so the engine cases *should* have been stamped with line-bore numbers having a "35" prefix (35-1234). None of the 1936 61 specialists I have spoken to have ever seen cases so marked—which, of course, proves nothing, but hints that either the bikes were scrapped after testing, that they have all disappeared, or that they were marked with "36" line-bore numbers.

With the assembly-line procedures debugged, it would seem that H-D was potentially ready to begin full-scale production of the 61 OHV, but did it? Along with this question, many others come to mind. Did pilot production just gradually ramp up after the December 16, 1935, meeting to become regular production of demonstrator models for the dealers, or was production delayed while further changes were instituted to the 61 design or assembly-line procedures? If there was a delay, was it caused by the need to solve the rocker-oiling problem? Was the rocker-oiling problem even solved by the time production began? Unfortunately, documentation to conclusively answer these questions has yet to surface, but a few clues to the time line for production were found in the Harley-Davidson archives, which I'll get to in due course.

Given their lack of experience with production OHV systems and the truly wretched economy at the time, Harley-Davidson took a big gamble in introducing its new OHV Big Twin. The enthusiastic reception the motorcycle had received at the dealers' convention had to ease Harley-Davidson's fears somewhat, but only the sales year to come would really reveal whether American riders would pay extra for the new engine design—and whether the new engine was really ready for those who would.

Window to the World, 1936

The withering effects of the Great Depression and the Dust Bowl continued in 1936, but in the United States the New Deal was really starting to seem like a better deal. For the third straight year, unemployment was down, although at 16.9 percent it was still shockingly high by modern standards. And the Dow and GNP were both up for the second year in a row. In an overwhelming vote of confidence for his policies, President Roosevelt was reelected in an electoral landslide.

Around the world, the Fascists began to march. Francisco Franco led his army against the republic for control of Spain. Germany and Italy joined in to test their burgeoning military might and help out their ally. And Mussolini's Italian Army continued its march across Ethiopia, occupying all of that country before the year was out.

After claiming dictatorial power in 1933, rubbing out his competitors in 1934, and instituting a state program for breeding perfect Aryans in 1935, Hitler began to reclaim lands Germany lost in the Treaty of Versailles.

Hitler also sought conquest in the world of sports, turning the 1936 Olympics, held in Berlin, into a shameless showpiece for Aryan superiority. Despite the best efforts of the "superior" elite of Aryan manhood, the "inferior" African-American athletes on the U.S. team dominated the prestigious track-and-field events.

Dale Carnegie's *How to Win Friends and Influence People* became a best-seller by simply telling people how to succeed by getting along with others. Apparently Hitler did not buy a copy.

If any two groups needed Carnegie's book, it was the United Auto Workers and the automotive industry management. Strained relations between them broke down, resulting in crippling strikes at a Fisher Body plant, at Midland Steel, and at Kelsey-Hayes Wheel. Fortunately, Harley-Davidson had an adequate supply of rims before the Kelsey-Hayes strike.

Production Begins

One of the great mysteries of the enigma that is the 1936 Knucklehead is when production really began. Some say it began in December 1935. Others maintain that it wasn't until March or April. The principals who had firsthand knowledge are all dead, and definitive documentation from within the Harley-Davidson archives has yet to surface. If it is there, I couldn't find it on two separate research visits, so I don't have the definitive answer—but I have uncovered some interesting facts that shed some light on the timeline.

Remember that admonition in the December 2, 1935, dealer news bulletin that "Under no circumstances should this model be ordered as a demonstrator!"? Well, just over one month later, the factory had obviously taken orders for the demonstrators and was well on its way to filling those orders. The January 27, 1936, dealer news bulletin trumpeted the headline "61 Overhead Twin Demonstrators Now Being Shipped!" The article beneath the headline went on to say, "Demonstrator orders for the new 61 Overhead Valve Twin are moving out at a healthy rate and production in the factory is gradually picking up." Of course, "healthy rate" and "picking up" are not very illuminating, but they do indicate that 61s were definitely rolling off the production line by the deadline date for the bulletin.

And the bikes shipped on or near that deadline date were obviously not the first machines out the door because that same news bulletin went on to say, "Reports from dealers who have already received their 61 demonstrators indicate that the new model is proving a real sensation and is exceeding all expectations."

Even more revealing is an actual report from a dealer, Kemper Motorcycle Company in Chicago, Illinois, because it reveals that the factory was by this time (late January) allowing the dealers to sell, or at least take orders for, the new 61s: "Just got in the 61 floor sample this A.M. Everybody likes it. Sold one today and expect two more to trade."

We also know that at least one 61 OHV had been shipped as far west as Portland, Oregon, on or before February 2, 1936, because a rider named "Butch" Quirk used a sidecar-equipped 61 to win the 350-mile endurance run sponsored by the Rose City Motorcycle Club, as reported in the March issue of *The Enthusiast*. Surely, this bike was shipped from Milwaukee no later than the last week of January.

The February 10, 1936, bulletin showed that favorable reports had been returned to the factory from as far away as California and Texas. The firm of Graves & Chubbuck in Pasadena wrote: "There never has been a motorcycle put out that has set the boys to talking so much as the 61. The news of its arrival was broadcast by the boys from the treetops, and five hours after its setup there was 120 miles on the speedometer." From Fort Worth came the report that "this is the first machine that no rider or prospect could find fault with, as they have nothing but praise for it." These bikes must also have left Milwaukee no later than the end of January.

The next issue of the news bulletin lends some credence to the notion that the demonstrators were really just the first production configuration machines and implies that regular series production began some time around mid-February. A headline in the February 24 bulletin announced, "We Are Surging Right Along on the 61!" The article beneath said, "Demonstrator orders for the 61 have all been taken care of and we are now making satisfactory deliveries on dealers' subsequent orders."

Apparently, the factory was not yet mobbed with orders by the deadline for the February 24 issue, so at long last the factory began prodding their dealers to get out and sell the 61 because the much-anticipated new model was at last available. The article continued: "We can't guarantee this state of affairs will continue indefinitely, but right now there is no very long delay in getting out orders. If some of your good customers have been under the impression that they couldn't get their 61's for a long time, better tip them off that if they place their order right away, they can get their machine before long. A little later when the remarkable qualities of the new model are better appreciated and when the real riding season opens, there may be considerable delay in getting deliveries."

About the time the dealer bulletin exhorted the dealers to push the 61 OHV, the new bike received its first official mention in the national press when it was shown in an ad in the March 1936 issue of *The Motorcyclist*. Even in this first ad, however, the 61 was given no special mention, let alone hype. Earlier, in January, the company had not even shown or mentioned the 61 in the new-model introduction issue of *The*

Enthusiast. In fact Harley-Davidson would make no official mention of the 61 in their own magazine until June 1936.

So where does this leave us? We still can't say for sure exactly when series production began, but it probably started slowly in early January and began ramping up from there until late February, when the factory was able to crank out new bikes at least as fast as the orders came in. By that time, the factory was confident enough about the 61 that it was asking its dealers to actually sell it, but it was still hesitant to give it the usual sales hype. The first hint of sales hype came in the June issue of *The Enthusiast*, which featured a back-cover ad for the 61.

Another big mystery is the exact configuration of the demonstrators. Were they regular production machines? Did they have the valve-spring covers? The glowing reports would seem to indicate that they did, for how could a rider not fault a motorcycle that slung as much oil as the 61s without valve enclosures are reputed to have?

Then comes the mystery of configuration of the first production models—indeed, the configuration of all the 1936 61s. During the production year, many parts of the 1936 61 were changed in subtle and not-so-subtle ways to improve the function of the machine and to fix problems that became apparent as the bikes were used in competition and on the street. A complete list of all the changes for 1936, with even the most cursory description of the parts and what was changed, could easily fill a book this size. Since the scope of this book is much broader, covering all the Knuckleheads from 1936 through 1947, the discussion presented here is incomplete, by necessity, and will concentrate on the changes that are obvious or important in describing later model Knuckleheads.

1936 Models and Prices

Although the new OHV model did not appear in the January issue of *The Enthusiast*, which introduced the rest of the 1936 line, order blanks featuring the model had been quietly sent to dealers. The order blanks listed the OHV Big Twin in three versions: the high-compression 36EL Special Sport Solo, the medium-compression 36E Solo, and the medium compression 36ES twin with sidecar gearing. All were listed at a retail price of $380, but this was without such essential equipment as a jiffy stand or a steering damper. These items were available at additional cost or as part of the option groups. Interestingly, a Model 36EM "Twin Motor For Midget Car Racing" is listed in the back of *The Legend Begins*, published by H-D.

Wheelbase for all models was 59.5 inches and weight was 515 pounds. The main differences between the models was in compression ratio and gearing. The EL engine was fitted with high-compression pistons for a compression ratio of 6.5:1 and a power output of 40 horsepower at 3,800 rpm, according to Harley-Davidson specifications. The E and ES engines were fitted with medium-compression pistons for a compression ratio of 5.66:1 and a power output of 37 horsepower at 3,800 rpm. Interestingly, the compression ratios for the E and ES are listed as being the same, even though the

Here's 35E1003 again, this time with its rear wheel removed. The wheel hub is fastened to the brake drum by lug bolts. Each lug has a safety-wire hole. Lugs with safety-wire holes were fitted for at least part of the 1936 production run. The 7 1/4-inch rear brake shown was used on the 1936 61 only. The type of rear mount for the rear chain guard shown did not make it into production. It did not even make it onto one of the other preproduction machines, 35E1002, which is shown later in this chapter with the type of mount used on the production machines. *Copyright Harley-Davidson Michigan, Inc.*

ES was fitted with 0.050-inch compression plates that should have lowered both compression ratio and power. The E and EL were fitted with a 23-tooth engine sprocket, a 37-tooth clutch sprocket, a 22-tooth transmission sprocket, and a 51-tooth rear sprocket, for an overall ratio of 1:3.73. On the ES with a four-speed transmission, the engine sprocket was changed to 20 teeth, for an overall ratio of 1:4.29. On the ES with the three-speed-with-reverse transmission, the engine sprocket was changed to 19 teeth, for an overall ratio of 1:4.51.

A four-speed transmission was standard, but a three-speed transmission could be ordered at no additional cost. For $5.00 extra, the three-speed-with-reverse transmission could be ordered. Early in the year, only standard handlebars

RIGHT: A 1936 EL that was repainted, chromed, and accessorized by its owners over the years. It is now owned by Jeff Coffman of Jeff's American Classics of Dundee, Oregon.

A close-up of the 1936-only shifter gate showing the shift pattern: 1-neutral-2-3-4, from front to back. For 1936 only, the shifter-gate slot is smooth sided, without notched detents to hold the lever in gear position. Rather, the tapered top of the spring-loaded plunger shown through the slot, around the shift lever's shaft, engages scallops along the edge of the slot. With this gate, the shifting motion is straight forward or back, no jockeying to the side to clear notched detents.

were available, but Speedster handlebars became available March 3, 1936.

Two option groups for solo machines were offered. The Standard Solo Group included the front safety guard, steering damper, ride control, and jiffy stand; it listed for $14.00. The Deluxe Solo Group included all the items in the standard group, plus the Chrome Plate Group (chrome handlebars, headlamp, kickstarter lever, muffler [but not the muffler clamps], exhaust pipes, clutch inspection cover, and safety guard), fender lamp, stop light, dice shift knob, foot-pedal rubbers, and saddlebags and hangers; it listed for $34.50.

Styling

Production 1936 61 OHVs carried on the same sleek styling that had been so obviously right on the 1935-serialed 61 shown at the dealers' convention. The new machine featured smooth, streamlined, almost organic lines from front to rear. Perhaps more than any other feature, the styling of the 1936 61 shaped the future of Harley-Davidson. For model year 1937, all H-D models from the 45 to the 80 were updated to look like the 61. The basics of this style carried through on all H-D Big Twins through the mid-1960s. It became more and more muted in the 1970s, but was revived almost in its entirety on the Heritage Softails beginning in the mid-1980s, and helped spark a second renaissance for the company. In the 1990s, the styling cues set on the 1936 61, which proved once again so popular for Harley-Davidson, were also imitated by the Japanese manufacturers on their increasingly Harley-like and popular big cruisers.

Gas Tanks

The twin, saddle-type gas tanks were the most obvious styling improvement on the new OHV models. Gone were the boxy lines of the earlier Harley-Davidson Big Twin tanks, replaced by rounded, teardrop-shaped tanks that carried through the tapered line traced by the frame from steering head to rear axle. Each tank has its own separate filler cap and petcock. The left tank holds 2.0 gallons and the right holds 1.75 gallons. Switched to the down position, the petcocks retain a reserve capacity of 1/2 gallon. Switched to the up position, the reserve capacity is available to take the rider those last miles to the next gas station. The left gas tank has a mounting lug for the gearshift-lever pivot and threaded holes for the shifter gate.

Instrument Panel

Perched on top of the tanks is a stylish, all-new instrument panel that encloses the speedometer, ammeter, oil-pressure indicator, and ignition switch. The shape of the panel suggests the shape of a skull—with the large round opening at the front for the speedometer being the cranium, the two gracefully curved apertures for the ammeter and oil-pressure indicator being the eye sockets, and the round opening for the ignition switch being the mouth. It has thus been nicknamed the "skull-face" instrument panel among enthusiasts. The panel was painted black on the outside and white on the inside.

Skull-face-style panels were used on 1936–1938 61s, but the 1936 panel is unique in that it lacks a hole for a speedometer-light switch (a small hole just aft of the ignition-switch hole) that appears on the 1937 and 1938 panels. If a speedometer with a trip odometer was originally fitted, a hole was drilled in the right side of the panel for the trip-odometer reset stem. A rubber grommet was fitted over the stem to keep moisture from getting inside the panel through the reset-stem hole.

The 1936 61 was the first Harley-Davidson Big Twin to be fitted with a speedometer as standard equipment, and the speedometer was given pride of place at the front of the instrument panel. Built by Stewart-Warner, the 100-mile-per-hour speedometer has a brass face plate with etched silver plating for a background. The numerals 10 through 100 are in black, with long hash marks for the numerals and short hash marks in between for the intermediate 5-mile-per-hour positions, also in black. A black pointer revolves around a pivot in the center of the face. The odometer window is forward of the pointer pivot. On tripmeter-equipped speedometers, the main odometer window displays five digits, all for miles and none for tenth miles, in black numerals on a white background. On nontripmeter speedometers, the odometer displays six digits, five for miles (in black numerals on a white background) and one for tenth miles (in red numerals on a white background). The tripmeter window (if a trip odometer was fitted) is aft of the pivot and displays three digits, two for miles (in black on a white background) and one for tenth miles (in red on a white background). A black H-D bar and shield is aft of the odometer. The glass is flat, and the bezel around the glass is chrome plated.

The 100-mile-per-hour speedometer was a 1936-only part for the 61. In stock form, a well-tuned 61 could just about bury the speedometer needle, so for 1937 the speedometer face was revised to read to 120 miles per hour.

The ammeter and oil-pressure indicator are situated aft of the speedometer, the ammeter to the left and the oil

Another view of Dave Banks' 36EL1374. Banks has owned his bike since the early 1970s. While others were still chopping such early machines, Banks restored his in 1974 and stuck it away in his basement. Twenty years later he pulled it out and began riding it. Today, it shows some wear and dirt from use, but is still in great shape. The chrome-plated exhaust was available as part of the Deluxe Solo Group, but the muffler hangers were still painted black when they left the factory. It also has the later, one-piece front safety bar. Early machines such as this one were probably fitted at the factory with the three-piece safety bar.

indicator to the right. The ammeter's needle indicated charge or discharge rates from plus-15 to minus-15 amperes. The oil-pressure indicator was little more than a mechanical version of the "idiot lights" that later became common. When the engine was off or oil pressure fell below 4 psi, the word "OFF" became visible through the indicator window. When oil pressure was above 4 psi, the word "RUN" became visible. The indicator was operated by a small oil line that connected the indicator to the oil pump. The ammeter and mechanical oil-pressure indicator were used on 1936–1937 61s.

Aft of the indicators is the ignition switch, which is key-lockable and has four positions: left position routes electricity to the front-fender lamp and taillamp, the center position is off, the next position to the right is for running the bike without lights, and the rightmost position is for normal operation with lights on.

Fenders

The swoopy, valanced front and rear fenders on the 1936 61 are two of the few example of parts carried over onto the new model from the Series V side-valve Big Twins. These fenders, first introduced on the 1934 models, look more at home on the sleek new 61 than they do on the Series V machines, which makes one wonder whether they were conceived as part of the overall design effort for the 61. Both fenders were constructed by spot-welding side valances to the center crown piece.

The front fender is attached to the fork by two braces on each side. Front and rear braces are riveted to a common brace clip on each side, and the brace clip bolts to the fork's rigid legs. Each brace is formed from a single piece of 5/8-inch wide steel, with the center section riveted to the inside surface of the fender and the left and right legs extending down to the brace clips. The attachment of the brace to the fender is reinforced by a butterfly-shaped plate spot welded over the center of each brace and fender, on the bottom side of the fender. These reinforcements were used for 1936–1938. The rest of the fender was carried over largely unchanged through the end of Knucklehead production (in 1939, stainless steel fender trim was added, and the braces were made wider in late 1946). The rear fender is hinged so that the rear section can be swung up and out of the way for easier tire changes.

Carman Brown's EL, one of the first 20 built, was fitted with an early version of the left crankcase. Identifying features of the early case include a small-diameter timing hole plugged with a straight-slot screw (just below the serial-number boss) and the lack of the small "eared" boss on each side of the crankcase's top stud (located just above the serial-number boss). This bike shines like new. It is one of the rare early Knuckleheads that still has the correct cup-type valve-spring covers. The rear exhaust cover is just visible at the right edge of the photograph.

Like the front fender, the rear fender has two fender braces on each side, both of which are riveted to a brace clip. The front brace is one piece, like those on the front fender, and is riveted to the underside of the fender and reinforced with a butterfly plate. It attaches to the fender just in front of the fender hinge. The rear brace consists of three pieces that form a detachable brace that can be unbolted to allow the hinged rear fender section to be swung up and out of the way.

The rear mount for the rear chainguard is unique to the 1936 61 (although a similar mount is used on the side-valve twins). The mount is riveted to the rear fender's left front brace. On 1937 and later 61 fenders, the mount was made part of a redesigned left-side brace clip.

Paint and Graphics

The paint and graphics on the 1936 61 OHV were nothing short of stunning. The gas tanks were painted a solid color, without panels, but with a contrasting pinstripe that curves gracefully around the Art Deco transfer on the side of each tank. The fender crowns were painted the same color as the tank, but the fender valances and braces were painted the color of the tank pinstripe. The valance panels wrapped around the front tip of the front fender and around the rear tip of the rear fender. A pinstripe of the main color parallels the curve of the valance's lower edge, about an inch up from the edge. Some bikes shown in the black-and-white photos taken in 1935 and 1936 clearly show a second pinstripe that separates each fender's main section from its panel; others don't. Was the upper pinstripe painted on standard-paint bikes for the whole year or for only part of the year? Or only with certain color combinations? And what color was the upper pinstripe. Dave Minerva, owner of an original-paint 1936 61 in the Venetian Blue and Croydon Creme combination reports that the upper pinstripe is gold on his bike.

Standard 1936 color choices were Sherwood Green with silver panels and wheel rims, Teak Red with black panels and red rims, Dusk Gray with Royal Buff panels and rims, Venetian Blue with Croydon Cream panels and rims, and maroon with Nile Green panels and rims. If one of these fetching color combinations didn't appeal to the buyer, custom colors were also available.

Though the order blanks don't list the option of custom colors, the dealers were well informed that just about any combination of colors and designs was available for the asking. The January 27, 1936, dealer bulletin featured the headline, "Please be explicit about special color specifications!" The accompanying text suggested that dealers describe thoroughly or even send a sketch for any special panels, striping, lettering, or designs the customer desired on his or her new machine.

Photos from the period show a wide variety of paint schemes on new machines, suggesting that many buyers took advantage of the option. Some were all white, with just the pinstripes on the tank and panels. Others had solid-color tanks (without even the pinstriping) or VL-style, thick tank stripes (the February 1937 *The Motorcyclist* shows a photo of "Red" Wolverton's 1936 61 with these stripes). Other riders didn't care for the color-matched wheel rims and chose black-painted rims or even cadmium-plated ones. Surely there is enough documentable variety to give any Antique Motorcycle Club of America (AMCA) judge heartburn.

The Knucklehead Engine

The 1936 61 was more than just a styling exercise, however. It was a completely new motorcycle with features that were modern in almost every way—features that proved so functional that many are still in use on Harley Big Twins today. And most of these were in the motor.

The left side of Banks' EL shows that by the 374th bike off the line, the left crankcase had changed slightly compared to the one shown on Carman Brown's bike. Note the eared boss on each side of the top crankcase stud and the hex-headed plug in the larger-diameter timing hole. Rubber spark-plug caps are a functional update for a bike that is ridden frequently, but are not correct. Note the primer cups just to the inside of the V from each spark plug. A special gas cap was used in conjunction with these cups to prime the intake tract with fuel for cold starting. Banks' bike also retains the cup-type valve-spring covers.

Before we get heavily into the details of describing the individual parts and the myriad details of what changed during 1936, let's discuss the fundamental design of Harley-Davidson's new motor, little of which changed during that first year, and little of which has changed on H-D Big Twins to this day. The 1936 61 was powered by a 45-degree V-twin with a bore of 3 5/16 inches and a stroke of 3 1/2 inches, for a total displacement of 60.32 ci (988.6 cc). Harley-Davidson's copy writers naturally rounded this displacement up to 61 ci, the origin of its common name during the era. Almost every part in the engine was new, the result of the relentless pursuit of the two main design goals Bill Harley had set for it: OHV cylinder heads and a dry-sump, recirculating oil system. Neither overhead valves nor recirculating oil systems were revolutionary features on motorcycles then, but they represented a big, long-overdue step forward for Harley-Davidson in 1936. Since these features drove the overall design of the new motor, let's examine them first.

Harley's OHV System

Overhead valves had become common on British and European road bikes such as those built by Ariel, BMW, Brough, Douglas, Matchless, Triumph, and others in the late 1920s and early 1930s. These companies had switched to the new system because overhead valves provide a straighter path into the engine for the fuel-air mixture supplied by the carburetor and a straighter path out of the engine for the spent exhaust gasses. This results in higher volumetric efficiency, producing greater engine power from a given engine displacement.

Overhead valves had even been tried on American machines before 1936, but mostly on limited production racing iron built by Cyclone, Indian, and even Harley-Davidson. Harley also had used overhead valves on some of their small singles, but overhead valves were strangely absent from the big American twins until the debut of the 1936 61, because this greater efficiency came at the price of greater complexity, which meant greater manufacturing expense and more potential for problems. The OHV system Harley-Davidson chose—two valves per cylinder, operated by a train of rockers, pushrods, and a cam mounted in the crankcase—seems pretty low-tech by today's standards, but the system was thoroughly modern for 1936.

Cylinder Heads

The 1936 61's cylinder heads are castiron and are virtual mirror images of each other, with the intake ports of each pointing to the center of the V formed by the cylinders and the exhaust ports pointing out from the V. The intake ports are fitted with a removable intake nipple that threads into the intake port and is locked in place with a rivet. The outer portion of each nipple is also threaded, and the nuts that secure the intake manifold to each head thread onto this portion of the nipple. The exhaust header pipes slip inside a flange in the exhaust port.

The combustion chambers are hemispherical (a configuration later made famous on the high-performance Chrysler "Hemi" engines of the 1950s and 1960s). Each head carries two overhead valves set at an included valve angle of 90 degrees. Valve seats and guides are replaceable. On the left side of each head is the spark-plug hole. Also on the left side of the head, but on the underside of the lowest cooling fin, is the casting number 119-35 (front head) or 119-352 (rear head). On at least some of the 1935-serialed OHV motors, and possibly some of the very-early-1936 cylinder heads, the casting numbers were raised from the surface of the fin; on later heads, the numbers were recessed into the fin.

An air-brushed photo of 35E1002 shows the three-piece front safety guard fitted to early 1936 61s. The guard consisted of a center top mount and two side loops that clamped at the top to the center mount and at the bottom to the sidecar lugs on the frame. Obviously, this made the rider choose between a safety guard or a sidecar. A new safety guard was introduced during the 1936 production run that eliminated the either-or situation. Note that the small round covers on the end of the rocker shafts have been airbrushed over to show the large hex nuts that replaced the round tin covers early in the production year. Underneath the footboard, the 1936-only brake rod is visible. This rod has a 90-degree bend at each end, one inserted into a hole on the brake pedal and the other inserted into a hole on the crossover lever. For 1937, clevis ends were fitted to the rod. *Copyright Harley-Davidson Michigan, Inc.*

Each head and its attached rocker housing also provide support for the rocker-arm shafts. The right side of each head has three lugs for mounting the aluminum rocker housing that gives the engine its shape and provides the right-end support for the rocker-arm shafts. On the left side of each head, inboard of the spark-plug hole, is a 90-degree-V-shaped bracket that provides the support for the left end of the rocker-arm shafts. This bracket is integral with the head casting. Each "ear" of the bracket is rounded off on top and has a rocker shaft hole on the centerline near the rounded top.

The rocker shafts insert through the holes in the ears and are fixed in place by a nut. Each ear also has a short reinforcing rib rising vertically (with its axis at a 45-degree angle to the axis of the bracket) from the base of the V to about the height of the head's cooling fins.

To the rear of the spark-plug hole on the front cylinder head and to the front of the spark-plug hole on the rear head is a round, cast-in boss. The bosses were drilled and tapped for the optional primer cups, which seem to have been fitted to most low-serial-number 1936 61s but not to many later machines. Turning the primer cup opens a passage into the intake port, into which a shot of raw gas can be squirted from the special priming gun in the right gas tank cap to ease the task of starting the bike on a cold day. Primer cups on the early 61s were a curious holdover from the days of truly primitive carburetors and seemed archaic and out of place on the sleek, new machine. If the primer cups were not ordered, the holes are plugged by screws.

Rocker Arms and Shafts
Each valve is opened by its own rocker arm and closed by a set of nested, coil-type valve springs. Each rocker arm rotates on its own shaft. The rocker-arm shafts are threaded at each end for fixing the shaft to the cylinder head and to the rocker box. Oil for the rockers and valves is carried by the rocker shafts through a ring groove around the shaft's right end, through a central passage that ends at an oil passage on the left end of the shaft, and along a groove on the bearing surface of the shaft.

Each rocker-arm casting has two arms, a pushrod arm and a valve arm, that are on opposite ends of the casting and point in opposite directions. The valve arm ends in a radiused pad, which is the surface that bears on the top of the valve stem. The pushrod arm's end is fitted with a replaceable pushrod ball socket, which is the surface that bears on the top of the push rod. The bottom end of the pushrod socket is a ball end that slips into the concave top end of the pushrod. Each rocker is drilled for an oil passage that picks up oil from the bearing surface and carries it to an opening near the valve-arm pad to lubricate the valve stem.

Valve-Spring Covers

The key to finally solving the oiling mess that had been the bane of the prototype and preproduction 61s was in integrating the two systems that defined the new motor: overhead valves and recirculating oiling. This was done through the design of a clever new cover for each valve that catches the oil from the valve gear and returns it to the engine.

Each cover consists of an upper and lower section. The lower cover is basically a stamped-steel cup with a center hole through which the valve guide is pressed to secure the lower cover to the head. A steel oil return line from each cover connects to the left side of the aluminum rocker housing. The upper part of the cover is a stamped cap with a slot through which the valve arm extends to push on and open the valve, and the cap is secured with a light press-fit over the lower cup. The rocker arms remained largely exposed because the valve-spring covers enclosed only the end of each rocker's valve arm.

After lubricating the rocker arms and valve stems, the oil drips into the lower valve-spring cover. A return line is attached at the low point of the cover, and the engine vacuum sucks the accumulated oil out the lower valve-spring covers and back into the engine.

These covers were the 1936 61's most controversial and trouble-prone feature. When the oil supply to the rocker mechanism was properly adjusted to supply just enough oil to keep the valves from squeaking, relatively little oil escaped the covers. Problems were mostly the result of dirt and water that were sucked into the covers through the valve-arm opening by the same engine vacuum that scavenged the oil out of the lower covers. This dirt and water accumulated inside the covers, mixing with the scavenged oil to form an abrasive sludge that contributed to valve-guide wear and was sucked into the engine, where it remained in circulation until the next oil change. Of more immediate concern, the sludge sometimes clogged the return line, so that oil filled the valve-spring cover and spilled over onto rider and machine.

Yes, the design of these covers was less than perfect, but they were certainly better than no covers at all. Remember, the covers were a last-minute fix, added some time after the preproduction models were built in late 1935 but before the bulk of production bikes were built. Consensus among 1936 61 enthusiasts seems to be that most production 61s were fitted with the valve-spring covers. This conclusion is based on the fact that no shop dopes have surfaced with retrofit instructions to add the covers to machines not fitted with them at the factory. Plus, the rave reviews that the dealers sent back to the factory about the very first production machines in late January and early February suggest that these machines had the covers. But others think the very first production machines lacked the covers. At least one of them has an early 61 that he claims was never fitted with the covers because none are on the machine and fins on the cylinder heads were not relieved to allow clearance for the covers. It is interesting to note that the break-in instructions for the 61, dated April 14, 1936, instructs riders to "put a few drops of oil around upper end of valve guides, particularly inlet valve guides." This implies that the valve-spring covers were not yet fitted at the time the instructions were written because the valve guides are not readily accessible when the covers are fitted, and the rear exhaust cover is almost impossible to remove when the motor is in the frame.

Which faction is right? Until definitive proof surfaces, I won't weigh in with an opinion on the issue, but I will say this: If the oft-repeated stories about the early 1936 61's propensities for coating the rider's legs with oil are true, they could just as easily be attributed to clogged return lines or maladjusted oiling as to a lack of valve-spring covers. I'll also cite a couple of documents that provide a "no-later-than" date for introduction of the covers. The first is *Shop Dope No. 140*, dated April 20, 1936, that mentions that "overoiling will be indicated by oil splashing from the spring covers." The second is the patent drawings for the oiling system submitted on William S. Harley's behalf by the law firm of Wheeler, Wheeler, and Wheeler on May 16, 1936. These drawings show valve-spring covers, but the covers are shaped differently than those on the production machines, and the oil return lines join together. The common line winds around one of the covers so that the viewer cannot see where it connects to the engine, but it appears *not* to attach to the rocker housing (where the return lines from the production covers are attached).

Rocker Housings

Besides being an integral part of the styling for the engine, the aluminum rocker housing attached to each head serves three purposes. First, it supports the rocker shafts. Second, it serves as the conduit that distributes oil to the two rocker assemblies. And third, it routes engine vacuum to the valve spring covers for use in returning the oil to the engine.

To support the right end of the rocker shafts, each rocker housing has two tunnels from the right side to the left side. At each end, the tunnel openings are about 1 1/2 inches. The left side of the rocker-tunnels are each sealed by a cork seal that is sandwiched between two steel washers and held in place by a spring clip that is inserted into a groove around the left side of the rocker tunnel opening. The right end of the shaft tunnel on the early-1936 61s is covered by a round, slightly domed chrome-plated cover that is fastened to the right end of the rocker shaft by a small center screw. These covers are the "knuckles" of the early rocker housings. On later 1936 61s, the round covers and the rope packing were replaced by large, chrome-plated nuts that threaded onto the exposed right end of the rocker shaft and a small seal.

Passages in each rocker housing route the oil to the rocker shafts. Oil return lines from the valve spring covers attach to the left side of the housing, which is drilled through to the pushrod tunnels that rise upward from the bottom of the housing. The return oil also provides the only lubrication to the pushrod ball sockets. The oiling and scavenging systems are discussed in more detail in their own section later in this chapter.

Prototype, preproduction, and possibly very-early production rocker housings are not drilled for the oil return lines because valve spring covers were not fitted. Early housings were

The kickstarter cover shown was introduced in mid-year, and has a boss for the transmission vent, just visible above the starter spring. The large shaft rising vertically out of the top of the cover connects to the clutch release lever on the outside of the case and to the release fingers on the inside of the case. The chrome-plated kickstarter arm was included in the Deluxe Solo Group or as part of the Special Chrome Plating package offered separately for $13.50. The cadmium-plated "hockey puck" inboard of the kicker arm is the stoplight switch, also included in the Deluxe Solo Group. A chain connected the switch's pull to the brake rod.

drilled for the fittings but the castings did not have bosses around the holes. Sometime during the production run, the castings were modified to include the bosses, and an air nipple was added to the front rocker housing. This air nipple is used to blow obstructions out of the return oil lines from the valve-spring covers and will be discussed in more detail later in the chapter.

Pushrods, Pushrod Covers, Tappets, and Tappet Blocks

The tappets, one per pushrod and valve, have a roller lower end that follows the eccentric surface of each camshaft lobe and converts the eccentricity into vertical motion. The tappets rise and fall within the two cast-iron tappet guide blocks (one per cylinder) attached to the top of the right crankcase to transfer the up-and-down motion to the pushrods, which then transfer the motion to the rocker arms.

Each pushrod is fully covered by a two-piece, telescoping pushrod cover with cork seals. The unflanged bottom of each lower cover nestles inside one of the ridged crowns of a tappet guide and rests on a cork seal. The flange at the top of each lower cover is fitted with another cork seal, a washer on top of the seal, a spring on top of the washer, and a spring cap on top of the spring. The lower end of the upper cover fits inside the spring cap and seal.

Each upper cover has a flange at its top end that slips inside a pushrod tunnel in the bottom of the rocker housing and is sealed with a cork washer. The upper and lower covers are prevented from telescoping together by a spring-cap retainer that bears against the flange at the top of the top cover and against the spring cap that rests atop the lower cover. When the retainer is removed, the upper cover can telescope inside the lower cover so that the adjuster screw on the tappet can be accessed during valve-lash adjustment.

The new OHV system wasn't perfect, and many parts of it changed that first year and in the years that followed. But the valve gear gave the 61 unprecedented performance for an American production twin. Even in its purposely mild state of tune, the OHV engine could propel the 61 to an honest 95 miles per hour. Unfortunately, it didn't remain the fastest American twin for long. That title was wrested from Harley's grasp by the 61-ci OHV Crocker V-twin that appeared later in 1936. While the high-priced Crocker didn't pose any real sales threat to Harley's 61 OHV (probably less than 20 Crockers were produced per year), it trounced the Harleys—and Indians, too—whenever they met.

But the superiority of the limited-production Crocker does not in any way diminish the importance of what Bill Harley and his design staff had accomplished. After all, the Crocker firm is long gone, while Harley-Davidson thrives, and the OHV configuration Harley uses in the 1990s has far more similarities to the configuration set on the 1936 61 than it does differences.

Pressure Oiling System

Like overhead valves, recirculating oil systems had been in use for many years before 1936, when the 61 OHV introduced the feature to the Harley line-up. Unlike overhead valves, recirculating oil systems had been common even in America. Harley's main competitor in the U.S. market, Indian, had introduced the feature on its big twin Chief in 1933—and Indian's advertisements and sales brochures often pointed to this feature as evidence of the superiority of machines, which no doubt fueled the competitive fires in the boardroom in Milwaukee. Although Harley was just playing catch-up with this feature, catch-up was all that was really needed because the OHV top-end of the motor put H-D in the technological lead against Indian, and Indian would not survive long enough to close the gap.

The recirculating oil system Bill Harley and his staff designed for the 61 is of the dry-sump type, meaning that the oil is stored in a separate tank and not in the engine's sump.

Dry-sump systems had been used on many other motorcycles, including Indian, but few of the period were as elegant as Harley's turned out to be.

Oil Tanks

One of the main problems for designers of motorcycle dry-sump systems had always been the location of the oil tank. The tank had to be accessible so the rider could check, add, and change the oil, but it also had to be close to the pump to reduce problems with routing vulnerable oil lines. It also had to be large enough to hold a usable oil supply. Some manufacturers had taken the easy way out and haphazardly hung the oil tank to a frame downtube or anywhere it would fit. These systems worked, but they tended to detract severely from the looks of the machine. Others, including Indian, had partitioned the fuel tank to hold the oil. This, too, performed acceptably, but the oil lines tended to be long and the oil tank's capacity came at the cost of fuel capacity.

The best dry-sump systems were on the British OHV models of the late 1920s and early 1930s, such as the Norton Model 18 and Sunbeam Model 90, which had their oil tanks under the seat, an area that was close to the rear of the engine. Bill Harley chose this location also.

What set Harley's design apart was the way it perfectly blended form and function. The 1-gallon oil tank on the 61 is U-shaped, with the open end of the U pointing to the rear. It is perfectly placed to deliver oil by the shortest route to the oil pump, but it also wraps around the battery, hiding the blocky battery from view, contributing to the rounded, streamlined, almost organic lines of the bike. This classic, functional styling cue still contributes to the "Harley look" on such current models as the Heritage Softail. During its development and first year, the Knucklehead oil tank evolved through at least four versions. The first version, apparently used on some of the prototypes and maybe a few other very early machines, has smooth top and bottom surfaces. It is also identified by one banjo-type fitting at the right rear for the oil feed line to the pump, two banjo-type fittings at the front for the oil return and vent lines, a filtering screen at the front of the right lobe of the oil tank, and a plugged hole on each side of the tank. The fittings and plugs are welded in place.

The second type of oil tank, used on some early machines, is just like the first, except that it does not have the welded-in plugs on the sides. Later in the year, a third type was introduced. This tank differed from the second in that its top surface was embossed with reinforcements. Still later, the fourth type was introduced. The fourth type has the embossed top of the third type, but the banjo fittings are swaged on, not welded on. A decal with oil-change instructions was attached to the front right side of the oil tank, below the oil return and vent fittings. These oil tanks and the oil-change decal were used only for 1936. At least, some of the 1936 61s were fitted with a dipstick that differs slightly from dipsticks used in later years. The 1936-only dipstick has a longer ridge, which runs from edge to edge.

This view shows the mounts for the updated safety guard and the sidecar lugs on the frame. Note the accessory tire pump mounted along the frame's right downtube.

Oil Pumps

The all-new, gear-type pump on the 1936 61 is the heart of the recirculating oil system. The pump is contained in a separate housing attached to the outside of the rear end of the gear case and is really two pumps in one—a pressure-feed pump to force oil throughout the engine, and a scavenge pump to return oil to the oil tank. The oil pump body and cover are cast iron and are painted silver.

The oil tank is mounted higher than the oil pump, so gravity assists the pump in drawing oil through a feed line from the back of the oil tank to the oil pump inlet, where the gears of the pump force it to the pressure side of the pump. When oil pressure reaches about 1.5 psi, the oil unseats the ball in the check valve (which prevents oil from flowing out of the oil tank and into the crankcase while the engine is shut off) and flows to a branched passage. One branch leads to the oil-feed passages in the crankcase, and the other to the maximum pressure regulating valve (which remains closed until the oil pressure reaches about 15 psi, when the oil unseats the valve's check ball and bleeds off past the valve to the gear case). The oil pump also directs a small amount of oil to lubricate the primary chain and to actuate the oil-pressure indicator on the instrument panel.

LEFT: Carman Brown's 36EL. The finish on wheel rims was color matched to the fender panels, except when the panels were black, in which case the wheels were red. Black wheels were optional for no extra charge, or cadmium-plated wheels could be specified at the time of order for 50 cents each. Starting in 1937, black wheels became standard. Note the way the fender panel wraps around the front lip of the fender. Photos of the preproduction machines show two pinstripes on the fenders—the one along the lower part of the fender valance shown on this bike and another along the top of the fender panels. Period photos sometimes also show the second pinstripe, almost invariably on machines with valance panels in a darker color than the fender-crown color. This second pinstripe may have been used only for part of the year or only with certain paint combinations.

Bottom-End Oiling

Oil to the lower end is forced through passages in the pinion gear shaft to lubricate the gear-shaft bearings and lower connecting-rod bearings. After lubricating these parts, the oil is slung around by the spinning flywheels, forming an air-oil mist that helps lubricate the cylinder walls, the wrist pins, and the left main bearing.

The flywheels spin clockwise (when viewed from the right side of the powerplant), so flywheel action tends to sling a lot of lubricant on the rear cylinder's walls but little on the front cylinder's walls. To counteract this tendency, H-D engineers used a system of baffles to create more vacuum under the front piston when it rises (which draws in more of the air-oil mist to lubricate the cylinder) and to partially block the spray of oil to the rear cylinder. The front cylinder baffle plate completely covers the opening to the cylinder, except for a slot for the connecting rod. The rear cylinder's baffle covers only the rear half of the opening, again, except for a connecting-rod slot. This basic configuration for cylinder oiling was used through 1939.

Top-End Oiling

Oil to the top end is carried from the gear case by an external, tubular-steel oil line that bends inward toward the cylinders, hiding itself behind the carburetor. The oil line branches to a fitting on each rocker housing, near the intake rocker shaft cover. In each cylinder head, the oil flows through a passage in the rocker housing and to the rocker-arm shafts. A groove running down the shaft distributes oil along its length to lubricate the rocker bearing. The hollow rocker shaft also carries oil to a passage in the rocker's valve arm to lubricate the valve pads and valve guides.

The oil supply to the valves can be adjusted after removing the large, chrome, domed "knuckle" covers or later chromed "knuckle" nuts to expose the right ends of the rocker shafts. Oil supply is increased by turning the end of the rocker shaft toward the valve-arm side of each rocker (that is, clockwise for the front cylinder exhaust and rear cylinder intake valve shafts, or counterclockwise for the front cylinder intake and rear cylinder exhaust valve shafts) or reduced by turning it toward the pushrod arm. After lubricating the rocker shafts, the oil bleeds out the valve-arm end of the rocker arm (and the oil passage to the intake valve guide on some machines).

"Direct Oil Injection" to the Combustion Chambers

Sometime early in the production run, the rocker-arm shaft support brackets on the cylinder heads were drilled with an oil passage to the intake valve guides. The special intake guide fitted to these machines has a groove all the way around its outside diameter and is cross-drilled to distribute the oil to the valve stem. This was apparently an attempt to ensure that the valve guides got enough lubrication even when the overhead oilers were adjusted for the lowest possible oil flow to keep oil spray to a minimum. As you can probably imagine, this was an ill-fated modification because engine vacuum sucked the oil right into the combustion chambers to foul the plugs and burn into billowing clouds of blue smoke. Ever light on their feet, Harley-Davidson stopped drilling the passages on new machines after the problem was discovered, sometime during the middle of the production run.

Scavenging and Breathing Systems

The heart of the 61 OHV engine breather system is the rotary breather valve in the gear case, which allows crankcase pressure to escape and routes engine vacuum where needed to help scavenge oil. The heart of the scavenge system is the scavenge section of the oil pump, which draws scavenged oil out of the gear case and returns it to the oil tank.

The geared rotary breather valve is driven at crankshaft speed by the cam gear and is timed to open a passage from the crankcase to the gear case each time the pistons are on their down stroke. Crankcase pressure blows accumulated oil and the air-oil mist created by all the rapidly moving parts from the crankcase through the breather-valve opening and into the gear case, where the oil mist lubricates the gears. Early engines were fitted with a breather that had a flat screen held to the valve with a stamped metal bracket. Later engines were fitted with an updated valve with a tubular screen that was much more likely to stay in place than was the flat screen.

Crankcase air is vented out of the main gear-case chamber through an integral breather pipe in the gear-case cover and into the breather oil trap chamber at the rear of the gear case. In this chamber, oil is separated from the crankcase air by a screen and separator in the breather oil trap. The air is then vented out of the chamber through a separate breather pipe that extends to the left through both crankcases and into the primary-chain housing. Air expelled into the primary chain case still is mixed with a minute amount of oil, and this air-oil mixture is deflected onto the chain by the slotted, domed head of the breather pipe.

On the pistons' upstroke, the rotary breather valve is timed to close the passage to the gear case and connect a passage from the crankcase to the pushrod tubes and another passage to the breather oil trap. Vacuum created by the rising pistons pulls oil from the valve-spring covers through the pushrod tubes and into the gear case. Vacuum also sucks out the oil from the breather oil trap into the gear case. Oil

This view of Brown's EL shows the round covers over the right ends of the rocker shafts. A center screw threaded into a hole in the rocker shaft's end and fixed the cover in place. Rope packing behind the cover sealed the end of the shaft. With the covers removed, the rocker shafts could be turned to increase or decrease oil supply to the rockers and intake valve guides. Also shown is the 1936-only slash-cut air-intake horn. This air horn (not a filter) attaches to the carburetor with two screws. Early-1936 carburetors have a two-hole mounting boss for the air horn, but later carburetors have a four-hole boss for the accessory round air cleaner, which attaches with four screws. The carburetor should be nickel-plated, and the removable cap at the bottom of the fuel strainer (shown just below the air horn) should have cross-hatched, rather than straight, knurling.

trapped in the gear case is sucked out of the case and returned to the oil tank by the oil pump's scavenge section.

Proper sealing of the pushrod covers is vital to keep out dirt and keep vacuum and return oil in. If any of the seals leak, vacuum will be lost, return oil will leak out, and dirt could be drawn in by vacuum. If the seals leak too much, the remaining vacuum will be too weak to pull oil out of the valve-spring covers and back into the engine.

The whole oiling-scavenging-breathing system did its job well, keeping the parts well lubricated and most of the oil within the engine. A patent application for the system was filed on May 16, 1936, with William S. Harley listed as the inventor. The patent for the system (number 2,111,242) was granted on March 15, 1938. Normal oil consumption on the new 61 varied between 200 and 400 miles per quart, which seems very poor by today's standards, but it was much better than the total-loss oil system of other Harleys.

Pistons and Piston Rings

The 1936 Knucklehead used conventional cam-ground, slotted, aluminum pistons. They were offered in two versions: high compression and medium compression. The high-compression pistons, fitted to the Model EL, have a high dome, giving a compression ratio of 6.5:1. Medium-compression pistons were fitted to Models E and ES and have a much flatter crown, giving a compression ratio of 5.66:1 (the Models ES are also fitted with compression plates, lowering their compression further, but the specifications do not say by how much). Medium-compression pistons were fitted in 1936 and 1937 only, according to the parts book. Thereafter, the medium-compression Models E and ES were fitted with high-compression pistons with compression plates to lower compression.

The front piston is fitted with two compression rings but no oil-control ring, whereas the rear piston is fitted with the two compression rings and an oil-control ring. This odd configuration was dictated by the aforementioned clockwise rotation of the flywheels, which slings a lot of oil onto the wall of the rear cylinder, but relatively little onto the wall of the front cylinder. Baffles described earlier in this chapter helped somewhat to even out the oiling to the cylinders.

Carburetor and Intake Manifolds

Fuel and air for the 1936 61 OHV motor were mixed by a side-draft-type 1-1/4-inch Linkert M-5 carburetor with a 1-1/6-inch, fixed venturi. These carburetors have three mounting holes on their manifold-end flange and two mounting holes in the air-horn flange. Sometime during the production run, a four-hole air-horn flange was introduced. The M-5 with two-hole air-horn flange was used for 1936 only. The M-5 with the four-hole flange was used from late 1936 through 1939.

On all 1936–1938 Linkert M-5 carburetors, the float bowl lacks a drain plug and has the number 7-64 in raised letters on the inside surface of the bowl. In 1939, a drain hole was added to the float bowl. M-5 carburetors were cast of bronze and were nickel plated, but the bodies were not polished before plating.

The Y-shaped intake-manifold assembly delivers the intake charge from the carburetor to each cylinder head's intake port. The manifold assembly includes the manifold, two large (2-inch) "plumber" nuts to attach the manifold to the each cylinder head's intake nipple, and two brass bushings to seal the plumber-nut connections. Incidentally, the plumber nuts and bushings were among the few parts the designers of the 61 borrowed from Harley's side-valve Big Twins. The time-proven design outlasted the Knucklehead itself, being used on Harley Big Twins into the 1950s. Some manifolds have a hole drilled in their underside. According to Chris Haynes, these holes were drilled for an aftermarket backfire valve. The valves were apparently of poor quality and eventually leaked, so they were replaced by a bolt to plug the hole. For 1936–1938, the manifold and plumber nuts were unpolished and nickel plated, matching the finish on the carburetor. For 1939, the manifold and nuts were cadmium plated.

The opening and closing of the carburetor's butterfly throttle valve is controlled by the spiral on the right handlebar, acting through a coil-protected control wire. (For those readers who are more familiar with modern motorcycles, a few terms need to be defined. The twistgrips on vintage Harleys are called "spirals." The two-piece cable that leads from the spiral consists of the "coil" and "control wire." The coil is a protective outer sheath consisting of a coil of wire covered in fabric. The control wire is a cable that slides freely inside the coil.) Harley-Davidson motorcycles had long been given a right-hand throttle, while some other motorcycle manufacturers, including Indian, favored left-hand throttles. For those who wanted them—mainly police officers, who wanted their right hand free, say to shoot their pistols at fleeing suspects—left-hand throttles were optional, and were usually sold on bikes with right-hand shift levers.

Air Intake Horn and Air Cleaner

Rounded at the front, squared off at the sides, and slash-cut at the rear, with three speed-lines embossed along its length, the standard air horn for the 1936 61 was another triumph of Art Deco styling. It was the mirror image of the air horn used on the 1935 side-valve Big Twins, which is further evidence that the 61 was originally planned as a 1935 model. The air horn was chrome plated and mounted to the carburetor with two screws. Although this horn was beautiful and distinctive, it wasn't really functional because it had no air-filter element. Worse, it was prone to rattling itself apart because the two mounting points were insufficient to hold it securely to the carburetor. This air horn was used only for 1936.

For those who wanted or needed an air filter, an optional 6-inch round air cleaner with a filter element was available for at least part of the production year. The cover is chrome-plated and has the H-D bar-and-shield stamped into the round face and an instruction plate riveted to the rim. The cover is fastened to the backing plate by four screws, and the backing plate is attached to the carburetor by four bolts. The copper-mesh air cleaner wraps around a mesh support welded to the steel backing plate. The backing plate is Parkerized. This air cleaner was also optional for 1937.

The early-1936 ignition timer used through serial number 1421. This and all Knucklehead timers use one set of points to time the spark to two cylinders. A two-lobed cam opens the points and both spark plugs fire each time the points break. Note the bolt head on the underside of the timer control strap lug, which differs from that shown on one of the other preproduction bikes, 35EL1003. The strap was updated again early in the production year. *Copyright Harley-Davidson Michigan, Inc.*

Cylinders

Cast iron was the standard material for motorcycle cylinders before World War II. It was inexpensive, easily cast into the complex shape of a finned cylinder, and easy to machine for a smooth cylinder bore. The material was also durable, so a liner of another material was not necessary, and its slight porosity allowed it to retain oil for good cylinder lubrication. Consequently, iron was the natural choice for the 1936 61 OHV's cylinders. Nearly 50 years passed before H-D would switch to aluminum cylinders on the Evolution Big Twin introduced in 1984.

The 61's cylinders were an all-new design. At the top, around the edge of the 3 5/16-inch bore, is a raised ridge that fits into a recess in the head to help seal the head gasket. Outside the ridge is the gasket surface with five head-bolt holes spaced around the circumference. A boss for each of the head bolts runs down from the gasket surface through the top four fins. Each head is clamped to the cylinder by bolts inserted from below, through drilled bosses, through holes in the head gasket, and into the threaded holes in the head.

The front hub of Dave Banks' EL showing cable-adjustment mechanism. Nuts threaded onto the control coil were used to adjust for slack in the cable. The operating lever, to which the cable attaches, has four round holes, as shown. The word "SOLO" is stamped between the closest-in two holes and the letters "SC" (for sidecar) between the two outer holes. This lever was used through 1941.

The cylinder bases are each held to the crankcases by four studs and nuts, with a base gasket between the cylinder base and the crankcase. External surfaces of the cylinders were painted black. The basic configuration of the 61's cylinders remained unchanged until 1940, when the headbolt bosses were changed so that they passed through the top five fins.

Compression Plates

Additional tuning of compression ratio was offered for specialized uses. For motorcycles to be used with sidecars or under heavy load or extended low-speed operation, Harley-Davidson offered compression plates that could be used to create what is effectively medium-high and medium-low compression ratios. These plates are simple metal spacers, 0.050 inch thick, that are fitted under the cylinder base to raise the deck height, lowering compression ratio. The 1936 and 1937 Model ES was fitted with medium-compression pistons and a compression plate beneath each cylinder. Starting in 1938, only the high-compression pistons were fitted, so compression plates were used with the high-compression pistons to create medium-compression engines.

The Bottom End

The 1936 61's lower end was far more conventional for its day than was the top end. Like those on the other Harley-Davidson Big Twins, the 61's connecting rods run on a common crankpin sandwiched between two flywheel halves, and a pair of mainshafts (one per flywheel half) serve as the axle

A left-side view of 35E1002. Although not as grimy as 35E1003 was shown to be, this machine shows signs of having been ridden—the dirt and wear on the white handgrips, rear sprocket, and oil tank. The oil tank on this bike also has the welded-in plug (the shiny spot near the top rim of the tank, about halfway back from the front of the tank). Look at the frontmost of the two stays for the rear fender. Note the riveted-on mount for the rear chain guard and how it differs from the one shown earlier on 35E1003. The type of mount shown here was used on the production machines for 1936 only. Note the three pinstripes on the safety guard—a thick one down the center and a thinner one on each side that end about halfway down the guard in an arrow-point flourish. The early-style steering damper knob is shown in profile ahead of the speedometer. It is the squared-off type used on most or all 1936 61s, but it lacks the welded-in reinforcement plate that seems to be present on the damper levers on most production bikes. *Copyright Harley-Davidson Michigan, Inc.*

about which the whole flywheel assembly rotates. Each flywheel half is 8 1/8 inches in diameter and has a tapered central hole for a center shaft and an off-center tapered hole for the crankpin. These flywheels were used on the 61s from 1936 through 1940.

The front cylinder rod's big end is "forked," and the rear cylinder rod's big end was designed to nestle inside the fork. Forked connecting rods were used on most V-twins of the era. Engine designers liked them because they are narrower than two connecting rods placed side-by-side, which then allows the engine designer to use a short, stiff crankpin. The only real disadvantage to the knife-and-fork arrangement is that it also puts both cylinders on the same centerline, to the detriment of rear-cylinder cooling. (If the big ends are placed side-by-side, the crankpin must be longer, but the front and rear cylinders could be offset, allowing a more direct flow of cooling air to the rear cylinder.) The tapered crankpin fits through the big-end bearings of the connecting rods, into the tapered, offset holes on the flywheel halves, and is secured on the outer side of each half by a crank-pin nut and lock plate. This basic arrangement was used through 1939.

The mainshaft from the left flywheel is called the "sprocket shaft." It is secured to the left flywheel on the inner side by the sprocket-shaft nut and lock plate. Supported by roller bearings in the left crankcase half, the sprocket shaft extends into the primary-chain case to drive the primary-chain sprocket. The sprocket then transfers engine power through a three-row primary chain to the clutch sprocket.

The center shaft from the right flywheel is called the "gear shaft." This shaft consists of two pieces, a stub shaft and a pinion shaft. The stub shaft is secured to the right flywheel on the inner side by the gear shaft nut and lock plate and extends through the roller bearings in the right crankcase. The pinion shaft, attached to the stub shaft by means of an eccentric tongue-and-groove joint, extends into the gear case on the right side of the engine to drive the oil pump, cam gear, breather valve, ignition circuit breaker, and generator. Attached directly to the gear shaft are two gears: the oil-pump drive gear and pinion gear.

The oil-pump drive gear is the innermost of the two gears and is machined into the shaft. It is a worm-type that meshes with a gear on the end of the oil pump drive shaft, to change the direction of drive 90-degrees toward the rear of the bike to turn the shaft for the oil pump. The shaft extends through the rear of the gear case to drive the two-section pump that is mounted at the rear of the crankcase on the right side.

The outer gear is the pinion gear, which is a separate piece that is press-fit onto the pinion shaft. This small diameter gear is comparatively wide. The width of the pinion gear allows it to mesh with two larger diameter gears that are thin and overlap each other—the cam gear (which is vertically above the pinion gear) and the intermediate gear (which is to the right of the pinion gear as viewed from the right side of the bike). The cam gear turns the single, four-lobed camshaft and drives the rotary crankcase breather valve gear that is aft of the cam gear.

The intermediate gear is driven off the inner portion of the pinion gear at half speed. Mounted on the intermediate gear's shaft, on the crankcase side, is another gear that drives (also at half speed) the ignition circuit breaker. (See the ignition discussion for more details.)

To the right of the intermediate gear is the idler gear. The idler gear transfers drive from the intermediate gear to the generator drive gear. The generator is mounted transversely on the front of the engine, its drive shaft extending into the gear case on the right side of the motorcycle and its end cover on the left. (See the charging system discussion for more details.)

"Lightning" Camshafts

The 1936 61 came with a new camshaft arrangement that was unlike the arrangement used on the side-valve Big Twins. The side-valves had a separate camshaft and gear for each valve because the flat valve angle and short pushrods of the side-valve engine prevented the use of angled-in pushrods necessary for a common camshaft. The long pushrods and 90-degree included valve angle of the new OHV engine allowed all four pushrods to be angled into a single four-lobed cam.

Besides the obvious benefits of reduced manufacturing cost and complexity, the single-cam arrangement ran quieter and gave more consistent and precise timing because only one gear was needed instead of four.

The cams fitted to the 1936 61 OHV are different from most that followed and have gained a reputation as being especially "hot." In later years, these cams were much sought after by savvy performance tuners who knew the cam's reputation and how to pick them out of the milk crates full of lesser cams at swap meets. These special cams are identified by the measures taken to lighten the cam gear—six holes and metal machined away on the front and back. References to these lightening measures and the performance offered by the cam resulted in the description "lightening" being misconstrued into a nickname for the cam: "Lightning."

Some sources report that at least three versions of this cam were offered in 1936. The cam fitted to the early 61s was reportedly so far advanced that the bikes were prone to backfiring while being kickstarted. Sports-oriented riders could overlook the occasional backfire because these cams gave great performance, especially at higher rpm. Later, the cam timing was reportedly retarded to reduce this tendency. Still later, some say, a third cam was released that had two sets of timing mark, one for solo machines and another for those equipped with a sidecar.

Crankcases

All unaltered 1936 61 OHV left engine cases have a cast-in baffle covering the rear half of the rear cylinder hole (except for the slot running fore and aft for the connecting rod), a full baffle covering the front cylinder hole (except for the con-rod slot), and the casting number 112-35 (in raised numbers) below the primary-cover boss. Early-1936 left cases have a small-diameter timing hole,

Carman Brown's 36EL is at least as shiny and beautiful as the day it left the factory. This view shows how sleek and slim a sports machine the first Knucklehead really was. In later years the basic design set in 1936 would gain much weight and girth, better suspension, and accessories—and would evolve into the classic American touring bike. Very few bikes Harley-Davidson has built in the last 60-odd years have equaled the looks of the first Knuckleheads.

which is usually plugged by a cad-plated, straight-slot screw, Later cases have a larger timing hole (plugged by a cad-plated bolt) and two small raised "ears" above the serial-number boss, one on each side of the hole for the top crankcase stud. This second style of left case remained in use through mid-1939.

Only one style of right crankcase was used in 1936. It has the baffles and the casting number 112-352 below the gear cover. This case was used through 1939.

"Line-boring" Numbers

At the start of engine assembly, each Knucklehead crankcase set was bolted together and the mainshaft holes were line-bored through both cases at once, ensuring that the holes were in good alignment. The matched set of cases were then each stamped with a "line-bore" number. The number consisted of two digits for the year and four digits to denote the engine's place in the production run, separated by a hyphen. For example, 36-1234 indicated that it was the 234th set of 61 cases line-bored in 1936. In later years, when production was higher, five digits denoted the engine's place in the production run. The line-bore numbers seldom match the serial number because the line-bore numbers were applied at the start of assembly, whereas the serial numbers were applied near the end of final engine assembly. However, line-bore numbers and serial numbers seldom differ by more than 100 or so. The two-digit number apparently indicates the year the case was line-bored, which is not necessarily the model year of the motorcycle. For example, some 1937-serialed cases have line-bore numbers that begin with "36" because they were line-bored in 1936.

Gear-Case Covers

At least three different gear-case covers are known to have been used on 1936 61s. The earliest style is called a "notched" cover, in reference to the recessed notch at the rear end of the cover. Inside, this cover has a steel baffle riveted on to shield the inlet to the gear-case breather pipe that is cast into the cover. The rivets that secure the baffle often were leaded over at the factory, but the lead plugs work lose from the vibration and heating-and-cooling cycles of decades of use, so the rivets are often visible on the outside of the cover.

Later covers are "smooth," in that they lack the notch of the earlier covers. The first smooth covers still had the riveted-on baffle, and the rivets sometimes show on the outside of the cover. Still later, the gear cover casting was revised to feature a cast-in baffle. Rivets were not used on the last style of cover, and it was used on subsequent 61s through 1939.

Exhaust System

The 1936 61 was fitted with a two-into-one exhaust system consisting of a front header pipe, an S-pipe, a rear header pipe, and a muffler with an attached collector pipe. Exhaust gases flow from the front cylinder through the front header pipe, through the S-pipe, and to the front connection on the pipe. Gasses from the rear cylinder flow through the rear header pipe to the top connection on the muffler pipe.

The tubular muffler is 2 1/2 inches in diameter and has a pretty flamboyant fishtail at its back end. Photos of preproduction bike 35EL1002 show the name "Burgess Battery Co." in large, raised letters on the muffler's side. Apparently, the Burgess name was too conspicuous for Harley-Davidson's liking because the name was moved to the bottom of the muffler, in much smaller letters, on the mufflers fitted to the regular production machines.

All components of the standard exhaust were painted black, but a chrome-plated exhaust was available as part of the Chrome Plate Group. Even with chrome-plated mufflers and pipes, however, the black clamps were fitted.

Charging System

The 1936 Knucklehead's charging system was one of the few systems on the new machine that was carried over from Harley's earlier twins. The system consists of a generator, external generator cut-out relay, and a battery.

The generator is the Model 32E 6-volt DC unit with a rotating armature, two magnetic field coils (regulating and

The forks and horn were new designs for 1936 and contributed to the bikes' classic lines. The only damping on these spring forks was provided by the optional "ride control" plates shown on Dave Banks' bike. Ride control was just friction damping that could be adjusted by tightening or loosening the lower knob. Note the grease fitting pointing forward on the spring perch, above and to the side of the upper horn mount. One such fitting is on each side. The fittings were in this location from 1936 through 1938. In 1939, the grease fittings were moved to the side of the spring perch and point to the sides.

shunt) fixed to the generator case, and three brushes (positive, negative, and current-regulating) contacting the commutator. This generator is used without an external voltage regulator because the third brush regulates the current output. Moving the third brush toward the negative brush increases current output and moving it away decreases output.

Like the plumber nuts discussed earlier, the Model 32E worked so well that it was both borrowed from earlier Harleys and passed on to later Harleys, after the Knucklehead engine was discontinued. It was the standard generator for Harley-Davidson Big Twins from 1932 to1952.

For riders who needed more current than the Model 32E could supply—mainly police users with bike-mounted radios—Harley-Davidson offered an optional generator, the Model 32E2, that had longer armatures and fields to supply the extra current. The Model 32E2 generator is also a 6-volt,

three-brush design that is used with a cut-out relay but without a voltage regulator. It was optional for 1936–1938.

The external cut-out relay's function is to disconnect the generator from the rest of the electrical circuit until the voltage produced by the generator exceeds battery voltage (preventing the battery from discharging through the generator windings). This cut-out relay looks much like a voltage regulator and mounts just forward of the ignition circuit breaker, on the forward part of the right side of the motor. The cut-out relay was also carried over from earlier Harley-Davidson motorcycles (having been in service since 1932). This relay has two terminal posts and is correct for 1936 and 1937 Knuckleheads.

Ignition System

Magneto ignitions were common in the motorcycle industry in 1936, especially on serious sporting machines. Magnetos are simple, light, and relatively trouble free. But Harley-Davidson had abandoned the magneto on its Big Twins in favor of a point-and-ignition-coil system with a distributor, because coil-stoked ignitions give a hotter spark at start-up, and made the kick-start ritual more of a sure thing, especially in cold weather.

In 1927, the company again modified the ignition to create a curious style of coil ignition. By use of a clever concept known as "wasted spark," Harley created a coil ignition system that is nearly as simple as a magneto system because it requires just one set of breaker points and one coil to operate both cylinders (no distributor or second set of points and coil). The coil fires both spark plugs each time the points open, igniting the fuel-oil mixture in one cylinder and "wasting" the other spark on the burned gases being expelled from the other cylinder on its exhaust stroke. Naturally enough, Harley-Davidson chose to fit its new 61 with its wasted-spark system.

Looking much like an automotive distributor, the 61's ignition circuit breaker or timer is mounted to the right of the front cylinder. The timer's main functions are to open the breaker points, and to time the break so that it occurs at precisely the right instant. Inside the breaker cover is a set of breaker points, a two-lobed cam, and the condenser. The cam lobe for the front cylinder is narrower than the lobe for the rear cylinder. The timer shaft and cam are spun at half of the crankshaft speed (so the plugs fire every other stroke).

The ignition timer assembly fitted to the first 1936 61s was basically just a longer version of the timer fitted to the side-valve Big Twins. After motor number 1422 was built, a new timer was introduced. The new timer has larger diameter (45/64-inch, versus 5/8-inch) holes for the shaft. On both of these timer assemblies, the circuit-breaker wire feeds into the side of the assembly through a notch in the side of the timer base, and the wire connects to the top of a terminal on the base. Timers with the notched timer base were used only for 1936, because the timer was revised for 1937 to route the timer wire out through a hole in the timer housing, which made the wire less vulnerable to chafing.

A single twin-lead ignition coil generates the spark, and it is mounted on the motorcycle's left side, in front of the oil

Jeff Coffman's 36EL also has the notched gear cover, in addition to a lot of extra chrome and a red-painted oil tank. In 1937, oil tanks were painted the main color of the bike and were fitted with the patent decal, as shown here.

tank. One spark-plug lead goes to the front spark plug and one to the rear plug, but both spark plugs fire each time the points are opened by the points cam. In greatly updated form, with electronic black boxes replacing the points and advance mechanism, the wasted-spark system is still in use on the 1990s Harleys.

Transmission and Shifter

Just as the OHV motor signaled the dawn of a new age for The Motor Company, so, too, did the new bike's transmission—an advanced, four-speed, constant-mesh design that was quieter, stronger, and more durable than the sliding-gear transmissions found on the competing Indian and foreign motorcycles. Although a constant-mesh transmission had been used on a few earlier 45-ci Harleys, the 1936 61 was the first Harley-Davidson Big Twin to use a constant-mesh transmission.

The all-new transmission was carried in its own housing separate from the engine, and this basic transmission proved to be one of the 1936 Knucklehead's most enduring features. In fact, it was passed on largely unchanged to all the Harley-Davidson Big Twins through 1964, except for those built during the 1939 model year when a curious new four-speed was used that was a hybrid of the constant-mesh and the older sliding-gear types. Optional transmissions included a three-speed and a three-speed with reverse.

Transmission Cases

The components of the new transmission were housed in at least two different transmission cases for 1936, neither of which had a cast-in support for the kickstarter side of the transmission. The early 1936 case has four frame mounting studs and is not drilled for the mounting holes for the countershaft end cap fitted to later cases. In mid-1936 H-D began drilling the transmission case for the four countershaft-end screws. The case was supported on the starter side by a bracket attached to the two lower studs for the starter cover and a bolt that butts against the lower frame tube. In late 1936, a new starter-side support bracket was introduced. More details on these mounts are provided later in this chapter.

Shifter and Linkage

In traditional Harley fashion, the new transmission was shifted through a gear-change lever that pivoted fore and aft on a bracket on the bottom of the left gas tank (although right-side shifters were optional). The gear-change lever moved within a shifter gate attached to the left gas tank. All the shifter parts were new for 1936. The gearshift lever was round in section, tapered from bottom to top, and featured a spring-loaded plunger near its top. The plunger mated with scallops in the underside of the gate to hold the gearshift lever in each gear's

The constant-mesh four-speed transmission was all-new for 1936 and would provide the basis for all Harley-Davidson Big Twin four-speeds to follow, except for the 1939 hybrid transmission with sliding second gear. Note the bolt and bracket that serves as the transmission support on the kickstarter end. The bolt extends down from the sheet-metal bracket, which is bolted to the lower two studs for the kickstarter cover. When properly adjusted, the bolt should just touch the lower frame tube. Problems arose when the bolt was over- or under-adjusted, so a new bracket and a mount on the frame was added late in the year. The new sheet-metal bracket was larger and stouter and extended down to butt against the frame mount, and the two were clamped together by a cap screw, providing a nonadjustable transmission mount on the kickstarter end. *Copyright Harley-Davidson Michigan, Inc.*

A rear view of the cutaway transmission showing the operating mechanism of the shift drum at top. At right are the kickstarter and clutch release mechanisms. Note the release fingers, the three-piece throw-out bearing, and the starter clutch. The three-piece, six-ball throw-out bearing had been carried over from the earlier singles and 45s. In mid-year, this bearing was replaced by a larger bearing with eight balls. Although the updated bearing was better, it still wasn't stout enough. It, too, was replaced, in late 1938, by an even larger bearing. *Copyright Harley-Davidson Michigan, Inc.*

position. From the rider's perspective, first gear was the farthest forward position, then came neutral, second gear, third gear, and fourth gear. To shift, the rider just pushed the lever forward or pulled it back. Both lever and gate are chrome-plated and were used only in 1936.

The shift lever is connected to the transmission's shifter shaft by a shifter rod with a clevis at the front end and a 90-degree bend at the back end. This shifter rod and clevis were cadmium plated and remained in use virtually unchanged through the end of the Knucklehead line in 1947.

Clutch

The transmission is connected to engine power via a conventional multiplate clutch and a primary chain. This clutch and drum proved to be nearly bullet-proof, able to handle much more than stock horsepower. Aside from a few changes to the discs, the assembly was carried forward onto the subsequent 61s through 1940.

The clutch disc pack consisted of five fiber friction discs, three flat steel discs, and one "humped" steel disc. The fiber discs have notches on their outer circumference that mate with the splines on the inside of the clutch drum. The flat steel discs have splines on their inner circumference that mate with the splines on the outside diameter of the clutch driving disc. Drive is transferred through splines on the inside of the clutch drum to the friction discs.

When the clutch is engaged, 10 clutch springs force the friction discs into contact with the steel discs, and the steel discs transfer the power to the clutch driving plate through their splined mating surface on the outside circumference of the driving disc's hub. And the driving plate transfers the power to the hub through another splined mating surface, this one on the inside circumference of the driving disc's hub.

The disc pack worked well under normal use, but under hard use or lots of stop-and-go driving, the discs sometimes would stick and drag. Even so they were carried over onto the early 1937 61s.

In traditional American practice, the clutch was foot operated by a pedal on the left side of the motorcycle. The pedal had toe and heel pads, the operation of which was the opposite of that used on cars and some other motorcycles, including Indian. Push down on the toe pedal, and the linkage would engage the clutch. Push down on the heel pad, and the linkage would disengage the clutch. The pedal is cadmium plated through about mid-1937 and is Parkerized thereafter. The foot-operated clutch-release mechanism was used on all Harley Big Twins through 1951.

The pedal connects to the transmission's clutch release lever by a rod that is threaded on the front for the clevis and is slightly flattened at the rear to slip into one of the two slots on the clutch release lever's end. The release lever is made of two pieces brazed together. The larger piece is a round rod with a dogleg bend, and the rod is flattened at the dogleg. The second piece is the right end, which has a square hole that mates with the release-lever stud, that extends through the kickstarter cover to attach to the release finger. This lever is cadmium plated and is used for 1936 and 1937.

The weak link in the 1936 61's clutch system was its throw-out bearing. Two different throw-out bearings were used in 1936 alone, and neither of these really proved satisfactory. On the first 1936 61s, Harley-Davidson reused the six-ball throwout bearing that was first used on the side-valve 45s introduced in late 1928. While the bearing was adequate for the loads imposed by the 45, it proved to be too weak to stand up to those of the 61, so it was replaced in midyear by a larger bearing with eight balls. This new bearing was used until mid-1938, when it was replaced with a still-larger bearing. And even this bearing wasn't stout enough, so it, too, was replaced for the 1939 model year.

Kickstarter Assembly

The 1936 61 was fitted with a conventional kickstarter assembly that includes a crank arm with pedal and return spring, a starter clutch, and gears to turn the transmission mainshaft and transfer the kickstarting force through the clutch to turn over the engine. The starter clutch disconnects the gears when the crank arm is in its rest position and again at the bottom of the stroke. Thus, if the rider pauses and holds the kicker arm at the bottom of the stroke, there is no danger of the engine kicking back through the crank.

The assembly is housed in the kickstarter cover on the transmission's right side. At least two covers were used during 1936 production, and the only significant difference between them is that the early 1936 cover has a milled flat for (but no boss for) the transmission vent tube, which is located above the starter-crank tunnel, while the late 1936 cover does have a cast-in boss for the vent. The later cover was also used on early 1937 61s.

On both covers, the starter, crank tunnel carries a one-piece bushing for the starter crank's shaft and the outer end of the tunnel is sealed by a cork washer held in a machined-in recess in the boss around the starter, crank tunnel. The tunnel boss is reinforced inside the cover by five ribs around the boss.

Early starters on four-speed transmissions used a 26-tooth starter-crank gear that meshed with a 14-tooth mainshaft starter gear. The gears were changed sometime early in the production run to 24 teeth on the starter-crank gear and 18 teeth on the mainshaft gear. This revised gearing was used on all four-speed transmissions through 1947 and on 1939-and-later three-speed and three-speed-with-reverse transmissions. The starters for 1936–1938 three-speed and three-speed with reverse transmissions use yet another gearing combination: 22 teeth on the crank gear and 18 teeth on the mainshaft gear.

Primary-Chain Housing

A two-piece guard covers the primary chain, keeping dirt off the chain and lubricant inside it. At least two different inner covers and three different outer covers were fitted at various times during the 1936 production cycle.

The inner cover used through mid-1936 lacks an oil drain hole because it is used in conjunction with an outer cover having a drain hole. Later 1936 inner covers are like the previous cover, except that a nipple for a drain pipe is added to the lower rear surface of the cover and two more reinforcement ribs are stamped in—a medium-length rib aft of the crankcase-breather-pipe hole and an even shorter one just aft that. All inner primary covers were painted black. Drain pipes were cadmium plated.

The first type of outer primary cover was probably fitted to only the preproduction 61s. It is unique in that it has a screw hole on each side of the primary-chain inspection-cover hole. The purpose of these holes is not known, but they probably fastened some sort of baffle. This outer cover also had a drain hole under the clutch derby.

The second type of primary cover used on the 61 is like the previous cover, except that it lacks the two screws fore and aft of the primary-chain inspection cover. This outer cover was first fitted sometime early in the production run, and may even have been fitted to the first production machines. It, too, has the drain hole. Some time during the production run, a third outer cover was introduced. The third 1936 outer cover was the same as the second type, except that the drain hole was omitted because this outer cover was used in combination with a new-type inner cover that had a fitting for a drain pipe. This third outer cover was then fitted to all subsequent Knuckleheads through 1940.

Outer primary covers were painted black. Standard chain inspection covers were chrome plated for 1936 and 1937, but were painted black for the following years (although plated covers were optional for most years). Standard clutch inspection covers were also painted black, but chrome-plated covers were part of the Chrome Finish Group for 1936 and 1937. Inner and outer covers are fastened together using 10 Parkerized fillister-head straight-slot screws.

Rear Chain Guard

Covering the rear drive chain is a stamped steel guard that is formed of two pieces riveted together near the front of the guard. It is attached at the front to a tab on the top of the inner primary cover and at the back to a mount riveted to the fender brace. This two-piece chain guard is correct on 1936–1938 61s. The guard is painted black.

Frame

The 1936 Knucklehead came with a frame as different and as modern as its engine. Previous Harley frames had all been single-downtube types that were really just descendants of turn-of-the-century bicycle frames. Single-downtube frames were light and easy to build, but they lacked the rigidity to handle higher weights and more horsepower. The new Knucklehead frame had twin downtubes that cradled the engine in a cage of chrome-moly tubing that stretched from the steering-head forging at the front to the axle-mount forgings at the rear. And its 28-degree steering-head angle gave a perfect balance of steering and stability with the stock 18-inch wheels and 4.00x18-inch tires. Unfortunately, the only rear suspension provided was the spring-mounted seat.

The top of each of the two main downtubes was single-butted to a slash-cut, larger diameter tube extending down

The two best-looking stock paint schemes on any of the Knuckleheads—1936 and 1939. The 1936 is owned by Dave Banks, and the 1939 by Ron Lacey. Note the chrome-plated clutch inspection cover on Banks' bike, which was included in the Chrome Plate Group, which was also part of the Deluxe Solo Group, as was the front fender lamp shown. Note the mount on the front stay for the rear fender. It is the type used beginning in 1937. The correct mount is a separate tab riveted to the back of the stay, about halfway up, as shown in the next photo.

from the steering head. From the butted joint, each tube sweeps down and back, around the engine and transmission, to join with the axle-mount forging for its side. The backbone tube is larger in diameter than the downtubes and angles down and back from the steering head to join with the seat-post tube.

Sidecar mounting loops are brazed to the front side of each down tube, and a mounting strap for the toolbox is brazed between the upper and lower tubes just forward of the right axle clip.

The engine mounts to the frame at three points: to a lug from the backbone tube, to a casting that bridges the down tubes underneath the front of the engine, and at the shelf-like rear motor mount attached to the front side of the seat-post tube. The transmission mounts to a plate that allows the transmission to be adjusted fore and aft to tighten or loosen the primary chain.

Sidecar Mounting Lugs

All production and pilot-production 1936 61 frames are thought to have come from the factory with sidecar mounting loops fastened to the front downtubes, but some of the prototype and preproduction frames apparently did not have them, as shown in the disassembly photo of 35E1003. The sidecar lugs also served as the lower mounting point for the three-piece safety guards that were optional for most of the 1936 production year. Sidecar loops on early frames are brazed on, while those on some of the later frames appear to be welded on. When asked how the lugs on one of his frames was attached, Chris Haynes said they appeared to be tack-welded in place and brazed. It is possible that some very, very late 1936 61s were fitted with the updated frame for 1937 with the new-style sidecar-mount forgings that were introduced for that year. See chapter 2 for more details on this frame.

"Fifth" Transmission Mount

Anyone who has ever kicked over one of H-D's Big Twins knows first-hand how much force is transferred through the kickstarter's crank arm to the transmission, especially at the end of the stroke, when the rider's full weight bears down on a lever that is hard against its stop. The transmission on all 1936 61s had four studs for fastening it to the frame. On the kickstarter end of the transmission, unfortunately, the tranny case was not bolted to the frame. Rather, it was loosely supported by what seems to be another one of the under-thought quick fixes that were necessary to get the bike into production for 1936: a sheet-metal bracket was bolted to the kickstart cover and an adjustable support bolt extended down from the bracket to butt against the frame tube.

When properly adjusted, the bolt and bracket provide adequate auxiliary support to the four solid mounts on the transmission. But when improperly adjusted, a number of problems can result. If the bolt is not adjusted far enough down to contact the frame, kickstarting loads are transferred to the other transmission mounting studs and to the frame's transmission mounts, eventually resulting in studs torn loose from the transmission case and cracks forming near the mounts. If the bolt is adjusted too far out, it "cocks" the transmission so that the engine and the sprockets are no longer in line, causing binding and accelerated wear.

Harley-Davidson made the kickstarter-end support "idiot proof" late in the 1936 production run by introducing a "fifth," nonadjustable transmission mount to support that end of the transmission. The new mount consisted of a support pad brazed onto the frame and a revised support bracket that was more rectangular and stout, but which still attached to the lower studs on the kickstarter cover. The bottom of the bracket butted up against the top of the support pad on the frame and a cap screw clamped the two together, providing a fairly good fifth transmission mount.

The new mounting pad and bracket were carried over into 1937 production, but the bracket was eventually replaced by a cast-in lug on the revised transmission case that was introduced in mid-1937. Some authorities say that very, very late 1936 61s were fitted with the revised transmission case and thus do not use the bracket. This is unlikely, however, because the 1937 parts book states that the second type of bracket, part number 2263-36A, was used on the later 1936 61 and "first 1937—61, 74, & 80 twins."

Frame Cracking

In keeping with the sporting nature of the machine, the 1936 61's frame was made as light as possible. The main tubes are 7/8-inch diameter, which, it turned out, were too light. Because of this, the frames were prone to cracking at the seat post, the transmission mount, and on the left rear stay when the machines were ridden hard—especially off-road, as riders of the day often did. Cracks were fixed by welding the broken pieces, either at a dealership or at the factory. If the work was done at the factory, a number was often stamped in the reinforcement webbing behind the seat post.

When a sidecar was fitted, the front downtubes often cracked from the extra torsional strain transferred to the tubes through the sidecar mounting lugs. Anecdotal evidence exists that a fix for the latter problem was sometimes performed at the factory by brazing in a longer slash-cut reinforcement on the downtubes. The reinforcement on these frames extends far below the normal slash-cut joint, sometimes to a point just above the sidecar mounts. At least one example exists of a frame that was apparently fitted with the longer reinforcements at the time the frame was built, as this frame shows no sign of modification. Were these frames built for the ES models for sidecar use? Or for the later ESs? Future research may supply the answer.

The real fix for the problems with frames cracking came in 1937, when a new frame was introduced that was heavier duty all around. Some authorities say that the new frame was fitted to the very last 1936 61s and they cite the fact that many 1936 61 engines reside in these frames today (including the 1936 61 in the Harley-Davidson collection) as proof. Since no documentation exists to prove conclusively when the new frame was first fitted, the most I can offer is an opinion: Some very, very late 1936 61s may have come with the 1937 frame, but more likely the 1936 engines that are in these frames are there because the original cracked frame was replaced under warranty with the updated frame or because the owner upgraded the bike at a later date when it cracked or was damaged in an accident. It is very unlikely that Harley-Davidson stocked the trouble-prone 1936 frame as a replacement part.

Tool Boxes

The 1936 61 was fitted with a toolbox that is similar to but not exactly the same as the one fitted to the side-valve models. It mounts to a bracket on the right side of the motorcycle. The box is rectangular and mounts so that the long dimension is vertical. Its cover is held closed by a keyed lock.

Box and cover are painted black and a Harley-Davidson patent decal is attached to the cover. This rectangular toolbox is correct for 1936–1939 61s.

Forks and Handlebars

The new forks on the 1936 Knucklehead were leading link, spring-suspended forks with about 2 inches of travel. They differed little in concept from the forks on previous Harley Big Twins, but they were a bit stouter. Externally, the main difference was that the legs of the rigid fork on the new 61 look smoother and more streamlined because they were made of extruded, oval-section tubing, rather than of the drop-forged I-beams that the forks on the side-valve Big twins were made of.

The 1936 61's forks had no built-in damping, but optional friction plates, called "ride control," could be ordered. These plates, one on each side of the fork, could be tightened or loosened for more or less friction, much like the steering dampers of the day. On the 1936–1937 61's ride control, the adjusting knob was on the right side. On later machines, the adjusting knob was on the left side.

Only minor changes were made to these forks from 1936 to mid-1946, when they were replaced by the new "offset" springer forks. Distinguishing features of the early forks include two forward-facing grease fittings on the front of the spring-perch forging, and narrow, unreinforced mounting tabs for the front fender. The grease fittings remained in this location until they were moved to the outside left and right edges of the spring perch in 1939, so that the fittings point out to the sides. The narrow fender tabs were used through 1937, but for 1937 they were reinforced by a plate spot-welded underneath each.

Handlebars and Hand Controls

The 1936 61's handlebars were also new, to fit the new fork. The left and right bars are brazed to a center forging that has a center hole and two smaller-diameter flanking holes, into which the tops of the fork's rigid-leg tubes slip. Pinch bolts clamp the forging around the fork tubes. At the start of the model year, only the Standard bars were available, but the March 3, 1936, dealer news bulletin announced the availability of new, Speedster bars for the sport-oriented 61 rider. According to the bulletin, "The rider using them leans forward just a little and presents a race-like, speeding appearance." Speedster bars were available in place of the standard bars for no extra cost after this date. Bars were painted black unless the Deluxe Solo Group or Chrome Plate Group was ordered, in which case they were chrome plated.

The inner diameter of each bar end is threaded for a screw that retains the throttle spiral on the right and spark-control spiral on the left. The outer portion of the spirals show a 2 3/8-inch-wide chrome band inboard of the rubber grip. Correct grips swell in the midsection and have a pattern of ridges running the length of the grip. Standard grips were white rubber, but black grips were optional. Throttle and spark-control coils and control wires are routed through the bars and emerge from holes in the bosses near the ends of the handlebar's center forging. These spirals and grips are correct for 1936–1942.

The left bar also has a headlight dimmer switch, a horn switch, and the front-brake hand lever and bracket. The brake hand lever assembly consists of an S-shaped, chrome-plated steel lever and a Parkerized lever bracket and clamp bracket. This hand lever and bracket were used from 1936 through 1940.

Fork Top Plate

On at least the early-1936 61, the chrome-plated fork top plate has four 13/64-inch holes in it. Unfortunately, no one has been able to uncover their intended purpose. Later in the year (or possibly at the start of 1937 production?) this top plate was replaced by a stainless steel plate that lacks the holes.

Safety Guards

Two different optional front safety guards were fitted to 1936 61s. Early guards were made of three pieces—the top center clamp/mount and the two side loops. The top end of each loop slips into the center piece, and bolts are tightened to clamp the three pieces into a unit. The guard attaches at the top to the motorcycle's frame and at the bottom to the sidecar mounting lugs. Thus, a rider had to choose between having a sidecar attached or having a safety guard. The guard is painted black. Some photos show that the guards were pinstriped, but others show that they were not, so the pinstripes may have been an early-season feature. I have been able to locate only one unrestored machine that has pinstripes on the guard. Its owner reports that it has two stripes on each loop and that they are gold. These stripes may be original or they may have been added at a later date.

Some time during the production year (possibly coinciding with the introduction of the LE sidecar, which was first ready to ship on March 16, 1936, according to a dealer news bulletin), the three-piece guard was replaced by a new one-piece guard with revised lower mounts that attached to the footboard mounts. This arrangement freed up the sidecar mounting lugs so that a sidecar and a safety guard could be mounted simultaneously. The four bends in the guard are symmetrical, giving it a squared-off, boxy look that kind of clashes with the lines of the bike and limits cornering clearance. The new safety guard was also painted black, but was probably not pinstriped. This new guard was optional on 61s through 1938.

Lights and Horn

The Cycle-Ray headlight is fitted with a prefocused 21/32-candlepower bulb and separate reflector and lens. This lamp is identified by the names "Cycle-Ray" and "Guide" inside a circle stamped on the outside at the rear of the steel bucket and "Cycle-Ray" and "Made in the U.S.A." raised out of the face of the glass lens casting. The standard steel bucket is painted black for all years (but chrome-plated buckets were available as part of the Chrome Plate Group) and the lens doors are chrome plated for all but 1943 to mid-1946 models. The headlamp mounted to a bracket that is bolted to the headlamp lugs on the fork's rigid-leg's spring perch and to the handlebar center section.

The taillight is the "beehive" style that had been introduced on the 1935 Big Twins. The taillamp assembly includes a stamped-steel bracket with integral license-plate bracket, a stamped-steel lens bucket, and a red glass lens. The bracket is painted black, and the bucket is chrome plated. This taillight is correct for 1936–1938 61s.

The horn was a new part for 1936. It is a Delco-Remy Model 16 horn with winged-face cover and bolt-on brackets. The horn body is painted black, and the cover is chrome plated. A separate bracket attaches the horn to the headlight mount so that the horn rides underneath the headlight. This horn is correct for 1936–1941 Knuckleheads.

Although these 6-volt lights and horn are anemic by today's standards, they were as good as any of the day, and if a rider needed any more light, the optional Little King or Little Beauty spotlights were available. These accessory lights mounted to a crossbar on the handlebars and were listed at retail prices of $9.75–$11.75 for the Little Kings or $11.50–$13.50 for the Little Beauties (prices depending on which order blank was in effect at the time of order).

Wheels and Brakes

The Knucklehead was introduced when tall, narrow wheels and tires were still fashionable on American motorcycles, and the Knucklehead was still in production when fashion switched to fatter, softer-riding tires.

The first Knucklehead's rims were 2.15x18 inches, stamped steel, laced with cadmium-plated spokes, and fitted with 4.00x18-inch tires. Front and rear wheels and hubs are identical and interchangeable once the brake and drive parts are detached and interchanged.

The 1936's star hub has a step on the inside surface of the brake-side flange. These "stepped" hubs were used through

Carman Brown's 36EL. Note the correct 1936-only mount for the rear chain guard on the frontmost fender stay. Also note how the pinstripe angles forward and down at the front, paralleling the line of the fender's chain-guard recess.

1938 and turn on roller bearings. The brake-side flange is stamped steel. The hub star cover used on the 1936 61 was used only that year on the Knucklehead. The cover has two small, square holes 180 degrees apart, near the axle opening. These holes were omitted from the star covers used on 1937- and-later Knuckleheads. The cover was cadmium plated on 1936 and some 1937 Knuckleheads.

For 1936, the wheel rims were painted the color of the fender panels (except when the color scheme was Teak Red with black tank panels—then the rims were painted red). Cadmium-plated or black-enameled rims were optional that first year. Hubs were painted black.

The 1936 Knucklehead was fitted with front and rear mechanically actuated, internal-expanding brakes with two shoes each. Both brake drums are 7-1/4-inch inside diameter and are made of pressed steel. Upper and lower brake shoes are lined with an asbestos material and are interchangeable. The brake drum is attached to the hub by five lug bolts. For at least part of the 1936 production year, the lug nuts were drilled with a "safety-wire" hole. The holes may have been a response to all the problems experienced with the 1935 45 "demountable" rear wheel and brake hub, which were almost identical to those used on the 61. According to *Shop Dope No. 123* (dated March 15, 1935), "Demountable rear wheel clamp screws must be securely tightened two or three times within the first few hundred miles after a machine goes in service." Lug nuts were probably not safety wired at the factory, but a dealer or owner who experienced problems with lugs that repeatedly loosened could wire them if necessary.

The front brake on the 1936 61 was a new unit designed for the bike's new spring fork, but it used the same cable adjusting mechanism that had been used on other H-D Big Twins since 1928—a hollow bolt threads onto the brake coil, the coil and adjusting bolt are inserted through an unthreaded lug on the brake backing plate, and a nut locks them into adjustment. The backing plate also has a peened-on stud for the brake shackle. This backing plate is used for 1936–1937. The front drum was used from 1936 through 1939. The brake shackle has a grease fitting on each end, each pointing up. This shackle is correct for 1936–1938.

The 1936 61's rear brake drum and backing plate are one-year-only parts, used only on the OHV. The brake is 7 1/4 inches in diameter, the same as the front, and uses the same shoes as the front. About the only part of the assembly that was carried over to following years was the operating-cam lever, which was used on all the OHV rear brakes through 1957.

The pedal and linkage for the 1936 61's rear brake also had many one-year-only parts, including the pedal, pedal pivot, front operating rod, and the right-end lever for the crossover. The stamped-steel brake pedal has only three holes—the pivot hole at the bottom, a 5/16-inch upper hole into which the operating rod's end is inserted, and a 1/4-inch lower hole for the pedal return spring. (Pedals for 1937 and later had a fourth hole for the brake-lock lever's pivot bolt.) The pedal is cadmium plated.

The 1936-only operating rod has a 90-degree bend at each end; one end is inserted into a hole in the pedal, and the other end is inserted into a hole in the crossover shaft's right-end lever. The hooked ends were not ideal connections, however. Under hard braking, the ends would flex and bind, so the rod was replaced for 1937 by a rod with clevises at each end.

The basic front brake setup introduced in 1936 proved to be satisfactory, so it was carried over into the following years largely unchanged. By today's standards it would be called pathetic, but it was about as good as the brakes offered by the competition—and it was probably as powerful as the period tires could handle under normal road conditions. Anyway, riders of the day didn't know that front brakes offered far greater braking potential than rear brakes, for these were the days when the rear brake was considered to be the main brake by most motorcyclists. Thus, many riders who considered the front brake perfectly acceptable were less than satisfied with a rear brake of the same size. They had reason to be dissatisfied because the rear brake on the 61 was conspicuously weak and tended to chatter and squeal, so the 7-1/4-inch rear brake was used for 1936 only. In fact, many owners of 1936 61s upgraded to the larger rear brake when it became available in 1937, so the original 7-1/4-inch rear brake parts are scarce today.

Brown likes to restore his bikes and preserve them perfectly, seldom riding them but showing them at various meets so they can still be appreciated. Note the holes in the chrome plate atop the handlebar's center section. These appear only for 1936, and they are one of the many mysteries of the 1936 61. I have never heard a plausible answer for why the holes were drilled.

Continuing Problems

The 1936 Knucklehead was a basically sound design but a number of circumstances—H-D's understandable eagerness to recoup the new bike's high development costs, the cumulative financial squeeze of the Depression, labor laws that prevented H-D engineers from working overtime—combined to force H-D's management into ordering the new model shipped to dealers in a form that was essentially an advanced prototype. Predictable difficulties ensued, but the company rushed to correct these teething problems with updated parts and tuning information, sometimes modifying a single part three or more times during the production run. The daunting number of such changes made during the 1936 model year attests to the fact that its configuration had been far from finalized when the first bikes were shipped

The most chronic problem was the same one that is thought to have delayed the 61's introduction for so long—oil control. Even after the valve-spring covers were put into production, oil leaks were still prevalent. One of the main causes of leaks was improper adjustment of the oil supply to each rocker arm. A little well-intentioned tinkering could easily result in over- or under-oiled valves.

The consequences of over oiling were unpleasant but not catastrophic: excessive oil consumption and extreme leakage from the valve covers (they all leaked a bit anyway). Even so, it is easy to understand why a customer would be disappointed when his shiny new Knucklehead trailed a thick blue cloud of oil smoke, saturated his legs with oil, or consumed more lubricant than the previous Harleys with total-loss oil systems.

If the adjustment erred on the side of under-oiling, the consequences were much more serious, ranging from what *Shop Dope No. 140* described as "squeaking" valves, to rapid and excessive wear of the valves, rockers, shafts, and pushrods.

Even when valve oiling was properly adjusted, the valve spring covers sometimes overflowed with oil, because with each engine cycle the vacuum used to pull oil out of the covers

sucked debris into the cover to form a sludge that could plug the return lines. As a quick fix, an air fitting was added to the front rocker housing in late 1936, according to *Shop Dope No. 140A*, revised July 20, 1936. Pressurized air applied at the fitting unclogged both scavenge lines. The shop dope also gave instructions to add the air nipple to earlier engines. Of more catastrophic consequence, water could enter through the valve-arm slot, freezing the valve in a block of ice if the temperature dropped below freezing. These problems would not be fully fixed until 1938, when new covers

A photo of a 1936 police bike showing many of the features common to late-1936 machines: the "knuckle" nuts in place of the round chrome "frog-eye" covers over the ends of the rocker shafts, the air fitting on the front rocker housing, the one-piece front safety guard, and the unnotched gearcase cover. The speedometer is apparently equipped with a tripmeter, as inferred from the reset knob and rubber cover on the right side of the instrument panel. A look under the kickstarter return spring shows that even at the late date this machine was built, the adjustable support for the transmission was still in use. The fender pinstripes are worth noting in that a second pinstripe is painted along the junction of the black panel and white crown of the fenders, and the lower pinstripe on the front fender ends in a flourish at the rear. This photo also shows the "star" cover on the front hub, with a small 1936-only notch on each side of the axle. *Copyright Harley-Davidson Michigan, Inc.*

were introduced that fully enclosed each rocker arm and valve in its own housing.

The two-piece pinion-shaft assembly (through which oil passed to get to the crank pin and connecting-rod bearings) was also a cause of excessive oil consumption. Starting with engine number 36EL1755 (and 88 engines with lower serial numbers), a new stub shaft (the part of the pinion-shaft assembly that mounts to the flywheel) was fitted that reduced oil flow to the bottom end, according to *Shop Dope No. 142*. Harley-Davidson suggested that the new stub shaft be retrofitted in all earlier engines and made it available free of charge, on an exchange basis. The shop dope also reiterated that proper adjustment of oil to the rocker arms was critical to making the engine run well and get acceptable oil mileage.

Listed in the Shop Dope are the 88 earlier engines that were also fitted with the new stub shaft. Interestingly, the list includes *all* engines from 1722 to 1754, which makes me wonder, why didn't the Shop Dope say that the modification began with engine number 1722 instead of 1755? Also, the engines listed include six from the first 100 serial numbers (including 1018, ostensibly the 18th engine built) and some from each subsequent 100. Why would all these very early engines still be at the factory when the engines with serial numbers over 1700 were being built? Had the earlier engines been returned for warranty work or had they remained at the factory for reworking of problems?

Competition

Even though the factory was unwilling to officially campaign the 61, private riders took up the mantle. As already mentioned, the Knucklehead was piloted to its first victory by "Butch" Quirk, who used a sidecar-equipped 61 to win a 350-mile endurance run sponsored by the Rose City Motorcycle Club. The March 23, 1936, dealer news bulletin announced that the 61 had been ruled eligible for Class C competition in the 80-ci class, and Knucklehead riders soon began competing and winning in numerous TTs, hillclimbs, and road races across the country. A rider even piloted a sidecar-equipped 61 to a gold medal in the grueling International Six-Day Trials, which were held in Germany that year. Though it wasn't a dominant racer in its first year, it would soon make its mark.

1936 Production

Just as the start date of 61 production is a mystery, so, too is the ending date and the number actually produced. As with the start date, I haven't found definitive answers for those questions. I have, however, gathered some information on these topics that I hope will add to the body of knowledge and spark further discussion on the issue.

Consensus among the many experts on the 1936 61 is that production began in March or April and ended in July. Information from dealer news bulletins suggests that both of these dates are suspect. As the dealer news bulletins quoted earlier in this chapter suggested, production probably began in early January and quickly ramped up. As winter turned to spring, orders began rolling in faster than they could be filled, as the February 24, 1936, dealer news bulletin had predicted.

The May 18 issue reassured dealers that "the 61 OHV delivery situation is getting better all the time!" and that production was "getting to a better stride." It went on to predict, "This is going to be welcome news indeed to our dealers who have been . . . fearful to give this model full selling justice because they were afraid of the delivery situation." It went on to state that orders could be filled in 8 to 10 days and also hinted at what a difficult task it had been to get the new model into production: "To us here at the scene it is nothing short of a miracle the way this factory has handled and brought on production of the new 61." Because the principles are all riding Harleys in the clouds, we'll never know what miracles were worked!

The immediate future. Demand grew for the 61 as the production year went on. The 1936 61s were built into at least late August 1936 (the August 10, 1936, dealer news bulletin specified that delivery time for 61s was "about two weeks"). The bike on the right, also owned and restored by Carman Brown, shows what the second-year Knuckleheads looked like.

As mentioned previously, the June issue of *The Enthusiast* contained an ad featuring the 61 OHV. The ad called the 61 the "Sensation of the motorcycle world," and accurately alluded to the conspicuous lack of promotion: "Minus fanfare and ballyhoo, a new motorcycle has come on the scene and has taken the world by storm." It also featured a photo of Bill Cummings, the winner of the 1934 Indianapolis 500, on his all-white (including frame, oil tank, and toolbox) 1936 61. This first official notice about the new model, in Harley's own magazine, came almost six months after the first 61s hit the streets.

The June 15 bulletin stated that orders could be filled in 7 to 10 days if standard colors and equipment were ordered—more evidence that custom colors were available.

By the deadline for the August 10 issue, delivery time for 61s was up to "about two weeks." This is interesting not so much to show that orders were still coming in as strong at the end of summer as at the beginning, but because it implies that the 1936 61s were still in production in early August and that the final orders in at that time would not be filled until at least mid-August. The bikes discussed in the bulletin were almost certainly 1936 models, because the 1937 models were not announced to the dealers until the October 19 dealer news bulletin, and not to the public until the November issue of *The Enthusiast*.

From the information in these bulletins, a rough timeline can be drawn. Production of 61 demonstrators began no later than mid-January and finished sometime around the middle of February. Production of 61s to fill customer orders began in middle to late February and ended no sooner than mid-August.

So how many were built? Production figures compiled by Harley-Davidson and published in its book, *The Legend Begins*, suggest that 1,704 Knuckleheads were sold in 1936, including 152 Model Es, 1,526 Model ELs, and 26 Model ESs. Consensus among many experts (based on their observation of serial numbers of existing machines) is that closer to 2,000 were built, and this figure is supported by the November 1936 issue of *The Enthusiast*, which boasts that, "In the short time it has been out nearly 2,000 of these sweet jobs have been placed in owners' hand and are rolling up millions of economical miles on American highways." According to Jerry Hatfield, the company's board minutes said 61 sales totaled 1,836 through the end of the business year on September 30, 1936. The highest serial number I have heard of on an existing bike is 2903 (the 1,903rd built).

For some reason, the early machines seem to have survived in greater numbers than the later machines. Gerry Lyons, founder of the 36 EL Registry and editor of the club's newsletter, divided the serial numbers of the 1936 61s known to exist into two lists—those up to 2000 (e.g., the first 1,000 1936 61s built) and those over 2000. In theory, at least, survival rates should have been uniform across the serial-number range, resulting in a one-to-one ratio if 2,000 machines really were built. In fact, the ratio is two to one, in favor of the early bikes.

Why would almost twice the percentage of the early bikes survive? I can't think of an *obvious* reason for this to be the case, but there must be one, or else actual production was substantially less than 2,000. Several theories to explain the skewed ratio have been floated in the club's newsletter. Some theorize that whole blocks of late-serialed motorcycles may have been shipped overseas. Others theorize that Harley-Davidson skipped blocks of serial numbers to trick rival Indian into thinking the 61 was selling in greater numbers than was actually the case.

I find the first theory plausible. It is not inconceivable that Alfred Rich Child or another foreign franchisee would order 50 to 100 or more machines at once, all of which probably would have been built as a block, with consecutive serial numbers. According to the book *Harley-Davidson: The Milwaukee Marvel* by Harry Sucher, Child had exclusive sales rights for Japan, Korea, China, and Manchuria and could order machines on open account, with payment not due until 90 days after the shipment reached Japan. Sucher also says that Genijiro Fukui, a representative of Sankyo, "purchased several hundred sidecar outfits from [Child] in 1936" to "fill out their Rikuo line." Sankyo was by this time building the Rikuo, a license-built copy of the Harley-Davidson VL side-valve Big Twin, so it is unlikely that Sankyo would purchase side-valve sidecar rigs. It is quite possible that many of them were 61s. Similarly, other importers may also have bought large blocks of 61s, all or most of which were probably destroyed or ground up for scrap during World War II.

The second theory I find implausible. Why, when it had just released a motorcycle that set the lead in the big-twin market, and one it couldn't build fast enough to keep up with orders, would Harley-Davidson skip serial numbers just to fool the competition? I don't think they would.

Whatever the actual production figure was—1,704, 1,836, or 2,000—it exceeded Harley-Davidson's original sales projections. And demand exceeded the factory's production capacity. Clearly, the 61 was a hit. More important, the Knucklehead gave H-D a firm technological lead over arch rival Indian and their flat-head Chief. It also gave them an engine that was in the same technological league as the best European twins. Even though the Depression was far from over in the country at large, the future looked bullish from the boardroom in Milwaukee.

CHAPTER TWO

1937-1939

The Knucklehead Takes Over

Today, we have a wonderful term that perfectly describes the reason for Harley-Davidson's reticent approach to publicizing the 1936 61: "plausible deniability." While the company hoped that the 61's unique combination of style and performance would bring success, it also knew the bike still had many flaws. Consequently, H-D did its best to keep the bike under wraps to ensure that if failure came, at least it would be a quiet one.

Fortunately, the 61 sold itself, and H-D did a superb job of fixing problems on the fly. Even so, some dealers and customers wondered whether they'd been used again as unpaid testers, a practice that is now common, especially in the software industry. And today, we have another term to describe less than fully developed products, such as the 1936 61, that are put onto the market for comment and debugging by favored customers: the "beta" release.

For 1937, H-D's efforts and its customers' patience were rewarded by the introduction of Knucklehead Version 1.0, a much-improved machine that was the product of lessons learned that first year. At the start of its second era, the Knucklehead began to take over. That year, all of the company's models were remade in its image, with revised, dry-sump motors clothed in 61-style finery. With full confidence in its OHV at last, H-D threw back the cloak of silence; the first year's lack of "fanfare and ballyhoo" gave way to a blizzard of promotion in the second, and sales of the 61 began a steady climb that accelerated in the following years. By the end of the decade, the 61 was poised to become Harley's best-selling motorcycle, even though it was also the company's most expensive.

Window to the World, 1937

By the start of the 1937 model year, most Americans believed that the worst days of the Depression were behind them, but the Depression was far from over. For 1937, unemployment and inflation were up slightly, and the Dow was down.

On January 20, FDR was inaugurated for his second term as president. His New Deal was given a big boost when conservative justice Willis Van DeVanter resigned and was replaced by Hugo L. Black. This swung the balance of the court to the left and promised an end to a string of New Deal acts that had been overturned by the Supreme Court.

On May 6, the German zeppelin *Hindenburg* was consumed by fire and crashed to Earth as it attempted to moor at Lakehurst, New Jersey, after a flight from Frankfurt-am-Main, Germany. More than 30 people were killed in the conflagration. Herbert Morrison's heart-wrenching eyewitness report of the tragedy was relayed around the country to become the first coast-to-coast radio broadcast.

On July 2, Amelia Earhart disappeared somewhere over the Pacific Ocean on her much-hyped attempt to fly around the world.

The 1939 models came closer to recapturing the sporty styling of the original Knuckleheads than did any other year. Note that the patent decal was moved back to the toolbox cover for 1939, where it had been in 1936. This stunning 1939 EL is owned and was restored by Eldon Brown. The solid Wolfe Safety wheels, made by Wolfe Accessory Mfg. Co., of Akron, Ohio, are period accessories that have been on the bike since it was new, according to Reg Shanks, the Vancouver Island, British Columbia, dealer who originally sold the bike in 1939.

LEFT: A gorgeous 1937 EL owned and restored by Elmer Ehnes. Although the paint combination shown—black with red stripes edged in gold—was not listed as a standard paint combination, custom color combinations could be ordered, and some almost certainly were ordered in this striking combination.

New for 1937 was the 120-mile-per-hour speedometer with hash marks at the intermediate 5-mile-per-hour positions. It was available with or without a trip odometer. The trip-odometer version shown was used only for 1937. The version without the trip odometer was available through 1940. Also new for 1937 was the speedometer light switch, which is at the aft end of the skull-face dash.

On July 12, the U.S. Navy got a taste of things to come when the *USS Panay* was sunk by Japanese aircraft while in China's Yangtze River, killing two Americans. Two days later, Japan apologized and agreed to reparations.

In one of the more remarkable ironies of the era, amphetamines were introduced to "cure" hyperactive children in the same year that the Marijuana Taxation Act prohibited the importation, sale, or possession of the weed.

Labor unrest continued as nearly half a million workers participated in sit-down strikes. Industry responded with a heavy club. Labor organizer John L. Lewis uttered the most memorable mouthful of the year: "No tin-hat brigade of goose-stepping vigilantes or Bible-babbling mob of blackguarding corporation scoundrels will prevent the onward march of Labor." The song, *Whistle While You Work*, became a major hit.

The labor unrest was as strong in Milwaukee as it was elsewhere. In March, Harley-Davidson employees unionized under the United Auto Workers. On April 21, William A. Davidson, one of the four founders of the company, died. His son, William H. Davidson, was made a company vice president and was selected to eventually succeed Walter Davidson as president.

The 1937 Knucklehead

Harley's OHV Big Twin was offered in three versions for 1937: the high-compression 37EL Special Sport Solo, the medium-compression 37E Solo, and the medium-compression 37ES twin with sidecar gearing. All were listed at a retail price of $435.00. Essential equipment such as a jiffy stand and steering damper had to be ordered separately or as part of one of the option groups, at additional cost.

Two option groups for solos and one group for sidecar haulers were offered. The Standard Solo Group, which listed for $21.75, included the front safety guard, steering damper, ride control, stop light and switch, jiffy stand, trip odometer, and front fender light. The Deluxe Solo Group included all the items in the standard group plus a colored shift knob, foot-pedal rubbers, the Chrome Plate Group, a license-plate frame, the 6-inch round air cleaner, and the Deluxe Saddlebags. It listed for $49.00. The Standard Group for sidecar or commercial motorcycles, a $20.00 package, included a front safety guard, a steering damper, a stop light and switch, the ride control, and the three-speed transmission with reverse gear.

Styling Changes

The 1937 models came with a new paint scheme. The art deco gas-tank transfer was retained, but for 1937 the transfer was bracketed above and below by thick stripes edged in a complementary color. Gone were the 1936's fender panels, replaced by solid-color fenders with stripes matching those on the tank running along each side of each fender's crown. And the 1936 OHV's gorgeous color-matched rims were replaced in 1937 by black-painted rims.

Two regular civilian color combinations were listed in the November 1936 issue of *The Enthusiast*, which introduced the new-models for 1937: Bronze Brown striped in Delphine Blue and edged in yellow and Teak Red striped in black and edged in gold. The brown scheme proved to be unpopular, so a third combination was soon introduced: Delphine Blue striped in Teak Red. Police models were offered in Police Silver with black stripes edged in gold.

Of the three regular civilian combinations, the red and blue schemes proved to be the overwhelming preference of riders then and restorers now. Viewed from today's perspective on what is clearly an antique machine, the Bronze Brown and Delphine Blue is a handsome combination that seems suitable for the machine. But at the time, the brown paint projected a somewhat military or utilitarian image—not at all what most riders wanted on their expensive new sport machine—so it was never popular.

To compensate for the loss of color-matched wheel rims, the 1937 OHV was given a color-matched oil tank in place of the black tank of 1936, resulting in a motorcycle that "is one continuous sweep of color," according to the November 1936 issue of *The Enthusiast*. The new "sweep" of color might have been too much of a good thing, however. Color-matched oil tanks were discontinued at the end of 1937 and would not again be offered on the Harley-Davidson Big Twins until the special Hollywood Green paint package offered for the 1955 Panheads.

Engine Updates

Aside from the tendency to spit a bit of oil out of the minimal rocker covers, the new OHV mechanism introduced in and refined throughout 1936 proved to be remarkably

The frame for 1937 was much-improved over the 1936 frame, but it also was much heavier. The front downtubes are no longer continuous from a slash-cut single-butted joint below the steering head to the axle clips. Instead, stiffer straight tubes stretch from the steering head to the new sidecar-mount forgings. Separate tubes run back from the forgings to the axle clips. Many of the mounts were also made stronger to eliminate the chronic frame-cracking problems experienced with the 1936 Knucklehead frame. This frame also has the mount on the right lower frame tube for the kickstarter-side transmission mount that had been introduced on late-1936 frames. The transmission case was updated early in 1937 to have a cast-in boss to mount directly to the frame mount, eliminating the need for the separate bracket attached to the kickstarter cover that had been used in 1936.
Copyright Harley-Davidson Michigan, Inc.

trouble-free. A weak point in the system was the somewhat willowy rocker-shaft support arms cast into the cylinder head. For 1936, the two support arms on each head had only a partial reinforcement rib that extended barely halfway up the arm, ending far below the level of the rocker-shaft holes. The problem with the design only came to light when the bikes were out on the street, being revved in friendly competition and fixed by owners and mechanics who had no experience with the new OHV system. During service work, these support arms are easily broken or over stressed if the shaft nuts are cinched up when everything is not correctly aligned or if the thrust washers are left out during assembly.

The solution? The support arms were increased in width, the reinforcing rib on each rocker-shaft support was lengthened, (now reaching vertically to the level of the rocker shaft,) and the ribs were cast integrally with the cooling fin to the left of the bracket. Other than this change to the support brackets, the heads were unchanged, retaining the cup-type valve-spring covers. This cylinder-head design is correct for 1937 only. They would be redesigned the following year to solve the other major problem with the OHV's cylinder heads—oil leaking out and dirt and water leaking in through the valve enclosures.

Another chronic source of oil leaks was the cork rocker-arm seals in the aluminum rocker housings. Starting with serial number 37E1672, the cork seals were replaced by synthetic rubber seals. While these seals came into regular production on 37E1672, they were also fitted on 28 motors with earlier serial numbers that apparently had not been shipped yet for whatever reason; these serial numbers are listed in *Shop Dope No. 153*. That Shop Dope also instructed dealers to throw away any cork seals in stock and to only use the updated rubber seal on future repairs.

Just as in 1936, an air horn was standard on the OHV's carburetor, but the 1937 air horn was a new design. The new OHV air horn was a mirror image of the horn on the flathead Big Twins, a rounded, streamlined shape that tapers from front to rear. The 1937-style air horn was standard on OHVs through 1939.

Starting in 1937, an air cleaner was supplied as part of the Deluxe Solo Group, or it could be ordered separately for $3. This air cleaner is the 6-inch round air cleaner that had been optional for at least part of 1936. The cover is chrome-plated and has the Harley-Davidson bar-and-shield stamped into its round face and an instruction plate riveted to the rim. The cover is fastened to the backing plate by four screws. The oiled-copper-mesh air cleaner wraps around a mesh support welded to the steel backing plate. The backing plate is Parkerized.

The ignition timer was also slightly revised for 1937. The new timer base is like the previous base, except that the notch in the side of the base for the circuit-breaker wire is omitted, and the wire attaches to a terminal post below the base. The wire is routed out of the timer through a hole added to the revised timer housing. This new timer base and housing were used through the end of the Knucklehead line in 1947.

About midway through the 1937 production run, the rocker arms were revised to include an oil passage to positively lubricate the pushrod ball socket. Prior to this modification, the pushrod-to-pushrod-ball bearing surface was oiled only by scavenged oil pulled from the valve-spring covers by engine vacuum. If the return oil lines from the valve-spring covers were plugged or if the oil supply to the valves was adjusted down for minimal overspray, the pushrods would be under-oiled and would wear prematurely. These revised rocker arms were used for the remainder of the 1937 production and through early-1939 production.

Frame and Fifth Transmission Mount

Like the rest of the 1936 OHV, that bike's double downtube frame was a radical departure for a Harley-Davidson street bike. And like the rest of the bike, the frame needed a good bit of tweaking to get it right. Hard use on street and track, and especially under heavy-duty police and sidecar duty, quickly proved that the original design wasn't stout enough for the job. The frame tended to crack under the seat post and at the transmission mount, and the left rear stay sometimes snapped off behind the clutch, so a substantially

The streamlined air horn shown replaced the slash-cut air horn used in 1936. Elmer Ehnes restored this machine for himself, but he does some of the nicest Knuckle and Panhead restorations out of his home shop and that of Kokesh Motorcycles in Spring Lake Park, Minnesota.

redesigned frame made its appearance for the second year of 61 OHV production.

Gone were the two continuous downtubes that swept down and back from the steering head to the axle clips. Replacing them were larger diameter tubes that make the same sweep, but each is formed in two sections. The first section on each side connects the steering head to the top of a new drop forging that has integral sidecar mounting loops. The second section connects to the bottom of the sidecar-mount forging and sweeps down and back to the axle clips. The new frame is stiffer in torsion, improving handling, and it proved much more resistant to cracking than the 1936 frame had been.

The sidecar-mount forgings replace the sidecar loops that were brazed or welded onto the continuous downtubes in 1936. The new mounts strengthen the frame and provide a much more durable mounting location for the sidecar.

The 1937 and later frames were also fitted with the brazed-on clamp bracket for the starter-end, "fifth" transmission mount that had been fitted to a few of the last 1936 frames.

To further strengthen the attachment of the transmission to the frame, the transmission mounts were made stronger, and the transmission mounting plate was twice as thick as that used in 1936. All these modifications helped tremendously, but the problem wasn't really fixed until midyear, when a new transmission case was introduced that had a starter-support boss designed into the casting, which replaced the support bracket bolted to the kickstarter cover. This new transmission case was not replaced until the 1940 model year.

Transmission and Clutch Updates

At about the same time as the transmission case was revised, the starter cover was also modified. The new cover looks, externally, like the previous cover, but is substantially revised internally. The machined-in area for the cork seal on the old cover was replaced with a slight recess for the starter-crank washer. The seal was no longer needed because the one-piece crank bushing used with the old cover was replaced by a two-piece bushing with a neoprene seal between the inner and outer length of bushing. Also, the reinforcing ribs around the starter-shaft tunnel were made thicker and a fifth rib was added.

The new cover continued in production through midyear 1938. This new cover and bushing, in concert with the fifth transmission mount, made the whole starter system stout enough to withstand the vigorous kicking sometimes required to start the OHV.

But it wasn't just the transmission mounts and frame that were prone to breakage under severe use. On rare occasion, the transmission mainshaft would crack at its clutch-hub end, so about midway through the production run, a revised transmission mainshaft and mainshaft nut were phased in. The new mainshaft differed from the old only in that the clutch-hub end of the shaft was increased to 3/4 inch in diameter (it

A 1937 EL restored and owned by Carman Brown. The fender stripes shown replaced the fender panels used in 1936. Standard wheel rims for 1937 were painted black, but cadmium-plated rims were available for 50 cents each, or bolt-on chrome wheel rings were available for $5. Note that the rear mount for the chain guard is now part of the fender-stay clip, unlike the 1936-only separate bracket that was riveted to the fender stay.

had been 11/16 inch), and the nut was increased in inside diameter to fit the new shaft. These revisions apparently fixed the problem because the mainshaft and nut were not revised again until mid-1950, when it was being used on the Knucklehead's successor, the Panhead.

The Knucklehead's clutch also suffered under severe use, especially under the incessant stop-and-go use motorcycles were subjected to in traffic-control or escort service with police departments. Under such use, the driving disc heated up from friction with the outermost fiber disc and conducted the heat to the clutch springs, ruining their temper.

To solve the problem, Harley-Davidson engineers revised the clutch pack that was incorporated into new machines starting after May 1, according to *Shop Dope No. 166*. The outer fiber disc was replaced by a steel sprung disc of a new design, and the original "humped" sprung disc was replaced by a plain steel disc. The new sprung disc has eight long, thin, L-shaped slots cut into its outer circumference and notches on its inner circumference to mate with the splines on the driving disc. This disc pack has one fewer fiber disc, one more steel disc,

and a redesigned sprung disc. Unfortunately, the revisions to the clutch pack didn't really solve the problem, so the clutch would be redesigned again in mid-1938.

New, Larger Rear Brake

The 1936 61's brakes, however anemic by today's standards, were as good as most of the day. But they still had some shortcomings, especially the rear brake. Though the 1936 rear brake is the same size as the front brake (7 1/4-inch drum inside diameter), and in theory just as powerful, it was considered too be too weak. The standard way to make brakes more powerful was to increase their size. So for 1937 Harley-Davidson introduced a new rear brake with an 8-inch inside diameter, larger and more powerful than the front brake.

While this bias toward rear brake power on a sport bike may seem odd in light of today's sport bikes with huge, full-floating twin front discs and much smaller rear discs, it was not unusual in the 1930s. Back then, the rear brake was still considered by most riders to be the primary brake, and the larger brake would remain in the rear through the end of Knucklehead production in 1947.

The 8-inch rear brake assembly fitted to the 1937 models was all new, from the drum and backing plate to the shoes. The new rear-brake backing plate was stamped steel, with a six-pointed star pattern around the axle hole. Its anchor tab on the plate's outside surface is reinforced by a plate that wraps about 1/3 of the way around the flat part of the backing plate and is attached with nine rivets to the inside surface of the backing plate. This backing plate was painted black and was used for 1937 only.

The rear brake drum was also stamped steel. Its swept surface is 8 inches in diameter for a substantial increase in braking surface over the previous rear drum. As before, the brake drum featured five dowel pins and five holes for the screws to attach the drum to the wheel hub. With this increase in power, the Knucklehead's rear drum had reached its final form, being used until the line was replaced by the Panhead series for 1948. Rear drums were painted black.

In addition to increasing the diameter of the drum, Harley-Davidson engineers gave the new brake shoes longer linings. Unlike the shoes on the 1936 brake, the shoes on the 1937 brake are not interchangeable. These shoes have a-1 11/64-inch-wide pivot end for the early-style pivot stud and use a return spring for each shoe. These shoes and spring were used through early-1938 production.

The pedal and linkage for the rear brake were also updated for 1937. The brake rod was redesigned to substitute stout clevis connections for the 90-degree bends used in 1936. The 1937 rod was given a shallow S bend to allow for the horizontal offset between the foot pedal and the crossover lever, and the rod was threaded at each end for the clevises. This new rod remained in use through 1947. The rod's front clevis is 2 7/16 inches long; its rear clevis is 1-7/8 inches long. The longer front clevis was used for 1937 and 1938, but the 1 7/8-inch rear clevis was used through 1947. Brake rods and clevises were Parkerized.

The brake pedal and crossover-shaft lever were subtly revised for use with the new clevises. Like the 1936 pedal, the

Brown's 1937 EL wears what Harley-Davidson hoped would be their signature paint combination for 1937—Bronze Brown with Delphine Blue striping edged in gold. To popularize their new models, they printed up a two-color brochure printed in the new color and touting the beautiful appearance it gave to the 1937 machines.

early 1937 pedal has only two holes (for the operating rod and the brake return spring) near the large pivot hole. For 1937, the operating-rod hole was reduced from 5/16 inch to 1/4 inch for the clevis pin. The crossover-shaft lever's brake-rod hole was also reduced in diameter to 1/4 inch, and another hole was added to the lever for attachment of the sidecar brake rod. The brake pedal is cadmium plated on early machines but was Parkerized on later machines.

According to *The Enthusiast* of November 1936, the new brakes and linkage prevented "bending and bucking" and loss of power. "You get real braking action and you can 'whoa' your iron hoss down in a hurry," boasted the magazine.

More changes were made to the rear brakes as model year 1937 progressed because some rear brake units were prone to chattering and "self-energizing" under severe braking.

The main cause of these problems was thought to be excessive clearance between the brake's operating shaft and the shaft's nonreplaceable steel bearing sleeve, and the problem only got worse as time and use increased clearance further. If the chattering became severe enough, "[t]he shock wave . . . sometimes breaks off brake cover torque stud or lug which allows the cover to turn, and breakage of operating shaft follows putting brake completely out of commission," according to *Shop Dope No. 157*. To help solve the problem, a replaceable bronze bushing that was finished-reamed to a closer tolerance was added to the operating shaft hole in the rear backing plate starting on January 11, 1937. The new bushing could also be fitted to earlier machines if the backing plate was reamed for the new bushing.

The new bushing and tighter clearances went a long way toward curing the chattering problem but did not reduce the brake tendency to "self-energize," or grab and lock. On April 13, 1937, *Shop Dope No. 157-A* was released that suggested that the solution to the problem lay in grinding back the brake linings 5/8 inch from the pivot-stud end and 1 3/4 inches from the operating cam end on those brakes that self-energized. The shorter linings were able to bear more evenly on the drum and greatly reduced brake squeal and sudden lock-up.

Late in 1937, a new, optional rear parking brake lock was offered, and the foot pedal was drilled with an additional hole, about halfway up the lever, for the pivot bolt of the parking brake lock's saw-toothed lever.

Several updates for 1937 are featured in this photo. Underneath the footboard is the improved brake rod with clevises at each end. Holes on both the brake pedal and crossover lever were reduced in diameter from 5/16 inch to 1/4 inch for the clevis pins. Early in the year, the brake pedal was cadmium-plated, as shown, but later pedals were Parkerized. For 1937, the main oil feed line to the oil pump connects to a fitting on the bottom of the tank at the drain hole, rather than at a separate fitting at the back of the tank. While the new fitting configuration may have simplified construction of the oil tank, it made oil changes messier, so it was used for 1937 only. Oil tanks were painted the main color of the bike for 1937 (instead of being painted black) and had a patent decal on each side of the tank. Note the air nipple on the front rocker housing. This feature had been added in late 1936 and was used again in 1937 because the 1937 models were fitted with the same cup-type valve-spring enclosures that had been used in 1936. The return lines from the enclosures were prone to clogging, resulting in the covers filling with oil and spilling it all over the machine and rider—hence the tall boots worn by this rider. Air pressure applied at the nipple would (if the rider was lucky) clear all four return lines at once. *Copyright Harley-Davidson Michigan, Inc.*

New Oil-Tank Feed-Line Connection

For 1937 only, the oil tank's feed-line attached to a special connection on the tank's drain opening underneath the right side of the tank, rather than at its former position on the back of the tank's right side. The new drain plug is really a valve with a banjo fitting on its side for attachment of the feed line and a special internal valve that prevents the oil from draining when the feed line is disconnected.

The 1937 oil tank is like the late-1936 tank, with the embossed top and swaged-in banjo fittings, but the feed-line fitting at the back is omitted on the new tank. And, as previously mentioned, the tank was painted the same color as the gas tanks and fenders. In addition, patent decals were applied to both sides of the tank.

In use, the new valve and feed-line configuration proved troublesome and leak-prone and made maintenance more difficult, so it was used only for 1937. The 1938-and-later models were again fitted with oil tanks having the feed connection on the right back of the tank.

A screen was fitted from top to bottom inside the oil tank to filter out large particles of debris before they reached the feed line to the oil pump. In cold weather, frost from condensation in the oil sometimes partially or wholly clogged this screen, keeping the cold-thickened oil from reaching the feed fitting and starving the oil pump. Harley-Davidson fixed the problem on new machines starting on January 20, 1937, by cutting out the screens on tanks so fitted and omitting the screens on subsequent tanks. *Shop Dope No. 159* recommended that owners of earlier machines who rode their machines in subfreezing weather cut out the screen with a screwdriver or chisel. For riders who rode in consistent temperatures of 15 to 20 degrees or colder, Shop Dope recommended adding up to 1 3/4 pints of kerosene to H.D.'s medium-heavy oil to keep it from congealing. It gave no advice on how to keep the rider's blood from congealing.

Speedo Light Switch and 120-Mile-Per-Hour Speedometer

The tank-mounted instrument console and speedo-meter introduced in 1936 became instant classics, so Harley-Davidson wisely made only minor revisions to them for 1937. The instrument-panel cover benefited from the addition of a hole just rearward of the ignition switch for the newly added speedometer-light switch. This new switch allowed the rider to turn off the speedometer light independently of the main headlight switch. The new switch's knob is tube shaped, with a ball on each end, kind of like a barbell. The tubular portion is

knurled, and the whole knob is cadmium plated. This style of knob was used only for 1937 and 1938.

All 1937 instrument-panel covers had a hole on the right side for the trip odometer reset shaft, whether or not the motorcycle was fitted with a tripmeter-equipped speedometer. The hole for the reset was sealed with a rubber grommet that had an opening for the reset rod if one was fitted.

In a somewhat optimistic move, but one in keeping with the sporting image of the machine, a new, 120-mile-per-hour face was added to tripmeter and nontripmeter speedometers for 1937. The styling of these speedometers is like the styling of the 100-mile-per-hour speedometer of 1936, except that the numerals 110 and 120 were added. A speedometer without a tripmeter was standard, but a speedometer with tripmeter was fitted if either of the two option groups were ordered, or it could be ordered in place of the standard speedometer for $3. The 120-mile-per-hour speedometer with 5-mile-per-hour hashmarks and a tripmeter was used only for 1937, but the same speedo without a tripmeter was used from 1937 through 1940.

New Tankshift Lever and Gate

The 1936 OHV's shift lever, with its spring-loaded-plunger detent mechanism, was elegant. After disengaging the clutch by rocking the clutch foot pedal back, the rider would just push the shift lever forward or pull it back to change gears. The action was smooth, and shifts could be made more rapidly than on any other hand-shifter of the period. But over time and after many shifts, the plunger and its mating recess in the tank-mounted shifter gate sometimes wore to the point that the tankshift lever could skip or be bumped past its detent, possibly nudging the transmission out of gear under certain conditions. Truth be known, this shifter system was probably too elegant to be practical on a hard-ridden street machine. It was also expensive to produce and assemble, so Harley-Davidson engineers simplified the tankshift assembly with the introduction of a new tankshift lever and shifter gate for 1937.

The new tankshift lever was oval in section, making it more streamlined and stiffer for less fore and aft flex than was the tubular lever it replaced. The new lever was held firmly in each gear position by an individual detent notch in the new shifter gate.

The shifter mechanism on the transmission received a new shift gear on the shift cam for 1937. The new gear has teeth only one-third of the way around its circumference. The new shift gear was used from 1937 to 1947.

Miscellaneous Changes

The narrow, unreinforced fender tabs on the 1936 front forks were prone to cracking, so a plate was spot-welded on the underside of each tab for 1937. While this helped delay the onset of cracking, it didn't entirely cure the problem. As a result, the fender tabs were redesigned for the following year; the fork with narrow, reinforced tabs is a 1937-only part. Also, the fork's top plate was updated for 1937 to omit the four small holes that it had for at least part of 1936.

For 1937, the rear fender's left brace clip was fitted with a slotted, hook-shaped tab that served as the rear mounting point for the rear chainguard. This new tab replaced the separate mounting bracket that was riveted to the rear fender's frontmost brace on the left side on 1936 Knuckleheads.

Like the brake pedal, the clutch pedal was cadmium plated for at least part of the 1937 production year. Later pedals were Parkerized. The chrome-plated chain-inspection cover was standard for 1936 and 1937 also. Starting in 1938, it was painted black.

Square slots near the center hole of the star-shaped hub cover were omitted on all 1937 models. (These holes were part of the speedometer-drive mechanism on the 45-ci solo models for 1935–1936.) This revised star cover was used through the end of Knucklehead production in 1947. It was cadmium plated through about midyear and Parkerized thereafter.

Redesigned spokes were introduced to reduce problems with stretching and breakage under severe use, according to *Shop Dope No. 162*. The new spokes had a shorter head end (7/32 inch versus 11/32 inch) that was bent at a 105-degree angle (rather than a 90-degree angle). The shop dope specified that only the new-type spokes be used on all future service work and that any old-style spokes be returned for exchange on new-style spokes.

Finally, a terminal post was added to the seat-post mast to provide for a short wire to the battery, and oil-soaked felt washers were fitted to each battery post to retard corrosion.

RIGHT: Note the way the chain pull for the brake-light switch attaches to the brake rod. Also note the swaged fittings on the oil tank. These fittings had been introduced in late 1936, changed from welded-on fittings. Nineteen thirty-seven was the last year for the oil sending line (the cloth-covered line stretching up and back from the oil pump) from the oil pump to the mechanical oil-pressure indicator on the instrument panel.

Competition

In its second year, the 61 OHV began to make its way into the winner's circle and into the record books. On March 13, Joe Petrali piloted a specially prepared 61 to a new AMA straightaway record of 136.183 miles per hour. On April 8, a true iron-man named Fred Ham took a day off from his job as a motorcycle cop to try to break the world record for the number of miles ridden in 24 hours. He used a stock 61 that he had purchased in October 1936, and he planned to do all the riding himself. With the help of a crew of over 20, oil flares to mark the course at night, and quarts of cold milk to keep him alert, Ham rode 1,825 miles, an average of 76.6 miles per hour, for the record (he also broke 44 other intermediate records). On May 16, Al Aunapa rode his 61 to victory in the 100-mile TT National Championship.

1937 Production

The 61 OHV found even wider acceptance in its second year, as did the flathead 45s and Big Twins that were given the OHV's styling for 1937. Overall, Harley-Davidson's sales rose by a satisfying 19 percent. Of the 11,674 Harleys built that year, 2,205 were 61s. This total includes 126 E, 1,829 EL, and 70 ES. The following year would bring further improvement to the Knucklehead, curing at last the problem that had contributed so much to its delayed introduction and had given owners of 1936 and 1937 Knuckleheads such fits: oil leaks from the valve gear.

Window to the World, 1938

The U.S. economy was in a recession within a depression for most of 1938. In an attempt to pull the economy out of its extra-deep doldrums, Congress passed the Revenue Bill of 1938, an early version of supply-side economics that centered around corporate tax relief.

Americans had even bigger problems emerging overseas. In Europe, the Fascists were on the march. German forces "annexed" Austria. Not satisfied, Hitler then pressed for a takeover of the Sudetenland, which was then part of Czechoslovakia. In September, Britain and France agreed to give it to him. British Prime Minister Neville Chamberlain predicted "peace in our time." But Winston Churchill foresaw what was to come and rose to prominence, decrying Chamberlain's "appeasement" of Germany.

FDR wasn't fooled, either. He requested and received more than $1 billion in additional military spending.

In the United States, labor unrest continued, but subsided to a whimper after passage of the Wages and Hours Act,

Record-Breaking Knucklehead

Once sales success of the 61 was certain, the company decided to build a special Knucklehead to go after the AMA straightaway record, with Joe Petrali as rider. The bike they built was almost completely custom-built for the record attempt, with a twin-carb engine, lightened frame, and shrouds and tailpiece with classic 1930s streamlined styling.

Interestingly, the engine in the restored machine is not the one shown in photos taken at the time. That engine, 37EL1002, is missing, and was replaced by the present engine, with the nonsensical engine number 36EL9991001, sometime after the record runs. Several engines were likely built, and the present engine may have been pieced together from spare parts because it is not complete, lacking pistons, connecting rods, and flywheels. Still it does have many of the special parts made just for the record-attempt bike. Its stroke was about 3/4-inch shorter than stock, so shortened barrels were fitted. Shortened pushrod retainers allowed the pushrods covers to telescope inward to accommodate the stroke.

Each head has a cast-in manifold on the left side for its own carburetor. The end of each manifold was drilled with a pattern of five holes to accommodate a two- or three-bolt carburetor. The carburetors fitted to this engine are Linkert MR-2 "barrel" racing carburetors—each had a revolving barrel rather than a butterfly valve in the throat—that fed special racing fuel to the engine. A magneto mounted in place of the generator supplied the ignition. Exhaust pipes were bobbed, ending just below the lower frame rails.

To save weight, the primary chain was replaced by a single-row 520 chain that transferred engine power to a VL clutch, which was engaged or released by a cut-off foot lever in nearly the same location as on a stock machine. Instead of a transmission, a special "in-or-out" single-ratio gear box was fitted. The box could be shifted in or out of gear, but the lever was not accessible to the rider; five pieces of shrouding had to be removed to access the lever. A VL kicker cover was fitted to the right end of the box, but the kickstart lever was omitted. Curiously, the hole for the lever's shaft was plugged by a wine cork. According to accounts of the record run, the bike was towed up to speed by another vehicle, then Petrali engaged the clutch to start the engine.

The frame had double downtubes, but it had no seat post, and the rear of the axle clips were bobbed to allow quick tire changes. Special rearset brackets were added to the frame for the bicycle-style pedals that served as foot pegs. Standard Knucklehead gas tanks were mounted on the frame. Curiously, the gas tanks and the handlebar fairing were chrome plated before painting.

In another effort to save weight, the Knucklehead forks and front wheel were exchanged for the slimmer and lighter pieces off a 1915 H-D.

Although H-D's efforts at streamlining ultimately proved counter productive, the shrouds dominated the look of the machine. Streamlining the front end were a small fairing and shrouds over the fork legs. The fairing was formed of a Knucklehead gas tank that had been cut and reshaped. In addition, the front wheel was also shrouded, giving it the look of a disc wheel. Wheel spokes were wired where they crossed with six wraps of wire, which were then soldered in place. The streamlining was completed by a boattail tailpiece that extended under the crankcase. (When the bike was disassembled for restoration, the extension had a layer of what appeared to be real Daytona sand). Shrouds and tailpiece were made of aluminum, but the joints between pieces were often leaded, which would seem to cancel out any weight savings. A seat built into the tailpiece placed Petrali much farther back than the normal riding position so he could bend forward, resting his chest against a pad on the gas tanks, arms stretching forward to the downwardly bent bars. Recesses for Petrali's legs were designed into the tailpiece and are similar to those later used on the original Harley-powered Buell motorcycles.

From his crouched position, Petrali had a good view of the handlebar-mounted tachometer, the bike's lone instrument. The tachometer was made from a stock speedometer by laying a hand-painted face over the speedo's face. A drive cable for the tachometer was spliced into the right crankcase's ignition-timer hole. The tach read from 2,000 to 7,000 rpm, with a 5,500-rpm redline.

Petrali made his first record-run attempts on March 12, 1937, on Daytona Beach. On the first day, heavy winds slowed him on the northbound leg of his runs, and spray from the surf sometimes wet the

On March 13, 1937, Joe Petrali rode this specially built Knucklehead to a new AMA straightaway record of 136.183 miles per hour on the sand at Daytona Beach. His efforts to break the record the day before had been foiled by ocean spray, heavy winds, and instability caused by some of the bike's streamlined bodywork. The tailpiece was removed for the record runs on the 13th. *Copyright Harley-Davidson Michigan, Inc.*

spark plugs and caused misfiring on the southbound leg. Worse, Petrali was forced to back off the throttle on the last northbound leg because the bike's front wheel was lifting off the sand. The record attempt was postponed until the next day. That night, the tailpiece and wheel covers were removed.

The wind eased somewhat by the time Petrali started his first run on the 13th. This run, too, was spoiled by ocean spray. The next run gave Petrali the new record, with an average speed of 134.83 miles per hour, beating the old record by just 2.81 miles per hour. The 61 was parked, and Petrali climbed aboard a 45 to set a new speed record for that class.

Even though he had already set two records that day, Petrali was not yet through. He climbed aboard the 61 again for another run. When the V-twin roared to life, he rocketed away from the pull-start vehicle on his way to a run with a two-way average of 136.183 miles per hour, beating his own record by about 1.5 miles per hour.

The bike Petrali rode was recently restored by Harley's on-staff restoration expert, Ray Schlee, and is part of H-D's traveling display. If anyone out there knows where the record-breaker's engine is, the factory has made it known that they'd like to buy it and bring it home.

The most obvious change for 1938 was the new striping on the tank. Rather than stripes above and below the tank transfers, the 1938 machines had a single stripe on each tank, extending forward and back from the tank transfers. This 1938 EL is owned by the enigmatic "Farmer Fred." Although it has a lot of extra chrome and nonstandard parts, it illustrates well the style of the 1938 Knuckleheads.

which raised the minimum wage to 40 cents per hour and limited weekly hours to 44.

Aviation was in the news. On July 14, Howard Hughes completed an around-the-world flight in 3 days, 19 hours, and 14 minutes. On July 17, Douglas "Wrong Way" Corrigan became a national celebrity when he took off for California, but landed in Dublin, Ireland. The part he left out of his story was that he had been denied a permit to fly to Europe.

On a visit to Milwaukee some time after his wrong-way flight, Corrigan asked for a ride on the machine of his dreams, a 1938 EL. After trading a limousine for 38EL3325 at the city limits, Corrigan raced south for the airport, leaving his entourage and police escort far behind. When the speedy flier reached the airport, he was heard to exclaim, "There is a real motorcycle!" Others raced their 61s to good effect that year, too. Sixty-ones carried their riders to victory in the 80-ci Pacific Coast TT Championship, the Southwestern TT Championship, and the Jack Pine Endurance Run.

The 1938 Knucklehead

As the October 1937 issue of *The Enthusiast* pointed out, the changes for 1938 were an "inside story" and one whose main theme was "smoother, quieter, cleaner." And, as we shall see, these were apt descriptions of the updated model.

The OHV Big Twin model line was paired down to just two offerings for 1938: the high-compression 38EL Special Sport Solo and the medium-compression 38ES twin with sidecar gearing. Accordingly, all nonpolice solo models should be marked 38EL and all nonpolice bikes marked 38E (remember, the S in ES was not marked on the crankcase as part of the serial number) should be sidecar or commercial machines. Most police solo models were probably 38Es, however, and some civilian solo 38Es were probably special ordered, so solo-models marked 38E undoubtedly were built.

Both the EL and ES were fitted with the high-domed, high-compression pistons for 1938 because the low-domed, medium-compression pistons had been discontinued at the end of the 1937 model year. The ES was given a lower compression ratio by fitting a compression plate underneath each cylinder. Gearing for the two models was unchanged.

All models were listed at a retail price of $435 (the same price as in 1937) but, for the first time, had to be ordered with one of the option groups, at additional cost.

Two option groups for solos and one group for sidecar haulers were offered. The Standard Solo Group included the front safety guard, steering damper, stop light and switch, jiffy stand, trip odometer, and front fender light and listed for $16.70 (which was about $5.00 cheaper than in 1937, probably because the ride control was no longer part of the package). The $49.75 Deluxe Solo Group included all the items in the standard group plus four-ply tires, ride control, a colored shift knob, the 6-inch round air cleaner, the Deluxe Saddlebags, and the Chrome Plate Special (includes chrome-plated handlebars, headlamp, instrument panel, wheel rings, parking lights, fender strips, and license-plate frame). The Standard Group for sidecar or commercial motorcycles, a $14.25 package, included a front safety guard, a steering damper, a stop light and switch, and ride control. (Note that the three-speed transmission with reverse gear was no longer part of the package.)

Color Harmony

The standard paint scheme was revised for the new model year. Once again, the art deco gas-tank transfer was retained and the gas tanks and fenders are painted in a solid color without panels, but for 1938 a thin stripe outlined in a complementary color runs down the centerline of the tank sides and aft of the tank transfer. A similar stripe curves along the top of the fender skirt, much farther down the sides of the fenders than the stripes used the previous year. And the oil tank is painted black for 1938, reversing the change to a color-matched tank that had been made for 1937.

Standard 1938 paint colors were Teak Red with black stripes edged in gold, Venetian Blue with white stripes edged in Burnt Orange, Hollywood Green with gold stripes edged in black, and Silver Tan with Sunshine Blue stripes. Police models were painted silver with black stripes.

Color harmony was the stated goal of some plating changes for 1938. "Chrome parts which only dazzled and did not carry out the color harmony of the machine were eliminated," according to an ad in the October 1937 issue of *The Motorcyclist*. The ad went on to specify that the timer cover was now plated in cadmium rather than chrome and that the "chain inspection cover on all models is now black and adds to the color harmony of the lower part of the machine." Most cadmium plating was also eliminated. According to the ad, "as soon as possible all nuts and bolts will be Parkerized instead of cadmium plated."

Fully Enclosed Rockers and Valves

Even when the adjustable rocker-oiling system was properly adjusted on the 1936 and 1937 machines, a fine mist of oil was continually vented out the rocker-arm opening in the valve-spring enclosures. It was nothing serious, but irritating nonetheless. As an ad in the October 1937 issue of *The Motorcyclist* admitted, "Oil seepage resulting in dirty motors and making for soiled clothing has been an evil that has been the source of much complaint in the past. With the growing popularity of light-colored riding clothing, especially club uniforms, the need for clean motors is self-evident."

Of greater import, if oil spray could leak out, dirt and water could leak in, quickly ruining valves and guides—not to mention the rockers and shafts, which were almost completely exposed to the elements. Worse yet, the dirt did not just leak in; it was actually sucked in by the engine vacuum used to scavenge oil from the valve-spring enclosure. And this dirt was then ingested into the engine along with the scavenged oil.

After two full years of complaints and warranty repairs, Harley-Davidson chose to fix the problem once and for all, by introducing truly effective full enclosures for the rocker arms and valves for 1938. One of these new enclosure assemblies was used for each valve, and each assembly consisted of a lower cover, a cover cap, a gasket, two screw plates, and screws.

The lower cover was a curiously shaped stamping with a lower cup that enclosed the valve stem and spring. An oil-scavenge line was attached to the right side of the cup, and a "trough" extended to the right to hold the rocker seal in place and cover the lower half of the rocker and shaft. A flange on the valve guide fastened the lower cover to the cylinder head, and an asbestos gasket was sandwiched between the cover and the cylinder head.

A separate cap completed the valve enclosure, covering the top of the pocket and the trough. The cap-to-cover junction was sealed by a gasket, then fastened together by screws that were inserted through holes in the cap, gasket, and lower cover and tightly cinched into threaded holes in two separate screw plates for each enclosure.

The oil lines from the lower cover were larger in diameter than the lines used the previous year (to reduce the tendency for them to clog) and attached to larger-diameter fittings on the rocker boss. A small vent hole allowed air to enter the enclosure when engine vacuum scavenged oil from the lower cover. Its location on the lower cover prevented water from dripping in, and its small size kept dirt ingestion to an acceptable minimum.

The new enclosures were a welcome improvement over the old type. Oil consumption decreased, and the bike stayed cleaner, inside and out. They worked so well that the enclosure stampings remained unchanged through 1947. (The screws and screw plates were updated in 1939, however.) Rocker enclosures were painted black.

Harley-Davidson even offered a kit to retrofit the new enclosures to 1936–1937 cylinder heads, and most of the older machines that exist today have these enclosures. *Shop Dope No. 172* gave instructions for the retrofit, and even mentioned that the factory would perform the work if the heads were returned to Milwaukee.

Cylinder-head cooling fins were relieved to allow clearance for the enclosures, but the castings were otherwise unchanged on early- through mid-1938 machines. Later in the 1938 production run, the cylinder head castings were again modified, this time to further stiffen the rocker-arm supports on the left side of the castings and provide more clearance for the rocker covers. The revised supports still joined in the center to form a V, but the V now had a flat atop each branch of the V, running from the reinforcing rib on the inside of the V to its rounded outside tip. The rocker-shaft

For 1938, the fender stripes were moved down to the top edge of the valance. Chrome-plated rims, hubs, and forks are not standard.

holes were no longer on the centerline of each ear of the V; rather, they were to the outside of the centerline, centered on the radius of the outer rounded tip. Head castings with the new rocker supports and drilled primer-cup bosses were used only on later-1938 machines.

Because the new rocker enclosures also held the rocker-arm seal in place in the aluminum rocker housing, the snap ring that held the seal in place on 1936–1937 motors was no longer needed. Consequently, both the front and rear rocker housings were revised to omit the groove that held the snap ring in place. The new rocker covers were so efficient at keeping out dirt and water that the oil-scavenge lines from the covers were no longer prone to clogging up with oil-dirt-water sludge, so the new front-head rocker housing was further revised to omit the air nipple that had been added in mid-1936. The rear head's rocker housing was fitted with an adapter for its exhaust valve's rocker enclosure. Rocker housings with these revisions were used through mid-1939.

The final top-end update for 1938 was to the exhaust valve's lower spring collar. The 1936 through early-1938 collar with an inside diameter of 21/32 inch was replaced in mid-1938 by the same lower spring collar (with an inside diameter of 27/32 inch) used on the intake valve.

Only a minor update was made to the engine's lower end, and it, too, continued the themes of "smoother, quieter." In a move to make their timing gears more round and the teeth more precisely shaped, Harley-Davidson purchased a new machine that shaved the gears to their final shape with greater precision, reducing runout and "high spots," which the company claimed reduced operating noise and made the engine's overall operation smoother.

Oiling System Updates

Another common source of oil leakage was the banjo-type oil fittings that secured the oil lines to the oil tank, especially the under-tank oil feed line fitting that was integral with the drain valve on the 1937 models. Continuing the theme of "cleaner" for 1938, Harley-Davidson moved the oil feed line fitting to the back of the oil tank's right side and changed the oil tank's oil-line fittings to better sealing compression-type fittings. This new tank is correct for 1938 and 1939 and is again painted black. Of course, the oil line fittings were also updated for the compression-type connections.

To improve breather action and help prevent clogging of the breather line in cold weather, the vent line from the oil tank to the crankcase was increased in size from 1/4 inch to 3/8 inch.

For 1938, the rear brake was again substantially modified. The backing plate was given a larger reinforcement plate, and the shoe pivot was replaced by a cup bearing that clamped both shoes together at the rear. The frame and forks were also made stouter for a better-handling machine. Note the rear stand. The old stand was half-round in section; the new stand was stamped with a channel down each leg and was lighter and cheaper to produce. *Copyright Harley-Davidson Michigan, Inc.*

The oil pump was updated for use with the diaphragm-type oil-pressure switch that was introduced with the new oil-pressure indicator light housed in the instrument cover (more on this later). The major modification to the pump was that the boss surrounding the sensing hole was lengthened to allow clearance for the switch. This style of oil pump was used only for 1938. The switch breaks the oil pressure indicator light circuit when the oil pressure reaches 3 psi, shutting off the indicator light. This switch threads into an adapter, which threads into the oil-pressure-sensing-hole boss on the oil pump. The switch is correct for 1938–1947, but this specific adapter was used on the OHV models for 1938 (but also on later side-valve models).

Stiffer Frame

The new, stronger frame that had been introduced in 1937 was a vast improvement over 1936's willowy frame, but the 1937 frame still exhibited signs of flexing when ridden at its limits or when lugging a sidecar. And its relatively lightweight rear frame tubes and open slot on the left axle clip's brake stay were also thought to contribute to the rear-brake chatter.

For 1938, Harley-Davidson fitted their Big Twins with a revised frame that was markedly stouter than its predecessors. The following reinforcements were made: The frame strut that triangulates the frame between the backbone tube and the lower part of the steering-head forging was made of larger diameter tubing (1 inch instead of 7/8 inch), the rear tubes that connect the axle clip forgings to the front portion of the frame were made of heavier-gauge steel (14-gauge instead of 16-gauge), the seat-post braces were made of heavier-gauge steel and were 1/2 inch wider, the transmission mounting bracket and rear support were made of heavier-gauge steel, and the brake stay on the left axle clip has a cap brazed on to close the end of the brake-stay slot.

The frame's steering head was also improved with the addition of a lower self-aligning head cone that has a convex base. Over the 1938 production run, the forging hallmarks on the left side of the steering head were phased out, and all subsequent Knucklehead steering heads lacked these marks.

The frame's toolbox strap was also revised for 1938—not to make it stiffer, but to make it easier and cheaper to manufacture. On the previous frame, the mounting bolts for the

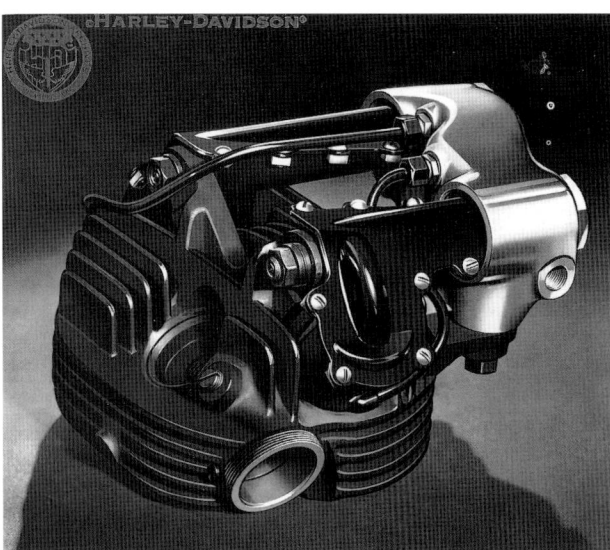

The big change for 1938 was the new valve enclosures. Unlike the old cup-style covers used in 1936 and 1937, the new covers enclosed the rocker arms as well as the valve springs. These covers kept out dirt and water and kept the oil in far better than the old covers had. For 1938, the upper and lower covers were fastened together by roundhead screws with threaded screw plates below, rather than the individual nuts shown here. Return lines from the new covers were made larger in diameter than those on the cup-type covers; the new lines seldom plugged up, so the air fitting on the front rocker housing was omitted on 1938 and later motors. The rocker-shaft mounts show the larger reinforcement rib (which was cast integrally with the cooling fin to its left) that was introduced in 1937. In late 1938, the rocker-shaft mounts were made even stronger. *Copyright Harley-Davidson Michigan, Inc.*

toolbox were each inserted through a hole in the toolbox strap and threaded into holes in the rectangular plates spot-welded to the wheel side of the strap. On the 1938 frame, the spot-welded plates were replaced by swaged-on threaded fittings. These fittings were used on all subsequent frames.

Sometime during 1938 production, the frame was improved yet again when a new left axle-clip forging was phased into production. The new forging no longer needed the brazed-on cap to close the end of the open slot for the brake stay because the slot's end was not left open on the new forging. Left-axle-clip forgings with closed brake-stay slots were used on all subsequent Knucklehead frames.

Brake Updates

While certain inadequacies of the early frames may have exacerbated the previously mentioned problem of rear-brake chatter and squeal, the real solution to these problems was in updates to the rear brake itself. the company actually began these changes in 1937, but the measures taken were only partly successful, so Harley-Davidson finally got serious about fixing the problem on their 1938 models.

First, the company followed up on its recommendation in the Shop Dopes by shortening the rear brake linings, which reduced the tendency for the brakes to chatter and self-energize, and made the brake more powerful by allowing more of the lining's surface area to contact the drum. The updated linings were used on all 1938–1947 Knuckleheads. Then, Harley-Davidson added a larger anchor-tab reinforcement plate to the inside surface of the backing plate to reduce its tendency to flex under braking load. The new reinforcement plate wraps 2/3 of the way around the flat part of the backing plate and is secured with 14 rivets. This reinforced backing plate was also used from 1938 through the end of Knucklehead production in 1947.

Early in the 1938 production run, "interconnected" brake shoes were fitted to the rear brake. The shoes were interconnected by a new, two-piece cup bearing on the redesigned pivot stud. The pivot pads of the shoes were made wider to fit the new inner bearing and included a raised, semi-circular boss around the circumference of the pad, over which the cup-shaped outer bearing piece was fitted, securing the pivot end of the two shoes together. A cotter pin was then inserted through a hole in the stud, securing the top cup of the bearing to the stud. Because the new bearing connected the shoes together, the upper spring was omitted. With these final changes, the Knucklehead rear brake had reached its final form, far smoother and quieter than ever before.

The front brakes were also refined for 1938 to improve power and reduce squealing. "Softer" metal was used in the manufacture of the front drum, and the shoes were lined with "Rex-Hide" material. And maintenance was made easier through the addition of a grease fitting on the backing plate to lubricate the center bushing.

Revised Instrument Panel and Speedometer

Long before 1938, car and motorcycle manufacturers had begun to realize that by making their machines more sophisticated and easier to operate, they could make them appeal to a new group of buyers who were not necessarily interested in, or knowledgeable about, mechanics. These buyers were not interested in tinkering with their machine—they just wanted reliable transport. To these new customers, finicky features such as ammeters and adjustable oiling for the valve gear were unnecessary anachronisms that at best only confused them with more information than they knew what to do with—and at worst were like an open mine shaft that lay in wait to entrap them.

Anticipating the next stage of this trend, but years ahead of standard practice in the automotive industry, Harley-Davidson made an unpopular but wise move in 1938, when it abandoned the ammeter and mechanical oil-pressure indicator in favor of what are today called "idiot lights."

The ammeter was an elegant device that had been a popular feature because it provided useful information about the condition of the motorcycle's charging system. So why would Harley-Davidson risk alienating their customers by deleting it and the less-useful, but charming mechanical oil indicator?

The most important reason was probably cost—the two gauges were far more expensive to manufacture than were indicator lights—but the new system brought with it some very real benefits: reduced complexity and vulnerability of the oiling and electrical systems.

The mechanical oil-pressure indicator had required a steel oil line that connected to the oil pump and was routed along the frame to the gauge. This routing protected the line well, but the potential was there for vibration to cause the line to crack or to abrade through, or for the connections to leak, with potentially catastrophic results for the engine. The new oil-pressure indicator light used a sensor switch on the oil pump and a wire to the indicator light. When oil pressure drops below 3 psi, the switch closes the circuit, lighting the indicator lamp and illuminating the red lens that covers the opening on the right, where the mechanical indicator was formerly mounted.

Similarly, the entire current of the electrical system had to be routed through the ammeter for it to operate. Again, the added wiring was well protected, but Murphy's Law sometimes wins out even over slim odds. Instead of current, the new indicator light responds to the voltage difference between the battery and the new third terminal on the generator cutout relay. When battery voltage is higher than generator voltage, current flows through the lamp and illuminates the green lens in the opening formerly occupied by the ammeter. When generator voltage reaches battery voltage, the light goes out. According to an ad in the October 1937 issue of *The Motorcyclist*, "The [instrument-panel] lights are distinctly arresting, even in the daytime."

In addition to the new indicator lights, the 1938 instrument-panel cover was given two other noteworthy modifications: the tripmeter-reset hole was replaced by a slot and a 3/8-inch hole was added on the left side for a police speedometer hand lock.

The new tripmeter-reset slot is covered by a solid (for nontripmeter models) or cutout (for tripmeter models) metal cover that is attached by two screws. The hand-lock hole is sealed by a clip-on cover on civilian models. The wiring underneath the cover was revised for the new indicator lights, and the horn and light-switch wiring were rerouted between handlebar switches and the instrument panel to eliminate chafing. The instrument cover was painted black on motorcycles ordered with the standard option groups or was chrome-plated on motorcycles ordered with the Deluxe Solo Group or the Chrome Plate Special.

The standard speedometer on the Knucklehead for 1938 was equipped with a tripmeter (based on the fact that all models had to be ordered with one of the option groups and all the option groups for the Knucklehead included the trip odometer). This speedometer looks like the earlier speedometer, except that hashmarks were added for the 2-mile-per-hour intervals between the numerals, which are spaced at 10-mile-per-hour intervals between 10 and 120. These new hashmarks replaced the 5-mile-per-hour hashmarks formerly used. This new speedometer is correct for 1938–1940 61s.

Some 61s may have been fitted with nontripmeter speedometers. If they were, they were equipped with the old-style speedometer with 5-mile-per-hour hashmarks because the speedometer with 2-mile-per-hour hashmarks was made only with the tripmeter.

Transmission and Clutch

At the start of the 1938 model year, a number of small, largely invisible changes were made to the Knucklehead transmission and clutch. These included a new starter cover; a larger, stronger clutch release finger and revised finger stud with a longer bushing; a higher oil-level communicating hole between the starter cover and the gear case (to keep foreign particles from entering the gear case); reinforced mainshaft second gear ("fully 75 percent" stronger, according to an ad in the October 1937 issue of *The Motorcyclist*); wider lugs on second-gear shifter clutch; wider lugs and beveled engaging surfaces on the fourth-gear shifter clutch; and a third-gear engaging clutch with more clearance from the side of the lugs. Externally, a revised clutch operating lever and a revised clutch-pedal spring were also introduced. The release lever is like the previous lever, except that the left end has only one slot (instead of two),

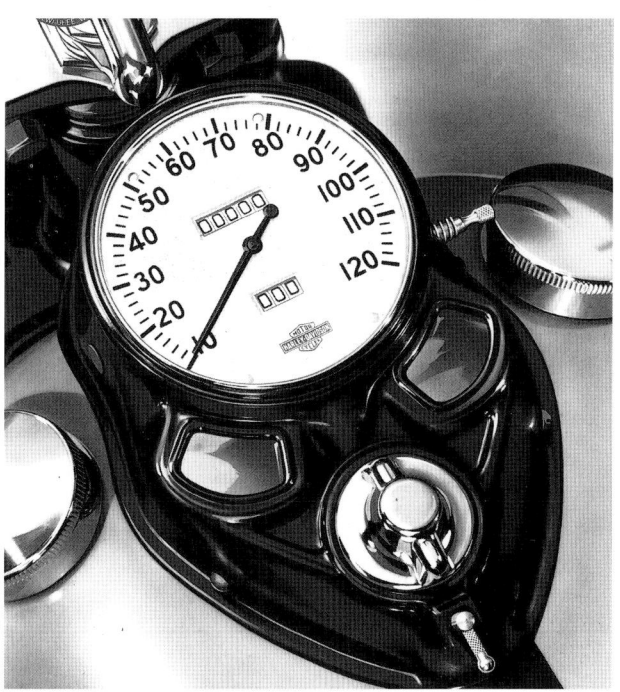

A revised speedometer and instrument-panel were introduced for 1938. The speedometer still had a 120-mile-per-hour face, but the hash marks were now at the intermediate 2-mile-per-hour intervals. The instrument panel shows the new "idiot" lights that replaced the ammeter and mechanical oil-pressure indicator in 1938. The left indicator (voltage) has a green lens, and the right indicator (oil-pressure) has a red lens. The skull-face panel with the colored lenses is correct for 1938 only. Standard instrument covers were painted black, but a chrome-plated cover was included in the Chrome Plate Special. *Copyright Harley-Davidson Michigan, Inc.*

A 1938 Knucklehead for the California Highway Patrol. Starting sometime during the middle of the model year, the Model 32E2R generator was introduced for radio-equipped police bikes. The 32E2R generator was a two-brush design that needed a separate voltage regulator, unlike earlier police generators, which were three-brush designs that did not need a separate regulator. The regulator is shown on this bike, just aft of the coil. California Highway Patrol bikes had the tool box on the left side to allow a rear-wheel siren on the right side. Note the arrowheads at the front of the pinstripes on the front fender. *Copyright Harley-Davidson Michigan, Inc.*

and the two pieces of the lever are welded together (rather than being brazed). This lever is Parkerized. The 1938 clutch-pedal springs are like the previous springs, except that they have only 19 coils (versus 22). These springs are painted black.

Most of the aforementioned changes were inconsequential in and of themselves, but they were necessary to implement a series of midyear changes that would constitute yet another attempt to fix two nagging problems with the Big Twin clutch: overheating and a weak throw-out bearing.

To make the clutch more resistant to overheating under police use, the clutch was given a new disc pack, an asbestos insulating gasket for the driving disc, a revised hub locknut, and new clutch springs. These parts were fitted to new machines after February 1, 1938, according to *Shop Dope No. 175*.

The new clutch-disc pack used two lined steel discs, two plain steel discs, one notched fiber disc, and one sprung disc. The plain steel and notched fiber discs were the same type that had been used on previous clutches, but the lined discs and spring disc were new parts. Each lined disc consisted of a steel disc with notches around the outer circumference (to mate with the splines on the clutch drum) and fiber linings riveted onto each side of the disc. The new spring disc still has the L-slots on its outer circumference but lacks the spline notches on its inner circumference. This new disc pack was used through the 1940 model year, after which an all-new clutch made its debut.

Shorter, stiffer, and wound of thicker wire, the new clutch springs were protected from clutch heat by the new asbestos gasket, installed between the new clutch springs and the driving plate. Also added in this update were a longer clutch-hub locknut and a longer adjusting screw. All these parts were used through the 1940 model year.

The second big change was to introduce the second update to the throw-out bearing and a revised clutch pushrod for the new bearing. Curiously, the new pushrod was first fitted to new machines more than two weeks before the new bearing (after February 25, 1938, for the pushrod, and after March 8, 1938, for the bearing, according to *Shop Dope No. 174*). The 8-ball clutch throw-out bearing that had been used on Knuckleheads since late 1936 was replaced by a 10-ball throw-out bearing that was less prone to seizing. In the *Shop Dope*, dealers were instructed to retrofit any unsold machines with the new bearing and pushrod and to return for exchange any of these parts replaced under warranty.

This throw-out bearing was much larger and stouter than the previous bearing, but it still wasn't good enough and would be replaced the following year. Consequently, late in the 1938 production run, the starter cover was revised yet again, this time to include a reinforcing rib between the filler hole and the boss for the clutch-release-shaft opening—and for added clearance for the 25-ball clutch throw-out bearing that replaced the 10-ball throw-out bearing.

Finally, a new clutch pedal and bracket were introduced in midyear. The new clutch pedal is taller (5.75 inches versus 4.25 inches) but shorter in length (9 inches versus 9.125 inches) than the previous pedal. It, too, was only used for the latter part of 1938. The new clutch-pedal bracket is like the previous bracket, except that it is taller (9.75 inches versus 8 15/16 inches) and has four 0.75-inch holes in a square pattern on the bracket midsection instead of the former bracket's two holes. This bracket was used again for 1939.

J-Slot Air Cleaner

The optional air cleaner was revised for 1938 to make the cover easier to install or remove. It is no longer fastened to the backing plate by four screws—rather, four J-shaped slots in the new cover mate with four capped studs on the new backing plate to fasten the cover. This 6-inch-diameter air cleaner is correct for 1938–1940.

Forks and Handlebars

The 1938 forks were formed from stronger tubing to make them less prone to flexing. The fork was also fitted with wider front-fender mounting tabs, to make the tabs even more resistant to cracking from vibration. These forks, with the larger tubing and the old-style spring perches with the grease fittings on the front part of the spring perches (rather than on the sides), were used only in 1938.

Also for 1938, the bend on the handlebars was revised to allow more clearance for the rider's legs when the bars are turned. These bars are correct for 1938 to mid-1946. The individual bars are brazed to the cast center section on 1938 through mid-1945 Standard bars and on 1938–1942 Speedster bar. The bars are welded to the center section on late-1945 to mid-1946 Standard bars and 1943 to mid-1946 Speedster bars. Bars are painted black.

Redesigned Rear Stand

For 1938, a totally redesigned and lighter rear stand was introduced. Instead of being half-round, the legs on the new stand are stamped from sheet steel with rounded reinforcing channels. Although it was lighter, it was "amply strong for all requirements," according to the October 1937 issue of *The Enthusiast*. And the magazine continued, with a sentiment any rider could agree with: "Anyway, a motorcycle shouldn't be left on a stand—it was built to roam the highways and once you try one of these new '38 jobs you won't need a stand."

Other Small Changes

In addition to the more momentous changes already outlined, many other smaller changes were made, including the following: the Alemite grease fittings were replaced by Zerk-Alemite grease fittings; a third post was added to the generator cutout relay (correct for 1938–1947); the speedometer cable sheath was cadmium plated (rather than painted black); and the horn brackets and bolts were painted black (rather than being Parkerized).

Police-Bike Updates

Police bikes were given two major new convenience features for 1938. The first and most important was the magnetic speedometer hand stop available for mounting on the handlebar. With this new device, an officer could pace a car and press a button to freeze the speedometer needle at the pace speed. The second was a streamlined, polished-aluminum siren.

The steady increase in electric-powered police accessories, especially radios, was the impetus for the introduction of a new high-output police generator in mid-1938. The Model 32E2R had longer armatures and fields to produce more current than the standard Model 32E generator. The new generator was a 6-volt, two-brush generator that was used with a voltage regulator instead of with a cut-out relay.

Mature Design

After the hundreds of running changes implemented in 1936 and 1937, the design of the Knucklehead stabilized somewhat starting in 1938, as many of the modifications introduced that year fixed nagging problems well enough that they were not to be changed again during Knucklehead production. And for the first time the Knucklehead design lived up to its early promise. From 1938 on, the improved brakes, the use of indicator lights, and the finish on many of the parts remained unchanged, except on the rare wartime bikes, through the end of Knucklehead production in 1947.

1938 Production

After the 20 percent rise in sales that had so pleased Harley-Davidson in 1937, the 1938 sales were a big disappointment. Overall sales declined 30 percent—the result of flagging interest in the 45s, 74s, and 80s as the excitement initiated by their restyling in 1937 dissipated. The one ray of hope was that the 61 was even more popular, its sales rising more than 20 percent to 2,478. Of this total, 2,289 were ELs

LEFT: This particular color combination was not offered as standard for 1938 but was probably available as a special order. Standard colors were Teak Red with black striping, Venetian Blue with white striping, Hollywood Green with gold striping, Silver Tan with Sunshine Blue striping, and Police Silver with black striping.

and 189 were ESs. The 61s accounted for about 30 percent of overall Harley sales (up from 15 percent the year before), and this trend would continue in the following years.

Window to the World, 1939

For 1939, Europe was again the center of attention, and the march toward war continued. On March 14, Germany invaded Czechoslovakia. On April 7, Italy invaded Albania. Germany took the irrevocable final step on September 1, when it invaded Poland. On September 3, Britain and France declared war on Germany. That very day, the first American war casualties occurred when a German sub torpedoed and sunk the British passenger ship *Athenia*. Thirty Americans were killed. Even so, the United States declared neutrality two days later.

On September 17, Russia joined the fun and invaded Poland. The conquest complete, Germany and Russia partitioned Poland on September 28.

The big movie of the year was *Gone with the Wind*, starring Clarke Gable and Vivien Leigh. The movie was the longest and most expensive movie ever made and won 10 Academy Awards.

The starting gun sounded in the nuclear race when Enrico Fermi and John Dunning use a cyclotron to split uranium for the first time.

By the start of the 1939 production year, Harley-Davidson's bold new designs were really beginning to pay off. The September 1938 issue of *The Enthusiast* trumpeted the fact that, based on the 1937 registration lists, 67 percent of all motorcycles in the United States were Harley-Davidsons. And the new Harleys continued to make their mark on the tracks as well. A 1937 61 sidecar rig ridden by Robert Tinoco won the 24-hour Bol d'Or race in France on June 5, 1938. During the 24 hours, Tinoco horsed his sidecar rig around the 5-kilometer Montlhery over 400 times, logging 1,252.5 miles. This was the first time that the Bol d'Or was won by a sidecar rig. Knuckleheads also carried their riders to victory in the Southwestern TT Championship and several classes in the Jack Pine.

The 1939 Knucklehead

The OHV Big Twin model line for 1939 included only the high-compression 39EL Special Sport Solo and the medium-compression 39ES twin with sidecar gearing. In addition, a special police package was offered combining the medium-compression motor, the three-speed transmission, and medium gearing. All models were listed at a retail price of $435 (the same price as in 1937 and 1938) and had to be ordered with one of the option groups, at additional cost.

Two option groups for solos and one group for sidecar haulers were offered. The Standard Solo Group included

For 1939, Harley-Davidson introduced a new set of transmissions with a sliding-gear first (in three-speed and three-speed-with-reverse transmissions) or second (in four-speeds). This shifter gate for a three-speed-with-reverse transmission is on a 1939 EL owned and restored by Ron Lacey. On the four-speed gate, neutral was placed between second and third gear. The new transmissions were unpopular because the rider had to go through the nonsynchromesh second gear every time he shifted from neutral to first (on four-speeds), or through the nonsynchromesh first every time he shifted to reverse (three-speed-with-reverse).

the front safety guard, steering damper, stop light and switch, jiffy stand, trip odometer, front fender light and four-ply tires; the package listed for $15.50. The Deluxe Solo Group for 1939 was expanded, and included all the items in the standard group, plus ride control, colored shift knob, 6-inch round air cleaner, deluxe saddlebags, deluxe solo saddle, and Chrome Plate Special (which included chrome-plated handlebars, headlamp, instrument panel, taillight cover, relay cover, exhaust-pipe covers, and license-plate frame, fender strips, and stainless steel top fender strips). It listed for $47.00. The Standard Group for sidecar or commercial motorcycles listed for $14.00 and included a front safety guard, a steering damper, stop light and switch, trip odometer, fender light, and four-ply tires. It is interesting to note that the three-speed transmission with reverse gear was no longer included in the package.

Styling Changes

Changes for 1939 took Knucklehead styling to heights it had not reached since 1936, and would never reach again. Elements of the new style that made it so stunning included the new paint scheme, streamlined "cat's-eye" instrument panel, "boattail" taillight, and new stainless steel fender trim.

New Paint

With the possible exception of the 1936 scheme, the paint scheme introduced for 1939 is the most handsome scheme ever used on a Harley-Davidson Big Twin, in my opinion. Like

For 1939 another new instrument panel was introduced. The new panel was nicknamed the "cat's-eye" because of the almond-shaped windows for the generator and oil warning lights. Shadows highlight the V-shaped ridge that ends just aft of the restyled speedometer-light knob (which was also new for 1939). Although the cat's-eye cover was used through 1946, this V is only apparent on covers through model-year 1942. The disc-shaped light knob with the domed top was also used through 1942.

the 1936 scheme, the 1939 paint scheme was again two-tone, but this time the contrasting panels were on the sides of the gas tanks, rather than on the fenders. From a side view, the top edge of the panel continues the long diagonal line of the frame, from the steering head to the axle clips. From a front view, the top lines of the panels are seen to curve downward and toward the center of the bike in a V shape. A pinstripe accentuates the curved top line of the panel. The art deco tank transfer was used for the last time with the new tank panels.

Standard paint colors for 1939 were Airway Blue with white panels, black with ivory panels, and Teak Red with black panels. Police models were available in Police Silver with black stripes.

"Cat's-Eye" Instrument Cover

A restyled instrument cover added to the impact of the new tank panels. This new cover is longer and more streamlined than the previous cover and has a pronounced V-shaped ridge aft of the ignition-switch hole. The rectangular apertures for the warning lights were replaced by cat's-eye-shaped openings, giving rise to the nickname of this dash. Lenses over these openings were green and red.

Also restyled was the speedometer-light switch knob at the rear of the instrument panel. The 1937–1938 barbell-shaped knob was replaced by a disc-shaped knob, slightly rounded on top, with a knurled edge. It was cadmium plated. This instrument panel and speedo-light knob are correct for 1939–1942.

Rather than being painted black or chrome plated like previous covers had been, the 1939 cover was painted to match the color of the tank top and fenders, adding further to the distinctive new look. As the September 1938 issue of *The Enthusiast* bragged: "From front to rear there is a continuous flow of color!" Chrome-plated instrument panels were optional.

"Boattail" Taillight

For 1939, the small "beehive" taillight was replaced by a larger, more streamlined assembly. It was dubbed the "boat-tail" because its shape evoked the image of the sterns used on the streamlined muscleboats of the era. Standard taillight bodies were painted the color of the fenders, but chrome-plated bodies were available. This taillight is correct for 1939–1941 (in 1942 the taillight unit was only slightly revised).

The rear fender was revised for 1939 to omit the taillight shroud that had been necessary for the old-style taillight, and to add mounting holes for the new taillight and stainless steel trim pieces.

Fender Trim

Icing on the whole 1939 styling cake was the bright stainless steel strip along the top of each fender valance. These trim strips are correct for 1939–1942 and late 1946 through 1947.

The final styling change of note was a nod back to the 1936 Knuckle. In 1936, the patent decal was on the toolbox cover. In 1937 and 1938 two were fitted, one on each side of the oil tank. For 1939, the patent decal was once again on the toolbox—but for 1939 only. For 1940 and later it was fitted only to the left side of the oil tank.

Engine Updates

Several subtle changes were made to the exterior of the 1939 engine. Primer cups were no longer offered as an option, so the primer-cup bosses on the cylinder heads were not drilled and tapped for the cups. Parker-Kalon self-tapping screws and unthreaded lower screw plates were used to fasten the rocker covers' top caps. Neoprene-covered spark plug wires were introduced.

A plate with date markings was added just forward of the casting number on the left crankcase. Intake manifold and plumber-nut finish was changed to cadmium plate (instead of nickel plate). A drain screw was added to the carburetor's float bowl, and because this was the last year

A prototype of the 1939 Knucklehead. New features for 1939 that did not make it onto this prototype include the stainless steel fender side trim strips (note that they are painted in on this bike) and the 1937–1938 style of speedometer-light knob. The photo does show the 1939-only deluxe solo saddle and saddlebags. *Copyright Harley-Davidson Michigan, Inc.*

the Linkert M-5 was fitted to the Knucklehead, it is a one-year-only carburetor. And the adapter base for the oil-pressure switch was revised, which resulted in a reversion to the 1936–1938-style oil-pump body. Late in the production run, the rocker housing was revised to incorporate a casting date plate and to thicken the casting in the area around the intake pushrod hole.

Internally, a redesigned one-piece pinion shaft was fitted. The 1936–1938 pinion shaft was a two-piece shaft with the helically cut drive gear for the oil pump machined into the outer shaft stub and the pinion gear press-fit on the shaft. Over time, the joint between the two stub shafts would incrementally wear, allowing flex in the shaft, which resulted in slight misalignment of the gears.

For 1939, the new shaft was machined from a solid bar with six splines running along the axis of the shaft, and the oil-pump gear was a separate piece. The pinion shaft assembly consisted of a one-piece pinion shaft, an oil-pump gear spacer, an oil-pump drive gear, a spring, and a pinion gear. The new pinion gear for the oil pump is larger in diameter (1 3/16 inches versus 1 inch) and is splined, but still has five teeth. This one-piece shaft kept the gears in almost perfect alignment. It was used through 1953. The pinion gear was used through 1950.

Mating with the pinion shaft's new, larger-diameter drive gear for the oil pump is a new, smaller-diameter gear (1 3/8 inches versus 1 9/16 inches) on the oil pump's driveshaft. The result is that the oil pump spins much faster, bringing the system up to operating pressure at lower rpm and generating higher overall oil pressure and flow. Unfortunately, this was a mixed blessing. A quicker rise to operating pressure was certainly advantageous, but the increased flow that came with it resulted in oil-fouled spark plugs and increased oil consumption at low rpm.

To solve the problem, a new, relief-valve spring was introduced early in the production run that allows the relief valve to open at 4–6 psi, venting the excess oil into the gear case, from which it is returned to the oil tank by the scavenge pump. This went a long way toward reducing the severity of the over-oiling problem at low rpm, but it was really just a band-aid fix that brought its own penalty—it also limited the oil pressure available at high rpm and wasted much of the output of the pump. Harley's engineers must have been satisfied with it, though, because the next attempt to fix the problem would not occur until the 1941 model year.

The old-style straight crankcase breather pipe that had been used since 1936 was replaced by a new pipe with a double elbow that bends forward and then to the left, through a hole in a revised inner primary cover. Inside the primary enclosure, a separate oil deflector attached to the end of the breather tube deflects the oil onto the primary chain. The new inner primary cover is like the previous cover, except that a new hole for the revised crankcase breather pipe was added to the bulge at the rear of the front reinforcing rib, a dimple appeared at the location of the former crankcase breather-pipe hole, and the stamped-in boss around the transmission mainshaft hole was made larger.

Standard Knuckleheads for 1939 were dressy machines, but Eldon Brown's machine is dressed up even more, with the disc wheels, white-wall tires (which were not offered on new machines that year), spotlamps, stainless steel trim strips for the top of the fenders (included in the Chrome Plate Special), and an accessory rear safety guard. This is a beautiful restoration, but a few parts were incorrectly cadmium plated when they should have been Parkerized, including the front brake cam lever and brake-mounting hardware, the rear brake rod, the stand hardware, and rear axle and nut.

Rounding out the motor changes for the start of 1939 were pistons that were reinforced with thicker metal behind the third ring grooves, and a revised screen on the breather valve. Improved valve springs were also introduced.

Nonadjustable Rocker-Arm Oiling

But another major change to the engine was made during the production year. Continuing the trend toward simplification and making their machines "idiot-proof," Harley-Davidson finally got rid of adjustable rocker oiling in 1939. With the advent of the fully enclosed rocker covers in 1938, the consequences of over-adjustment were no longer as critical because the oil remained inside the covers rather than spraying out to coat bike and rider—yet the risk of squeaking valves and accelerated valve-gear wear from under-adjustment remained.

The solution was to fit all new machines after 39EL1902 with new rocker arms and rocker shafts, with factory-set oiling. The new rocker shafts lack the previous shaft's oil grooves, and the central oil passage ends at two oil holes on the bearing surface, near the right end. The new rocker arms are like the previous arms, except that the oil passage to the valve-pad stem ends at a hole on the side of the stem, rather than under the stem. With these new parts, top-end oiling problems were cured at last.

Frame and Forks

The 1939 61 OHV frame was the same as the previous frame, except that the steering head was fitted with a self-aligning upper cone to match the self-aligning lower cone that had been introduced in 1938.

The 1939 fork was made easier to service by moving the grease fittings on the spring perch from in between the headlight bosses to the sides of the perch, where they are easily accessible. (The original grease-fitting bosses between the headlight bosses remain, but they are not drilled for the fittings.) To improve the ride, lighter cushion springs were fitted on forks for solo machines. Forks for sidecar machines were fitted with the same cushion spring, but an additional cushion spring was fitted in place of the buffer spring. This fork is correct for 1939 through early 1942.

Sliding-Gear Transmission

Even though the sliding-clutch four-speed, three-speed, and three-speed-with-reverse transmissions introduced on the 1936 Knucklehead had proved to be just about the only major system that was trouble-free, Harley-Davidson introduced a whole new set of Big Twin transmissions for 1939 that incorporated old-style sliding gears for second gear on the four-speed and for first gear on the three-speeds—a seemingly retrograde step. The September 1938 issue of *The Enthusiast* claimed that the change "will make for easier, smoother shifting." In fact, the opposite was true.

So what was the real reason for the change? Second gear in the four-speed and first gear in the three-speeds was the gear used most by police and commercial users, and the gears didn't stand up to such constant use as well as they should have. These users were in the minority, however, and the more sport-minded riders who were in the majority didn't care for the delay in shifting caused by the sliding gear. In a compromise Harley-Davidson hoped would satisfy both groups, the sliding-gear second was used only for 1939, while the pair of three-speeds kept the sliding-gear first through the end of Knucklehead production in 1947.

The new transmissions had a revised shift pattern, so the shift gates were revised. On the sliding-gear four-speed, the neutral position was between second and third (rather than between first and second), so the markings on its shift gate were changed accordingly. Depth of the gate's high-gear notch (fourth on four-speeds; third on three-speeds) was reduced by half to ease shifting out of high. This four-speed transmission gate was a 1939-only part. The gate for the three-speeds was used through 1946.

The final changes to the 1939 transmissions were a new starter clutch designed to work with the new 25-ball throw-out bearing (discussed in the next section), shifter fingers revised to include rollers, and a midyear shifter-cover revision to include a cast-in date mark on the inside. These changes were carried forward to the next year's transmissions.

25-Ball Throw-Out Bearing

After numerous updates that ultimately proved unsatisfactory (most recently in mid-1938), the throw-out bearing was finally fixed for real in 1939. The all-new throw-out bearing is much larger than the old bearing and has 25 ball bearings instead of the former bearing's 10. The bearing is cone-shaped, tapering toward the redesigned clutch release fingers, and its retainer has four scooper cups to supply lubricant. A new starter clutch was also fitted. The designs of the bearing and release fingers were so sound that they were used on Harley-Davidson Big Twin transmissions into the 1970s.

The 25-ball throw-out bearing may be fitted to some earlier machines because a kit was released in the spring of 1939

The new "boat-tail" taillight for 1939 did not use the metal shroud that had been used on the 1936–1938 "beehive" taillight. The new taillight had a red lens at the rear and a frosted lens on top to illuminate the license plate, which mounts to a separate bracket. Standard taillight covers were painted the color of the fender, but a chrome-plated cover was included as part of the Chrome Plate Special.

to allow use of the bearing on earlier machines. As described in *Shop Dope No. 191*, the kit included a new starter cover, release finger, release-finger shaft, thrust bearing, starter clutch, and oil deflector, and retailed for $7.50.

Clutch Pedal and Springs

The clutch footpedal was revised in 1939 by moving the stud for the clutch rod one inch upward on the side of the pedal's vertical center section. The hole in the pedal for the lower stud position remained on the new pedal. This pedal was Parkerized and is correct for 1939 and 1940.

Clutch-pedal balancing springs were also revised. The springs are like the previous springs, except that one end is no longer bent into a hook. Instead, it tapers and connects to a separate wire loop. These springs were painted black and are correct for 1939–1942.

Another California Highway Patrol bike, this one a 1939 model. Note that the toolbox is now mounted sideways, below the radio, but that the special strap for mounting the toolbox on the left side of the frame remains. *Copyright Harley-Davidson Michigan, Inc.*

Brakes

The 61's front brake received several improvements for 1939. The front linings were shortened to reduce chatter and the tendency to self-energize, as the rear shoes had been in 1938. To accommodate the new linings, the shoes were drilled in different places. These new linings were used through the end of the Knucklehead line in 1947.

To make the task of lubing the front brake shackle easier, the grease fitting on the fork end was relocated so that it points rearward when the shackle is installed. On the shackle stud, the screw-slot head was replaced by a hex head. Both shackle and stud were one-year-only parts.

The final change to the front brakes was the addition of a larger cable oiler on the cable's coil. The oiler has a Parkerized body and a spring-loaded plunger. The new oiler was fitted through 1947 production.

Foot controls for the rear brake were also revised. The brake pedal is about 1/4-inch shorter than the previous pedal and is slightly reshaped. This pedal body remained in production through 1947. The pedal was Parkerized. To simplify assembly, the pedal support was revised with a peened-on pivot stud (rather than bolted-on).

New Fuel Filter

Though the old-style fuel filter, with its side connection for the fuel line, had worked fine, Harley-Davidson replaced it for 1939 with an all-new filter that had the gas line connection at the bottom. To clean the strainer, the fuel line must be disconnected, allowing the gasoline to drain out over the cleaner's hands and onto the engine case and exhaust pipes. It should be obvious why the design was disliked. Even so, it remained in production through 1941. A tapered-flare-nut fitting connected the gas line to the filter.

An unrestored 1939 sidecar rig owned by Dave DeMartini, proprietor of Northwest Custom Cycle, in Snoqualmie, Washington. DeMartini has owned this bike since 1972. After he and his wife, Joanne, were married in 1976, they drove away from the church on this machine.

Eldon Brown's 1939 Knuckle shines from any angle. The wheels were made by welding the discs and rim onto a rider's H-D hubs sent in at the time of order. Wheels with 5.50 x 16 General Dual-10 tires, tubes, and flaps sold for $59. Shipping weight was listed as 94 pounds.

The 1939 transmissions came with numerous internal changes, some of which were improvements and some of which were definitely retrograde. Among the improvements was yet another (the fourth in four years) throw-out bearing, shown in this photo as the truncated-cone-shaped part inside the kickstarter cover. The new bearing for 1939 was much larger and had 25 ball bearings instead of 10. This new bearing was finally strong enough; it would be used on H-D Big Twins for more than 35 years. *Copyright Harley-Davidson Michigan, Inc.*

A 1939 EL owned and restored by Ron Lacey of British Columbia. In addition to the black-with-ivory-panels scheme shown on this bike, standard colors included Airway Blue with white panels, Teak Red with black panels, and police silver with black striping.

Brown Saddles

The 1939 standard solo saddle was like the previous saddle, except that the leather was rhino-russet-grain horsehide instead of black cowhide. This seat is correct for 1939 only.

The 1939 deluxe solo seat was also covered in brown horsehide, but it featured a three-piece leather skirt. The rear part of the skirt is shorter than the longer side-skirt lobes for clearance between the skirt and the fender. The two side skirts are sewn to the center skirts. At the center of the rear skirt is a trim piece that has a floral design under a clear piece of convex glass. Near the lobed tip of each side skirt is a leather, two-layer rosette with a short leather tassel, matching those on the optional saddlebags. This seat is also correct for 1939 only.

Sportier Front Safety Guard

As befits its name, the front safety guard was meant to prevent damage to bike and rider in the event of a crash. But the early safety guard was a safety hazard to the really brave riders of the day who tried to test the limits of the bike's cornering clearance. When it touched down, the stout tubing of the safety guard gave a sideways jolt to the bike that was not at all unlike that given when a forgotten sidestand touches down.

For 1939, Harley-Davidson revised the bend on the guard to address the problem. The new guard was almost identical to the old, except that it is bent so that it loops a bit farther forward (instead of more nearly straight out to the sides), which reduces the effective width of the crashbar, resulting in slightly more cornering clearance. The September 1938 issue of *The Enthusiast*

Obviously, the springs should not be chromed, but this photo does show two subtle new features of the 1939 and later machines: the grease fitting sticking out of each side of the rigid leg's spring perch and the larger oiler on the front brake coil (shown just above the top nut of the forks).

LEFT: Eldon Brown restores his machines with great care and rides them little so they stay pristine.

reassured riders that "you can sure lay the Big Twins over on the curves now." This new safety guard was fitted for 1939 and 1940.

1939 Production

Overall sales of Harley-Davidson motorcycles made a slight gain in 1939 of 1.6 percent—nothing to rejoice over, but far more satisfactory than the 30 percent decline in sales in 1938. Once again, the 61 was the star of the line-up, and it was also the only bulwark preventing another sales catastrophe. Sales of the Knucklehead increased by almost 20 percent to 2,909. Of this total, 2,695 were ELs and 214 were ESs.

Since its shaky debut, the 61 OHV had been refined to become the great American motorcycle of its era. Among American production motorcycles, it offered unmatched speed, sophistication, and power, and it even stood up well against limited-production specialty machines such as the Broughs, Vincent-HRDs, and Crockers. No longer was the Knucklehead more delicate, leaky, or trouble-prone than its peers—even those with the much simpler and less powerful flathead motor. As a result, its sales grew steadily between 1936 and 1939, while sales of its less sophisticated—read, flathead—stablemates and competitors were stagnant. By the end of the 1939 model year, the sexy 61 had clearly proved the Harleys and the Davidsons right in their belief that OHVs were the future. And a bright future it would be!

CHAPTER THREE

1940-1946

The Big Port Engine

Nothing jump-starts an economy like a good war—or preparations for one. And the United States had been gearing up for several years. On September 1, 1939, as Harley-Davidson began assembling its 1940 models, Hitler took the final, irrevocable step toward world war when his troops invaded Poland.

The U.S. economy really came alive in the fall of 1939, as defense spending rose and factories struggled to meet the demand for war materiel for the United States and Allied forces. Ever eager to do its part, Harley-Davidson was already hard at work designing the WLA and other military motorcycles that kept it busy during the war years.

The United States was not yet in the war, however, so H-D did not neglect its civilian line-up. For 1940, the company introduced the first extensive revamp of its crown jewel, the 61 OHV, since the design had stabilized for model year 1937.

Window to the World, 1940

Not relishing the job but realizing that the coming conflict would require a steady, experienced hand at the helm, FDR ran for an unprecedented third term as president. In November, he won in an electoral landslide.

In Britain, Winston Churchill replaced Neville Chamberlain as prime minister and became the symbol of British resolve to fight and win.

On the continent, the Nazi blitzkrieg rolled on, overrunning Denmark, Norway, Holland, Belgium, Luxembourg, and France. Soon after, the Battle of Britain began as German planes daily attacked London.

Relations between the United States and Japan continued to deteriorate as the year went on, and accelerated in July when FDR banned export to Japan of scrap metal and oil.

FDR vowed to turn America into the "Arsenal of Democracy." Early in the year he asked for and got the funds to build 50,000 warplanes. In July, he asked for and got $4 billion for new Navy ships. In November, he convinced Congress to agree to allocate half the military production to England.

Realizing late in the year that it takes soldiers—not just planes, tanks, and ships—to win a war, Congress passed the Selective Service Act, instituting the first peacetime draft for the United States.

Fred Ham, the California bike cop who set the 24-hour record in 1937 on a Knucklehead, was killed on December 9 when a car crossed in front of his bike during a high-speed chase.

The 1940 Knucklehead

The OHV Big Twin model line for 1940 included only the high-compression 40EL Special Sport Solo and the medium-compression 40ES twin with sidecar gearing. For the second year, a special police package was offered, but for 1940 it included only the three-speed transmission and medium gearing, not the medium-compression motor. All models were

After the war ended, civilian production gradually resumed. The first bikes built were like the few built during the war—very plain, with almost no chrome- or cad-plated parts and limited paint selections. Like almost all wartime-through-1946 bikes, this one was updated with many of the normally plated parts when it was restored, rather than with all the Parkerized parts. It was also given a nonstandard two-tone paint scheme using the two regularly offered colors available early that year: red and gray. On February 5, 1946, the gray color was replaced by Skyway Blue. It is owned by Larry Engesether of Wisconsin.

LEFT: For 1940 the Knucklehead was restyled and given updated cylinder heads. This unrestored machine is owned by Wayne Pierce, Sr. and Wayne "Whiz" Pierce, Jr. of Pierce Harley-Davidson in DeKalb, Illinois.

A major part of the restyle was the switch to metal tank badges, replacing the art deco transfers that had been used since 1936. For 1940, the two tanks were interconnected by a balance tube from the right tank to the left. Individual petcocks for each tank were replaced by a single "instant-on" fuel valve that gave the rider quick access to the main and reserve fuel supplies by turning a knob on the top of the left tank, just to the left of the speedometer.

listed at a retail price of $430 ($5 less than in 1939) and had to be ordered with one of the option groups, at additional cost.

For 1940, the option groups were reshuffled and a new one was added. The Standard Solo Group was no longer offered, its place as the most basic trim package taken by the new Utility Solo Group. Included in this package were only the most rudimentary "options," such as front safety guard, steering damper, jiffy stand, and four-ply tires, which should have been included in the base price, but were $11 extra. The basic package for sidecar and package-truck machines was renamed the Utility Group, and it included the front safety guard, steering damper, and four-ply tires for $8.50.

The mid-level option package, also new, was the Sport Solo Group, which included a front safety guard, steering damper, jiffy stand, air cleaner, trip odometer, fender light, chrome rims, chrome exhaust-pipe covers, colored shift ball, and four-ply tires, all for $22.50.

For a really "doggy" machine, the Deluxe Solo Group was offered. This group ($46.00) included a front safety guard, steering damper, jiffy stand, air cleaner, ride control, trip odometer, fender light, deluxe saddlebags, deluxe solo saddle, colored shift ball, four-ply tires, and Chrome Group (chrome-plated rims, handlebars, headlight, instrument panel, relay cover, exhaust-pipe covers, license frame, and top fender strips).

Styling Changes

With model year 1940 came the first major restyle of the Knucklehead. Unlike earlier restyles, this one was more than paint deep. The machine's look was modernized through use of revised gas tanks, new tank emblems, all-new footboards, and a reshaped toolbox. Overall, the restyle could be called "speed-lined and streamlined." Like the styling cues set on the first series of Knuckleheads, those set in 1940 would be resurrected by the company in later years, most recently and conspicuously on the 1997 Springer Heritage Softtail.

Tanks and Fenders

The most obvious styling changes were the new paint scheme and tank emblems. Gone with the 1930s were the art deco tank transfers that had fit the mood of the prior decade so well, replaced by teardrop-shaped emblems in chrome-plated stamped brass. The company name is debossed down the centerline of the emblems, and the name is framed above and below by a pair of tapered "speed-lines." Speed-lines are painted black, and letters are painted red. This emblem is correct for 1940 to 1946. Each gas tank was fitted with a single, horizontal mount for the tank emblem.

Also gone were the tank panels that had made the 1939 61 so distinctive. Instead, tanks were painted one solid color, except for a pinstripe that starts just forward of the tank badge and sweeps up and back toward the aft end of the tank before jogging forward horizontally, ending several inches aft of the tank emblem. Overall, the pinstripe suggests a projected shadow that frames the emblem perfectly.

Standard colors were black with Flight Red stripe, Clipper Blue with white stripe, Squadron Gray with Bittersweet stripe, Flight Red with Black stripe, and Police Silver with black stripe (police only). Fenders were painted the same color as the tanks, and were fitted with the same classy stainless steel trim stripes as in 1939.

In addition to the tank emblem, the left tank features the "instant-reserve" fuel valve, an innovative feature that controls the flow of fuel from both tanks through one valve, replacing the separate petcocks that had been standard since 1936. This new valve makes it much easier for the rider to turn the fuel on and off—and especially to access the reserve fuel supply without burning his or her hands on the cylinder head. The valve mechanism is fully enclosed within the tank, with only the knob visible on the top of the tank, just to the left of the speedometer. Unscrew the knob to the top of the threads to access the main gas supply. Lift the knob up and away from the tank to access the reserve. A spring-loaded neoprene backing holds it in the reserve position. Reserve capacity is 3/4 gallon.

Left and right fuel tanks are interconnected by a coiled balance line that attaches to a nipple fitting on the front underside of the right tank and the fuel valve on the left tank. They act as one tank when the bike is upright and draining. Unfortunately, they still act as one when the bike is on its sidestand and is being filled. If the right tank is filled first, the gas will flow through the balance tube and fill the left tank, too—and this tendency sometimes results in a bit of Harley hilarity. At their first fill, neophyte Knucklehead riders often get a lesson they'll never forget when, after completely filling the right tank, they then pull off the left tank's gas cap. Their eyes bug out as fuel unexpectedly gushes out and over the hot

A late-1940 police Knucklehead. Two different gear case covers were fitted to 1940 Knuckleheads, and both have eight 1/4-inch-wide cooling fins. Early- and mid-1940 Knuckleheads came with a thick, sand-cast cover with a somewhat rough surface texture and a flat surface behind the cooling fins. The late-1940 style is shown on this machine. It is die cast, giving it a much smoother texture, and it is thinner than the earlier gear cover. Because it is thinner, the surface behind the cooling fins shows the diagonal boss for the breather-tube passage and the circular boss for the pinion bushing. *Copyright Harley-Davidson Michigan, Inc.*

engine of their new mount. It's pretty comical watching them trying to decide whether to run for their lives from what they imagine will be an imminent explosion, or run for the nearest paper towel to wipe the gas off the bike's paint.

Like the balance line, the fuel line is an all-new part. It runs unbranched from a tapered-flare-nut fitting at the tank's fuel valve to a tapered-flare-nut fitting at the bottom of the fuel filter. This gas line was used only for 1940 and 1941; in 1942, a revised line was fitted for a side-feed gas filter.

Ribbed Gear Cover

After four years of plain, flat, featureless gear-case covers, the gear-case cover was revised for 1940 to harmonize with the flowing lines of the rest of the motorcycle. The new, sand-cast gear cover is internally the same as the previous cover (with cast-in baffle plate and breather tunnel), but the outside of the casting was given eight 1/4-inch-wide horizontal "cooling" fins. "Strength is added and heat is dissipated," according to the September 1939 issue of *The Enthusiast*.

Most 1940 machines were fitted with these sand-cast covers, but the cover was revised again very late in the production season, and the very last 1940 machines were fitted with a completely redesigned cover. This cover is die-cast, resulting in a smoother appearance. Externally, bulges for the breather-tube passage and pinion-bushing boss project beyond the base surface of the cover, but not beyond the level of the ribs. Internally, a riveted-on baffle plate replaces the cast-in baffle plate used on the previous cover, and the word "ALCO" and the number "97-403" are cast in relief. This cover is correct through 1947.

This bike is reported to be an original-paint machine, which means it must have been special ordered in this color. Standard colors for 1940 were Clipper Blue with white stripe, Flight Red with black stripe, Squadron Grey with Bittersweet stripe, Black with Flight Red stripe, and Police Silver with black stripe. This bike has most of the features of the Chrome Group for 1940, which was part of the Deluxe Solo Group and included chrome-plated rims, handlebar, headlamp, instrument panel, relay cover, exhaust-pipe covers, license frame, and top fender decoration. This machine also carries the "airplane-style" speedometer that is correct for 1941–1946 Knuckleheads. The correct tripmeter-equipped speedometer for 1940 is the "white-face" 120-mile-per-hour speedometer with 2-mile-per-hour hash marks that was introduced in 1938.

Teardrop Toolbox

Continuing the trend toward a more streamlined look for the new decade, the 1940 models were given a racy new tool box to replace the boxy, rectangular toolbox used on the 1936–1939 61. The new toolbox is a streamlined teardrop with five ribs embossed on the cover. "The ribbing on the toolbox harmonizes with the new lines on the crankcase and adds plenty of sweep and dash to the entire motorcycle," gushed the September 1939 issue of *The Enthusiast*.

Unlike the previous tool box, this one mounts horizontally, wide end forward, the taper of the box's top line gracefully following the line of the top right rear frame tube. The cover is secured by a lock, and the toolboxes is painted black. This style of toolbox is correct for 1940–1947 Knuckles and on the Panheads through 1957.

For 1940 only, the toolbox bracket is riveted to the frame's tool-box strap. On 1941 and later machines, the bracket is a separate piece.

Half-Moon Footboards

After the toolbox, the last real square corners to be rounded were the footboards, which also were redesigned for a more streamlined effect. The new footboards are D-shaped and have redesigned rubber floorboard mats riveted on. With only minor changes over the years, these footboards were standard on all Harley-Davidson Big Twins through 1965. Footboards are Parkerized for 1940–1942 and have rubber mats.

At the same time Harley-Davidson updated the footboards, they cured a nagging problem in the clutch-pedal mechanism. On pre-1940 clutch-pedal assemblies, the pivot-bearing cover rattled almost constantly because it was only loosely held in

For 1940, "half-moon" footboards replaced the rectangular footboards that had been used on Harley-Davidsons since 1914. The half-moon footboards soldiered on almost as long as the rectangular boards had, until they were replaced on the 1966 Shovelhead Electra Glide with a new, semirectangular design.

place by the pedal bracket's spring stud and spring. For 1940, a revised clutch-pedal bracket was fitted. Its spring stud was threaded for a new nut to firmly fasten the cover in place. The bearing cover was revised to omit the "step" that had been embossed around the spring-stud hole, and the hole was increased to 27/64 inch in diameter (rather than 5/16 inch). The cover was painted black, and the bracket was Parkerized.

Fat Tires

It doesn't matter whether they're on a Deuce Coupe hotrod, a lifted four-by-four truck, or a 1940 Harley—fat tires can give the meekest machine the aura of performance. Usually, the aura is all you really get, but the millions of "sticker-package" performance cars sold during the 1970s proved convincingly that the look is all most people really wanted anyway. The bike we're talking about here, the 1940 Knucklehead, was one of the early pioneers of this trend, but it was an accidental trend-setter. And actually, H-D was following the lead of aftermarket companies such as Wolfe and Goulding. G. R. Wolfe was first, designing a special disc wheel and talking General into building a special 5.50x16-inch tire

called the Dual 10, with "squeegee action" tread, and offering them for sale in the April 1938 issue of *The Motorcyclist*. The Wolfe Safety Wheels were custom-built on the customer's hubs and a set of wheels, tires, tubes, and flaps sold for $59. They were heavy, though; shipping weight was listed as 94 pounds! These wheels are shown on Eldon Brown's 1939 61 in this chapter.

For 1940, fat 16-inch tires were made optional on all Harley-Davidson models. While style was almost certainly considered, the fatter tires were fitted for a more functional reason: the fatter tires could be run at lower pressure so that the sidewalls could flex more than those on the 18-inch tires, absorbing the effects of small road bumps and compensating somewhat for the lack of damping on the front fork and for the complete lack of suspension in the rear.

Problem was, the frame's 28-degree steering, head angle had been set up for the standard 18-inch tires, so machines fitted with the 16-inch tires didn't handle properly. At low speeds, the steering was heavy. And at high speed the front end gave poor feel and could easily go into a scary wobble on bumpy roads. Savvy riders cured the problem by having their frame "bumped"—bent using a frame jig and press, or by simply hitting the frame's backbone just behind the steering head with a heavy mallet—to increase the steering-head angle slightly. Harley-Davidson even recommended that its dealers resort to such measures to fix bikes with chronic handling problems, but I doubt the dealers really told their customers the disturbing details of the fix.

Despite the handling problems, most riders opted for the bigger tires, probably because they liked the look. But opinion was mixed on the looks at the time, and still is today. More traditional riders felt that the fat tires disrupted the OHV's sleek lines and were the ruin of a fine-handling machine. The factory liked what their customers liked, so fashion won out, and the 16-inch tires became standard the following year.

As alluded to earlier, the fat tires started a trend, and that trend came to be the great equalizer among American motorcycles, for Indian began fitting its machines with the fat tires in 1941, transforming their looks and ruining their handling forever, too.

A Few More Horses

Styling, schmyling, I say. The real changes for 1940 were all inside the motor. This was a bike for the new decade, after all, and Harley-Davidson intended to start the new era right. "Harley-Davidson engineers corralled a few more horses and packed them into the new 61 OHV motor," bragged the September 1939 issue of *The Enthusiast*. And all they had to

RIGHT: In addition to all the correct chrome bits included in the Chrome Group, this bike has many extra chrome-plated parts, including the primary cover and the rear chain guard. Like most 1940 Knuckleheads, this one was fitted with 5.00x16-inch tires, which first became optional for 1940. Fatter tires changed the look of the motorcycle substantially.

Like the footboards, the toolbox was restyled for 1940 from its old rectangular form to a more rounded, streamlined shape. The black air-cleaner cover shown is a war-time part; the optional air cleaner for 1940 was chrome plated.

do to get those extra horses was to open the gate a bit wider by enlarging the intake ports, intake manifold, and carburetor.

Large-Port Cylinders Heads

New head castings were introduced for 1940 with larger intake ports and a larger diameter threaded hole for the new, larger intake nipple for the new, larger manifold. Missing from the new casting was the boss for the primer cups, since the cups were no longer offered. Except for these changes, the head castings were like the 1939 castings. These head castings are correct for 1940 through 1947 civilian Knuckleheads (the few military OHVs built had a unique set of head castings with small ports on large-port castings).

Carburetor and Intake Manifold

The real key to opening the corral gate was the Linkert M-25 carburetor fitted to the 1940 Knucklehead. The M-25 is a 1-1/2-inch carburetor with a 1-5/16-inch venturi, replacing the venerable Linkert M-5 1-1/4-inch carb with a 1-1/16-inch venturi. Four bolts (instead of three) mount the new carburetor to a flange on the manifold. With its 1/4-inch-larger venturi, the M-25 added noticeably to the Knucklehead's top end, but at a cost in low-end power and throttle response, so it was used on the 61 only for 1940 (but it was also used on the early-1941 74-ci OHVs). In a cost-cutting move, the new carburetor was painted silver instead of being nickel plated.

Better performance was the goal, so the intake manifold was completely redesigned to carry the increased flow from the larger carburetor. Previous manifolds had been Y-shaped, but the 1940 manifold was reshaped to a T section, with 1 9/16-inch-diameter brass tubes (rather than 1-3/8-inch cast iron) in each section. The manifold's carburetor flange is drilled for four mounting bolts, and the cylinder-head ends have a smooth bushing surface. New, larger-diameter plumber nuts and brass bushings slide onto the bushing surfaces to fasten the manifold to the new, larger-diameter intake nipples. Manifold and plumber nuts were cadmium plated.

While the new, larger intake provided the gateway for more fuel-air mixture to flow from the carburetor to the intake ports, a flaw in its design also allowed air to leak in, resulting in backfires, misses, and poor performance. The problem was that the bushings and manifold were both made of brass. Time and vibration would make the bushing gall and seize on the manifold, ruining the seal. Because of this problem, the brass manifold was used for 1940 only; it would be cast iron starting in 1941.

Other Top-End Changes

To handle the increased horsepower produced by the new carburetor and intake tract, the cylinder castings were revised so that the tunnels for the head bolts extended

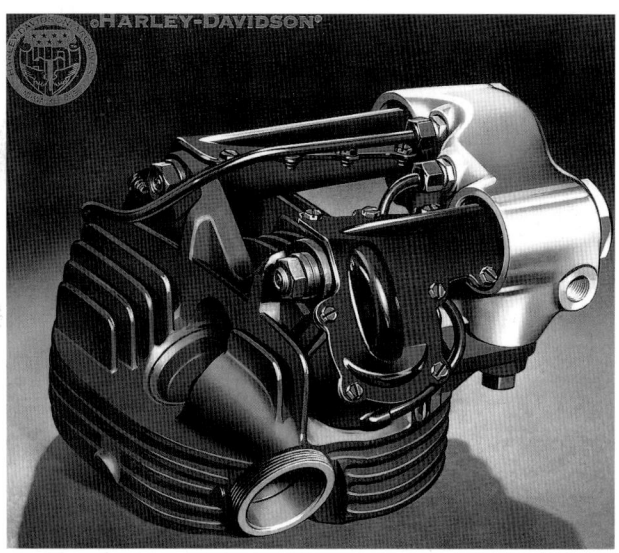

This air-brushed photo from the Harley-Davidson archives shows how the company would often have an older photo retouched to show new features, in this case the revised valve cover screws added in 1939 and the large-port heads introduced in 1940. This is essentially the same photo as the one printed in chapter 2, except that hex-head screws (Parker-Kalon self-tapping, introduced in 1939) were airbrushed over the round-head screws, the individual nuts for each screw were airbrushed out (screw plates were used), the rounded boss over the intake tract was airbrushed larger to show its size on the large-port heads, and the primer-cup boss was airbrushed out (it was deleted from the casting starting in 1940). The airbrush artist neglected to change one prominent feature, however. The rocker-shaft brackets shown were used only through about midyear 1938. The large-port heads were fed by a larger carburetor and intake manifold. *Copyright Harley-Davidson Michigan, Inc.*

through five cylinder fins, rather than through four. Except for this one change, the cylinders are unaltered. New head bolts, 5/16 inch longer than the superseded bolts, pass through the tunnels to fasten the heads to the cylinders. These cylinders and bolts were fitted for 1940–1947.

With the advent of fully enclosed rocker covers in 1938, problems of oil leaking out had been solved. But there was still the matter of over- or under-oiling of the intake valves. Too much, and the bike would suck oil in past the intake valve stem to smoke and foul the spark plugs. Too little, and the valves would squeak and wear.

The underoiling problem was solved when fixed oiling for the valve gear was introduced in mid-1939, but some individual engines were still prone to sucking in oil when used hard. This problem was finally solved on the 1940 engine by the use of revised guides for the intake valves. The new guides have a taper at the top that deflects oil spray away from the valve stem and also causes accumulated oil to flow away from the stem. The new guide was used only in the intake position and for 1940–1947.

To seal another source of oil seepage, the lower pushrod covers were redesigned for 1940 to have a flange at the bottom to rest on top of the lower cork seal (previous covers lacked the flange and were pushed down inside the cork seal). To make removing the pushrod-cover retainer easier, the retainer was revised to have a small "handle," through which a small screwdriver blade could be inserted to pry out the retainer. The new lower cover and retainer were chrome plated. These parts are correct for 1940–1947 (except that they were Parkerized for 1943–1946).

Bottom-End Updates

The 61's bottom end was extensively revised for 1940 to strengthen it and to equalize the amount of oil reaching the two cylinder walls. The strength was provided by a beefier crankpin and bearing, and the oiling was improved through revisions to the crankcases, connecting rods, and pistons.

Larger Crankpin and Bearing

To handle the added power supplied by the new top end, a new, larger-diameter crankpin was introduced. The 1940 crankpin was given a 1 1/4-inch-diameter bearing surface (1/8 inch larger than before). It is the same length as the previous crankpin, retains the oil hole and passage from the end to the bearing surface, and tapers at each end from 1 1/8 inches to 1 inch, but now it "steps down" suddenly from the outboard ends of the bearing surface to the start of the taper, so that the new crankpin could be used with the old flywheels. The new, matching main bearing is 1/8 inch larger in diameter and has 54 rollers (instead of 42) for a substantial increase in strength. Both crankpin and bearing remained in use through the end of the Knucklehead line in 1947.

New lapping machinery at the factory was put to good use for 1940 production by line lapping the pinion and sprocket shaft races to ensure perfect sizing and perfect alignment. To make line lapping possible, new bearing races were introduced that did not have the steel plate formerly used with each race. After the crankcases were bolted together and line bored, the new bushings were installed and lapped together. The crankpin and roller bearings were also lapped to "glass smoothness." The result? Smoother, quieter, longer lasting motors.

Crankcase Oil Control

Because the flywheels spin clockwise, when viewed from the right side of the engine, much more oil is slung off them onto the walls of the rear cylinder than onto the front cylinder. To block the bulk of this spray, the 1936–1939 motors had a half baffle covering the rear of the rear cylinder opening. The front cylinder opening had a full baffle to increase vacuum below the piston, with the hope that the vacuum would draw in enough air-oil mist to lubricate the cylinder. This arrangement had worked fairly well—the extra oil on the rear cylinder tending to carry away heat, compensating somewhat for their lack of direct cooling air—but Harley-Davidson decided it could do better, so the company gave a new system a try on the 1939 side-valve Big Twins.

On the 1939 side-valves, the baffles at both cylinder openings were removed, the positions of the connecting rods were reversed (the female rod was moved to the rear cylinder position and the male rod to the front), and half of the slot around the big end of the female rod was closed. Why? The new rod positions tended to sling much less oil on the rear cylinder, so the rear baffle wasn't needed to block direct oil spray. And the half-filled slot on the female rod's big end tended to catch oil and throw it on the front cylinder, so the front baffle plates were no longer needed.

The revised female rod slung enough oil on the front cylinder that Harley-Davidson found it necessary to fit the front piston with an oil-control ring for the first time, so now both front and rear pistons had the same ring configuration: two compression rings and one oil-control. Side benefits were more consistent vacuum throughout the lower end and less oil mist, easing the burden of the crankcase breather valve and oil separator. This system worked so well that Harley-Davidson introduced it to the OHV Big Twins for 1940, and the same basic system is still in use on Harley-Davidson Big twins today.

The new system for the Knucklehead required new left and right crankcases and front and rear connecting rods. The 1940 crankcases are similar to the previous case, but the baffle plates and steel plates for the sprocket- and pinion-shaft bearing races were omitted and the casting number and date plate were moved to inside the case. The left case bears the new casting number 112-406, and the right case bears casting number 112-404. These cases (set up for the new rod positions and bearing races, but still designed for 8-1/8-inch-diameter flywheels) are correct for 1940 only. The new rods bear casting number 40A 706 (male) and 40A 705 (female) and were good enough to remain in service through the early 1970s.

The final lower-end update for 1940 was to the pinion-shaft assembly. The spacer that had been in between the left side of the oil-pump gear and the bearing was replaced for 1940 by a seal ring. Also, a spacer was added between the right side of the pump gear and the spring that fills the space between the pump gear and the pinion gear. Both these changes were used thorough the end of Knucklehead production in 1947.

Transmission and Clutch

For 1940, the standard transmission was once again the constant-mesh four speed because 1939's four-speed transmission with sliding second gear had not been popular among solo riders. Shifting between the constant-mesh first gear and sliding second required more deliberate effort than between the constant-mesh first and second of the pre- and post-1939 four speeds. Perhaps worse than the slower shifting, neutral was in an odd position on the 1939 transmission—between second and third—making it necessary to shift through second when shifting from first to neutral or from neutral to first.

Although it meant swallowing a bit of pride and a lot of design effort, switching back to the constant-mesh four speed was the right thing to do. It was the standard transmission through the end of Knucklehead production in 1947. Returning with the four speed was the 1-N-2-3-4 (front to rear) shifter gate. This gate is correct through 1946.

The sliding gear transmissions were more popular with police and commercial users, however, so the three-speed and three-speed-with-reverse transmissions with sliding-gear first were optional again for 1940-and-later Knuckleheads.

Front brake drums were cast nickel-iron (rather than being stamped steel) with an integral stiffening ring for 1940. The brake shackle was slightly updated, as well. The new shackle has only one grease fitting, at the backing-plate end of the shackle. The fitting for the fork end of the shackle was moved to the fork-end mounting stud, pointing out to the left, as shown. The fender-top trim for 1940 included a chevron and stripes for the front fender. The chevron is visible just ahead of the fender light.

All the 1940 transmissions were updated with the breather on the transmission case (rather than on the starter cover) for 1940. This change required a new transmission case with a boss for the transmission vent plug, and a new starter cover with an undrilled vent boss. The case and cover were otherwise unchanged.

To reduce chatter and to take up slack to prevent rattle, four-slotted spring keys were added to each lined clutch disc. These spring keys fit into the keyways of the clutch ring.

Frame

Only one significant change was made to the frame for 1940: a horizontal toolbox bracket is riveted to the frame's toolbox strap. Starting in 1941, the bracket became a separate piece.

The rear fender of the Pierces' 1940 Knucklehead shows the three fender-top trim pieces that were included in the Deluxe Solo Group, an accessory rear fender tip, and an aftermarket bumper. The saddlebags appear to be aftermarket, too.

Front Brakes

Front brakes were further refined for 1940. The flimsy stamped front brake drum was at last replaced by a cast, nickel-iron drum with an integral stiffening ring to reduce vibration and chatter caused by flexing of the drum. The stiffer drum allows use of a new brake-shoe operating shaft that is 9/32 inch narrower. It also made possible smoother, more uniform grinding of the braking surface for even smoother braking action. Although the front brake was still next to worthless, the 1940 changes made it as good as it would ever get. This drum was used on all spring-fork civilian Big Twins from 1940 through 1949. Interestingly, the Empire Electric Brake Company began marketing the Magdraulic Electric Brake for H-Ds, promising increased stopping power with "The light touch of a Woman's Hand!" All for $22, according to an ad in the April 1940 *The Motorcyclist*.

Front-brake shackles and studs received minor updates to make maintenance easier. The fork-end grease fitting was omitted on the shackle. Replacing it was a grease fitting on the new nut that secured the shackle to the fork stud. The grease fitting extended to the left from the end of the nut for unrestricted access. Grease pumped through the fitting was channeled through the nut and along a flat ground into the stud's shaft to grease the shackle. The new shackle and stud are correct for 1940–1947.

Saddles

Also updated for 1940 were the standard and deluxe solo saddles. The standard saddle is like the previous saddle, except that the leather covering was changed to tan, smooth-grained cowhide (rather than horsehide) and the pan was made with vent holes. This saddle is correct for 1940–1946.

The 1940 deluxe solo seat was covered in cowhide (again, rather than horsehide) and was given a restyled valance. This saddle was fitted with a short, one-piece leather valance (replacing a longer, three-piece valance). The 1940 valance was made of "walrus grain" leather, to which several jeweled pieces were attached. The valance is fringed, and the fringes grow gradually longer from the sides to the back. The seat was available in tan or black leather—and only for 1940.

Minor Updates

In addition to the major changes already described, the 1940 Knucklehead came with many minor improvements that deserve only brief mention. The forks were heat treated. The top of the oil tank has a raised, vertical rim but lacks the embossed pattern of the previous oil tank. The patent decal is applied to only the left side of the oil tank. The center reinforcement rib on the inner primary cover was lengthened, and a forward-facing bulge was added near the top of the rib. The rear chain guard has its front section spot-welded (rather

They're smiling a bit too broadly to be just watching birds. My guess is that the road they are on ends at Wisconsin's only nudist colony. Binoculars in hand, the young lady on the lightweight 45 takes a closer look. The couple on the powerful "big-port" 61 smile coyly and look but are already planning their get-away from the naked and vengeful posse that will surely follow. The 61 is outfitted with the top-of-the-line Deluxe Solo Group, which added $46 to the $410 cost of the basic machine. Deluxe items shown include the air cleaner, chevron front-fender trim, fender lamp, and chrome-plated instrument panel, wheel rims, handlebar, and relay cover. The spotlamps were accessories available outside the Deluxe group. Note that this bike has the early, sand-cast gear cover. *Copyright Harley-Davidson Michigan, Inc.*

than riveted) to the rear section. The base for the cutout relay was revised to move the relay slightly to make room for the accessory chrome exhaust-pipe covers that had been introduced in 1939. Finally, the brake-side flange of the interchangeable star hub was made of forged steel and its inner surface was redesigned to omit the "step" that had been on earlier hubs. All of these updated parts are correct for 1940–1947.

1940 Production

As the U.S. economy improved, more people had the money to spend on motorcycles. Harley-Davidson's sales rose 26 percent overall to a total of 10,461, the highest total since 1937. Knucklehead sales rose almost 40 percent, to 4,069. Of this total, 3,893 were ELs and 176 were ESs. Most significantly, the 61 OHV—the most expensive model in the line-up—was also the best selling for the first time ever.

Window to the World, 1941

FDR saw the United States' entry into the war as inevitable, so the preparations continued at full throttle. In January, FDR asked for a defense budget of $10.8 billion. In March, Congress passed the Lend-Lease Act, empowering the president to "lend" arms and equipment to the Allies.

In June, U.S. Army troops were sent in to break up a strike, so that production of new warplanes was not interrupted.

The most obvious changes for 1941 were the addition of stainless trim strips fore and aft of the tank badge and the new, "rocket-fin" muffler and exhaust Y-pipe (the pair replacing the fishtail muffler with integral pipe). Other more-subtle changes include a steering-head angle increased to 29 degrees to help stabilize the 16-inch tires, main battery ground attached to a tab on the frame (rather than to the oil line), a new oil pump with centrifugally controlled bypass, and a redesigned brake hand lever. This 1941 Knucklehead is owned by the Trev Deeley Motorcycle Museum in suburban Vancouver, British Columbia. It is a very nice machine, but has a few incorrect bits, including the 1955-and-later deluxe solo saddle and the chrome-plated exhaust pipes (although the chrome header-pipe covers shown were available) and fork springs. The patent decal shown on the right side of the oil tank should be only on the left side of the tank.

Hitler, flush with confidence over the successes of his armies, launched the invasion of Russia.

In September, the USS Greer was attacked by a German U-boat, and FDR ordered U.S. forces to attack on sight any Axis vessels in U.S. waters. Taxes were sharply increased to raise money for the defense buildup.

In October, the hawkish General Hideki Tojo took over control of the Japanese government. In November, the U.S. ambassador to Japan warned of an imminent attack on the U.S. military, but the warnings went unheeded. In early December, FDR forwarded a personal appeal for peace to Emperor Hirohito. On December 7, well, you know what happened. Pearl Harbor. And the end of civilian motorcycle production for the duration.

The 1941 Knucklehead

The OHV Big Twin model line expanded in 1941 to include four models, the high-compression 41EL and 41FL Special Sport Solos and the medium-compression 41ES and 42FS twins with sidecar gearing. The new F-series machines were identical to the E-series, except that the F series were fitted with a 74-ci version of the OHV engine.

The EL and ES models were listed at a retail price of $425 ($5 less than in 1940), the FL and FS models at $465. All models had to be ordered with one of the option groups, at additional cost. The 5.00x16-inch tires that had been optional in 1940 were standard for 1941 (except when the Standard Group for sidecars was ordered); the 4.00x18-inch tires were optional for no extra cost.

For 1941, the Utility Solo Group and Sport Solo Group were unchanged. The Deluxe Solo Group included a front safety guard, steering damper, jiffy stand, air cleaner, ride control, trip odometer, fender light, deluxe saddlebags, chrome saddlebag plates with jewels, deluxe solo saddle, colored shift ball, 5.00x16-inch tires, and Chrome Group (chrome-plated rims, handlebars, headlight, instrument panel, taillight housing, relay cover, exhaust-pipe covers, license frame, and top fender ornament).

The 1941 Knuckleheads were available in six standard colors: Brilliant Black, Skyway Blue, Flight Red, Cruiser Green, or Police Silver (police only).

Styling Changes

Styling for 1941 was largely unchanged from that of 1940, the major exceptions being the addition of trim strips to the gas tanks, a restyled speedometer, and a redesigned muffler. In addition, the taillight cover was painted gloss black (rather than the color of the tanks and fenders).

New Tank Trim

The new stainless steel gas-tank trim strips extend horizontally on the centerline of the gas tanks, fore and aft of the same chrome-plated gas-tank emblems that had been introduced in 1940. The result is that, "The stainless steel strips on the tanks blend the front and rear of the motorcycle in one pleasing sweep and add emphasis to the beautiful nameplates," according to the September 1940 *The Enthusiast*. The tank strips replace the pinstripes used on the gas tanks in 1940 and are correct on 1941–1946 Knuckleheads.

"Airplane-style" Speedometer

After five years with the "white-face" style of speedometer, a restyled speedometer was released for 1941 that was influenced by the modern instrumentation in the prominent high-performance aircraft of the day. This new face is difficult to describe; see the photos of it in this chapter. Overall, the face is two-tone, black and silver, in a bull's-eye pattern.

The speedometer's glass is convex, to allow clearance for the thicker pointer, the bezel is chrome plated, and the Harley-Davidson bar and shield is printed in silver at the aft end of the speedometer face. As the September 1940 issue of *The Enthusiast* boasted, "Even the sleek ships that dart through the skies don't have any smarter-looking dials than this one." This speedometer is correct for 1941–1946.

"Rocket-Fin" Muffler

Like the "white-face" speedometer, the fishtail muffler had been carried over essentially unchanged from 1936 through 1940, and the both had definitely begun to look dated on the restyled 1940 machines. For 1941, the Knucklehead's muffler was completely redesigned for a more modern, "Buck Rogers" appearance, with a stylish rocket fin replacing the fishtail of the old-style muffler.

The new muffler is 3 1/4 inches in diameter, much larger than the previous muffler, and was redesigned internally. This muffler departed from standard design practice of the day by not using any steel wool or other internal packing to absorb sound. Instead, it used a resonating chamber to attenuate the exhaust note. The new design had two practical benefits: it didn't grow louder over time because there was no packing to burn up or blow out, and it reduced back pressure for better engine performance. Even without packing, the new muffler was quieter than the old muffler and had a lower, mellower tone. This muffler is correct for 1941–1949 Big Twins. Standard finish was black.

The 1941-and-later muffler lacks the collector pipe that is attached to the front of the 1936–1940 muffler, so a new, separate exhaust pipe was introduced to connect the front and rear headers to the muffler. Because of its shape, the new pipe is called the Y-pipe. This pipe was used on all 1941–1947 Knuckleheads. Like the rest of the exhaust, the Y-pipe is painted black.

Big-Inch Knuckle: The FL

Being the quintessential American motorcycle company, Harley-Davidson eventually came around to raising displacement of the Knucklehead to create a new flagship Big Twin, the 74-cubic-inch Series. Except for its motor, the new model was identical to the venerable Series E.

The extra displacement in the new motor was obtained by increasing the bore by 1/8 inch (from 3 5/16 inches to 3 7/16 inches) and the stroke by 15/32 inch (from 3 1/2 inches to 3 31/32 inches). To obtain these new dimensions, the 74s used new cylinders. The result of the displacement increase was about 5 extra horsepower. To handle the extra power, the lower end and clutch were redesigned for greater strength.

The longer stroke of the 74 made it necessary to use larger-diameter flywheels. The flywheels were made 3/8 inch larger in diameter than the previous flywheel (8 1/2 inches versus 8 1/8 inches) and 4 pounds heavier. In the interest of parts commonality, the 61 engine also used the larger flywheels. Flywheels for the 61 retain the same crankpin-hole dimensions that were used on the previous flywheels (tapering from 1 1/8 inches to 1 inch) so that the crankpin was not changed. Flywheels for the 74 are the same as the 61 flywheels, except that the 74's crankpin holes are placed farther out for the longer stroke and taper from 1 1/4 inches to 1 1/8 inches for the 74's beefier crankpin. These flywheels were used through the end of the Knucklehead line in 1947.

The larger flywheels for 1941 would have been too tight a fit in the existing crankcases, so revised cases were fitted for 1941. The left crankcase was substantially revised, with the top two reinforcement ribs extending up to the cylinder bases and the flywheel cavity increased in size for the 8-1/2-inch flywheels. Except for the larger cavity for the new flywheels, the right case was unchanged. Both cases were used from 1941 through 1947.

The stronger crankpin for the 74 OHV has a cylindrical bearing surface that tapers at each outboard end without a "step" to a threaded end (like the 1936–39 61 crankpin), the larger diameter bearing surface of the 1940–1947 61 crankpin (1.249 inches versus 1.124 inches), and a new taper, from 1 1/4 inches to 1 1/8 inches. It has the same overall length (3.85 inches) as both previous crankpins. This crankpin was used for 1941–1947.

New Clutch

Although the clutch used on the 1936–1940 61s was plenty stout for the added power of the new 74, it displayed a nagging tendency to stick and drag as the many small splines in the hub and notches on the clutch plates wore with use. Harley engineers cured these problems forever with an all-new clutch for 1941.

New Components

The redesigned clutch drum was an all-new part that is larger in diameter than the previous drum and has six keys riveted on the inside of the drum, replacing the 30 keys milled into the inside ring of the previous clutch. These keys mate with notches on the clutch's new plain steel discs. This clutch drum was used without change for 1941–1947.

The 1941 hub was also an all-new part. It is larger in diameter than the previous hub and mates to the clutch's friction plates by a new, more-direct method. The new hub has three long studs (threaded at both ends) and seven long pins (threaded at one end). The new lined discs have 10 matching holes and slide over the studs and pins to mate them solidly to the hub. Ten new clutch springs are used, one on each stud and pin, outboard of the new releasing disc, and the springs are retained by the clutch pressure plate. Nuts threaded onto the ends of the three studs fasten the pressure plate. The outer diameter of the hub is filled with two staggered rows of ball bearings that form the bearing on which the clutch drum freely revolves when the clutch is disengaged. Each row has

For 1941 the speedometer was given a facelift to the "airplane-style" shown. This particular speedometer is the one supplied when the Utility Group was ordered and lacks the trip odometer. When the Sport or Deluxe Solo Group was ordered, a speedometer with a trip odometer was fitted. The upgrade speedometer was just like the one shown except that it had a trip odometer window just aft of the pointer pivot that displayed three digits (two for miles in black on a white background, and one for tenth miles in red on a white background) and the main odometer displayed only five digits, all for miles and none for tenth miles.

18 ball bearings (7/32 inch in diameter). This clutch hub was used without change for 1941–1947.

The 1941 clutch disc pack consisted of a releasing disc, a sprung disc with an asbestos lining on one side and 10 holes for the studs and pins on the hub, three plain steel discs with notches on their outside diameter to mate with the keys on the clutch drum and two spring-loaded balls on each steel disc to reduce looseness and rattling, and three steel discs with asbestos linings on both sides and 10 holes for the studs and pins on the hub. This disc pack would be used without change for 1941–1947.

Clutch Operation

In operation, the new clutch was much different from the previous unit. On the new clutch, the drum transfers power to the plain steel discs. When the clutch is engaged, spring pressure clamps the plain discs to the lined discs, and the lined discs transfer the power to the clutch hub through the 10 pins on the hub. Overall, the new clutch provides seven total friction surfaces (versus five on the 1940 clutch) with a total of 121 square inches of friction area for an increase of 48 square inches or 65 percent. The new clutch was so effective that it was used almost without change through the end of Knucklehead production in 1947 and on to the Panhead and Shovelhead series of engines that followed.

Revised Clutch Pedal and Bracket

Clutch pedals are subjected to constant use when a bike is ridden in traffic, and the Knucklehead's pedal-pivot bushings were found to wear quickly under such use. For 1941, the problem was fixed through the introduction of a revised clutch pedal on a revised pedal bracket. The clutch pedal has a longer pivot shaft, and the stud for the clutch-rod end is also longer. The pedal's longer shaft inserts through a much longer boss on the revised pedal bracket, and this boss is fitted with two bushings and a grease fitting that provide twice the bearing surface and make for easy lubrication, resulting in much smoother, more durable clutch-pedal action. The bracket and pedal were Parkerized. This bracket is correct for 1941–1944, and the pedal is correct for 1941 through mid-1946.

Carburetors and Intake Manifolds

Because the 1-5/16-inch venturi on the Linkert M-25 had proved to be excessively large on the 1940 61, it was replaced

A new clutch was introduced on all the Harley-Davidson Big Twins for 1941, to handle the extra power of the 74 OHV. It was much stronger, less prone to chatter, and cheaper to produce than the earlier clutch, and it would be used almost without change on all subsequent Harley-Davidson Big Twins into the early 1980s. *Copyright Harley-Davidson Michigan, Inc.*

on 1941 61s by the Linkert M-35 1-1/2-inch carb with a 1-1/8-inch venturi. The new carb cured problems with low-rpm operation, so it was carried over and fitted to all 61s through 1947.

The M-25 was used on the early 74s but was soon replaced by the Linkert M-75, which was also a 1 1/2-inch carb with a 1 5/16-inch venturi. The M-75 carb was used through the end of 1941 production, but was then replaced for the following years by the same smaller-venturi M-35 used on the 61s.

In hot climates or in heavy-duty low-speed use, the OHVs were prone to vapor lock and percolation because the gas in the carburetor would heat up excessively. To fix the problem, the manifold's carburetor pipe was lengthened to space the carburetor farther away from the engine's heat.

Centrifugal-Bypass Oil Pump

For 1941, Harley introduced a new oil pump to fix a long-standing problem on the OHVs—how to properly regulate oil-pump output across the rpm range. To explain the root of the problem, we have to look back to model year 1939. On that year's Knuckleheads a new, larger-diameter drive gear for the oil pump was added to the pinion shaft and a new, smaller-diameter gear was added to the oil pump's driveshaft, effectively "gearing up" the oil-pump drive so that the pump spins almost twice as fast for higher oil pressure and greater flow. Unfortunately, the result was over-oiling at low rpm. Later that year, a lighter bypass spring was introduced to help control the overoiling by opening the bypass channel at 4–6 psi, bleeding off the excess oil. The lighter spring reduced the severity of the overoiling problem, but it was really just an expedient fix that also limited available oil pressure and flow at high rpm. Hardly desirable.

The solution for 1941 was both elegant and effective—a new bypass valve controlled by a centrifugal governor that gradually increases oil flow to the engine as rpm rises. At low rpm, the valve is open, venting most of the oil pump's output to the gear case. At high rpm, the valve is closed, sending all of the oil flow to the engine. The new valve gave the 1941 OHVs optimum oiling at all rpm. The pump worked so well, it was used through the end of the Knucklehead line in 1947. The pump is painted silver.

Frame

To avoid the handling problems associated with use of the now-standard 16-inch tires and a 28-degree neck angle, Harley-Davidson "bumped" the early-1941 frames at the factory, bending them for a 29-degree neck angle. Later frames were given a revised steering-head forging designed for the 29-degree neck angle. Both 1941 frames also came with two other updates: the toolbox bracket was no longer riveted to the frame's toolbox strap, and the battery was grounded on the frame, instead of on the oil line.

7-Inch Air Cleaner

Feeding air to the 1941 carburetors is a new, larger air cleaner. The new air cleaner is superficially similar to the previous air cleaner assembly—the cover fastens to the backing plate with four J-slots, has the bar and shield stamped on the flat surface in the center, and has a data plate riveted to the edge—but is 7 inches in diameter, rather than 6 inches. The backing plate was revised so that the filter's mesh and support are removable as a unit from the backing plate, to make changing or cleaning the air filter easier. The backing plate was Parkerized, and the cover was chrome plated. This air cleaner is correct for 1941–1947 (except that the 1943–1946 covers were painted black).

Small Changes

Many other subtle changes were made to smaller components for 1941. New, "positive-grip" brake hand levers and brackets replaced the old-style "spoon-tip" levers. These levers were die-cast aluminum and were polished for 1941–1942 and for mid-1946 through 1947. (Black-painted steel levers of the same design were used for 1943 through early 1946.) The front-brake backing plate was given a revised anchor with a threaded, 5/16-inch hole for the a new-style cable adjusting screw.

A new primary cover was fitted that is 1/2 inch deeper (3 1/4 inches versus 2 3/4 inches) to allow clearance for the 1941-and-later clutch assembly. This primary cover is correct for 1941–1947.

The front rocker housing was revised to have thicker metal in the area around the intake pushrod hole, and the boss around the motor side of the exhaust rocker shaft hole was lengthened to eliminate the need for the adapter sleeve introduced in 1938. This housing is stamped with the new casting number 7049-41.

The front safety guard was revised to allow more cornering clearance. The lower mounts are longer, and the lower bends begin immediately outboard of the lower mounts. From a frontal view, the lower curves are not symmetrical with the upper curves. This guard is correct for 1941–1947.

The deluxe solo seat was revised to again have a three-piece leather skirt with shorter rear skirt and longer side skirts. Each side skirt carries a faceted jewel trim piece near the front of each skirt. The seat is covered in tan or black cowhide.

To allow clearance between the starter-crank arm and the larger-diameter muffler, the starter arm's dogleg bend starts about a quarter of the way up (rather than halfway up) the arm. This crank arm is correct for 1941–1947.

Piston rings were oxide-coated to reduce scuffing and formation of ridges in the cylinder.

The gearshift lever was cyanide-hardened to prevent the shifter gate from cutting into the lever.

A heavier clamping ring was used on the horn to prevent distortion of the diaphragm at high speeds. The horn's tone is slightly lower.

The oil-pressure switch's diaphragm was made of DuPont "Fairprene" for longer service.

The valve stem of the gas shut-off valve was redesigned to give a 1.0-gallon reserve gas supply—1/4 gallon more than before.

The transmission mainshaft nut was redesigned to provide more contact area on the washer, reducing the tendency

ABOVE AND NEXT: The little Knucklehead that could have been. This experimental 45-ci OHV was developed and tested in tandem with the 74 OHV in the late 1930s. It was well-liked by testers but was doomed when a production analysis predicted it would be as expensive to produce as the side-valve 74. Owner Carman Brown reports that the bike is a pocket rocket, able to easily light up the rear tire when ridden hard. The 1941 styling is appropriate because like the 74 OHV, it probably would have been ready for production in 1941 had the project not been canceled.

for the washer to crack. The transmission mainshaft thrust bearings were redesigned for greater thrust strength and were fitted with shields on both sides to keep out foreign matter.

1941 Production

Much of the total Harley-Davidson production for 1941 was for the military. Yet Harley-Davidson still had the capacity to produce a record number of OHV Big Twins for the civilian market—5,149 in all. Of this total, 2,280 were ELs, 261 were ESs, 2,452 were FLs, and 156 were FSs. Then, as now, American riders can never resist bigger engines and more power: the 74 OHVs outsold the 61s 2,608 to 2,541—despite this prediction in the September 1940 issue of *The Enthusiast*: ". . . a limited number of 74 OHV Harley-Davidsons will be produced. However, as I have said, the number will be limited and production will not be nearly as extensive as on the other models."

Window to the World, 1942

By the time the 1942 models began rolling off the line in the early fall of 1941, America was perilously close to entering the war. American factories were churning out planes, tanks, guns, and other military equipment to the exclusion of almost everything else. And so was Harley-Davidson. With fat contracts to build bikes for United States and Allied forces, and increasing shortages of steel, copper, iron, and aluminum, Harley-Davidson only promised each dealer one new bike for the year. Then came December 7. On January 1, all production of civilian cars, trucks, and motorcycles was halted.

Initially, U.S. troops were steadily forced back all around the Pacific theater of war. In January, Manila fell and American and Philippine forces withdrew to the Bataan Peninsula. They surrendered there in April, and the Bataan Death March began.

In February, FDR ordered internment for all Japanese-Americans on the West Coast. More than 100,000 people were moved inland to internment camps in the following months. On the seventh, Harley-Davidson president Walter Davidson Sr. died. William H. Davidson took his uncle's place at the head of the company.

In June, the United States won its first major victory over the Japanese, in the Battle of Midway. The then-unknown Maj. Gen. Dwight D. Eisenhower was named commander of U.S. forces in Europe. And $42.8 billion was appropriated for the war effort that year—reportedly, more than the entire cost of World War I.

In August, the U.S. Army Air Forces began bombing raids on occupied Europe from bases in England

In December, gasoline rationing took effect nationwide. Fuel-efficient motorcycles once again appealed to the masses. Unfortunately, only used machines were available.

The 1942 Knucklehead

The OHV Big Twin model line for 1942 included the high-compression 42EL and 42FL Special Sport Solos and the medium-compression 42E and 42F twins. The 61s were listed at a retail price of $425, the 74s at $465—both prices the same as the previous year's. All models had to be ordered with one of the option groups, at additional cost.

For 1942, the same option groups were offered again. The Utility Solo Group and the Utility Group (for sidecar machines) were unchanged.

The mid-level option package was the Sport Solo Group, which included a front safety guard, steering damper, jiffy stand, air cleaner, trip odometer, fender light, chrome rims, chrome exhaust-pipe covers, colored shift ball, and 5.00x16-inch tires.

The top option package was the Deluxe Solo Group. This group included a chrome-plated front safety guard, steering damper, jiffy stand, air cleaner, ride control, trip odometer, fender light, deluxe saddlebags, set of jewels for saddlebags, deluxe solo saddle, colored shift ball, 5.00x16-inch tires, Chrome Group (chrome-plated rims, handlebars, headlamp, instrument panel, taillight housing, relay cover, exhaust-pipe covers, license frame, and top fender ornament), and several new items: chrome fender tips, clutch- and brake-pedal rubbers, chrome mirror, and chrome parking lamps. This option package made the Knucklehead flashier than ever—but wartime restrictions soon made it impossible to obtain.

Styling Changes

Styling was unchanged for 1942. Even the available colors were not changed. The lucky few customers who were able to get a 1942 Harley had their choice of Brilliant Black, Skyway Blue, Flight Red, Cruiser Green, or Police Silver (police only).

Parts Changes

Just as with the styling, the mechanical configuration of the 1942 civilian Knuckleheads was carried over essentially unchanged. The few changes that were made are briefly noted here.

For 1942–1947, the 74s were fitted with the same, smaller M-35 Linkert carburetor used by the 61s. The larger M-75 carburetor that had been standard on the later 1941 74s was still available as an option.

Because the fuel filter introduced in 1939 (with the fuel line connected to the bottom of the filter) was so unpopular, a new filter (with the fuel-line connection on the side of the filter) was standard for 1942. The new filter was just like the one used from 1936 to 1938, except that the new filter had tapered-flare-nut fittings instead of the older filter's compression-type fittings, and used straight—rather than cross-hatched—knurling. The gas line from the gas tank to the filter was also revised with a slightly different bend for the new

The Deeley 1941 Knucklehead outside the main warehouse and museum building. Trev Deeley is the Canadian importer for Harley-Davidson motorcycles and maintains one of the best motorcycle museums in North America. Starting in 1941, the redoubtable 61 was joined by a larger OHV stablemate, the 74-ci Models F and FL, created by boring and stroking the 61. Along with the 74 OHV came new, larger flywheels and redesigned crankcases, among other changes. The chrome clutch- and chain-inspection covers shown are not stock for 1941; chrome covers were available through the accessory catalogs. The chrome-plated taillight housing is not correct either. Starting in 1941, standard taillight covers were painted black.

connecting point on the filter's side. This filter and line were standard through the end of the Knucklehead line in 1947.

The front brake's cam-operating lever was slightly revised. The 1942–1947 levers are the same as previous levers, except that they have two holes instead of four on the shank and are no longer stamped with the words "SOLO" and "SC."

On 1942–1947 horns, the bracket is peened to the back rather than attached by a screw.

Rocker housings and the oil lines to them were given with nipple fittings (replacing leaky banjo-type fittings) starting in 1942.

The 1942–1946 boattail taillamp was given new spring clips to fasten the glass lenses to the body. The new clips are held in place by four straight-slot countersunk screws, so the taillight body was drilled for these screws.

Padding on the standard seat was changed to spun latex (replacing sponge rubber) padding.

Finally, a new standard gearshift knob was fitted. The new knob consists of a "squashed sphere"—not quite an oval, but slightly wider than it is tall—and a high, stepped ring that runs horizontally around the sphere, suggesting the rings around the planet Saturn. This knob is correct for 1942–1947.

Finish Changes

Shortages of aluminum and cowhide resulted in changes to some parts for 1942. Aluminum was used to manufacture silver paint and was strictly rationed even in late-summer 1941 when 1942 production began, so the tappet blocks and oil pump were painted white, instead. They remained white until the restrictions began to be lifted in 1946. And cowhide was needed to make boots for all the men who were being drafted, so the seats for 1942 were covered in horsehide.

Weathering the War

With numerous contracts to fill for military motorcycles, H-D was set up to prosper in 1942, despite the war. Not so the company's dealers. With no new machines or parts to sell and with most of their customers off to war, they would have to be clever to survive.

Knowing the plight of its agents, Harley-Davidson sought to help by including helpful advice in the dealer bulletins. The factory urged small, remote dealers to take war jobs and to invest their start-up money in war bonds so they would be ready with enough money to open their shops again when the war ended.

Many dealers took the advice, becoming police motorcycle officers, soldiers, and shipbuilders. The factory urged dealers to secure as much work on police bikes as possible. In the October 19 dealer bulletin, Harley-Davidson urged its dealers to convince their police chiefs to put motorcycles on their 1943 budgets because, "Then, later, if the War Production Board [WPB] should permit production of police motorcycles, your departments should have funds to purchase them." And Harley-Davidson helped woo these scarce customers by mailing out over 3,000 posters to police chiefs.

Other helpful advice? Of course. In the November 16 dealer newsletter, Harley-Davidson provided an answer to every dealer's most pressing dilemma, namely, "What can I get in the way of an appropriate Christmas gift for my police chief and other good customers?" The answer? An official Harley-Davidson memo holder, a mere $1.15 each with orders of five or more.

In the November 30 issue, dealers were advised to send letters or cards to their police customers to "capitalize on gas rationing and get more service work" by emphasizing how regular service work would minimize their bikes' consumption of scarce fuel. This issue also shared the secret for easy installation of the new hard, plastic handgrips: Soak them in hot water before installation.

The December 14 issue reminded dealers to pester the chiefs yet again, this time to have police motorcycles overhauled during the winter months.

To help secure bikes for their showrooms, Harley-Davidson urged the dealers to "try and buy Harley-Davidsons from the boys going to war!"

These bulletins also provide a look at how tightly controlled the supplies of strategic materials had become. Because rubber was so tightly controlled, seals for the rocker housings became unavailable in April 1942.

By May, Harley-Davidson was urging all dealers to send in ruined pistons so that the company could reclaim material to make replacement pistons. Dealers had to supply proof that they had sent in ruined pistons before they could qualify for replacement pistons. All the pistons sent in were pooled "for the common good of all Harley-Davidson dealers." In September, batteries and exhaust valves were restricted to an exchange basis, too.

1942 Production

Despite the shut down of 1942 production, Harley-Davidson records show that 1,743 OHV Big Twins were built. Of this total, 620 were ELs, 8 were ELAs (special ELs for the U.S. Army), 45 were ELCs (special ELs for the Royal Canadian Army), 164 were ESs, 799 were FLs, and 107 were FSs. Those who bought these bikes were fortunate indeed because no more new machines were made available to average civilians until late 1945.

Window to the War, 1943

Steadily gaining strength based on America's production abilities, the Allies began pushing back the German and Japanese advances that had previously seemed so easy in 1940 and 1941.

In January, FDR, Churchill, and Gen. Charles DeGaulle met at Casablanca to discuss war strategy. Sensing that they would ultimately triumph, the Allies agreed that they would accept nothing less than unconditional surrender from Germany, Italy, and Japan. They also agreed to start a second front against Germany by invading Sicily.

In June, income-tax withholding was instituted to improve government cash flow.

In July, the Allied armies invaded Sicily, and Mussolini resigned.

In September, Allied armies invaded Italy. Five days later, Italy surrendered. On September 18, chief engineer and company cofounder William S. Harley passed away.

By the end of the year, America was truly the "arsenal of democracy." Production of B-24 Liberator bombers topped 500 per month at Ford's Willow Run, Michigan, plant alone. American shipyards cranked out 1,949 ships in 1943, among them were 1,238 Liberty ships. And Harley-Davidson was doing its part, too. In 1943, H-D built more than 27,000 military motorcycles.

The 1943 Knucklehead

In principle, the OHV Big Twin model line for 1943 included the high-compression 43EL and 43FL Special Sport Solos and the medium-compression 43E and 43F twins. In principle because Harley-Davidson could build bikes only on special order for customers who had first received WPB approval, which was very difficult to obtain in 1943. Those bikes that were built were likely available with only the items in the Utility Solo Group—front safety guard, steering damper, jiffy stand, 5.00x16 tires, and black rims.

I could not find a source listing the standard colors for the year. Gray was probably the only option, but other colors may have been left over from 1942 production that were used up on the 1943 models. The only reference to colors for 1943 that I could find was in the September 13, 1943, dealer news bulletin, which stated that colors other than standard were offered on police orders for $5 extra.

The only real changes for 1943 were that use of chrome plating, cadmium plating, and silver paint were virtually eliminated. Nearly everything that had been plated on previous models was Parkerized or painted black for the duration of the war and through at least part of 1946, when restrictions on use of critical war materials were eased. The one notable exception to this rule is that the stainless steel tank strips seem to show up on the photos of wartime bikes. Harley-Davidson must have had enough left over from previous years to carry them through the war year. Some bikes may have been fitted with the earlier, chrome or cad-plated parts if any of those parts were left in inventory at the time the bikes were assembled.

So what would one of these wartime machines have looked like? The tank emblems, oil pump, and tappet blocks were painted white. Pushrod tubes, timing-hole plug, seat-post tube, and almost all screws and bolts were Parkerized. The bezel on the speedometer and around the dash's indicator lights were painted black, as were the ignition switch cover, speedometer-light knob, tankshifter and its gate, the handlebar spirals, gas caps, headlamp rim, horn face, front-brake hand lever, front-fender light cover, air-cleaner cover, covers for the horn and headlight switches, steering damper knob, and gas shutoff knob. The stainless steel fender strips were left off. The floorboards for 1943–1947 were painted black and were fitted with ribbed steel (instead of rubber) mats. The rubber blocks on the kickstart pedal were also omitted.

Just about the only chrome-plated parts left on the machine were the four rocker-shaft "knuckle" nuts. In short, the lucky few who were authorized to buy a new Harley got what most would consider an ugly duckling rather than a graceful swan.

Weathering the War

War continued to be hell for cash-strapped Harley-Davidson dealers in 1943, but the factory was there for the dealers again with more helpful hints in the dealer news bulletins.

Although oil was scarce and rationed, Harley-Davidson motorcycles didn't know it. They leaked just as much as they had during peacetime, so the oil needed to be washed off from time to time with a little Gunk. Cans and glass jars were in short supply, so Harley-Davidson was forced to discontinue selling Gunk in small containers. To solve the problem, the factory suggested that dealers buy Gunk in half or full barrels and recycle their old oil jars by filling them with Gunk for resale to customers.

For those dealers who had planned ahead and had heeded the factory's advice of the previous year to court police

Very little changed for 1942 because preparations for war-time production took up most of the time available to the company's design engineers. And then on December 7, 1941, just as production should have been hitting full stride in a normal year, the Japanese attacked Pearl Harbor. Virtually all civilian motorcycle production was stopped by the end of the year. Note the optional jewels covering the saddlebag mounting screws. *Copyright Harley-Davidson Michigan, Inc.*

business, good news was presented in the July 20 dealer newsletter: "A plan long under consideration has now been approved by the proper WPB officers, and police departments having a vital need for motorcycles will be allotted machines in late August or early September."

Even more good news and advice was offered in the August 16 issue: "War plants eligible for new Harley-Davidsons for guard and police duty!" Dealers were encouraged to visit gunpowder plants, air conditioning factories, gun factories, steel mills, and other essential defense manufacturers to encourage them to apply for WPB approval to purchase motorcycles.

Apparently, the police orders began rolling in, because the September 13 issue stated that police bikes ordered with nonstandard colors were $5 extra—implying, of course, that colors other than gray or silver really were available.

Asserting that more Harley-Davidson commercial motorcycles were "very definitely needed to promote the war effort," the November 1 issue urged dealers to court buyers for such machines. The dealers were told to promote the great potential "savings in rubber, gas, and time" these machines would offer to essential war industries for messengers and to deliver shipments. Once convinced of their obvious need for new Harleys, the bosses of these industries would then petition the WPB to allow Harley to build them. You gotta love circular promotion.

The November 15 issue gave the dealers a little pat on the back by trumpeting the results of the court-your-chief campaign: "137 police departments have qualified for new Harley-Davidsons!" Unfortunately, the bulletin gave no indication of how many bikes were allotted to these police departments or what models they were. However, it did include a "purchase proposal for police motorcycles" to show the dealers the proper way to submit a successful request to the WPB. Soon, even the flimsiest excuse would qualify a police department for new machines.

1943 Production

Harley-Davidson records list only 203 OHVs in their 1943 production of over 29,000 motorcycles. Of the total, 53 were ELs, 103 were Es, 33 were FLs, and 12 were Fs. These machines were available only to the very well connected (famous actor or general's son), and those who could demonstrate a compelling, war-effort-related need for a new motorcycle.

Window to the War, 1944

In January, the United States' march across the Pacific islands continued with the successful invasion of the Marshall Islands.

In late February and early March, the U.S. Eighth Army Air Force intensified the bombing campaign against Germany, in a campaign that would come to be known as "Big Week."

In April and May, U.S. forces continued pushing the Japanese from their island strongholds, successfully invading Kwajalein, Eniwetok, Hollandia, and Wake. In June, the Allies struck their most telling blows to date against the Germans. On the fourth, U.S. forces captured Rome. On the sixth, Allied forces invaded France with an amphibious landing at Normandy. FDR signed the GI Bill of Rights.

In August, Allied forces captured Brittany, invaded southern France, and liberated Paris.

In September, Allied armies pushed into Germany, truly taking the war to The Fatherland and signaling that the end was near. Unfortunately, the Germans still had a lot of fight left in them.

In October, U.S. forces returned to the Philippines, and the U.S. Navy thrashed the Japanese navy in the Battle of Leyte Gulf.

In November, FDR won his fourth presidential election. Harry S. Truman became vice president. The end grew near for Japan, and Hideki Tojo's military government fell.

In December, German forces began a surprise offensive—the Battle of the Bulge—in the Ardennes. The offensive initially forced back the overconfident Allied armies, but was soon routed. By the time the Germans retreated, almost 77,000 Americans had been killed or wounded.

One of the few things that did change for 1942 was a slight redesign of the taillight. To make it easier to assemble the taillight, the internal clips that held the lenses in place were replaced by spring clips fastened by the four straight-slot, cad-plated, countersunk screws down the longitudinal centerline of the taillight cover, as shown in the photo. The side screws shown are not correct. They should be straight-slotted and Parkerized.

For the next three and a half years, the company spent most of its time on military projects, including the manufacture of military motorcycles for the Allies, such as these WLAs for the U.S. Army. *Copyright Harley-Davidson Michigan, Inc.*

Throughout most of the desperate fighting of 1944, Harley-Davidson motorcycles were there. During the year, The Motor Company continued to contribute, building 16,887 military motorcycles.

The 1944 Knucklehead

According to the 1944 order blank, the OHV Big Twin model line for 1944 included the high-compression 44EL and 44FL Special Sport Solos for $425 and $465, respectively, and the medium-compression 44E and 44F medium-compression twins, also for $425 and $465, respectively. Non-police solo bikes were available with only the items in the Utility Solo Group—front safety guard, steering damper, jiffy stand, 5.00x16 tires, and black rims. The only standard color listed was gray or silver—the factory's option, not the orderer's.

Wartime restrictions once again prevented any significant changes. The only mechanical change was that a small spring was added to each of the clutch hub's long studs. Harley's stocks of rubber tires were depleted, so "S-3" synthetic-rubber tires were fitted. And Linkert's supply of silver paint was used up, so carburetor bodies were painted black and would remain black even after the war.

Weathering the War

As the Allies began to get the upper hand in 1944, the supply situation gradually loosened up at home. Still, the dealers had to scramble to secure enough business to support themselves. Again, Harley's news bulletins were there to help.

The March 20 issue announced triumphantly, "You can get OHV models on your essential civilian and police orders!"—providing the first proof, besides the notoriously unreliable production figures the company published, that OHV models were really made for civilian use during the war. The article went on to specify that even the top-of-the-line 74 OHV models were available.

The April 17 issue informed dealers that the resins used in paints were now even further restricted, so the factory could no longer guarantee that replacement tanks and fenders would be painted. Primed parts would be substituted, if supplies of paints were exhausted.

Although paint was in short supply, plastic for handgrips apparently was not. The May 1 issue announced that dealers could get all the handgrips they needed, and that these grips would not count against their "parts quota."

As the Allies marched to victory after victory, they naturally captured thousands of prisoners. Many of them ended up in prison camps in the United States and Canada. And all those hapless POWs presented the enterprising Harley dealer with still more opportunity for profit. The June 26 issue claimed, "War prisoner camps present added police problem!" and urged all Harley dealers near the camps to contact the security officials in the camps and police in the area to

Starting in 1942, certain materials became unavailable for use on motorcycles. First, it was silver paint (which contained ground aluminum), so the oil pumps and lifter blocks were painted white, as shown here, when stocks of paint ran out in late 1941. Later, chrome and cadmium became scarce, so pushrod tubes, tank badges, air-cleaner covers, screws, and other parts that would normally be plated were painted or Parkerized. Curiously, the pushrod retainers appear to be plated, rather than Parkerized. Perhaps there were still some plated parts left in the bins when this engine was assembled. The photo also illustrates several features that had been changed earlier: the nipple-type fittings for the oil line to the rocker housings that had changed in 1942 and the "handle" added to the pushrod retainers in 1940. Harley records label this as an advertising photo of a 1944 engine. *Copyright Harley-Davidson Michigan, Inc.*

This left-side view of the 1944 engine shows more examples of the wartime finish changes: Parkerized plumber's nuts on a white-painted manifold and Parkerized timing-hole plug, among others. It also provides a good overall view of engine features that are normally difficult to see on an assembled motorcycle: the extended reinforcing ribs on the crankcase (introduced in 1941), the updated crankcase breather pipe (lower right of photo, introduced in 1939), and the "flat-topped" rocker-shaft brackets (introduced in late 1938). *Copyright Harley-Davidson Michigan, Inc.*

"acquaint them with the procedures to obtain as many Harley-Davidson police motorcycles as their needs make necessary."

As these "tips" to the dealers show, the WPB's process of allocating machines where they were needed most had become a farce by mid-1944 and would only get worse (or better) as the year continued.

The October 9 issue recommended that dealers sell the 74 flatheads to all customers because orders could be filled faster than if 61 or 74 OHVs were ordered.

The October 23 issue suggested that dealers buy special Harley-Davidson pigskin wallets as Christmas gifts for police chiefs and other favored customers. A modest bribe, at $2.10 from the factory.

Although not spoken of in the news bulletins, Harley-Davidson dealers were gifted with a new source of motorcycles to sell in mid-1944. *Shop Dope No. 233* said, "During the past four months, the Government has sold a large number—possibly 3,000 to 5,000—Army surplus, used Harley-Davidson military-model motorcycles.... Included in the motorcycles already sold are 800 to 900 XA shaft-drive models.... A portion of both types of these motorcycles have been purchased by Harley-Davidson dealers."

Showing how loose the regulations had become, the November 20 issue featured a photo of a mine mechanic for the Sentry Coal Company of Madisonville, Kentucky, who shuttled between the company's mines on his new 1944 OHV. The issue also trumpeted that 380 police departments recently received approval to buy new motorcycles.

The November 30 issue presented the news flash that the following police departments received new bikes: Los Angeles got 59; Milwaukee got 21; Portsmouth, Virginia, got 5; Akron got 5; Kansas City, Missouri, got 15; and Waukegon, Illinois, got 1. It was almost beginning to resemble a normal production year.

1944 Production

Eligibility criteria were eased somewhat during 1944, so civilian OHV production more than doubled to 535. Of this total, 116 were ELs, 180 were Es, 172 were FLs, and 67 were Fs.

Window to the War, 1945

By the start of 1945, a swift end to World War II seemed a foregone conclusion. The American and British armies

LEFT: Although the factory never officially built the model, the 1940 "ELR" built by Jeff Coffman of Jeff's American Classics in Dundee, Oregon, is an intriguing idea. It is built on a 1940 frame and engine cases, with Panhead cylinders, a late-1965 police hand shift, and XA forks. Coffman has raced it at Rainier and at Davenport, where it was a crowd favorite.

were building a bridgehead to cross the Rhine, and the Russians were poised to sweep into Germany. And in the Pacific, the U.S. Marines were catching their breath before assaulting the last islands on the way to Japan itself.

In February, U.S. forces captured Manila. One of the epic battles of the war began with the United States' invasion of Iwo Jima. The Japanese defenders on Iwo had spent the previous three years preparing over 800 pillboxes to protect the defenders during the expected invasion. The 21,000 Japanese soldiers on the island had been supplied with over 22 million rounds of ammunition and were ordered to fight to the death. The battle would not end for another month.

In March, U.S. forces crossed the Rhine River, one of the last obstacles on the road to Berlin. In the Pacific, the U.S. Marines gain control of Iwo Jima after an incredibly costly battle.

On April 1, U.S. forces invaded the heavily fortified island of Okinawa. Although the landing went almost unopposed, the Americans soon ran into the fiercely determined Japanese defenders

On April 12, less than one month before the fall of Germany, President Roosevelt died of a cerebral hemorrhage as he posed for a portrait in Warm Springs, Georgia. Harry Truman was sworn in as president that afternoon.

On May 7 the war ended in Europe, when Germany surrendered unconditionally. The war on Japan continued.

In June, the American forces on Okinawa gained control of the island. It was one of the costliest victories of the war, however, with over 49,000 Americans killed or wounded. Only the Japanese home islands remained to conquer.

On July 16, the world entered the nuclear age when the first atomic bomb was detonated in New Mexico.

On August 6, a U.S. B-29 Superfortress dropped an atomic bomb on Hiroshima. The next day, Truman promised a "rain of ruin" if the Japanese did not surrender. They did not answer. On August 8, more than two months after the fighting stopped in Europe, Russia declared war on Japan. The next day, an atomic bomb was dropped on Nagasaki. On August 14, Japan surrendered unconditionally.

On September 2, almost six years after the war began, it officially ended when the formal Japanese surrender was signed on the deck of the battleship USS *Missouri*.

President Truman ordered a full return to consumer production. Back in Milwaukee, Harley-Davidson gladly followed Truman's order and prepared to grab their hard-earned share of postwar prosperity.

The 1945 Knucklehead

The OHV Big Twin model line for 1945 included three versions of each model, the high-compression 45EL

A very rare 1944 FL owned by Adolph Ogar. This bike is even more rare in that it is restored to subdued wartime finish. On the wartime machines, almost all parts that had been chrome or cadmium plated were Parkerized or painted. Their very "plain-ness" gave these machines a certain dignity that their tarted-up siblings lacked. *Sheryl Laws*

A Knucklehead even Gen. George S. Patton would have loved. This experimental twin-Knucklehead powerplant was designed for the Royal Canadian Army to power an experimental light tank. The project was canceled after prototypes had been built.

Although the Knuckleheads were considered too complex and costly for general military service, the U.S. Army bought eight Model ELAs, and the Royal Canadian Army bought 45 ELCs, both in 1942. Several other interesting military Knucklehead experiments were carried out. Among them were the XT three-wheeler project shown and an odd experimental powerplant for a Canadian minitank that used two Knucklehead motors. Both projects were canceled after demonstrators had been built. *Copyright Harley-Davidson Michigan, Inc.*

and 45FL Special Sport Solos for $463.67 and $465.00, respectively, the medium-compression 45E and 45F twins at the same prices as the EL and FL, and the 45ES and 45FS twins with sidecar gearing, again, at the same prices as the EL and FL. One has to wonder why anyone would order the 61 models when they were only $1.33 cheaper than the 74 OHVs.

Interestingly, an additional $4.08 ($2.04 per tire) surcharge was levied on the 74 OHV models for their synthetic tires, raising the base price to $469.08. The cost of these tires was built into the base price for the 61 models. The only standard color available was gray.

These bikes were available with the Utility Solo Group—front safety guard, steering damper, jiffy stand, 5.00x16 tires, and black rims—which cost $14.50 extra or the Utility Group for sidecar or package truck motorcycles (which was the same as the other utility group, minus the jiffy stand) for $12. Beginning in March, this option group also included a tripmeter because the nontripmeter speedometers were no longer available, according to the March 12 dealer news bulletin. The $1.50 extra that Harley-Davidson added for the tripmeter raised the price of the option group to $16.00.

The 1945 OHVs were also available with a new option group, the Special Solo Group, which included a front safety guard, steering damper, ride control, jiffy stand, air cleaner, rear safety guard, trip odometer, mirror, 5.00x16-inch tires, sheepskin saddle cover, solo windshield, and black rims—all for $44.50. Beginning in September, a shock absorber replaced the ride control in the Special Solo Group and the group price was raised to $55.00, according to the September 9 dealer news bulletin. The shock was also available for order without the group for $15.00. It is not clear whether the bikes built around September 9 were 1945 or 1946 models.

Production of military Harley-Davidsons had begun to slow, so time was available to make a few more mechanical improvements for 1945 than had been made in previous wartime years. The generator drive gear's outside diameter was increased from 1.0 inch to 1.022 inches. The new gear was used through 1947. The spring-ring groove was omitted from the clutch pushrod used from 1945 through 1947. And an Oilite bushing replaced the plain bushing and grease fitting on the 1945–1947 clutch-pedal bracket.

Weathering the War

Victory was at hand in 1945, but the dealers were still fighting a war of their own against shortages of bikes and spare parts—and, of course, government red tape. Once again, however, the dealer news bulletins gave hope that the dealers would survive.

The February 12 issue gave the first indication that parts and accessories would again be available when it announced the reintroduction of Speedster handlebars.

The April 9 issue boasted that 450 police departments were approved for new machines.

Even though the Nazis had already surrendered, the May 21 issue made it clear that "VE-Day has brought no change in production of current Harley-Davidsons!" Furthermore, the company asserted that there would be "no special priority on motorcycles for veterans," and that dealers should be "tactful" in explaining the situation to former GIs.

As the war wound down to its satisfying end, even more new surplus items were offered through the dealers. The June 4 issue announced that Army saddlebags would be available for $12.50 retail per bag.

The July 30 issue informed dealers that buddy seats were once again available for the 61s, which means they were available for all the Big Twins because they all used the same seat.

The August 27 issue proclaimed, "A new era dawns with war's end" and promises a swift resumption of civilian production.

Only a week after the surrender of Japan was signed, the September 10 issue revealed that "effective immediately" a shock absorber for the front forks was included with the new Special Solo Group; the shock was also available separately for $15. The price for the Special Solo Group was raised to $55. The November 12 issue announced the return of black rubber grips to replace the hard-plastic grips mandated by the WPB.

Option groups! Accessories! Rubber grips! Normalcy! Thank the Lord! Thank the Bomb! And FDR, God rest his soul. The hard times really were over!

1945 Production

As a result of eligibility requirements being further relaxed so that just about any police department could qualify, and the end of the war, Harley-Davidson's civilian production tripled to 1,430. Of this total, 398 were ELs, 282 were ESs, 619 were FLs, and 131 were FSs.

Window to the World, 1946

With the war over, life at home slowly returned to normal. FDR's New Deal was replaced by Truman's Fair Deal, as in "every segment of our population, and every individual, has a right to expect from his government a Fair Deal."

But after four years of restrictions on their right to strike and frozen wages, America's workers didn't think they were getting a fair deal. Four-and-a-half million workers struck during the year. Major strikes at GM, U.S. Steel, and in the coal mines resulted in major gains for the workers.

Prices rose rapidly because consumers had more money than ever, after four years of wartime thrift and little to spend the money on because American industry was slow to resume production of consumer goods. After so many years of austerity, people were in the mood to splurge.

As the U.S. military scaled back from 11 million to 1 million, birth rates rose 20 percent, starting the "baby boom."

Overseas, relations between the United States and the Soviet Union degraded into suspicion and hostility as Stalin closed borders, isolating eastern Europe completely from the West.

Justice was meted out to the surviving Nazi leaders at the conclusion of the Nuremburg war-crimes trials. The most prominent Nazi to be tried, Hermann Goering, cheated the noose by biting into a cyanide capsule one hour before he was to hang.

The big news in science was the invention of the computer. At the University of Pennsylvania, the world's first electronic calculator, the Electrical Numerical Integrator and Calculator (ENIAC), was demonstrated. Not quite portable, the new machine used 18,000 vacuum tubes to perform 5,000 steps per second.

With its commitments to the war effort successfully completed, Harley-Davidson eagerly resumed the business they new best, the production of America's best motorcycles.

The 1946 Knucklehead

The OHV Big Twin model line for 1946 included three versions of each model—the high-compression 46EL and 46FL Special Sport Solos for $463.67 and $465.00, respectively, the medium-compression 46E and 46F twins at the same prices as the EL and FL, and the 46ES and 46FS twins with sidecar gearing, again, at the same prices as the EL and FL. Again, the 61 models were only $1.33 cheaper than the 74 OHVs. All prices were the same as the previous year's, and the additional $4.08 ($2.04 per tire) surcharge was still levied on the 74 OHV models for their synthetic tires, raising the base price to $469.08. The cost of these tires was still built into the base price for the 61 models. For 1946, two standard colors were initially available: red or gray.

As in 1945, two option groups were offered, both unchanged. See the discussion that follows for more information on option groups.

The early 1946 machines, built in late 1945 and early 1946, were only slightly dressier than their wartime siblings

Some throwbacks to wartime austerity retained on Engesether's mount are the steel footboard mats and knurled buddy-seat pegs shown, which are thought to have been used into the 1947 model year. The rubber pedal pads may seem out of place with steel footboard mats, but they are not. The February 18, 1946, dealer news bulletin announced that the rubber pedal pads were once again included in the Special Solo Group.

had been because chrome and aluminum were still in short supply. The main difference was that red paint was offered in addition to the wartime gray.

Another color and several equipment options became available as the year progressed. Black rubber grips became available in November 1945, according to the November 12, 1945, dealer news bulletin. Availability of foot-pedal rubbers was announced in the January 21, 1946, news bulletin. On and after February 5, gray was dropped as a color option and was replaced by Skyway Blue, according to the news bulletin of that date.

The February 18 news bulletin heralded the return of aluminized paint, so the color Police Silver was once again available for police models. Aluminized silver paint was probably used again on the tappet blocks and oil pumps after that date, replacing the white paint that had been used during the war. A supplement to the February 18 bulletin also listed new accessories and changes to the Special Solo Group. Added to the group were chrome fender tips, deluxe saddlebags, colored shift ball, and rubber pedal pads, and the price was raised to $75. These new items were also available outside the group.

Apparently, the factory experienced a shortage of four-speed transmissions because the May 27 news bulletin announced that beginning on that date, without notice, an unspecified percentage of nonpolice orders would be shipped with the three-speed in order to maintain production.

Much later in the production run, such niceties as stainless steel for the fender trim and chrome for the pushrod tubes probably became available, and the machines gradually began to look like civilian motorcycles again. Even though many 1946 OHVs were wartime plain, they looked like

Harley's February 18 dealer news bulletin also specified that chrome fender tips, colored shift ball, and deluxe saddlebags were added to the Special Solo Group, so chrome was becoming available enough again by that date for use on frivolous decoration. Based on the fact that chrome was available for fender tips, it is likely that around this time chrome-plated pushrod tubes, tank emblems, air-cleaner covers, shift levers, shifter gates, and horn covers also became available once again. It seems that there was enough stainless steel available during the war that the stainless tank strips were fitted, yet, curiously, the company discontinued the stainless fender strips. These fender strips likely became available again in late 1946. The fringed buddy seat and saddlebags shown are aftermarket items.

sparkling jewels to motorcyclists who had been deprived of new machines for so long. But after the dressier bikes became available once again, the formerly sparkling jewels began to look as plain as they really were. Naturally enough, most of them were soon outfitted with the glossier parts. Original and restored machines with the wartime finishes on their parts are almost never seen.

"Bull-Neck" Frame

Stability problems with the 5.00x16-inch tires had been largely solved when the neck angle was changed from 28 degrees to 29 degrees in 1941. Even so, Harley-Davidson engineers introduced a revised frame for 1947 that had a more massive neck forging with a 30-degree neck angle. The new forging is more massive overall, and the diameter of the neck is larger than the diameter of the neck cup so that less of the cup is visible. Because of its stout construction, the new forging earned the nickname of "bull-neck." This new neck forging is correct for 1946 through mid-1947.

The 30-degree neck angle did give an extra margin of stability and safety, but at the cost of slower, heavier steering—but Harley-Davidson's customers didn't seem to mind. By another degree, the OHV sport bike Harley-Davidson had introduced in 1936 continued its evolution toward its destiny as a heavy, stable touring bike.

Mechanical Updates

After so many years with so few changes, the OHV Big Twin's design was in definite need of some updates, and most of the updates were made as running changes during the production year.

In midyear, a new tab for affixing the spark-control spiral to the frame was added to the lower tank mount on the left front downtube. The separate clamp for the coil was no longer used.

Early in the production run, the forks were given revised spring-rod-ball bushings and a ball-bushing retainer plate. After April 29, according to the October 21, 1946, dealer news bulletin, the inline forks were replaced by "offset" forks that are identical to the inline forks, except that the neck on the offset forks angled back so that it is behind the centerline of the rigid fork legs at the top of the forks. New handlebars were designed with a revised center section for use with offset springer forks. The center hole on the center section is offset to the rear of the two holes for the rigid fork legs. The offset forks and bars were also used in 1947.

About midway through production, the fenders were given wider braces. Still later, the fenders were once again drilled for the stainless steel trim strips that became available after wartime restrictions were lifted. The updated fenders were also used in 1947.

The headlight mount was redesigned to have an integral top horn mount, and the mounts were used again in 1947.

In late 1946, the front rocker housing was slightly revised. The new housing is like the previous housing, except that the bottom surface was milled flat and the mold was revised to thicken the casting in the area around the intake pushrod hole. It was used again for 1947.

Finally, in late 1946 the clutch pedal was recontoured so that the heel pad is offset to the left by about 1/4 inch. It was used again for 1947.

1946 Production

The war was won, the boys were coming home, and most prewar motorcycles were worn out because of the lack of spares during the wartime years. Harley-Davidson was able to sell all the motorcycles it could find raw materials to build. According to the September 1946 *The Enthusiast*, "The demand for new Harley-Davidsons has been so overwhelming that we found it necessary to allot motorcycles to dealers on a quota basis." Despite shortages, production rose to 6,746 OHVs, higher than for any preceding year. Of this total, 2,098 were ELs, 244 were ESs, 3,986 were FLs, and 418 were FSs.

Clearly, the market was still there in postwar America for Harley-Davidson's flagship Big Twin—all the company had to do was figure out how to make enough to satisfy the demand.

As mentioned in previous captions, most of the "civilian-shiny" parts shown here probably were available by the end of the 1946 production year. The plainer, earlier bikes have almost all been updated for a better appearance over the years—and who can blame the owners for having done so?

CHAPTER FOUR

1947

The Last Knucklehead

Optimism. That's the word that summed up the mood of the country for 1947. The economy was booming again. Unemployment was down to 3.9 percent, and the GNP was rising at the rate of 11 percent per year. Farmers were raising bumper crops, yet prices stayed high. The only blight was the high inflation rate of 8.4 percent, fueled by the housing shortage. The last real vestige of wartime shortages of consumer goods, sugar rationing, finally ended midyear, and meat consumption rose to five nights a week for the average American family. Over a million former servicemen entered college on the G.I. Bill and prepared for a more prosperous future.

If anything, the mood was even more jubilant at the Harley-Davidson factory in Milwaukee. After weathering the Great Depression, World War II, and the shortages and rationing that were the war's lingering legacy, the company was stronger than ever. And their OHV Big Twin, the flagship of the world's largest motorcycle fleet, was still the best and most technologically advanced American production motorcycle, 11 years after its introduction. Harley's main rival, Indian, was still peddling flatheads and was rapidly losing market share to Harley-Davidson's OHV. Despite shortages of materials that had kept Harley-Davidson from meeting demand, 1946 had been the best sales year ever for the OHV; more than 6,000 were sold.

As the 1947 models began rolling off the production line in the fall of 1946, the company was also busy preparing an extensively updated version of the OHV motor that would gain its own fame under the nickname "Panhead." If the Knucklehead was so popular and so technologically far ahead of the competition, why expend the effort to replace it? Because Indian wasn't the real competition anymore—heightened expectations and new machines from overseas were.

When the Knucklehead was introduced, biplanes were still the norm in the U.S. Army Air Corps. By war's end, even sleek, 400-mile-per-hour monoplanes like the P-51 Mustang looked obsolete compared to the jet fighters that were just entering service. By early 1947, jets were the norm, and the even-faster rocket-powered experimental planes were the leading edge.

At the same time, light, fast, sophisticated motorcycles were beginning to flood onto U.S. shores from Great Britain. The young and the reckless who had been the primary market for motorcycles—which in that era included thousands of discharged pilots, sailors, and soldiers who were looking for a new jag to replace the terrifying thrills of combat—were not going to be satisfied for long with Harley's old biplane.

While Harley-Davidson probably could not have guessed how thoroughly the middleweight British machines would come to dominate the U.S. market in the next 10 years, they didn't care because the testosterone-charged dare-devil was no longer the company's intended customer. After all, these customers were fickle, likely to switch to the hottest new machine to come along, whatever the brand. For better or for worse, Harley-Davidson abandoned these riders to the British and staked the company's future on making their motorcycles appeal to a larger segment of society and hooking their customers for life.

Turns out this was a great long-term strategy but a poor short-term tactic because there were more perfor-

Jeff Coffman's bagger probably would have won the "best-dressed machine" award at one of the AMA club events of the day.

After six years without much change, the styling of the Harley-Davidson Big Twins was updated in 1947. The most obvious change was the new, streamlined tank badges. These emblems were penned by famous industrial designer Brooks Stevens. Also updated were the taillight, instrument panel, and speedometer. This nice 1947 FL, owned and restored by Carman Brown, shows a top-of-the-line bike with almost every option, and even some extra chrome that wasn't available on a new machine, such as the exhaust pipes, muffler, and rear safety guard. The saddlebags are aftermarket bags designed to mount to the rear fender rack.

mance oriented customers waiting than Harley-Davidson would ever have guessed. More than 10,000 British motorcycles were sold in 1946, and another 15,000 in 1947.

As we have already seen, Harley-Davidson began trading performance for civility on the Knucklehead during its very first year, and by 1947 the design of the bike had evolved so far away from its sport-bike origins that there was no turning back. So when the company introduced its redesigned engine for 1948, it was one that would help carry the company further down the evolutionary path leading toward the big, reliable cruisers it still builds today.

In the meantime, Harley-Davidson kept its corporate fingers crossed. Barring any unforeseen shortages or a fresh outbreak of war, 1947 looked to be the year the company would cash in.

Window to the World, 1947

Tensions heated up between the United States and the Soviet Union and between the U.S. government and its few dissenting citizens. Bernard Baruch coined a chilling phrase when he implored: "Let us not be deceived. Today we are in the midst of a cold war. Our enemies are to be found abroad and at home." The United States embarked on its policy of "containing" the Soviets. As part of the containment strategy, President Truman requested $17 billion for aid to America's war-ravaged allies and enacted the Marshall Plan to rebuild Europe.

Who were the enemies at home? Like Kilroy was during the war, these enemies were everywhere, especially in government and in the movies. President Truman ordered FBI loyalty checks on federal employees to weed out "Socialists, Communists, and fellow travelers," and the House Un-American Activities Committee investigated the Communist infiltration of Hollywood. Instead of containment, suspected communists in Hollywood were "blacklisted."

The sport of motorcycling was given a black eye as a result of exaggerated publicity of a few instances of inebriated motorcyclists taking liberties in the town of Hollister, California, on July 4. The movie *The Wild One*, starring Marlon Brando, was later based on the incident.

Television continued its takeover of the air waves. The World Series (Dodgers versus Yankees) and a presidential speech (in which President Truman implored Americans to conserve on food so that more could be sent to Europe) were each televised for the first time. Exciting new shows like *Howdy Doody* mesmerized the first of the baby boomers, and the Kraft Television Theater proved the marketing potential of the new medium as sales of Kraft cheese skyrocketed.

Strife between labor and industry continued. Telephone workers and coal miners struck and made major gains before unions were neutered by the provisions of the Employers Rights Act. Henry Ford, perhaps the staunchest opponent of unions, passed away on April 7.

Advancing science, a new "cure" for schizophrenia was announced: the prefrontal lobotomy. Edwin Land invented the Land camera. Admiral Richard Byrd explored Antarctica.

Progress in aviation really took off. Pan American Airways began round-the-world service in the Lockheed

Here's one owner's vision of a custom 1947 Knuckle, mostly in stock form, but with blacked-out chrome on the spirals, air-cleaner cover, and gas caps, and no stainless fender trim. This machine was restored by Elmer Ehnes per owner Jim "Aard" Conklin's specifications.

Constellation *America*. The big one occurred on October 14, when the laconic Capt. Charles E. Yeager—flying the world's most dangerous aircraft despite having broken his ribs in a tumble from a horse—flew the Bell X-1 rocket plane through the "sound barrier" over Muroc Air Force Base to become the first hero of the supersonic age.

Jackie Robinson became the first African-American player to break the "color barrier" in the major leagues when he signed with the Brooklyn Dodgers.

And Harley-Davidson was poised to break through a barrier of its own, the 20,000-sales barrier. Not since 1929, the year of the stock market crash that started the Great Depression, had sales of the company's civilian motorcycles surpassed this mark.

The 1947 Knuckleheads

By 1947, the Knucklehead's major shortcomings had all been ironed out, so most of the changes were limited to restyling to give it a fresh, new, postwar look.

The OHV Big Twin model line for 1947 included the high-compression 47EL and 47FL Special Sport Solos, the medium-compression 47E and 47F solo twins, and the 47ES and 47FS twins with sidecar gearing. The EL, E, and ES models were listed at a retail price of $590 (almost $130 more than in 1946), and the FL, F, and FS models were listed at $605 ($145 more than in 1946). As the listing shows, retail prices had increased over 20 percent for 1947, mostly the result of the high prices Harley-Davidson was forced to pay for aluminum, steel, rubber, and chrome because of the easing of price controls and lingering scarcity. Other manufacturers were forced to raise their prices, too.

Putting the best possible face on the increase, Harley-Davidson called it "moderate," and boasted in the November

The shifter gate for 1947 was restyled to a boxier, more massive design than that used on the 1936–1946 Knuckleheads. The shift pattern was also reversed so that first was at the rear and fourth was at the front, getting the shift lever out of the way of the rider's knee once the bike was shifted into second or higher gear. Note the shift knob, which is the "Saturn" type introduced in 1942, with the raised ring around its belt line. *Copyright Harley-Davidson Michigan, Inc.*

All Harley models had to be ordered with one of the option groups, at additional cost. Again for 1947, only two major option groups were offered for solo motorcycles, but for 1947, two version of each were offered—with hydraulic shock absorber and without. The Utility Solo Group included a trip odometer, steering damper, hydraulic shock absorber, front safety guard, jiffy stand, chrome fender lamp, and 5.00x16-inch tires, all for $34.00 ($26.50 with ride control in place of the shock absorber). Sidecar and package-truck machines were fitted with the Utility Group, which came in two versions and included the same items as the Utility Solo Group, minus the jiffy stand—all for $31.50 ($24.00 with ride control in place of the hydraulic shock absorber).

The only upgrade package offered for solo machines was the Special Solo Group. This group included a trip odometer, steering damper, hydraulic shock absorber, front safety guard, jiffy stand, rear safety guard, set of three foot-pedal rubbers, colored shift ball, deluxe saddlebags, 5.00x16-inch tires, chrome fender light, chrome air cleaner, chrome headlamp, pair of chrome fender tips, chrome exhaust-pipe covers, chrome spotlights and fork bracket, and chrome parking lamps—all for $100.00 ($92.50 with ride control in place of the shock absorber).

The 1947 Knuckleheads were available in four standard colors: Brilliant Black, Skyway Blue, Flight Red, or Police Silver (police only).

Styling

For its last year, the Knucklehead was restyled to give it a more-modern, postwar look. The centerpieces of the restyle—new tank emblem, tankshift gate, instrument panel, and restyled speedometer face—were clustered on the tank, but subtle styling changes stretched all the way back to the new taillight.

"Ball-and-Banner" Tank Emblem

The most visible change for 1947 was the new, streamlined "ball-and-banner" tank emblem. This emblem was designed by noted Milwaukee industrial designer Brooks Stevens, who lent his distinctive style to everything from Evinrude outboard motors to the Excalibur car. Incidentally, when Willie G. Davidson, grandson of one of the company's founders and future vice president of styling, graduated from the Art Center College of Design in Los Angeles, he went to work for Stevens before joining Harley-Davidson in 1963.

At the front, the new emblem has a circular chrome rim with a large red ball in the center and a chrome "speed-line" running horizontally across the ball. Trailing the ball is a long chrome-plated banner that tapers slightly before ending in a blunt chisel point. The company name is debossed on the banner, and the letters are painted red.

Unlike all earlier tank emblems and decals, the 1947 emblems do not follow the rakish angle of the tank's side centerline. Rather, the new emblems are placed near the center of the tank's side, but the centerline of the emblem is perfectly horizontal so that it breaks with the overall flow of the bike's lines, which taper toward the rear axle. The new emblem, suspended alone on the expanse of paint on the side

1946 issue of *The Enthusiast* that, "It is only because of the forsight [*sic*; maybe they were still rationing the letter *e*?] and judgment gained by long experience, plus advanced manufacturing methods, that prices have been kept down to their present level."

Another decked-out 1947 Knuckle, this one owned by Jeff Coffman of Jeff's American Classics in Dundee, Oregon, and restored by Jeff and his employees, Mark Dencklau and Glenn Weyrauch. This bike, too, has just about every option offered that year, and some items that weren't, including the dual exhaust with the early-style mufflers. The fender-top trim, saddlebags, bumpers, and buddy seat are aftermarket items.

of the gas tank gave a clean—some would say stark—appearance that further emphasized how much the 16-inch tires had bulked up the bike. This style of tank emblem was also used on 1948–1950 Panheads.

Shifter Gate

The new shifter gate for 1947 was a radical departure in style. From a side view, it is flat and perfectly horizontal (not curved), like the tank emblem. It is also longer (stretching forward beyond the front end of the tank) and thicker (because the edge is bent down). This shift gate is chrome plated and was used through 1965 on hand-shift Panheads.

The markings on the top of the gate reflect another change for 1947—the shift pattern was reversed so that first gear is at the rear and fourth gear is at the front for more knee room. Because most riders do most of their riding in high gear, the gearshift lever is almost always in the rearmost position, where it could interfere with the rider's left knee if that person was long of leg or carried a passenger on the optional buddy seat. While the optional buddy seat was quite long and had an adequate seat area for two, the rider still had to scoot forward a bit so that even an average-size rider's left knee could run afoul of the shifter.

Sliding in the new gate was a revised shift lever. Because the shift lever used from 1937 to 1946 tucked in very close to the gas tank, it was not useable with the 1947 shift gate, so the bend on the shift lever was revised for 1947 to work with the new gate. The new lever was chrome plated. Although it was a one-year-only part on the Knucklehead, it was carried over onto the new Panhead for 1948.

At the transmission end, the revised shift pattern was implemented by rotating the position of the short gearshift lever on the left side of the transmission by 180 degrees. For 1936–1946, the lever was positioned to point nominally upward; for 1947, it was positioned to point nominally downward, reversing the movement of the transmission lever with respect to movement of the tankshift lever, thereby reversing the shift pattern.

Instrument Panel

Perched atop the gas tanks was a new instrument panel that echoed the lines of the tank emblem. At the front, the

Without all the extras, Jeff Coffman's other 1947 Knucklehead is a fairly trim machine. The speedometer and instrument cover were restyled for 1947, the panel to mimic the styling of the tank emblems and the speedometer with italic numerals and a silver center. Note the center of the speedometer. Factory photos show that the black gradually fades to silver at the very center, but every 1947 speedometer I have seen abruptly changes from black to silver, like the one shown here. This style of speedometer was used only for 1947.

instrument panel encircles the round speedometer dial, much like the front of the emblem encircles the red ball. And the rear of the instrument panel tapers gracefully before ending in a blunt chisel point, just as the emblem's banner does. The instrument panel is painted the main color of the tank.

The panel is fastened to the tank by a chrome-plated mounting bolt located just aft of the speedometer. Rather than separate lenses for the two warning lights, the new dash has just one red lens, located just aft of the mounting bolt. The wide, rectangular, red lens covers the generator- and oil-warning lights. The oil light is on the right, and the generator light is on the left. Aft of the lens is the ignition switch. A hole for the police speedometer lock is on the panel's left side, and a slot for the tripmeter reset lever is on the right side. The new hole and slot covers are retained by clips rather than screws. Also for 1947, the gap between the lower edge of the instrument panel and the gas tank was sealed by a rubber molding.

"Black-Face" Speedometer

Nestled in the front of the new instrument panel was a revised "airplane-style" Stewart-Warner speedometer with a restyled face and a new light position, all of which made the speedometer easier to read at night.

The main difference between the 1947 face and the 1941–1946 face is that the new face no longer has the concentric bull's-eye pattern in black and silver. Instead, the new face has a black background that fades to white at its very center. All the features that were formerly silver—the numerals, hash marks, circular pinstripes, bar and shield, and Stewart-Warner face part number—are now white. For ease of reading, the numerals are thicker and are slanted in italic style, and the pointer is painted red, rather than white. This speedometer is correct for 1947 only.

The light for the 1941–1946 speedometers shone through a plastic window on the edge of the back third of the face. Because of this position, it did a good job of illuminating the bar-and-shield logo and the numerals 10 and 20 on the left and 110 and 120 on the right, but left the numerals for normal operating speeds in the dark because they were at the front of the speedometer, at the farthest point on the face from the light.

On the 1947 speedometer, the light window was shifted clockwise so that most of the light shone on the numerals 10 through 60, the speed range most used. The repositioned light made the thicker, white numerals seem to glow against the black background, so the night rider could read his speed precisely.

Revised Gas Tanks

To accommodate the revised pieces attached to it, the gas tanks were revised with new mounts for the new emblems (and the stainless steel strip mounts were deleted), a recessed mounting area on the left tank for the new shift gate, and reshaped dash-mount bases for the restyled dash. These new tanks are correct for 1947–1950.

This close-up of the forks on Coffman's black 1947 shows the hydraulic shock absorber that first became optional in late 1945. It also shows the new-style horn mount that had been introduced in 1946.

This view with the carburetor removed on Mike Golembiewski's 1947 Knucklehead shows how the oil is routed from the top of the gear-case cover to the rocker housings atop each head.

"Tombstone" Taillight

At the rear, a new taillight was fitted to match the other, more angular styling cues introduced for 1947. Instead of tapering gracefully as the 1939–1946 "boattail" taillight did, the 1947 taillight was squared off at the rear. When viewed from the back, the taillight looks like a tall rectangle with a semicircle on top, a profile similar to that of simple tombstones—hence its nickname.

The taillight body was die-cast zinc alloy. The front of the body's top surface has a cast-in lug, to which the license-plate bracket attaches. On the top of the body, just aft of the license-plate bracket, is a window with a frosted-glass lens that allows light from the taillamp to shine through and illuminate the license plate. The tombstone-shaped red rear lens has a molded-in Stimsonite refractor pattern to diffuse the light.

The standard taillamp body, lens retainer, and license-plate bracket are painted black, but these items may have been available in an optional chrome-plated finish later in the year when chrome became more available. This taillight assembly was used on the 1947 Knucklehead and on all the later Panheads through 1954.

More Chrome and Cadmium Plating

"We are doing everything within our power to supply more chrome and there is more of it on our 1947 Harley-Davidsons than there has been for a long time," boasted the September 1946 issue of *The Enthusiast*. And the magazine wasn't lying. Chrome for plating was far more available than it had been since before the war, so the switch back to shiny finishes on the parts that had begun in 1946 was essentially completed by the start of the 1947 season.

Once again, the handlebar switches, ignition-switch cover, horn cover, front-fender light, instrument-cover mounting bolt, gas shut-off knob, gas caps, speedometer bezel, headlamp ring, and many other parts were chrome plated on the basic motorcycle, and chrome-plated optional accessories were offered, including front and rear fender tips, headlamp bucket, exhaust-pipe covers, and parking lamps.

Similarly, cadmium-plated parts were used in many of the same places as on the prewar bikes: kickstarter tube and end pieces, timer cover, seat-post tube, spoke nipples, light-switch knob for the speedometer, and other small parts. And aluminized paint was once again in steady supply, so the oil-pump body and tappet blocks were once again painted silver. Wartime's ugly duckling once again became peacetime's swan.

New Neck Forging

Late in the 1947 production year, the frame's steering-head forging was given another update. The bull-neck forging that had been introduced in 1946 was replaced by a much-slimmer forging. The neck of the new forging is about the same diameter on its upper and lower edges as the neck cups, but tapers to a much smaller diameter in the center section of the neck. This new neck forging was used only for late 1947.

Coffman wanted to keep this machine light and simple of line, so when he and his crew restored it, they left a lot of extra chrome off and even omitted chrome bits that came standard, such as the chrome on the handlebar spiral. He also left off the red paint that highlights the tank emblems. Authentic in every detail? No, but the few changes he made give the bike a very clean look. Note the low-mounted toolbox. Holes on the toolbox strap for 1947 allowed it to be mounted in either the low or high position.

A Knucklehead in Every Barn

Among the many secrets I unearthed during two visits to the Harley-Davidson archives is a reference to a top-secret sales strategy that allowed Harley-Davidson dealers to exploit the only segment of the youth market that was benefiting from the postwar inflation. The secret untapped market? Farm boys. Yep, farm boys.

Looking back on the economic conditions during 1947, it doesn't take a supply-side economist to appreciate the obvious genius of the plan. The main beneficiaries of the postwar inflation were farmers, who were still intensively farming every square inch of their land for bumper crops, yet were receiving record prices for the crops because the government was buying incredible quantities of produce to ship to war-ravaged Europe. Naturally, some of the new-found wealth trickled down to farm boys across the fruited plain.

In an article titled "$30 Hogs and Your Motorcycle Market" in the March 10, 1947, dealer news bulletin, Harley-Davidson's sales department outlined the new strategy and exhorted its dealers to exploit this untapped youth market because "farm boys really like motorcycles." Better yet, these boys had money because "dad has been liberal with them—has let them raise a calf or two—a hog—or put in a few acres of crop." Even better, "When they make up their mind to buy a new Harley-Davidson, they have the cash to put right down on the line. No extended payments for them."

Harley-Davidson's sales increased over 25 percent in 1947, compared to 1946, and sales of the OHV models, the most expensive in the line-up, almost doubled. Did farm boys make the difference? I'll leave that answer for an upcoming MBA thesis.

This factory photo shows the new speedometer and instrument panel for 1947. Note how the black speedometer face fades to silver at the very center. All 1947 speedometers I have seen change abruptly to silver at the pinstripes just outboard of the odometer windows. Speedometers with the gradual fade may have been only on the machines in the Harley-Davidson photos or on early production machines. Note that the top plate over the handlebar holes is not chrome plated, and that the fork is of the "inline" springer type used through mid-1946, which indicates that the photo is of a prototype machine based on one of the "plain" 1946 machines. *Copyright Harley-Davidson Michigan, Inc.*

Engine

Mechanical modifications for 1947 consisted of subtle refinements, rather than radical change. The 1947 tappet assemblies were fitted with an updated roller with needle bearings (replacing the roller bushing used from 1936 to 1946) for smoother operation and longer wear. Each new tappet roller assembly consists of a roller, a roller race, a roller axle pin, and 25 needle rollers. The new rollers were used again on the tappets for the 1948 Panhead motor.

The other notable engine update for the year was made to the ignition timer assembly. On the 1936–1946 timers, the cable from the advance spiral on the handlebar is attached to a post on the timer strap, which clamped around the timer's base. For 1947, a new base was fitted. The new timer base has an adjustable post sticking straight

With all the items available that year and later, the Knucklehead, which had been designed as an elemental sporting machine, could be transformed into a long-distance hauler.

to the side, to which the cable is attached, providing a more direct, simpler connection. The timer housing was revised with a 13/16-inch notch on its top rim. The new post on the timer base protrudes out to the side of the timer assembly through the slot. The slot allows clearance for the post to slide clockwise (retard) or counterclockwise (advance), and the slot's edges serve as the advance and retard stops. This style of advance mechanism was also carried over to the Panhead in 1948.

As part of the switch to the new timer assembly, a new cut-out relay base was fitted. Relay bases since 1936 had an integral slot that served as the advance and retard stops for the pre-1947 timer assembly. The new relay base for 1947 lacks the slot. A redesigned bracket was used to fix the control coil in place.

The new taillight introduced in 1947 was quickly dubbed the "tombstone" taillight because of its shape. It had an integral license-plate frame, a top window to illuminate the license plate, and a red "Stimsonite" refracting rear lens. The chrome-plated rear lens retainer was optional; the standard retainer was painted black.

Coffman's black 1947 Knucklehead has the "bull-neck" frame introduced in mid-1946 and used through most of 1947 production. Note how heavy the casting is around the lower cup for the steering-head bearing.

Clutch

To simplify assembly at the factory, the 1947 pressure plate and pressure-plate nuts were revised. On the 1941–1946 clutch, the pressure plate was secured by three nuts and lock washers to the three threaded studs that extend out from the clutch hub. For 1947, the pressure plate was redesigned to have a bump along the edge of each stud hole, and the nuts were redesigned to have notches. Each bump mates with a notch in its respective notched nut to prevent the nut from turning, so no lock washers are needed. The new pressure plate and notched nuts were good enough to be carried over to the Panhead series in 1948, then on to the Shovelhead series that followed in 1966, and all the way through the last Shovelheads in 1984.

Seats

With the war over, cowhide was available again. For 1947, the standard solo saddle was covered in black cowhide, replacing the brown horsehide that had been standard since 1942.

The optional deluxe solo seat was restyled for 1947. This seat is covered in black horsehide and has a black plastic valance that gets gradually wider at the sides and tapers to be very short at the rear. The valance is decorated by a row of small nickel dots along the lower edge of the skirt and has a plastic rosette on each side of the valance. Smaller nickel pieces flank the rosettes, three to the front and one to the rear. This seat was carried over onto the Panhead series for 1948–1954.

1947 production

As the company had hoped it would be, 1947 was the best year for civilian sales since 1929—despite the substantial increase in price. Harley-Davidson's records suggest that it sold 20,115 motorcycles in 1947. Of this total, 11,348 were Knuckleheads, including 4,117 ELs, 237 ESs, 6,893 FLs, and 401 FSs.

While sales of 11,000 Knuckleheads in a single year may not seem all that significant, comparison with sales figures

Brown's 1947 Knucklehead carries the deluxe solo seat that was optional from 1947 to 1954. Whitewall tires were not available on a new machine from Harley-Davidson in 1947, but may have been available from the aftermarket.

from other years shows just how important the OHV Big Twin had become to the company. In its first year, 1936, only 1,700–2,000 Knuckleheads were built, which represented about 20 percent of Harley-Davidson's motorcycle production. In its final year, 1947, Knuckleheads accounted for more than half of Harley-Davidson's sales. In its first four production years, 1936–1939, only about 9,300 Knuckleheads were built, almost 2,000 fewer than were sold in 1947 alone. In fact, almost one third of all Knuckleheads ever built were built in 1947. Even so, demand had not been met. What had once been a temperamental hot-rod for the devil-may-care few had become a workaday mount for motorcycling's equivalent to "the masses."

The Future

Fall of 1947 brought with it the end of the Knucklehead, but a new beginning for H-D. The November 1947 issue of *The Enthusiast* announced the "biggest motorcycle story of the year," the new OHV models that would carry the company into the future.

The big story? An updated top end for the OHV engine, consisting of aluminum cylinder heads, hydraulic valve lifters, redesigned cylinders with internal oil feed and return lines to and from the heads, and a chrome-plated, stamped-steel "pan" cover that completely enclosed the rockers and valves of each head. These updates made the motor smoother, quieter, more oil tight, cooler running, and more maintenance free, but not much lighter or more powerful.

Other than the top end, little else was changed for 1948. Even the styling was almost exactly the same as on the 1947 OHV. The changes that turned the Knucklehead into the Panhead were evolutionary, not revolutionary like those that turned Harley-Davidson's old flathead into the 61 OHV in 1936. Even so, the new model was even more popular than the old, and 12,924 were sold.

The evolution continued in the years that followed. For 1949, hydraulic forks were introduced, giving rise to the first official Harley-Davidson name for the OHV Big Twin: Hydra-Glide. During the early 1950s, the motor was gradually updated, the styling was changed slightly, and a foot-operated shifter and hand-operated clutch was introduced. In 1958, rear suspension was added, giving rise to the second official Harley-Davidson name for the Big Twin: Duo-Glide. In the late 1950s and early 1960s, the British invasion waned, and Harley-Davidson was forced to weather a new invasion, this time by the Japanese. Harley-Davidson stayed on course, however, and their Panhead continued to evolve into a larger, heavier, touring-oriented machine. In 1965, electric starting was added for the Panhead's final year, sparking the third official Harley-Davidson name for the Big Twin: Electra Glide.

In the beginning, the Panhead still was a fairly trim machine that many riders proved was capable of winning on

Coffman's red 1947 Knucklehead has the late-1947 frame with the much-slimmer steering-head casting.

This cutaway shows the internal workings of the Knucklehead engine. *Copyright Harley-Davidson Michigan, Inc.*

the tracks, on the hills, and in the swamps of America. By the end, it weighed over 700 pounds in stripped form and more than 800 pounds by the time it was outfitted with fiberglass saddlebags, windshield, dual exhaust, and all the chrome bits that were in fashion. In short, it had become the archetypal American touring machine.

For 1966, the Electra Glide was given a new motor featuring yet another redesign of the top end. It, too, was smoother, quieter, more oil tight, cooler running, and more maintenance free than its predecessor, but not much lighter or more powerful. And it, too, was eventually given a nickname: Shovelhead. Over time, many new features were introduced on the Electra Glide, including an alternator, disc brakes, and a real fairing. Then the chopper craze was given official sanction when Harley-Davidson devolved the Electra Glide into a series of more elemental customs that gave variety to the line-up and appealed to new customers.

The oldest living Harley rider in Milwaukee? Valentino "Vick" Domowicz, who was over 90 years old when this photo was taken, still kickstarts and rides his 1947 Knucklehead. After the photos were taken, I rode behind him over to the Juneau Avenue plant where he was to meet Willie G. Despite his age, Vick's still a pretty spirited rider.

Except for the cylinders and heads, the 1947 Knucklehead and 1948 Panhead are nearly identical. The Knuckle is owned by Jim "Aard" Conklin and the Pan by ace restorer Elmer Ehnes. Ehnes restored both machines.

In 1984 came the V2 Evolution engine, the first true fulfillment of the promise made in 1936. The new engine was lightweight and as reliable and as maintenance-free as the best of its competitors. When combined with restyled and updated chassis in new models such as the Softail and FLHT, the Evolution engine finally gave Harley-Davidson's Big Twin true mass-market appeal. As a result, by the early 1990s, the once-ailing Milwaukee firm would again achieve the same dominance in the American marketplace that they had enjoyed at the end of 1947.

But after almost 50 years of change, little really had. From Knucklehead, to Panhead, to Shovelhead, and on to Evo, the basics of the 1936 OHV engine that had made it so appealing remained. In fact, maybe we're all really being a bit myopic by encouraging the continued use of such distinctions.

The truth is, the Knucklehead was never really replaced by the Panhead—or by any of the others, for that matter. To Harley-Davidson and to the enthusiasts of the day, there were no Knuckleheads or Panheads, only 61 or 74 OHVs. Later came the official names, such as those already mentioned and a whole slew of later ones such as Super Glide, Low Rider, Tour Glide, Softail—on and on.

In fact, it wasn't until the V2 Evolution engine was introduced in 1984 that Harley-Davidson even gave an official name to any of its OHV Big Twin engines. The switch from Knucklehead to Panhead that today seems to be such a definitive dividing point in Harley-Davidson history was barely noticed by most riders—and it wasn't accompanied by a name.

As a result, somewhere along the way, enthusiasts found it convenient to coin names to distinguish between the variations on the OHV Big Twin motor. And the names are truly useful, in some ways. But let's not let them disguise the fact that what began with the 1936 61 continues today. The 1936 61 has far more similarities to the 1997 FLSTS Heritage Softail Springer than differences. And that is the Knucklehead's greatest legacy.

PANHEADS

BY GREG FIELD

pling of American industry. The Western powers and Russia jockeyed toward an uneasy coexistence in Germany and Eastern Europe while Communist forces marched toward victory in China. Before long, the terms "Iron Curtain" and "Cold War" gained everyday usage, and fear of Communist infiltration in the U.S. and in Europe began its rise toward the paranoiac levels reached during the 1950s.

Most damaging of all for Harley, the Marshall Plan was implemented to "contain" the Soviets by rebuilding the economies of Europe and England. Hundreds of millions of dollars in scarce raw materials such as steel and chromium went overseas to America's economic competitors. The U.S. government drastically lowered tariffs on imported goods, while American goods faced rising tariff rates overseas. The British government mandated that England's motorcycle industry export 75 percent of its output or face reduced quotas of scarce materials, so the trickle of British motorcycles reaching American shores became an incoming tidal wave.

Rewind to 1946. As a manufacturer of a "nonessential" good, H-D was given only a fraction of the materials they needed. Even so, they cranked out 16,222 motorcycles in 1946. But this number was far below capacity (production had reached 29,521 in 1942) and even farther below demand (civilian production had been rationed to dealers since fall 1941 when dealers were advised that they would each be allowed to order *one* new motorcycle, and delivery of even this one machine was not guaranteed). The base 74ci overhead-valve (OHV) Big Twin carried a suggested retail price of $469.08 with synthetic-rubber tires. The Special Solo Group cost an additional $55 and included such niceties as a hydraulic shock absorber for the forks, a solo windshield, and a sheepskin seat cover. Alas, chrome and rubber were still scarce, so even this top-of-the-line trim package left the motorcycle with painted tank badges and air cleaner, hard-plastic grips, and steel, wartime-spec mats for the footboards.

The supply situation improved somewhat in 1947, when 20,115 Harleys were produced. Lingering wartime restrictions on rubber and chrome usage had been eased, allowing Harley to tart up their bikes with chrome tank badges, chrome headlights, and chrome air cleaners for the first time since the war had begun, but H-D literature from the time made it very clear that the unpredictable chrome supply might still force them to revert to painted parts. The inflation that racked all segments of the American economy hit H-D especially hard: the retail price for the base 74ci OHV Big Twin rose by 30 percent to $605. Even so, demand still outstripped supply.

Meanwhile, nearly 10,000 British motorcycles had been imported in 1946 and more than 15,000 reached America's shores in 1947. Sure, these lightweight British twins and singles weren't "traditional" mounts for American motorcyclists, but there weren't enough Harleys to go around. How many potential Harley customers went over to the "dark side" can only be guessed.

Fortunately, by fall 1947 H-D dealers were in for some really good news. In an attempt to finally meet new Harley demand, production facilities were being expanded, and H-D announced the introduction of their first really new models in twelve years–new versions of the 61ci Model E and 74ci Model F OHV Big Twins.

At first glance, these new Big Twins didn't look very new. In fact, their external appearance was barely distinguishable from the previous year's Big Twins, or even from those of ten years previous. They retained the cradle-type frame, OHV V-twin engine, spring forks, and classic form first seen in the 1936. Even the streamlined, Brooks Stevens-designed chrome tank badges are carry-

The 1948 Panhead, the first of the breed, was a slim, low-slung machine that differed little from the 1947 Knucklehead it replaced. This top-flight machine is by Elmer Ehnes, who handles the fine restorations at Kokesh Motorcycles of Spring Lake Park, Minnesota. He restored this one for himself, but those he restores for others are just as nice.

An unrestored 1948 Panhead owned by Jan Berghoff. Berghoff bought this bike from its original owner and was wise enough to leave this fine machine as he found it. Nevertheless, this bike is not completely stock; it has the wrong speedometer and is fitted with D-ring reinforcements for the rocker covers, which were not introduced until 1951. Note the black-painted cylinders. Early 1948 Pans were fitted with black-painted cylinders and exhaust pipes, but later machines were fitted with silver-painted cylinders and exhaust pipes. Photos taken during the era suggest that the change in color for exhaust pipes and cylinders occurred at about the same time. Also noticeable here is the stainless steel muffler shroud, which was not introduced until 1949. Panheads for 1948 all were equipped with black-painted mufflers.

overs from 1947. (Stevens, a famed Milwaukee industrial designer who penned automobiles for Studebaker, and later designed the Excalibur luxury roadster, passed away January 4, 1995, as this book was being completed.) The most apparent difference was the shiny, new motor.

Continuing the tradition that began with the naming of the previous series of Models E and F OHV Big Twins—christened "Knuckleheads" because their rocker housings looked like the knuckles of a clenched fist—the new Big Twin was soon dubbed "Panhead" by enthusiasts because it looked as if a sparkling, chrome cake pan had been up-ended atop each cylinder head.

Harley's copy writers called the 1948 model line the "Biggest Motorcycle Story of the Year," and the Panhead motor was clearly the biggest part of that story. It would be easy to dismiss their statement as sales hype, but it wasn't, for these were the days when The Motor Company could still proudly boast that "Harley-Davidson leadership in the field of motorcycling has been achieved through hard work, devotion to duty and the sincere effort to build better and better." These were also the days when they could prove in iron (or aluminum) that they took seriously the related responsibility of "pioneering along new ways and blazing new trails."

The Motor Company has always been a favorite target of second-guessers—then and now. As we shall see, the direction in which Harley's new "ways" and "trails" were really leading the company would not be appreciated for nearly four more decades.

Flat-earthers of the time took the view that Harley should have saved the time and money spent on the Panhead's development and expanded production capability to meet demand for new Knuckleheads. (After all, they would argue, the Knucklehead had been developed into a fine machine and, in any case, hydraulic lifters were needlessly complicated and unnecessary because real men who rode Harleys didn't mind getting their hands greasy once in a while to adjust their valves.)

Cycle cynics of today dismiss the Panhead as just a Knucklehead with a few long-overdue refinements. They argue that the two most obvious improvements H-D engineers built into the Panhead—hydraulically operated lifters and cast-aluminum cylinder heads—were simply new icing on a stale, old cake.

Both groups fail to see the real significance of the Panhead. Harley-Davidson didn't spend their scarce development money to make their bikes more powerful to compete with big-inch hot rods such as the Vincent-HRD Rapide or even lighter and more sporting to compete with the scads of lesser British twins. Instead, H-D engineers concentrated on making their bikes quieter, more oil tight, and easier to maintain so they would appeal to a broader cross-section of Americans. In short, H-D took the first step on the long road to make their Big Twins *civilized*. The new Panhead was one small step for motorcycling but one giant step for The Motor Company.

The Knucklehead Harley

The starting point for the Panhead was the 1947 Knucklehead, which was the last in a distinguished line that had been introduced in 1936, just as America was starting the long recovery from the Great Depression. The Knucklehead was a masterpiece from any angle, a bold fusion of art deco and streamlining.

The first Knucklehead was more than just a styling exercise, however. It was a completely new motorcycle with features that were modern in almost every way—features that proved so functional that many are still in use on Harley Big Twins today. No other motorcycle, before or since, has debuted such a bold and enduring style.

Think I'm exaggerating? Just park a Knucklehead and a new springer Softtail side-by-side and take a walk around. Leading-link springer forks up front with a head light on top. Forty-five-degree V-Twin engine connected to the separate transmission by a primary chain on the right. Carburetor in the V of the cylinders with a chrome-plated air cleaner on the right. Twin, saddle gas tanks, one on each side of the frame backbone. Instrument panel with speedometer. The lines of the body, sweeping back on top from the steering head to the rear axle and sweeping up behind the motor to join up with the top tube in a classic hard-tail vee (of course, the Softtail's rear end is suspended, but it was designed to mimic the hardtail look). Horseshoe-shaped oil tank under the seat. Coil mounted just forward of the oil tank on the left side. Put a post-mounted seat, a two-into-one exhaust, and art deco tank decals on the Softtail, and the resemblance would be even more striking.

The Knucklehead Motor

Internally, the Knucklehead motor was almost

A nicely restored 1948 Panhead owned by John Burgin. Note the way the front downtubes of the frame bend out like a wishbone near where the front safety guard attaches. This new frame was nicknamed the wishbone frame and was fitted to all 1948 Panheads. Though slight changes to the frame were made during each production year, the wishbone-style frame was used from 1948 through mid-1954. The front safety guard is the 1948–50 style with the squashed center section drilled for two mounting holes. Both guards are also finished correctly; chrome-plated guards were not available until 1950. The Deluxe Solo Saddle is also the correct style for 1948–54, with three-piece leather skirt. The saddlebags are also the correct style, except that the buckles are the 1950–53-style plain buckles. Buckles on 1948–49 bags were "western" style (thicker at the top than at the bottom).

entirely new, having few parts in common with Harley's side-valve twins. It was the first H-D production twin with overhead valves and a recirculating oil system.

The 1936 Knucklehead was powered by a 45deg V-twin motor with a bore of 3-5/16in and a stroke of 3-1/2in, for a total displacement of 60.32ci (988.6cc). H-D's copy writers naturally rounded this displacement up to 61ci, and all Knuckleheads were 61s until a bored-and-stroked version was introduced in 1941 as the 74ci Model F. Three models with the OHV engine were listed for 1936: the Model EL Special Sport Solo with 7:1 compression, the medium-compression Model E Twin Solo with 6.5:1 compression, and the low-compression Model ES Sidecar Twin, with special "compression plates" on the cylinders to reduce compression to 5.5:1. Interestingly, a Model 36EM "Twin Motor For Midget Car Racing" is also listed.

Externally, the engine's most prominent features were the long, thin pushrod covers reaching up to polished-alloy rocker housings on the right side of the heads; the two round, dished chrome rocker-shaft covers on the rocker housings (these covers were changed to chromed hex nuts during the 1936 model year); and the sweptback air-intake horn between the V of the cylinders on the right side.

Top End

The Knucklehead's most innovative feature was its all-new, OHV top end. The cast-iron cylinder heads carry two valves per cylinder, with replaceable valve seats and guides. Hemispherical combustion chambers and domed pistons supply the squeeze, and a single 18mm spark plug per cylinder touches off the bang.

Opening the valves are rocker arms rotating on fixed rocker shafts that run between the polished rocker housing on the right side of each head and cast-in bosses on the left side of the head. Two nested coil springs per poppet close the valves. The rockers are rotated by four pushrods driven by tappets from the four-lobed cam in the gear case.

The rockers are exposed for their entire length; only the valve arm extends through a slot into the dubious protection of the two-piece, cup-type valve-spring covers. The lower cover is a stamped-steel cup with a center hole through which the valve guide is pressed to secure guide and cover to the head. An oil-scavenge line is attached to the bottom of each cup to return oil to the rocker housing. Each valve cover is topped by a stamped cap with a slot through which the valve arm extends to push on and open the valve, and the cap is secured with a light press-fit over the lower cup. These covers were prone to oil leaking out, and foreign matter often leaked *in* through the valve-arm slot in the top of the cover to clog the oil scavenge lines, which caused oil to fill the cup and overflow over the engine and rider. As a quick fix, an air fitting was added to the front rocker housing in late 1936. Pressurized air applied at the fitting unclogged both scavenge lines. Of more catastrophic consequence, water could enter through the valve-arm slot, freezing the valve in a block of ice if the temperature dropped below freezing. These problems were cured in 1938 when new covers were introduced that fully enclosed each rocker arm and valve in its own housing.

The Knucklehead uses conventional aluminum pistons. They were offered in two versions: high compression (7:1, Model EL) and medium compression (6:1, Model E). High-compression pistons feature a high dome, whereas medium-compression pistons feature a nearly flat crown.

The pistons were unusual in that the front piston was fitted with two compression rings but no oil-control ring, whereas the rear piston was fitted with the two compression rings and an oil-control ring. The rear cylinder wall was well lubricated by oil spun off the flywheels, so the oil-scraper ring was necessary to keep oil out of the combustion chambers. The front cylinder received no direct oil spray, so H-D engineers omitted the oil-scraper rings. For 1940, the lower end was revised to splash more oil on the front cylinder walls, and an oil-scraper ring was installed for that and subsequent years.

From 1941–47, only high-compression pistons were offered. Medium-compression motors used a 0.050in compression plate under the cylinder base to lower compression to 6.5:1.

Carburetor and Intake Manifolds

A chrome-plated air-cleaner cover in the middle of the V (when viewed from the right side) is a hallmark of H-D style. Hidden by that cover, of course, is a single carburetor, feeding both cylinders through a Y- or T-shaped intake manifold. All perfectly logical and perfectly functional—and that's why H-D still uses the same basic design today. It doesn't hurt that it just looks natural, either. That's why many of the early Japanese "cruiser" bikes imitated the look with a chromed plastic cover. No one was fooled, however. We all knew that plastic "blob" on the right side of the Virago was just a ripped off styling cue.

Even before the Knucklehead, H-D Big Twins had carburetors mounted in the center of the V, but the carburetor and air cleaner pointed to the bike's left side. This arrangement made sense for these side-valve bikes because the intake and exhaust valves were side-by-side in the exhaust pocket on the right side of the cylinders. If the carburetor and air cleaner had been pointed to the right, they would have stuck out far to the right of the engine. Pointing to the left, the carb snuggled comfortably between the cylinders, allowing the left-mounted air cleaner to tuck in tight to the cylinders on the bike's left side.

For the Knucklehead, H-D kept the tradition of having both exhausts exit the heads on the right side, which meant that the intake ports had to be on the left side of the heads. Naturally enough, they then turned the carburetor around, facing to the right, in a mirror image of the side-valve carburetor arrangement.

Fuel and air for the 1936 Knucklehead motor is mixed by a side-draft type 1-1/4in Linkert M-5 carburetor with a 1-1/6in, fixed venturi. In 1940, the M-5 was replaced with the 1-1/2in Linkert M-25 carb with a larger, 1-5/16in, fixed venturi (to feed the large-port heads introduced that year). The M-25 was also used on the 1941 74ci Knuckleheads (the model's first year), but the 61s for 1941 are fitted with 1-1/2in Linkert M-35, M-35T, or M-35TP carbs with a 1-1/8in, fixed venturi. The M-35 series were still the standard carburetor when the Panhead was introduced in 1948, although the Linkert M-75 was optional for 74ci models from 1942 to 1948.

The carburetor's butterfly throttle valve is opened and closed via the right twist grip. (H-D motorcycles had long had a right-hand throttle, while some other motorcycle manufacturers—including Indian—favored left-hand throttles.) Left-hand throttles were optional, and were usually sold on bikes with right-hand shift levers. For those of you who are more familiar with modern motorcycles, a few terms need to be defined. The twist

Elmer Ehnes' bike again. Elmer restored this bike to represent one ordered with the base-model Utility Solo Group and a few extra options, including chrome rims, chrome head lamp, chrome taillight, and oil filter. It is refreshing to see restorers building bikes that are not over-chromed and encumbered with every possible accessory.

grips on vintage Harleys are called "spirals." The two-piece cable that leads from the spiral consists of the "coil" and "control wire." The coil is a protective outer sheath consisting of a fabric-covered coil of wire . The control wire is a solid-steel wire that slides freely inside the coil.

A Y-shaped intake manifold delivers the intake charge from the carburetor to each cylinder head intake port. Three bolts fasten the carb to the manifold, and a large (2in) "plumber" nut secures the manifold to the threaded intake nipple in each head.

In 1940, a new, T-shaped manifold was introduced to match the large-port heads and the newer, 1-1/2in Linkert carburetors with four-bolt mounting plates. This manifold still used the plumber nuts on the cylinder-head ends, but the nuts are now 2-1/8in wide. The manifold measures 3-13/32in wide between the cylinder-head ends for 61ci and 3-5/8in for 74ci motors. Plumber-nut manifolds were one of many proven features passed down from the Knucklehead to the Panhead, and they continued in use through 1954.

Cylinders

Cast iron was the standard material for cylinders before WWII because it was inexpensive, easily cast into the complex shape of a finned cylinder, easy to machine for a smooth cylinder bore, durable so a liner of another material was not necessary, and slightly porous so it held oil well for good lubrication of the cylinders. Consequently, iron was the natural choice for the 1936 Knucklehead's cylinders.

The Knucklehead's cylinders were an all-new design with a 3-5/16in bore. At the top, around the edge of the bore, is a raised ridge that fit into a recess in the head to help the head gasket seal the juncture between head and cylinder. Outside the ridge is the gasket surface with five head-bolt holes spaced around the circumference.

A boss for each of the head bolts runs down from the gasket surface through the top four fins. Each head is clamped to the cylinder by five bolts inserted from below, through drilled bosses, through holes in the head gasket and into the threaded holes in the head. The Knucklehead's cylinders remained unchanged until 1940, when the head-bolt bosses were changed so that they passed through the top five fins.

In 1941, the 74s were introduced, so new cylinders were needed to accommodate their increased bore and stroke. The 74ci cylinders are similar to the later 61ci cylinders except that the bore was increased to 3-7/16in and the bore and head-gasket surface was raised up to the level of the ridge on the 61ci cylinders (lengthening the cylinder while allowing Harley to use the same basic cylinder casting).

The cylinder bases are each held to the crankcases by four studs and nuts, with a base gasket between the cylinder base and the crankcase. Also, depending on the compression ratio ordered, a 0.050in compression plate may be used between the cylinder base and the crankcase to create a lower compression ratio.

For 1936–40, the solo Model E had a 6:1 compression ratio. The solo Model EL had a higher dome on its piston resulting in a 7:1 compression ratio. Though not listed on some standard order blanks, a low-compression motor could be ordered that used one compression plate per cylinder in conjunction with the Model E's medium-compression pistons to achieve a ratio of 5.5:1. Similarly, a medium-high compression motor could be ordered that used one plate per cylinder in conjunction with the Model EL's high-compression pistons to achieve a ratio of 6.5:1. These low- and medium-high compression motors were intended for use with sidecars, or in areas where high temperatures and poor gas were common.

For 1941–47 models, the compression plate was used on all medium-compression motors because the medium-compression pistons were no longer offered. Medium-compression motors used one plate per cylinder with the standard high-compression pistons to achieve a compression ratio of 6.5:1 (versus 7:1 for high-compression motors).

The Bottom End

The Knucklehead lower end was a conventional design for its day. The connecting rods run on a common crankpin sandwiched between two flywheel halves, and a pair of mainshafts (one per flywheel half) serve as the axle about which the whole flywheel assembly rotates. Each fly wheel half has a tapered center hole for a centershaft and an off-center, tapered hole for the crankpin.

The front cylinder rod's big end was "forked," and the rear cylinder rod's big end was designed to nestle inside the fork of the front rod's big end. Forked connecting rods allow the engine designer to use a short, stiff crankpin, but it also puts both cylinders on the same centerline, to the detriment of rear-cylinder cooling. (If the big ends are placed side-by-side, the crankpin must be longer, but the front and rear cylinders could be offset, allowing a more direct flow of cooling air to the rear cylinder.) The tapered crankpin fits through the big-end bearings, into the tapered, offset holes on the flywheel halves and is secured on the outer side of each half by a crankpin nut and lock plate. This arrangement was changed for 1940, when H-D switched positions of the rods so that the forked rod is in the rear. In addition, the forked end was redesigned to splash more oil on the cylinder walls. In 1941, the flywheels were increased to 8-1/2in in diameter (from 8-1/8in) and made 4lb heavier. This revised lower end was carried over on the Panhead motor.

The centershaft from the left flywheel is called the "sprocket shaft." It is secured to the left flywheel on the inner side by the sprocket-shaft nut and lock plate. Supported by roller bearings in the left crank-case half, the sprocket shaft extends into the primary-chain case to drive the primary-chain sprocket. The sprocket transfers engine power through a three-row primary chain to the clutch sprocket.

Many of the chassis parts from the Knucklehead were carried over to the 1948 Panhead, including forks, wheels, headlight, fenders, horn, and front-fender light. The fender does not move up and down with the wheel as the suspension is compressed and rebounds. The fork provides about 2in of travel.

Bill Seber of Seber's Leavenworth Cycles in Leavenworth, Kansas, owns this nice 1948. The rocker covers and air cleaner were made of chrome-plated steel for 1948, but both were changed to stainless steel for 1949.

Gear Case

The main shaft from the right flywheel is the gear shaft or pinion shaft. It was secured to the right flywheel on the inner side by the gear-shaft nut and lock plate. Supported by roller bearings in the right crankcase half, the gear shaft extended into the gear case on the right side of the engine to drive the oil pump, cam gear, breather valve, ignition circuit breaker, and generator. Attached directly to the gear shaft were two gears: the oil-pump drive gear and the pinion gear.

The oil-pump drive gear was the innermost of the two gears, and the outer gear was the pinion gear, which was of small diameter, but was comparatively wide. The width of the pinion gear allowed it to mesh with two larger-diameter gears: the cam gear and the intermediate gear.

The cam gear turn the single, four-lobe cam at half the crankshaft speed. Each lobe was followed by a separate roller tappet that translated the rotary motion and eccentricity of the lobe into valve lift via the pushrod and rocker arm. This cam style and valve-operation scheme are still used on Harley Big Twins today.

The intermediate gear was driven off the inner portion of the pinion gear at half speed. Mounted on the intermediate gear's shaft, on the crankcase side was another gear that drove (also at half speed) the ignition circuit breaker.

To the right of the intermediate gear was the idler gear. The idler gear transfered drive from the intermediate gear to the generator drive gear.

Pressure Oiling System

The Knucklehead motor was lubricated by a recirculating oil system with a dry-sump. Oil was stored in a separate, 1gal oil tank under the seat.

The all-new, gear-type pump for 1936 was the heart of the recirculating oil system. The pump was contained in a separate housing attached to the outside of the aft end of the gear case and was really two pumps in one: a pressure-feed pump to force oil throughout the engine and a scavenge pump to return oil to the oil tank.

The oil tank was mounted higher than the oil pump, so gravity assisted the pump in drawing oil through a feed line from the back of the oil tank to the oil-pump inlet, where the gears of the pump force it to the pressure side of the pump. When oil pressure reaches about 1.5psi, the oil unseated the ball in the check valve and oil flows to a branched passage. The oil pump also directed a small amount of oil to lubricate the primary chain.

Oil to the lower end was forced through passages in the pinion-gear shaft to lubricate the gear-shaft bearings and lower rod bearings. After lubricating these parts, the oil is slung around by the spinning flywheels, forming an oil mist that helps lubricate the cylinder walls. Oil also dripped down the left crankcase wall and into a small hole to lubricate the sprocket-shaft bearings.

The flywheels spun clockwise (when viewed from the right side of the motor), so flywheel action tended to sling a lot of lubricant on the rear cylinder's walls and almost none on the front cylinder's walls. To compensate, H-D engineers used a system of baffles to create more vacuum (which would draw in more of the air-oil mist to lubricate the cylinder) on the front cylinder and to partially block the spray of oil to the rear cylinder. In 1940, the baffles were omitted, and the connecting rods were redesigned to sling more lubricant into the front cylinder.

Oil to the top end was carried from the gear case by an external, tubular-steel oil line that bent inward toward the cylinders, hiding the oil line behind the carburetor. The oil line branched to a fitting on each rocker housing, near the intake-rocker-shaft cover. In each head, the oil flowed through a passage in the rocker housing to oil the fixed intake and exhaust rocker shafts and to oil the valve guides (some early motors did not have the passages to the valve guides, whereas others only had passages to the intake-valve guides). Each rocker shaft is drilled to spread a layer of oil between itself and the rocker arm that revolved around it and to the top of the valve.

The oil supply to the valves can be adjusted after removing the large, chrome, domed "knuckle" covers or nuts on the rocker housing to expose the ends of the rocker shafts. Oil supply is increased by turning the end of the rocker shaft toward the valve-arm side of each rocker (that is, clockwise for the front-cylinder-exhaust and rear-cylinder-intake shafts, or counterclockwise for the front-cylinder-intake and rear-cylinder-exhaust shafts) or reduced by turning it toward the pushrod arm. In 1939, the rocker shafts were redesigned to deliver a constant oil supply (they are non-adjustable).

After lubricating the rocker shafts, valve ends, and intake-valve guides, the top-end oil drips into the bottoms of the cup-like valve-spring covers, and the oil is returned to the tank by the scavenging system.

Breather and Oil-Scavenge System

Since the breather and oil-scavenging systems work in concert, they will be described together. The heart of the breather system is the rotary breather valve in the gear case, which allows crankcase pressure to escape and routes engine vacuum where needed to help scavenge oil. The heart of the scavenge system is the scavenge section of the oil pump, which draws scavenged oil out of the crankcases and returns it to the oil tank.

The geared rotary breather valve is driven at crankshaft speed by the cam gear and is timed to open a passage from the crankcase to the gear case each time the pistons are on their down stroke. Crankcase pressure blows scavenged oil from the crankcase through the breather-valve opening and into the gear case, where the oil mist lubricates the gears. The crankcase air is vented out of the gear case and into the breather-oil-trap chamber at the rear of the gear case, through an integral breather pipe cast into the gear-case cover. Oil is separated from the crankcase air by a screen and separator in the breather oil trap while the air is vented by a separate breather pipe that extends through both crankcases and into the primary-chain housing.

On the pistons' upstroke, the rotary breather valve is timed to close the passage to the gear case and connect a passage from the crankcase to the pushrod tubes and another passage to the breather oil trap. Vacuum created by the rising pistons pulls oil from the valve covers through the pushrod tubes and into the gear case. Vacuum also sucks out the oil from the breather oil trap into the gear case. Oil trapped in the gear case is sucked out of the case and returned to the oil tank by the oil pump's scavenge section.

Charging System

The first Knucklehead used a generator, external generator cut-out relay, and a battery to supply current for lighting and ignition.

John Burgin's 1948 displays the correct outer primary cover for 1948 and 1949 Panheads. Note that the screws holding the chain inspection cover—the small, round cover in the middle of the "diamond"—are at 3 o'clock and 9 o'clock; on 1951–54 covers the screws are at 6 o'clock and 12 o'clock. The outer primary covers were all painted black from the factory, but chrome covers for the chain-inspection cover and clutch cover were optional.

The generator is a 6V DC unit with a rotating armature, two magnetic field coils (regulating and shunt) fixed to the generator case, and three brushes (positive, negative, and current-regulating) contacting the commutator. This generator is used without an external voltage regulator because the third brush regulates the current output.

The external cut-out relay disconnects the generator from the rest of the electrical circuit until the voltage produced by the generator exceeds battery voltage. This cut-out relay looks much like a voltage regulator and mounts just forward of the ignition circuit breaker. All non-police

Elmer Ehnes' bike displays the correct oil filter for 1948 and 1949. This filter attaches directly to the oil tank. Later filters are supported by a bracket bolted to the frame, and a short oil pipe connects the filter to the oil tank. Harley-Davidson later offered an update kit to convert tank-mounted filters to the new type. Nevertheless, only the tank-mounted filter is really correct for 1948 and 1949. Elmer's attention to finish is really evident in this view. Muffler hanger, rear brake pedal, footboards, fork springs, transmission filler bolt, and many other small parts are all Parkerized. The exhaust pipes are painted flat black, which is correct for at least the early part of 1948. Later 1948 Pans were fitted with silver pipes. The chrome header-pipe covers were optional. Spokes are cadmium plated. Instrument cover is painted the same color as the tank (chrome dashes were not available on a new bike until 1956). Cylinders are painted silver on this bike, but many early 1948 bikes were fitted with black-painted cylinders.

H-D Big Twins used a three-brush generator with cut-out relay and without a separate voltage regulator through 1957.

Ignition System

Magneto ignitions were still the rule for the motorcycle industry in 1936, because they have many positive qualities to recommend them. They are simple, light, and relatively trouble free. Harley bucked the trend and gave the Knucklehead a points-and-coil ignition because coil-stoked ignitions give a hotter spark at start-up, thus easing starting, especially in cold weather.

Then, as now, H-D motorcycles used a curious style of coil ignition. By use of a clever concept known as "wasted spark," Harley created a coil ignition system that is nearly as simple as a magneto system because it requires just one set of breaker points and one coil to operate both cylinders (no distributor or second set of points and coil). The coil fires both spark plugs each time the points open, igniting the fuel-air mixture in one cylinder and "wasting" the other spark on the burned gases being expelled from the other cylinder.

Like all coil ignition systems, the Knucklehead's has a primary and a secondary circuit. The primary circuit includes the points, condenser, primary coil, ignition switch, and battery. Although it operates at the battery's voltage (6V), the primary circuit acts to "excite" the secondary coil to produce the very high voltage (more than 15,000V) needed to fire the spark plugs when the primary circuit's points break open. The secondary circuit includes the secondary coil and the spark plugs.

The circuit breaker is mounted to the right of the front cylinder and serves two main functions: it opens the points, and it times the opening so that it occurs at precisely the right instant. The rider can manually advance or retard the timing of the circuit breaker by twisting the left handlebar grip.

Inside the breaker cover is a set of breaker points, a two-lobed cam, and the condenser. The cam lobe for the

Jan Berghoff's *other* 1948 Panhead. This one, Jan gussied up with lots of chrome. Though not original, it is a beautiful machine.

front cylinder is narrower than the lobe for the rear cylinder. Even though the cam lobes are of unequal duration, both have opening ramps of equal length so that the points are closed an equal number of degrees for each cylinder (which means that the condenser builds up an equal kick voltage for each spark).

A twin-lead ignition coil is used, mounted on the motorcycle's left side, in front of the oil tank. One lead goes to the front spark plug and one to the rear plug, and both spark plugs fire each time the points are opened by the points cam. This same basic ignition scheme was used through 1960, after which dual-point timers and twin coils were introduced. In 1965, the ignition was switched back to single points and single coil, but the circuit breaker was given an automatic advance.

Clutch and Transmission

Just as the OHV motor signaled the dawn of a new age for The Motor Company, so, too, did the new bike's transmission—an advanced, four-speed, constant-mesh design that was quieter, stronger, and more durable than the sliding-gear transmissions found on the competing Indian and foreign motorcycles. Although a constant-mesh transmission had been used on a few earlier 45ci

Harleys, the 1936 Knucklehead was the first Big Twin to use the new transmission. The all-new transmission was carried in its own housing separate from the motor.

After 1936, all standard H-D Big Twins used the same standard transmission through 1964, except during the 1939 model year when a curious new four-speed was used that was a hybrid of the constant-mesh and the older sliding-gear types. Optional transmissions included a three-speed and a three-speed with reverse.

In traditional Harley fashion, the new transmission was shifted through a gear-change lever that pivoted fore and aft on a bracket on the bottom of the left gas tank (although right-side shifters were optional). The gear-change lever moved within a chrome guide.

From the rider's perspective, first gear was the farthest forward position, then came neutral, second gear, third gear, and fourth gear. For 1939 only, the shift pattern changed to (front to back): first, second, neutral, third, fourth. For 1940, the pattern reverted to the original, which was not changed until 1947 when it changed to (front to back): fourth, third, second, neutral, and first. All hand-shift Big Twins retained this pattern through 1965.

The transmission was connected to engine power via a conventional multiplate clutch. In traditional American practice, the clutch was foot operated by a pedal on the left side of the motorcycle. The pedal had toe and heel pads and the clutch was engaged when the toe pedal was down and was released when the heel pedal was down. The foot clutch was used on all Big Twins through 1951.

Frame

Harley-Davidson's 1936 Model E came with a frame as different and as modern as its engine. Previous Harley frames had all been single-downtube types that were really just a descendant of turn-of-the-century bicycle frames. The new Knucklehead frame had twin downtubes that cradled the engine in a cage of chrome-moly tubing that stretched from the steering-head forging at the front to the axle-mount forgings at the rear. Unfortunately, the only rear suspension provided was the spring-mounted seat. The 28-degree steering-head angle gave a perfect balance of steering and stability with the stock 18in wheels and 4.00x18in tires.

Many detail changes were made to the Knucklehead frame over the years, including the following:
 • 1937: the one-piece lower frame tubes were cut, and new forgings with integral sidecar loops are brazed in between the new front and rear lower frame tube (replacing the loops that were brazed onto the front of the tube)
 • 1941: the steering head angle was changed from 28 degrees to 29 degrees because the old steering-head angle, while perfectly stable when used with 4.00x18in tires, was found to be unstable when used with the 5.00x16in tires that had been introduced as an option in 1940 and that became standard in 1941

 • 1946: the steering head was raked out to 30deg. All these frames were painted black, but archival photos suggest that custom colors could be ordered. Serial numbers were not marked on Knucklehead frames.

Front Suspension

The new forks on the 1936 Knucklehead were leading link, spring-suspended forks with about 2in of travel. They differed little from the forks on previous big twins, except that the legs of the rigid fork were made of oval-section tubing, rather than of I-beam section.

Many minor changes were made to these forks over the years, but only two are really worth pointing out. The first is the change from "inline" springer forks to a new type. When inline forks are viewed from the top, the centerline of the rigid leg tubes is in line with the centerline of the steering stem. Late in the 1946 production run, a new style of springer forks was introduced that is referred to as the "offset" springer because the centerline of the rigid leg tubes is forward of the steering head's centerline. Offset springer forks are used on all late-1946–1948 OHV Big Twins and on sidecar-equipped 1949 Big Twins.

The second significant change was the availability of an optional damper assembly. The only damping provided in the early years was the Ride Control friction-damping plates along the sides of the springs. In 1945, an optional hydraulic shock absorber was made available.

Wheels and Brakes

The Knucklehead was introduced when tall, narrow wheels and tires were still fashionable on American motorcycles and was still in production when fashion switched to fatter, softer-riding tires. The first Knucklehead's rims were 2.15x18in stamped steel, laced with cadmium-plated spokes and fitted with 4.00x18in tires (standard through 1940). New 5.00x16in tires were optional for 1940 and became standard in 1941.

For 1936, the wheels were painted the color of the tank panels (except when the color scheme was Teak Red with black tank panels, then the rims were painted red). Cadmium-plated or black-enameled rims were optional that first year. Black rims became standard in 1937, and chrome rims became optional in 1940 (replacing the optional chrome wheel "rings," which were plated strips attached to the rim).

An unusual feature is that front and rear wheels and hubs are identical and interchangeable once the brake and drive parts are detached and interchanged.

The 1936 Knucklehead was fitted with front and rear, mechanically-actuated, internal-expanding brakes with two shoes each. Both brake drums are 7-1/4in inside diameter and are made of pressed steel.

For 1937, the rear hub size was increased to 8in. For 1939, the linings of the shoes were made shorter to reduce chatter. For 1940, the drums were made of cast iron. Small changes continued, but the brakes passed on to the Panhead were essentially those introduced in 1936.

A hand lever on the left handlebar acted through a sheathed cable to operate the front brake. A new-style brake lever was introduced in 1940, but the front-brake actuating system remained essentially unchanged until the hand clutch and foot shift were introduced on the 1952 Panhead (at this time, the brake lever was moved to the right handlebar). A foot lever at the front of the right footboard acts through a linkage and crossover to operate the rear brake.

The Knucklehead's brakes state of the art for the era. Moreover, they were about as good as 1930s–era tires could handle.

Early Problems

The 1936 Knucklehead was a basically sound design but a number of circumstances—H-D's understandable eagerness to recoup the new bike's high development costs, the cumulative financial squeeze of the Depression, labor laws that prevented H-D engineers from working overtime—combined to force H-D's management into ordering the new model shipped to dealers in what was essentially advanced prototype form. Predictable difficulties ensued, and the daunting number of changes to Knucklehead components made during the 1936 model year attest to the fact that its configuration had been far from finalized when the first bikes were shipped. To H-D's credit, they rushed to correct these teething problems with updated parts and tuning information.

The features that made the Knucklehead so exciting were the ones that proved most troublesome. The Knucklehead's oil pump was more than adequate to pump oil all the way to the new OHV mechanism, but adjustment of the oil supply to each rocker arm was critical—and the standardized factory adjustment left some bikes with problems from over- or under-oiled valves.

The consequences of over-oiling were unpleasant but not catastrophic: excessive oil consumption and extreme leakage from the valve covers (they all leaked quite a bit anyway). Even so, it is easy to understand why a customer would be disappointed when his shiny new Knucklehead trailed a thick blue cloud of oil smoke, saturated his legs with oil, or got worse oil mileage than the previous Harleys with total-loss oil systems.

If the adjustment erred on the side of under-oiling, the consequences were much more serious, ranging from what *Shop Dope No. 140* described as "squeaking" valves to rapid and excessive wear of the valves, rockers, and shafts. These difficulties were exacerbated by the weak valve springs and problems with the pinion shaft (through which oil passed to get to the crank pin and connecting-rod bearings). H-D engineers fixed the valve-spring problem by switching to a new spring supplier and the pinion problem by releasing a new pinion shaft and gear, and H-D offered these parts to dealers free of charge to fix early motors.

It took nearly the whole production year to get the major problems straightened out, but even so, the Knucklehead was a major hit. Harley-Davidson sold 152 Model Es, 1,526 Model ELs, and 26 Model ESs, for a total of 1,704 first-year Knuckleheads. These sales figures exceeded H-D's projections, but, more importantly, the Knucklehead gave H-D a firm technological lead over arch-rival Indian and their flat-head Chief. It also gave them an engine that was in the same technological league as the best European twins.

Refining the Knucklehead

In classic Harley fashion, hundreds of subtle refinements were made to the Knucklehead over the years that made it more powerful, oil tight, and reliable. By the time the 74 was introduced in 1941, bombs were already falling on England, and H-D was already gearing up for what became known as World War II. The Knucklehead was seen as too expensive and too complex for military service, so only a handful were produced for the U.S. and Canadian armies. Production and development of civilian models were severely curtailed during the war, but even so, H-D records suggest that Knuckleheads were still produced in greater numbers than is generally acknowledged: 5,149 for 1941 (a record high); 1,743 for 1942; 203 for 1943; 535 for 1944; and 1,430 for 1945. These motorcycles (shod with synthetic rubber tires in the later war years) were sold to customers who could demonstrate wartime need or who had the right connections.

After the peace with Japan was signed in August 1945, production of the 61ci and 74ci Knuckleheads for the general civilian market slowly resumed. Despite government-mandated material shortages, H-D records suggest that they built 6,746 Knuckleheads in 1946.

Model Year 1948

Nineteen forty-eight was a year of big changes, even outside The Motor Company.

At home, the big story of the year is the resilience of President Harry Truman. Criticized for fighting tax cuts, for the worsening economy, and for promoting the mongrelization of America's Anglo-Saxon heritage with his civil-rights plans, Truman strikes back, vowing to "give 'em Hell" and calling Republicans "bloodsuckers with offices on Wall Street, princes of privilege, plunderers." Though he received the Democratic nomination for president, the "Dixiecrat" wing of his party splits off and nominates then-Democrat Strom Thurmond. Republican challenger Thomas Dewey is the predicted winner by 10–15 percent. Some newspapers are so sure of Truman's defeat that they actually print papers with the headline "Dewey Defeats Truman." More prudent editors wait for the results and print the headline "Truman Defeats Dewey in Giant Upset."

The State of the Art, 1936

Harley-Davidson EL vs. Vincent-HRD Series A Rapide

Across the Pond, another new 1000cc OHV V-twin made its debut in 1936—the Vincent-HRD Rapide. Though few, if any, of these amazing twins made the long trip from Stevenage, England, to the shores of the fruited plain, timing and technology lead me to the inevitable comparison between the two. After all, does anyone really want to read another comparison between Harleys and Indians?

To motorcyclists steeped in the Vincent's fearsome reputation for speed and unwilling to look past the Harley's reputation as a "Hawg," the comparison between the two may seem loony. Nevertheless, I think it will be enlightening to compare back and forth throughout the text to show how the different philosophies of the two companies resulted in similar initial designs being developed along quite different paths.

Compare the prewar, Series A Rapide and the prewar Knucklehead, feature by feature:

- Both are powered by four-stroke V-twins of 1,000cc nominal displacement (988.6cc for the Harley and 998cc for the Vincent) with cylinders splayed at a narrow angle (47.5deg for the Vincent and 45deg for the Harley). Very similar.
- Both have two overhead valves per cylinder, actuated by pushrods on the right side of the engine. The Vincent used exposed hair-pin valve springs; the Harley used nested, coiled springs inside a valve-spring cover. Both systems did the job admirably, but the Harley received updated valve covers that completely covered the rockers and valves in 1938, solving many of the problems with oil leaks, so we'll tally one point for Harley.
- Both followed the then-popular trend toward larger-bore, shorter-stroke dimensions: 84mm bore and 90mm stroke for the Vincent; 84.14mm bore and 88.9mm stroke for the Harley. No clear winner here.
- Both used a sturdy crankshaft consisting of flywheel halves and an offset crank pin, but the Vincent's connecting rods are positioned side-by-side so that the cylinders could be offset, allowing more cooling air to reach the rear cylinder. Was this difference of any consequence? Probably not.
- Both used alloy crankcases with cast-iron cylinder heads and cylinders. Again a tie.
- Both had dry-sump, recirculating oil systems, and each gained a reputation as oil leakers. No clear advantage.
- The Vincent uses two carburetors; the Harley uses one. This gives the Vincent a clear performance advantage, but also makes it harder to keep in tune. Even so, score one for Stevenage.
- At first, both used sprung front forks without hydraulic damping, and hydraulic damping for each became available at about the same time. Tie.
- The Vincent has an innovative sprung frame with a swinging rear end suspended on dual springs. The Harley has no rear suspension, other than the sprung seat. Score a big one for Stevenage.
- The Harley uses coils and points; the Vincent uses a magneto. Both bikes start easily when kept in tune, and there are advocates who claim advantage for each type of system, so I should probably call this a tie. However, the H-D's simple, wasted-spark point system is more modern and gives it an edge in cold-weather operation, so I'll score one for Milwaukee.
- The Harley uses a constant-mesh, four-speed transmission and multiplate clutch of its own design; the Vincent uses a heavyweight proprietary Burman transmission of an older, constant-mesh type and a clutch designed for the horsepower of a 500cc single. The Vincent's transmission and clutch were known for self-destructing under even moderately severe use, whereas the Harley transmission and clutch were stone-ax reliable. Score another for Milwaukee.
- The Harley uses a foot clutch and hand shifter; the Vincent uses a hand clutch and foot shifter. Some would disagree, but I score another point for the Vincent.
- The Harley's single-sided brakes were as good as any brakes except the Vincent's dual-sided brakes. Another big one for Vincent.
- Weight: 515lb for the Harley; 430lb for the Vincent. Big advantage Vincent.
- Wheelbase: 56in for the Vincent; 59.5in for the Harley. This is a tough call. Brits would call the nimble Vincent the clear winner here, but Americans tend to prefer bigger bikes, and thus would call the more stable Harley the victor. Both bikes feel "natural" at their wheelbase, so I call it a tie.
- The high-compression Model EL was rated at 40hp at 4800rpm; the Series A Rapide was rated at 45hp at 5500rpm. Not a huge difference despite the reputation. Nevertheless, score another for Vincent.
- Top speed: 90–95 for the Harley; 105–115mph for the Vincent. This statistic brings it all together, to show how a small advantage in horsepower, combined with far less weight, add up to a big top-speed advantage. No contest; one more for Stevenage.

So which was the better bike at the time? For hyper-velocity touring or for racing, the Vincent was the clear winner. But for everyday use on rough American roads, over long distances, at the hands of abusive American riders of the 1930s, I think the Harley prevailed. In any case, it is amazing how well the Knucklehead compares, especially when you look at the relative production of the two: about eighty Series A Rapides were built versus 8,000 Knuckleheads between 1936 and 1939. A final point worth noting is that a modified Knucklehead ridden by Joe Petrali held the American speed record (and fastest speed by any non-supercharged motorcycle in the world) from 1937 until the record was broken in 1948 by a specially tuned Vincent.

Bogart and Bacall star in *Key Largo*, and Ed Sullivan's *Toast of the Town* premiers.

National Football League games are televised. Baseball hero George Herman "Babe" Ruth dies.

Captain Charles "Chuck" Yeager becomes a national hero when the Air Force announces that Yeager had become the first person to break the sound barrier, on October 14, 1947. Aviation pioneer Orville Wright dies.

The transistor is developed at Bell Telephone Laboratories, and the electronic age begins.

Overseas, the great Indian leader and champion of nonviolence, Mahatma Gandhi, is assassinated.

Sunset by the river, and Bill Seber's 1948 Panhead catches the last rays.

Russia bans land traffic to West Berlin, and the West responds with a massive airlift of supplies. The country of Israel is created out of violence and chaos by a United Nations partition of Palestine. Before the ink dries on the agreement, the violence and chaos resume.

Meanwhile, forward-thinking companies around the world continue the race to take advantage of the myriad, amazing advancements in material science, engine design, production methods, and fuel technology that were pioneered during the war, not to mention the huge factories built with government aid to feed, clothe and equip Allied soldiers. Harley-Davidson was, among those companies looking toward the future, and its a good thing they were because by 1947—even though 11,648 Knuckleheads were sold and demand far out-stripped supply—there was no denying that the cast-iron Knucklehead was in need of a bit of updating, too. Which brings us back to the point of this long-winded digression: the 1948 Panhead Big Twins.

The 1948 Panhead

Three versions of the new model were offered in each displacement size for 1948: 48E (61ci solo twin with 6.5:1 compression), 48EL (61ci solo twin with 7:1 compression), 48ES (61ci sidecar twin with 6.5:1 compression), 48F (74ci twin with 6.6:1 compression), 48FL (74ci solo twin with 7:1 compression), and 48FS (74ci sidecar twin with 6.6:1 compression). Sidecar models differed from solo models in that they were fitted with sidecar gearing. (The "S" for sidecar was not stamped into the case as part of the serial number on any of the Panhead series motorcycles.) Sixty-ones were listed for $635 and 74s were listed for $650. The four-speed transmission was standard, but the optional three-speed and three-speed with reverse were available at no extra cost.

These prices were for bare-bones models (without an air cleaner, side stand, or front safety guard) intended only for use as the base bike for sidecar or package-truck use. Three solo option groups were offered, and one of them had to be specified at the time of order: the Deluxe Solo Group for $92, the Sport Solo Group for $59.25, or the Utility Solo Group for $24. For police bikes, the Standard Police Group was offered for $73. For sidecar and Package Truck bikes, the Utility Group was offered for $33.50, and the Deluxe Sport Sidecar Group was offered for the sidecar for $90.50. For information about what was included in the option groups for 1948 and for later years, see the tables in the Appendix. Many of the items in the option groups were available separately, as were many options not included in these groups. For more information on these options and their prices, see *The Legend Begins*, published by Harley-Davidson Inc., 1993.

Four different colors were available for 1948 Big Twins: Azure Blue, Flight Red, Brilliant Black, and Police Silver (Police Group only). The paint on 1948 H-D motorcycles was applied only after the parts were first "Bonderized" (a Parkerized coating that soaks up paint and bonds it to the metal, while also giving the metal an extra level of protection against corrosion).

The New Motor

Like the Knucklehead motor it replaced, the 1948 Panhead motor was a four-stroke, 45deg V-twin with pushrod-operated overhead valves. It was offered in two displacements, 61ci, and 74ci. Most of the updates were in the top end, so lets look at it first.

Hydraulic Lifters

Before this first Panhead was introduced, all OHV motorcycle engines had been built with mechanically-actuated valves. The Knucklehead motor employed pushrods to transfer thrust from the tappets (which ride the rotating camshaft's lobes) to the individual rockers that opened the valves. The whole system operated efficiently

Pistons and Rings

As on pre-1940 Knuckleheads, pistons for the 1948 Panhead were offered in high-compression (7:1 ratio) and medium-compression (6.5:1 for 61s or 6.6:1 for 74s). Compression rings on 61ci pistons were 3/32in (reduced from 1/8in on the Knucklehead) in width, but the oil-control ring was widened to 3/16in. Early 74ci pistons had an oil-ring groove 1/8in wide. From motor number 48FL10184 on, new pistons were fitted with a 3/16in oil-ring groove and an updated oil-control ring. Later 61ci pistons were also fitted with the updated 3/16in oil-control ring.

Pushrods and Tappets

Par for the course, nearly the entire pushrod system is new—not just the hydraulic lifters and pushrods, but the roller tappets and many pushrod housing parts, as well. Lets, look at them all, starting at the bottom and working up.

Two new tappet blocks mount to bosses on the top of the right crankcase and each block houses one intake and one exhaust tappet. The most apparent change is that these blocks are now cast of aluminum (rather than of iron) and are unpainted (the iron blocks had been painted silver during peacetime and white during the war when the aluminum necessary for the silver paint was being used to build war planes). Less noticeable, the new blocks do not have the oil-scavenging holes that the Knucklehead blocks had because oil from the heads is no longer returned to the cases through the pushrod tubes (oil return for the new heads is through an oil passage in the cylinder). However, they do have grooves in each tappet hole to drain off the excess oil that drains down the pushrods from the hydraulic lifters. These aluminum tappet blocks are correct for 1948–52 Panheads.

The front and rear tappet blocks are not interchangeable. The number "9-483" is cast in relief on the bottom of the front block, and the number "9-482" is cast in relief on the bottom of the rear block. Four straight-slot, cadmium-plated screws with countersunk star lock washers are used to secure each tappet block to the crankcase on all 1948 and 1949 Pan motors.

All four tappets are identical, and each consists of a roller at the bottom to bear on the camshaft, a cylindrical body, an adjuster screw (with lock nut) that threads into the tappet body (allows adjustment of valve lash), and an adjuster lock nut. The ball-shaped lower end of the pushrod seats in a socket on the top of the adjuster screw, and the top of the pushrod has a 1/4in hole for the stem of the hydraulic lifter. The new pushrods are 7-1/4in long (before the lifters are installed), and, as previously described, the hydraulic lifter rides atop the pushrod to complete the connection from tappet to rocker arm. This style of tappets, pushrods, and adjuster screws continued in use through 1952.

As on the Knucklehead motor, a pair of telescoping, chromed steel tubes cover the pushrods to seal out dirt and seal in oil. Both tubes were redesigned for 1948, however.

The lower tube is 5-1/8in long, is flanged at top and bottom, and has a "step" in the tube where the 3/4in diameter top portion is swaged to 7/8in diameter on the lower section. The flange at the bottom seats against the tappet block, with a cork washer to seal the gap. Another cork washer is fitted on the upper flange, then a steel washer, a spring, and a spring cap are fitted atop the seal. The upper tube slips inside the spring cap, through the spring, the steel washer, and the cork washer, into the lower tube. The upper tube is then extended up so that the flange at the top reaches the cylinder head (with a cork washer as the seal), and a spring-cap retainer snaps over the upper tube to keep the tube from telescoping down. At its lower end, the retainer seats against the spring cap, and at upper end, the retainer seats against the flange at the top of the tube. The spring-cap retainer acts as a removable spacer to spring-load the upper pushrod tube in place. When the retainer is removed, the tubes can be telescoped together so the pushrod can be adjusted or serviced. The upper and lower pushrod tubes introduced on the first Panhead were still in use on the last Panhead, more than seventeen years later. The cork seals eventually wear out and cause leaks, but the system seals well if the seals are periodically replaced.

Cylinders

Those shiny, new, aluminum cylinder heads are perched atop redesigned cylinders. The main difference between the new and the old cylinders is the internal oil passages in the new cylinders, bored from the base-gasket surface at the bottom to the head-gasket surface on the top. When the cylinder is viewed from the top, the oil-feed passage is on the right, and the oil-return passage is on the left. Oil is pumped from the right crankcase, through a hole in the new base gasket, through the internal oil passage, through a hole in the right side of the head gasket, and to a passage in the head. Similarly, oil is returned from the head to the left crankcase through the internal return passage.

Some familiar features returned, including the lip along the top of the barrel (it had always been there on 61ci barrels but not on 74ci barrels; now it was used on both) and four mounting holes in the base. The cylinders were made of cast iron and were painted black. Some time during the production run, H-D began painting the cylinders silver, and all Panhead cylinders from that point on were painted silver. This cylinder design was used, unchanged, through the 1952 model year.

Crankcases and Lower End

There is some truth to the notion that the Panhead motor was just a Knucklehead motor with a new top end. Only four significant parts were changed in the 1948 Panhead lower end and gear case: left and right crankcases, cam gear, and gear-case cover—and all of these changes were made to accommodate the new top-end components.

For 1948, the left case was modified to serve as part of the oil-return system. Return oil from the front head flows out of the internal passage on the left side of the front cylinder, through a hole in the base gasket, and into a new drain passage in the left crankcase. The new passage runs from the left side of the front cylinder's base-gasket surface to the scavenge sump. Return oil from the rear head flows out of the internal passage on the left side of the rear cylinder, through a hole in the base gasket, and into a new drain channel milled into the base-gasket surface. This channel runs from the left side of the left crankcase, around the back, to the inner edge of the case, where it meets with a similar channel milled into the base-gasket surface of the right case. Return oil flows along the channel to a drain hole into the right case.

The left case was also updated on the inner side to improve oiling of the sprocket-shaft bearing. A cast-in V-shape funnels the oil dripping down the inside of the case into the oil hole to the bearing. This left case has the number "112-481" cast in relief on the inside of the case, along with a casting-date plate. This style of left crankcase was used through the 1952 model year.

For 1948, the right case was modified to serve a new role in the oil-feed system to the cylinder heads. The new

In this front view of Jan Berghoff's 1948 Panhead, the eagle fender tip, chrome horn cover, and chrome spotlights are prominent. The spot lamps mount to a chrome-plated bar on the spring-fork Panheads. On the later Hydra-Glide, the lamps mount individually to each fork leg. Note the short hand grips and relatively long chrome part of the control spiral (what is today called a twist grip, used for the throttle and spark control on the Panheads). The only Panhead fitted with this type of spiral was the 1948.

right crankcase routes oil from the oil pump to a passage at the right side of each cylinder base, rather than out a boss to an external oil line. The right case also completes the oil return path from the rear cylinder head. The channel milled into the rear section of the rear-cylinder base transfers oil from the similar channel in the left case, and drains the oil through a passage to the crankcase. Unlike the last Knucklehead right case, the new right case has no oil-drain passages to the tappet-guide mounting bosses. This case has the number "112-48" cast in relief on the inside and was used into the 1952 model year (H-D literature says only that the case style changed with "about" engine number FL3529).

Cam and Gear Cover

The 1948 Panhead cam retained the familiar four-lobe configuration introduced on the 1936 Knucklehead, but the lobes were given revised profiles to work better with the hydraulic lifters. The cam for 74ci motors had a lift of 1.334in for 74ci motors and a 1.10in lobe width. The cam for 61ci motors had a lift of 1.328in and a lobe width of 1.10in. (For comparison, the cam used on Knucklehead motors from 1936–47 had 1.22in and

0.875in lobe width.) The cam for 61ci motors was used through the 1952 season (after which the 61ci motor was dropped); afterward, it was fitted to the 74ci FLE Traffic Combination motors built from 1953 to 1956. The new 74ci cam was used for all standard FL motors 1948–69 and in the 1955 FLH (first year of the FLH).

The gear cover for 1948 is basically the same as the die-cast gear cover used in 1947, except that the oil-feed hole on the top edge is plugged with a screw because oil to the cylinder heads is now routed through the cylinders, rather than through an external oil line. Later-1948 motors were fitted with gear covers having a steel plug pressed into the oil hole. Still-later 1948 motors were fitted with covers that were not drilled for the oil hole. On the outside, the case features eight cooling ribs cast in relief. Also visible from the outside are the breather tunnel (the tube-like ridge that goes across the cover from lower left to upper right) and the pinion-bushing boss. This last style of gear cover is used from late 1948 through 1950. The gear cover is fastened by straight-slot screws for 1948 and 1949.

Exhaust System

The exhaust system for the 1948 Panhead is basically the same as the Knucklehead's, except that the header pipes are swaged at the top to fit over the exhaust-port nipple. The system has four pipes (front header, S-pipe, Y-pipe, rear header) and a muffler. The muffler is the rocket-fin style that had been used since 1941. All 1948 mufflers were painted high-temperature black. The pipes on early 1948 Panheads were also painted high-temperature black, but sometime during the production run, H-D started painting the exhaust pipes silver. Observation of many photos in *The Enthusiast* of this year and inspection of several unrestored 1948 machines suggests that the change to silver-painted cylinders and silver-painted exhaust pipes occurred at about the same time. Optional chrome-plated-flex-pipe covers were available as part of the Deluxe Solo or Sport Solo groups or separately, but neither a chrome-plated muffler nor a stainless steel muffler cover was available on a new machine.

Chassis

Updating the motor rather than the chassis had been a logical decision for H-D. The last Knucklehead's chassis and suspension—tubular cradle frame with rigid rear end, sprung saddle, and offset springer fork–were not cutting-edge stuff, but were certainly adequate for the average road conditions and riders of the day and, more importantly, were in line with the Panhead's more conservative contemporaries.

Gas tanks, fenders, forks, wheels, primary-chain covers, tool box, oil tank, transmission, taillight, and many other parts were carried over from the last Knucklehead. Even so, several major components were upgraded to accompany the new motor.

Wishbone Frame

The 1948 frame was the first of the "wishbone" frames. Observed from the front, the downtubes of the frame bend outward and then back down, much like the shape of a chicken's wishbone. These tubes were not flattened on the motor side for 1948, as they would be on later frames.

A bracket for the front safety guard was welded between the two downtubes just above the wishbone bends. A new safety guard was introduced to mount to this bracket. The new guard consisted of two tubular guard loops connected in the center by a sleeve. This sleeve was flattened and two holes were drilled through it for the mounting bolts. All front safety guards were painted black for 1948 and 1949. This style of safety guard was used through 1950, and 1950 was the first year they were available in chrome finish on a *new* Panhead.

The frame was fitted with a new steering-head forging that was fitted with a steering-head tumbler lock on the right side and a boss for the steering-damper pin for the forthcoming Hydra-Glide steering damper.

The upper motor mount was also updated. The new mount curved forward, whereas the old mount dropped straight down from the backbone tube.

The frame carried over many familiar features, including the tool-box strap welded between the upper and lower rear frame tubes. Though the wishbone frame would be used through mid-1954, the frame fitted to 1948 and 1949 models with spring forks were the only wishbone frames that were neither fitted with horn mount blocks nor had downtubes flattened for these mounts.

New Speedometer

The 1948 Panhead was fitted with a Stewart-Warner speedometer of new design. The circular, recessed center panel was bluish gray and enclosed the odometer (forward of center) and trip meter (aft of center) and had hash marks at 2mph intervals (all equal length but thicker at the ten-mph marks) painted on the outside edge. The odometer and trip meter numerals were black for miles and red for tenths, both on white backgrounds. The speedo's outer ring was greenish gray and provided the background for the numbers, which were painted (10 through 120) on the underside of the glass in cream-ivory paint, along with the H-D bar and shield at the rear edge. The pointer was painted red, the glass was flat (glass was convex on previous speedometers), the bezel was chrome plated, and the case was cadmium plated. This speedometer was used through the 1952 season.

Terminal Box

The lighting and ignition wires lead to a new terminal box behind the spark coil. The terminal ends were crimped on (they had been soldered) and insulated with Vinylite plastic tubing.

The State of the Art, 1948
Harley-Davidson FL vs. Vincent-HRD Series B Black Shadow

The state of the art had advanced on both sides of the Atlantic. In April 1946, Vincent-HRD unveiled its new and much-improved Series B Rapide. Its many modern features—unit construction, aluminum cylinders and heads, servo clutch, redesigned four-speed transmission, and rerouted oil lines—had corrected almost all of the Series A's faults and made it the fastest and most technologically advanced motorcycle in the world when it was introduced—and one of the best looking, to boot. Serendipitous for comparison with the new Panhead, a new Vincent was released in 1948, a hopped up Rapide called the Black Shadow. (I know you Vincent fans will cry foul at my comparing the 1200cc Harley to the 1000cc Vincent when there is a 1000cc version of the Panhead to compare. If you do, you've proved yourselves to be no bigger than the H-D fans who will cry foul because I chose to compare the specially-tuned Black Shadow to the mass-produced Harley when the much milder Rapide is available for the comparison. No apologies to either group. Remember this is a comparison of the best big twins, not the best 1000cc twins.)

When we last compared, the differences between the H-D and the Vincent were surprisingly few. The Vincent's advantages were its light weight, higher power, better brakes, and sprung rear suspension. The Harley's advantages were its sturdier clutch and transmission, easier-starting coil ignition, and ease of maintenance. Rather than compare every point, lets look at what had changed for each since our last discussion and how these changes affect their ranking.

Both motors were modified to completely enclose the valvetrain, so they were both more oil tight on the top end. Tie.

The Vincent was updated with alloy cylinders and cylinder heads, whereas the Harley got alloy heads. Vincent opened a gap with this feature that Harley would not close until 1984. Score for Vincent.

The Harley had hydraulic lifters for reduced noise and maintenance. The Vincent's still needed adjustment. The maintenance gap grows. Score for H-D.

Both had oil lines rerouted to put them out of sight and reduce leakage. Again, a tie.

Harley's springer fork was available with hydraulic damping, while the Vincent's was still undamped (some 1948 Vincents were fitted with the new Girdraulic forks, which were hydraulically damped, but most 1948s were fitted with the undamped Brampton forks). Score a small point for H-D.

Vincent dispensed with its old multiplate clutch and Burman transmission in favor of a servo clutch and four-speed transmission of its own design. Both clutch and transmission were sturdy and reliable, but the Harley's always had been. Some would say the Vincent's two-finger servo clutch gave it a big advantage, but proper adjustment was critical and it was known to be grabby. The way I see it, Vincent had only caught up with Harley. I call the tranny-and-clutch wars a tie.

The Vincent's frame was a technical tour de force for its day that used the engine as a stressed member and had a swinging rear end with springs for suspension (some 1948s were fitted with the new hydraulic dampers that were fitted with greater regularity in 1949). The Harley also had a new frame, but it was just a warmed-over version of the duplex, hardtail frame from 1936. The rear "suspension" was still just a spring-post-mounted seat. The Vincent's rear suspension still carried rider and passenger as part of the sprung weight, but as before, poor rear suspension beats no rear suspension. Score another small point for Vincent.

In 1936, the Rapide had a 5hp advantage—45 to 40. In 1948, the specially tuned Black Shadow still only showed a 5hp advantage over the FL Panhead—55 to 50. Score again for Vincent.

Top speed for the Harley had increased to about 100mph. Top speed for the Vincent had climbed to nearly 125mph. Quite a difference in speed from such a small difference in horsepower.

The main reason for the performance gap was the Vincent's light weight. The Vincent had picked up a few pounds, but was still ultra-light at 458lb. The Harley always had been heavy and had picked up a few more pounds since 1936, to about 550lb in its most stripped-down form.

So how did the new Harley compare to the new Vincent? Not as well as it had in 1936 but better than it would in later years. Most of the Harley's strengths remained intact, as did most of the Vincent's. The comparison is most useful in pointing out the different paths on which each company was now treading.

With his postwar Rapide and Black Shadow, Phil Vincent served notice that his path was the freeway to the future of motorcycling. Through the late 1940s, Vincent's small British firm would advance the state of motorcycling at a rate that would not be equaled until the Japanese took up the quest in earnest in the 1970s. His goal had always been to build the perfect motorcycle—whatever the cost—and that became the single-minded quest that led to the company's ruin.

The Harleys and Davidsons steered their company down a different path. A path that took longer to reach the state of excellence Vincent achieved so quickly, but one that was ultimately more successful. Both paths led to a group of eager enthusiasts, but Harley's path to a much larger group because the Milwaukeeans were compelled to build better bikes by a businessman's self-interest, while Vincent was driven toward the same goal almost solely by an engineer's vanity. Harley drove in Ford's tire tracks, whereas Vincent drove off in Duesenberg's. The result was that Harley built more than 12,000 Panheads in 1948, while Vincent built no more than fifty or so Black Shadows in the same year, and only a few of them made it Stateside.

To H-D's chagrin, however, those that did make it to the U.S. were used to start their own legend at the Milwaukee marque's expense. On the salt flats of Bonneville, Rollie Free—an avowed enemy of Milwaukee iron—piloted a specially tuned 1948 Black Shadow to a new American speed record of 150.313mph on September 13, 1948, shattering the record set at Daytona in 1937 by Joe Petrali on a 1937 Knucklehead.

Accessories

Wartime restrictions resulted in plain motorcycles from 1942 to 1947. For 1948, dozens of options were available to dress up a new bike. I don't have room to list them all here, so I'll just list the most popular items.

Two optional seats were offered, the Deluxe Solo and Deluxe Buddy seats. The solo seat had thicker foam padding than the Standard Solo seat, was covered in leather, and had a three-piece skirt around the seat's rear. The skirt was decorated with a plastic rosette on each side,

Even top-flight restorers make a slight mistake once in a while. This bike is correct in nearly every detail. The major exception is the outer primary cover. It is fitted with the 1950–54 style cover, with the screws for the chain-inspection cover placed at 6 and 12 o'clock (rather than at 3 and 9 o'clock, as they were for 1949 and earlier).

a row of nickel pieces in line with the rosettes, and a line of nickel dots along the skirt's lower edge. It was included in the Deluxe Solo Group or could be ordered separately. This style of Deluxe Solo Seat is correct for 1947–54 Big Twins. The Deluxe Buddy Seat was a much larger seat, designed to hold both rider and passenger. It was covered in leather and had a plastic skirt decorated with nickel studs and nickel stars on yellow-plastic rosettes. This style of buddy seat was optional for 1947 and 1948.

New, chrome fender tips were optional for 1948. Both front and rear tips had a winged design that looked like a WWII bombardier's wings stamped in relief in the center of each. The front fender tip was optional for 1948 and 1949 spring-fork models. The rear tip was optional through 1958. The older style front fender tips with the embossed eagle on them were available in early 1948, as shown in some of the photos.

A rear safety guard was one of the most popular options. The 1948 guard was the same guard that had been used since the 1930s. It was offered only in black-painted finish (chrome-plated guards were not offered until 1950). This guard was an option through 1957.

Perhaps the most popular option for a spring-fork Panhead was the Silver King handlebar-mounted sport windshield, which did an excellent job of protecting the rider from the wind. The standard shield was clear plexi-glass without colored lower panels. Next most popular option was probably the King-Size saddlebags.

Panhead Production

By any measure, the first Panhead was a huge success. During the 1948 production run, 12,924 Panheads were built, and still H-D was unable to meet demand. This total included 198 Model ES, 4,321 Model EL, 334 Model FS, and 8,071 Model FL. Again, the "S" in "ES" and "FS" was not stamped into the motor as part of the serial number.

The Future

At the end of 1948, the future finally began to look really promising. Harley-Davidson's long-time rival, Indian, appeared to be preparing to abandon the Big Twin market to the more advanced H-D. Even though Indian produced substantial numbers of their Chief for 1948, it was no secret that Indian was gearing up to go head-to-head with the flood of lightweight OHVs from England by introducing their own line of modular OHV lightweights. For 1949 and beyond, it looked as if Harley's new big twin would not only be the most advanced big twin on the American market, it might just be the only big twin on the American market.

This overly-optimistic prediction did not come to pass, however, because Indian experienced immediate difficulties with their new models and resumed limited production of the Chief in late 1949 to keep cash flowing into company coffers.

During its first half century, H-D had really earned the title of The Motor Company. While many other motorcycle manufacturers in the U.S. and abroad had used proprietary engines, H-D had always built its own. It didn't always build the fastest and most powerful, but each series was more refined, reliable, and oil tight than the last. The Knucklehead motor had put Harley-Davidson in the technological lead against Indian, and the Panhead widened the gap.

CHAPTER TWO

1949-1957
The Hydra-Glide

Just one year after it had been introduced, the Panhead entered its second era, the Hydra-Glide era. "Hydra-Glide" was the name Harley-Davidson gave to its innovative new hydraulic forks—the star feature of the 1949 Big Twins. Before long, the bikes themselves were called "Hydra-Glides," and Harley-Davidson encouraged the trend by offering optional front-fender badges featuring the name. Little beyond the forks was changed to make the 1949 Hydra-Glide, but the model would receive hundreds of updates during the next nine years, before Harley took its Big Twin to stage three.

In many ways, the Hydra-Glides were the classic Panheads. They set a style that was just as striking as that of the first Knucklehead—and as enduring. Prove it to yourself: Compare the Hydra-Glide's form to today's extremely popular Heritage Softtails. I don't know whether Harley-Davidson had a styling director in the 1930s and 1940s or whether the shape was

Above: For reasons unknown, Harley-Davidson chose 1954 as the year of its 50th anniversary (it was their 51st year), and fitted all its Big Twins with a spiffy fender medallion to commemorate the event. These were a standard item, so no 1954 restoration is complete without one. This view also shows the front fender tip that was standard from 1949 to 1956.

Right: The right side of the 1950 EL shows the 1949–54 fork top front panel with four horizontal stripes. These tank emblems appear to be reproductions because the lettering is painted black, when it should be painted red. The oil filter shown was introduced in 1950 to isolate the filter from vibration. It features a short oil pipe to connect the filter to the oil tank; a mounting arm to the frame is bolted to a stud in the filter cap.

The big change for 1949 was the new, hydraulically damped telescopic forks, for which the bike was christened the Hydra-Glide. This 1949 Panhead is owned by Claire McCormick. The horn used on the Hydra-Glides was the same one that had been mounted atop the fender of the spring-fork models, but it was now bolted to brackets welded onto the back of the front downtubes.

purely function determining form. Whichever is the case, it worked. And it continues to work today. That is not to deny Willie G.'s role in reviving Harley-Davidson—his contributions to the company's success, as director of styling and as goodwill ambassador, are legion—but it is equally hard to deny that the classic styles set in 1936 and 1949 later played a big part in pulling The Motor Company's bacon out of the fire in the 1980s. Part of Willie G.'s genius was in recognizing H-D's rich styling heritage and in adapting those styles to motorcycles that were modern, functional, and nearly maintenance-free.

Model Year 1949

Nineteen forty-eight had been a record year for H-D. Despite opening the new plant in Butler, Wisconsin, where, among other things, the steel bodywork was made, production had not been able to keep up with demand. Even so, the Motor Company sold 29,612 new motorcycles, more than they had sold in any other non-war year.

In 1949, the Motor Company was riding high while its major domestic competitor was floundering. Indian was having difficulties getting its new modular OHVs launched, so production of the Chief was severely curtailed. Only a few (in his book *Illustrated Indian Motorcycle Buyer's Guide*, Jerry Hatfield estimates the number at between 50 and 100) Chiefs were built toward the end of the year to bring a few badly-needed dollars into the company coffers. These new Chiefs were officially listed as 1950 models and were vastly improved, with hydraulic forks, foot shift, and hand clutch.

But Indian wasn't entirely finished yet. To help increase revenue, Indian began importing AJS, Douglas, Excelsior, Matchless, Norton, Royal Enfield, and Vincent-HRD motorcycles and selling them through its formidable dealer network. These new imports further added to the rising tide of foreign machines lapping at H-D's knees. In 1946, there had been only about a dozen Triumph dealers in the U.S. By 1948, there were more than 100 Triumph dealers, and their sales would top 1,000 units in 1949. Also in 1949, BSA established a nationwide dealer network. And the foreign makers were increasingly going after H-D's Big Twin. In late 1949, Triumph increased the size of their big bikes from 500cc to 650cc, and the British government devalued the pound by over 20 percent, making the imports even cheaper in comparison to the Harleys.

John Burgin's 1949 Hydra-Glide, with his military surplus Mule in the background. Stainless steel was used in many new places for 1949. Polished stainless upper fork covers were available as an option (standard covers are black-painted steel). Most 1949 covers do not have the name "Hydra-Glide" stamped into the upper front panel, but all 1950 and later covers do have the name. The rocker covers and air-cleaner cover were made of stainless for 1949, and the rocker covers would remain stainless through 1956 whereas the air-cleaner covers would remain in stainless through 1965. For 1949 only many other items that were normally chrome-plated options were instead made of stainless, including the muffler shield, clutch-pedal pivot cover, primary-chain inspection cover, clutch inspection cover, and generator end cover (none of which are shown in this photo).

In America at large, 1949 was the on-ramp to the paranoid, but prosperous, 1950s. Lines were being drawn around the world that culminated in several bloody Cold War skirmishes over the next twenty years: the United States formally recognized the Republic of Korea and Israel, the North Atlantic Treaty Organization was formed, the Soviet blockade of West Berlin broke under the massive American airlift, France backed Bao Dai as the leader of non-Communist Vietnam, Russia tested its first nuclear bomb, and the Nationalist Chinese fled mainland China for Formosa.

Similarly, the beginnings of many national crazes of the 1950s also had their roots in 1949. Pizza fever began its spread to the heartland. Television began its rise toward becoming the new national pastime. Canasta swept America, and three of the year's best-selling books told eager neophytes how to win at the game and be the life of every card party. Bikini bathing suits shocked and titillated swimmers across America. The 33-1/3rpm, long-play record was introduced to confuse music fans everywhere. Polaroid's new Land camera was introduced at the shockingly high price of $89.75 and began spoiling Americans with photographs that self-developed in 60sec. Roller Derby put pro wrestling on wheels. The first Volkswagens hit America's shores. The first pre-fabricated suburb rose out of a Long Island field. And George Orwell's prophetic novel *1984* was published to critical acclaim.

Economically, America was poised for a boom. Prices actually fell during 1949 (overall inflation was at *negative* 0.7 percent). The Dow-Jones average was on the rise, even though unemployment was rather high at 5.9 percent.

So, with great optimism—despite the foreign competition—Harley-Davidson proudly introduced the second major update to their Big Twin in as many years.

1949 Hydra-Glides and "P-models"

Two basic versions of the 61ci and 74ci Panhead motors were offered for 1949—high-compression (EL and FL) and low-compression (E and F). Hydra-Glide forks were standard on all E, EL, F, and FL models, but spring forks were available by special order for sidecar-equipped motorcycles (although some 1949 springer Pans were probably ordered as solo models). All bikes so equipped were designated EP, ELP, FP, or FLP, depending on which motor was fitted. Sidecar gearing was also optional for both chassis, and bikes so fitted were designated ES, ELS, EPS, ELPS, FS, FLS, FPS, or FLPS, depending on which motor and front end was fitted. Though the "S" was not stamped on the motor as part of the serial number, the "P" sometimes was, but it was stamped at the end of the number (e.g FL1234P, *not* FLP1234). Even though H-D offered sidecar-equipped bikes with the Hydra-Glide forks, they recommended that all sidecar and package-truck bikes be equipped with the spring forks because the Hydra-Glide's had insufficient trail for good stability with a sidecar or package truck. The three-speed transmission was no longer an option for 1949 and later bikes; the only option to the standard four-speed was the three-speed with reverse.

All 61ci Hydra-Glides retailed for $735, and all 74ci Hydra-Glides retailed for $750. Spring-fork models, prices were not listed on the documentation available to me.

These prices were for bare-bones models (without an air cleaner, side stand, or front safety guard) that were only meant for use as the base bike for sidecars or package-truck applications. For solo use, the bike had to be ordered with one of the three solo option groups that were offered for bikes with each of the two styles of front forks. The Utility Solo Group was the cheapest option at $21.15 ($24.75 for springer models), thus the real base price for a stripper was a bit higher than Harley's figures indicate, and much higher if the rider ordered the usual touring accessories.

The 1949 Panheads were available in four standard colors and one optional color. Standard at no extra charge were Burgundy (described as a "rich, deep maroon color"), Peacock Blue ("a beautiful green-blue"), Brilliant Black, and Police Silver (for police bikes only). Optional for $8 extra was Metallic Congo Green ("a deep, attractive green accented by the metallic pigments"). Only Brilliant Black and Police Silver were carried over from 1948.

The Hydra-Glide Forks

The spring forks that had been carried over from the Knucklehead to the 1948 Panhead were as much of an anachronism as the iron heads that had been replaced. The spring forks still worked fairly well, especially when fitted with the optional hydraulic damper units, but they looked decidedly "prewar" and offered very limited suspension travel (about 2in).

The state of the art in suspension was changing as fast as any other aspect of motorcycle technology in the postwar world. The new wave in front suspension was clearly going to be oil-damped telescopic front forks, which had first been used in prewar Germany on the 1935 BMW R12 and R17 750cc flat twins. Triumph had switched to the new forks in 1946 on their 500cc Speed Twin, and BSA made the switch to telescopics in 1947 on their 500cc A7 twin. In late 1948, Vincent had taken a half-step by replacing their old Brampton spring forks with new "Girdraulic" forks, which were sprung girder forks with separate hydraulic damping units. With thousands of these new interlopers from England reaching these shores, H-D knew their Big Twin needed an immediate suspension and *image* upgrade to keep from being buried.

H-D chose to keep up by imitating its competitors, but, typically, the new forks were given Harley's unique style. Unlike the spindly-looking forks on the foreign bikes, the Hydra-Glide forks looked stout and muscular. The fork legs are spaced wide to clear the fat front tire and wide, valanced, Air Flow front fender. The upper tubes and whole top of the fork assembly are shrouded in black-painted, stamped-steel cover panels that give the front end the massive good looks that are still so much a part of Harley style. Chrome-plated or polished stainless steel covers were optional, but the bright covers looked so good that few bikes were ordered with the plain-Jane black covers. Most 1949–59 fork covers I have seen are made of stainless steel, but chrome-plated-steel covers are sometimes seen. It is unclear whether these covers were originally black painted and chromed later by their owners or whether chrome-plated covers were fitted for some years. The front cover panel has four horizontal stripes relief-embossed on each side of the headlight. This front panel style would be used through 1954. The name "Hydra-Glide" is stamped into the top front panel on 1950–59 models, but it is possible that some late 1949 fork panels were so stamped. The forks' tubes are chrome-moly steel, and the sliders are made of sand-cast aluminum that was heat treated and then painted black. Sand-cast sliders are a 1949-only item. Later sliders were die-cast and were available in painted or polished form.

Like most new features on H-D motorcycles, the forks went through several modifications in their first year. Early in the production run, vented caps with oil fittings were introduced, with a domed cap covering the oil fitting. Late in the production run, a new vented cap was introduced without the oil fitting. In this configuration, the forks were produced almost unchanged through 1959.

A new, friction-operated steering damper mounted atop the steering stem of the forks. Turning its large, starfish-shaped, stamped-steel knob increased or decreased (depending on the direction it was turned) the pressure on the unit's spider spring. This style of steering damper was used through 1959.

"Hydra-Glide sets a new standard in smooth-as-flying, road-hugging comfort. . . ." So said the October 1946 issue of *The Enthusiast*—and the ad copy was right. The new forks had 5-1/4in of fork travel (more than twice the travel of the spring forks) and velocity-sensitive valving that tamed bumpy roads much better than did the old spring forks. In addition, hydraulic stops in compression and rebound ensured that "it is impossible to make a metallic bottom on either the cushion or recoil strokes." Once again, the Big Twin was made more civilized.

Handlebars and Controls

Updated handlebars and control spirals were fitted to the new forks. Spring-fork handlebars had been rigidly attached to the top fork plate, so the handlebars lacked the capability for adjustment. The new Hydra-Glide bar was a one-piece, tubular bar clamped to the top fork bracket by a handlebar riser, thus the handlebars could be adjusted to accommodate rider preference. Standard handlebars were solid-mounted Speedster (short) bars. Longer Buckhorn bars were available as a no-cost option. Control coils from the spirals and wires from the horn and light switches are routed through the handlebars, out a slot in the bottom of the center section of the handlebar, through a phenolic resin housing between the handlebar and fork top cover, and through the fork top cover. The electrical wires attach to a terminal block behind the fork cowling, and the control coils are routed to the carburetor and circuit-breaker.

At the time the bike was ordered, rubber-mounted bars (really, rubber-mounted risers) were optional for an additional $18.75, in Speedster or Buckhorn style. They could also be ordered from the 1949 *Accessory Catalog* for $35. "Boy what a difference in riding ease and comfort the new chrome plated rubber mounted handlebars make," boasted the catalog. At the time new bikes were delivered, all rubber-mounted bars and risers were chrome plated and all solid-mounted bars and risers were painted black, but after delivery, an owner could install H-D or after-

Another 1949 Hydra-Glide, shown at the annual rally at Sturgis, South Dakota. This bike is a very nice restoration, and still has the correct Air Flow front fender with spot-welded fender brackets (1950 and later fenders have riveted-on front-fender brackets). The spot-welded fenders tended to crack, so most have been replaced in the forty-plus years since new. Not to criticize, only to point out to those who care about such things, this bike has a few non-stock items: the fork sliders should be painted black (polished sliders first became optional in 1950), the instrument panel should be painted the color of the tanks (chrome panels became optional in 1956), the safety bars should be painted black (chrome-plated guards were first offered in 1950), the muffler should be painted black (chrome-plated mufflers were first offered in 1950), the rear stand should be painted black, the exhaust pipes should be painted silver (chrome-plated S-pipes and Y-pipes were introduced in 1951), the Deluxe Solo Seat is the 1955 and later style, and the "Deluxe OHV" badges are correct only for 1952–54 Hydra-Glides. The front fender tip and side trim stripes are correct for 1949–56. This shiny machine is owned by Doug Rykel and has appeared in *Iron Horse* magazine.

market chrome-plated bars into the solid-mounted risers. Rubber-mounted bars were also optional for spring-fork models for an additional $23.

All solid-mounted risers and the early 1949 rubber-mounted risers used two separate riser "towers" with top clamps. Two screws cinch each top clamp over the handlebar, securing the bar to the riser tower, and one center bolt clamps each tower to the top fork bracket. Risers for rubber-mounted bars had a rubber bushing with a steel sleeve through the center of each riser and a rubber bushing under each riser tower.

In service, the rubber-mounted bars did help reduce vibration felt through the handlebars, but the steering feel

The rear fender of the 1949 springer Panheads was the same as the one on Hydra-Glide bikes. The new fender featured three stainless steel stripes on each side of the taillight and most have three vertical ribs on the flat of the chain recess (some early fenders did not have the ribs). The tombstone taillight is correct for 1948–54 Panheads. Standard taillight bodies and lens doors were painted black; chrome-plated taillights were optional. Correct taillight lenses feature the Harley-Davidson name curving along the top as shown. The rear bumper shown was a new option for 1949 and retailed for $6.95. The rear fender tip shown is probably an aftermarket item (the correct tip is the "bombardier" tip).

varied between "loose," "scary," and "dangerous," depending on how tightly the riser bolts were clamped and how worn the rubber bushings were. Harley fixed the problem by adding a chromed-steel riser link plate on all bikes with rubber-mounted bars produced on April 7, 1949, and after. Harley also issued *Shop Dope No. 287* to offer free parts and instructions to retrofit the new riser link on all earlier Hydra-Glides with rubber-mounted bars. They evidently saw the problem as serious because they urged "prompt action" in retrofitting the new parts.

This new plate links the two riser towers at the top, creating a nearly flex-free mounting between the bars and the top fork bracket, while still retaining the vibration-reducing qualities of rubber-mounted risers. The two mounting screws that had been used to secure each handlebar clamp were replaced (on the new bikes and with the parts in the retrofit kit) by two studs with acorn nuts, allowing tighter clamping of all parts.

Solid-mounted bars were not fitted with the new riser link.

The new-style spirals introduced in 1949 looked markedly different from the controls they replaced, and

No it's not a 1948. Harley-Davidson had learned from hard experience not to force change on its customers, so it offered the 1949 Panhead with spring forks. This FLP (the "P" is the designator for spring-fork Panheads) is ostensibly one of 486 that H-D records show were built that year. Important trivia: the "P" in FLP is not stamped into the serial number on all spring-fork 1949s, and when it is, it is stamped at the end of the serial-number string (e.g. FL1456P, not FLP1456). Harley recommended that motorcycles destined for use with sidecars or package trucks be purchased with the spring forks because the Hydra-Glide fork angle was too steep for good stability when such additional cargo was attached. The factory suggested that all solo machines be ordered with the Hydra-Glide fork because of its superior ride quality. Even so, H-D sold some sidecar bikes with Hydra-Glide forks and some solo machines with the spring forks. Note the "western" buckles that were standard on King Size saddlebags for 1948 and 1949 only. This special machine is owned by Dave Monahan.

THE HYDRA-GLIDE

the bars incorporated changes to accommodate the new spirals. The "twistable" part of the old spirals is a one-piece sleeve with a relatively short rubber grip and a relatively long (2-3/8in) chromed section, inboard of the grip. The sleeve slips over the handlebar end and is held on by a large end screw that threads into the end of the bar. The new spirals use a shorter twist sleeve that is held on by a chrome-plated retainer on the inboard end. Two screws secure the retainer to the handlebar. The grips are now 4-1/2in long and do not have end holes for the spiral end screws. This style of spirals was used through 1953.

The new handlebars lack the threaded ends for the end nuts, but have two threaded screw holes 180deg apart on each bar for the spiral-retainer screws. As before, the right spiral controls the throttle, and the left spiral controls the spark advance. The new style of controls was also used on the spring-fork Panheads for 1949, so a real P-model will have the new-style spirals. A fake one will simply have the 1948 forks, bars, and spirals in place of the 1949's Hydra-Glide forks and new-style bars. The new spirals were used on all Panheads from 1949 to 1953.

Head Lamp

Springer models for 1949 retained the old-style, 7in headlight with "pre-focused" 21/32-candlepower bulb and separate reflector and front lens.

Hydra-Glide models received a larger, more powerful headlight to go with the new forks. The new 8.19in bulb was a sealed-beam (called "sealed ray" by H-D) type with 32 candlepower for both low and high beam. Its low beam was "dipped to the right" and aimed lower than the high beam. Harley claimed that the new light put out 10–13 percent more light than the old. As *The Enthusiast* stated, "Better and more light for night riding is good." How true.

The new light is housed in a stamped housing that mounts to a headlight bracket mounted to the fork lower bracket. The bulb is held in the shell by a retaining ring that fastens to the housing with three screws, and the brightly-polished headlamp door covers the retaining ring and the edge of the light, tidying up the look of the headlamp unit. The headlight housing is painted black on standard bikes, but is chrome plated for bikes ordered with the Deluxe Solo Group or the Sport Solo Group. The chrome headlight could also be ordered separately for $2.30 extra. This style of headlight was used through 1959.

Frames for 1949

Two different frames were used for Hydra-Glide-equipped bikes during the 1949 model year. Both frames were based on the wishbone frame that had been introduced in 1948. The electric horn, which had been mounted on the spring forks, was moved to the front of the

"Van," presumably the original owner of this machine, went all out in decorating his bike. It has the correct 1949–52 style Deluxe Buddy Seat (red rosettes under the nickel stars), the optional seat rail that was new for 1949, and the King Size saddlebags. It is also fitted with many other aftermarket and accessory catalog items, including a fender rail, chrome shifter ball, chrome instrument cover, chrome fork-spring covers, chrome safety bars (these were not available on new machines until 1950), and too many other items to list.

frame between the two downtubes on Hydra-Glide-equipped bikes. On early-1949 frames, square-cornered brackets were welded to the backs of the downtubes. On later-1949 frames, the downtubes were slightly flattened on the back side where the horn mounts were welded. Spring-fork bikes appear to have been fitted with leftover 1948 frames or new-production 1948-style frames (these frames lack the new horn-mount blocks and the downtubes are not flattened for these blocks). The horn is the same horn that had been used on the spring-fork models. It was painted black.

In the interest of bearing longevity and obtaining "effortless ease of handling," H-D engineers used tapered Timken roller bearings in the steering head for 1949. Each bearing used fifteen 0.383in long Timken rollers instead of the seventeen ball bearings used top and bottom in 1948.

Air Flow Fenders

All-new front and rear fenders were fitted to 1949 Hydra-Glide models. Spring-fork bikes were fitted with the old-style front fender and the new-style rear fender.

The new front fender was stamped from a single sheet of 20-gauge steel and had deep, streamlined skirts, though not nearly as deep as those on the Indian motorcycles. H-D named the new-style fenders Air Flow.

The handsome new front fender was mounted to the fork sliders by streamlined brackets spot-welded to the fender skirt on each side. Air Flow front fenders were a hit with riders, both for the styling and for the excellent protection it offered. All was not perfect however. The fenders often cracked at the spot welds, so new fenders were released in late 1949 or early 1950 with riveted-on brackets. Many restored 1949 Hydra-Glides have the later, riveted brackets because their original fenders failed in use and were replaced (under warranty or later by the owner) with the riveted fenders.

Air Flow front fenders were fitted with a stainless steel tip that wraps around the sides of the fender, stretching back almost to the fork sliders. The design on the new fender tip continues the lines of the ribbed tire tread, adding a distinct, modern look to the fender. This style of tip was standard on all Hydra-Glides through 1956. A thin, stainless steel trim stripe at the fender's rear edge was standard on all Hydra-Glides through 1957. The front fender light that had been optional on spring-fork Pans was not offered for the Air Flow fenders, although it could still be ordered on spring-fork machines.

In late 1949, an accessory "roller" chrome front bumper was offered. This assembly consists of a tapered-cylinder bumper spanning two bumper rods that mount to the fender with two cylindrical lugs apiece. This bumper was a $5.75 option that really dressed up the fender and offered a modest amount of protection. No other front-fender trim was offered on new Hydra-Glides for 1949. Spring-fork-equipped Panheads could be ordered with the optional fender tip and fender light.

The rear fender was stamped in two pieces (front and rear) that were joined together by a hinge that allowed the rear portion of the fender to be pivoted upward during tire changes. The tombstone-style taillight was carried over from the old-style rear fender, except that the integral license-plate bracket was riveted on, rather than attached by screws. The taillight body was painted black on standard models but a chrome-plated taillight was available for the bargain price of 95¢, or when the Deluxe Solo Group or Sport Solo Group was ordered.

The most distinctive features of the new rear fender are the three stainless steel "sergeant stripes" that wrap around from the edge of the wheel well to the taillight and the three vertical ribs stamped into the chain recess. Some early-1949 rear fenders lack the ribs on the chain recess. The rear fender with sergeant stripes and the three ribs were fitted on 1949 and 1950 Panheads only.

To further dress up the rear fender, a chrome fender tip (the same one that had been offered in 1948) and a chrome rear bumper were offered. The Deluxe Solo Group and Sport Solo Group included the chrome rear

Even the front wheel and fender was given the chrome treatment. Note the chrome wheel rings, pivot cover, fender rails, turn signals, and fender light.

fender tip, but it was also available separately for $2.35. The bumper was available in the Deluxe Solo Group, or separately for $6.95.

New Front Brake

Harley-Davidson front brakes had always been so weak as to border on useless. For 1949, H-D engineers made an attempt at improving the situation by introducing a larger and more powerful front brake for the Hydra-Glide. (Spring-fork models made do with the old front brake.)

The Hydra-Glide front brake was an all-new design with an 8in drum (the old drums were 7-1/4in) and an internal brake actuating lever (the old brakes had an external actuating lever). Its cast-iron drum is painted black and attaches to the star-shaped wheel hub with five screws (front and rear wheels are still interchangeable). The

The 1947–50 tank emblems were penned by famed designer Brooks Stevens. Note that both the circle at the front and the lettering is painted red (many reproduction emblems have black-painted letters). Note also the plumber-nut manifold that is used on all Panheads through 1954. The manifold on this machine is the cad-plated, cast-iron manifold that was introduced in mid year (earlier manifolds had been polished, cad-plated steel). Note also the clutch-pedal pivot cover. This cover was made of stainless steel for 1949 only. Although it is difficult to see in this photo, a letter "P" is stamped lightly at the end of the serial number string in a larger letter size, as it is on most other P-models. Also of interest, the frame lacks the horn-mount blocks fitted to all 1949 Hydra-Glide frames, and the tubes are not flattened for these blocks as they were on later 1949 Hydra-Glide frames. It appears that H-D used leftover 1948 frames for this and other 1949 spring-fork Big Twins.

backing plate is cast aluminum and attaches to the left fork leg. The brake backing plate is unpolished on 1949 machines. The new 1/8in brake cable (the old cable was 5/64in) is housed in a flexible coil from the left hand lever to the back side of the lower steering stem. The cable is then housed in a steel tube that carries it along the left side of the fender to where the tube attaches to a boss on the top edge of the brake backing plate. This front brake assembly was used almost without change through the 1965 model year.

Harley-Davidson claimed the new brake had 34 percent more braking surface than the old brake. Even so, it still feels anemic compared to the rear brake and—despite Harley's claims of "instant stopping power"—the front brake is only marginally adequate for a 600lb motorcycle. To be fair, most front brakes of the era weren't much better. The one exception was the powerful, two-sided drum brake used on the Vincents.

Motor Updates

Harley-Davidson concentrated on updating the chassis for 1949, but a few minor changes were made to the powerplant to correct faults and complement the new running gear. Most significant was the addition of an oil-supply spigot that cured forever the problem 1948 Panheads had with oil-starved intake valve stems. The spigot picked up oil from the rocker bearing and dripped it on the intake-valve spring, from which it splashed on the valve stem to reduce valve-guide wear and keep the valve from sticking.

The appearance of the cylinders was improved with a new silver-silicone paint finish that made them look like they were cast of aluminum alloy. "Organo-silicon oxide polymers" in this special paint gave it the ability to resist heat and rust formation far better than the high-temperature paints previously used. All Panhead cylinders from 1949 through 1965 were painted silver-silicone.

To improve everyday rideability, updated carburetors and new breaker points made by H-D were fitted. The 1949 61ci bikes were fitted with the Linkert M-36 carburetor with a 1-1/8in venturi. Early 1949 74s were also fitted with the M-36, but later 1949–early-1950 74ci bikes were fitted with the M-45 carburetor with a 1-5/16in venturi. During the 1949 production run, the material used to make the intake manifold was changed to cast iron (it had been made of steel tubing), but the finish remained as cadmium plated.

Exhaust Pipes and Mufflers

All exhaust pipes on the 1949 Big Twins were coated with the same silver-silicone paint used on the cylinders, and the mufflers were painted in a black-silicone paint. The new paint proved far more resistant to rust than the previous high-temperature black paint used on the pipes and mufflers for 1948 and earlier twins.

Many owners opted for the chrome pipe covers to dress up the header pipes (available for $3.85 or as part of the Deluxe Solo and Sport Solo groups) and the stainless steel muffler cover (available for $5.75 or as part of the Deluxe Solo and Sport Solo groups). Chrome exhaust pipes and mufflers are sometimes seen on restorations of 1949 bikes but are incorrect. The standard, single-exhaust header pipes were painted in silver-silicone through 1965. The S-pipe and Y-pipe were painted silver-silicone for 1949–50, but were chrome plated for 1951 and after.

The Year of Stainless Steel

The 1949 Panhead is considered by many Harley enthusiasts to be the most handsome bike Milwaukee ever built. Mostly this is because of its classic form, but the impression is enhanced by the many brightly polished parts fitted to even the base model. In many ways, 1949 could be called the year of stainless steel.

For 1949, even the standard Utility Solo Group bikes were fitted with an unusual assortment of chromed and stainless steel parts, including a stainless generator end cover, a chromed generator-relay cover, and a stainless steel ignition-timer cover. These parts had been painted on 1948 and would again be painted on 1950 Utility models.

Other parts that had been chrome-plated on base-model machines in 1948 were made of polished stainless steel for 1949. Most prominent among these are the rocker covers and the air-cleaner cover. Stainless rocker covers would be standard through 1956, and stainless air-cleaner covers would be standard through 1965.

Still other parts that had been optional in chrome-plated form for 1948 were made of stainless steel for 1949 only. These include the primary-chain inspection plate, the clutch-inspection plate, and the foot-lever bearing cover, all of which were painted on the base-model bikes. These parts were changed back to chrome-plated on the 1950 option groups.

Finally, the optional muffler cover was made of stainless steel. As far as I have been able to determine, this is a 1949-only part because no optional muffler cover was listed on the H-D order blanks for 1948 that I have seen (though I have seen stainless steel covers on original 1948 Panheads) and because a new muffler style was introduced in 1950.

Optional Radio Generator

As two-way radios became more common on police bikes, the old Model 32E2R radio generator was found to be inadequate. It could usually supply enough current, but it often would overheat in the process, burning out the armature. For 1949, H-D engineers installed the new Model 48 generator. This new generator was capable of 20amp output (versus 15amp for the older radio generator) and was fitted with an integral cooling fan attached to the armature shaft. A voltage regulator was fitted to a special bracket on the left side of the bike.

Accessories

The most popular accessories for 1949 were basically the same as they had been in previous years: saddlebags, windshield, front spotlights, parking lamps, Deluxe Solo or Deluxe Buddy seat, rear safety guard, and chrome bits—but new models of many of these familiar accessories were introduced.

The optional King Size saddlebags were the same as for 1948, and cost $37.50 when ordered separately. They were also included in the Deluxe Solo Group.

The optional windshield was redesigned to wrap around the Hydra-Glide forks. The new windshield attached to the side of the fork (rather than to the handlebars), had plexiglass lower panels (rather than vinyl), and sold for $17.75. An adjustable panel over the headlight could be raised or lowered to adjust air flow to the rider. All panels were clear plexiglass through 1955, but blue or red lower panels were offered for 1956 and later models.

New front spotlight mounts were designed for the Hydra-Glide front end. The individual lamps are the same as for 1948, but the lights mount to separate brackets attached to the sides of the fork (rather than to a light bar). Spotlights could be ordered for $17. The lamps were used through 1961, but the new mounts were used only through 1959.

The Deluxe Solo Seat was the same style of seat that had been used in 1948, and was available for $11 (in place of the standard saddle). It was also included as part of the Deluxe Solo and Sport Solo groups. The Deluxe Buddy Seat for 1949 was the same as the 1948 version, except that the plastic rosettes were red (instead of yellow) and a new one-piece chrome hand rail was optional. The buddy seat could be ordered for $16 (also in place of the standard saddle).

The rear safety guard was the same as used on the 1948 Panhead and was offered only painted black (again, chrome-plated rear safety guards were first offered on new bikes in 1950).

As a replacement for the front-fender light on the spring-fork models, new bullet-shaped front parking lamps were introduced. These lights were chrome-plated and mounted to the sides of the fork, looking much like a turn signal. They had a clear lens and sold for $4.75 per pair (they were also included in the Deluxe Solo and Sport Solo groups). Rear parking lamps were also offered, and these rear lights were the same as the front, except that they had red lenses. They sold for $5.50 a pair.

1949 Production

Harley had another great sales year in 1949, selling a total of 12,685 Panheads (239 fewer than in 1948). As

Even the spring-fork bars used the same new-style spirals that the Hydra-Glide bars used. These spirals have a longer grip than the 1948 spirals and are held to the bar by the chrome retaining ring inboard of the grip (the old spirals had been held on by an end nut that threaded into the end of the handlebar); The retaining ring is fastened to the bar by two screws. The left spiral is used to manually advance and retard the ignition timing. The upper switch is the horn button; the other switch is the head-light dimmer. Note the spiffy hood for that mirror and green grips, non-stock items that show the range of accessories available to the Panhead rider.

This is the correct speedometer for all Panheads from 1948–52. The recessed center panel was painted bluish gray and enclosed the odometer and tripmeter. Odometer numerals are black on a white background; trip meter numerals are black for miles and red for tenths, both on a white background. Around the perimeter of the center panel are hash marks at 2mph intervals, with thicker hash marks at the tens. The hash marks are painted cream-ivory. The speedo's raised outer ring is painted greenish gray and serves as the background for the speed numerals, which indicate 10–120mph in tens and are painted cream-ivory on the underside of the glass. The H-D bar and shield is painted on the underside of the glass in white, toward the rear. The pointer is red, and the bezel is chrome plated. Chrome-plated instrument panels were not offered in 1949.

expected, Hydra-Glide models dominated sales. The best selling model was the Hydra-Glide FL, at 8,014 sold. Next best was the Hydra-Glide EL, at 3,419 sold. Despite Harley's recommendation against using the Hydra-Glide motorcycles with a sidecar, 177 ES and 490 FS Hydra-Glide sidecar models were sold. A total of 585 other buyers, apparently, opted against the Hydra-Glide front end, resulting in sales of ninety-nine ELP and 486 FLP spring-fork Panheads.

In my opinion, these production figures for sidecar- and spring-fork-equipped machines must be viewed as highly suspect. Harley-Davidson officially peddled the Models EP and FP with spring forks for use on *all* sidecar rigs—yet not one of these models is listed as having been sold! Meanwhile, the sales list includes 667 Models ES and FS Hydra-Glide sidecar bikes—which H-D actively discouraged its customers from buying—and 585 Models ELP and FLP solo springer bikes—which many enthusiasts and dealers insist were never offered for sale. Would so many customers really ignore H-D's recommendations, and would the factory really comply if the customers did? My answer to both questions: I don't think so.

So how do I explain it? My best guess is that the sales figures for the springer models actually represent a composite of the relatively large number of sidecar-equipment EPS and FPS bikes and whatever small number of ELP and FLP solo bikes were actually built, and that the sales figures for the sidecar bikes actually represent a composite of the relatively large number of EPS and FPS Springers and the relatively small number of ESs and FS Hydra-Glides. Such duplication in H-D's official figures is commonplace, especially for wartime figures.

Model Year 1950

For such a fondly remembered decade, the 1950s got off to a really rocky start. By midway through 1950, North Korea invades South Korea, and America is embroiled in another war.

Atomic anxiety becomes the leading cause of heatburn. President Harry Truman directs the Atomic Energy Commission to develop the H-bomb with all haste because of fears that Russia already possesses the bomb. A short while later, Russia officially confirms Truman's fears, and the U.S. government begins distributing a pamphlet titled *You Can Survive*, which includes do-it-yourself plans for a backyard bomb shelter. Not long after, realtors begin marketing rural properties as "out beyond atom bombs."

Senator Joseph McCarthy starts an anti-Communist witch hunt by accusing the State Department of harboring known Commies. Accusations of Communist ties become the second leading cause of heartburn and blacklisting begins. Universities, broadcasting companies, and government agencies make loyalty oaths a condition of employment. The word "McCarthyism" enters the American lexicon.

On a more positive note, the U.S. Army integrates white and black troops, setting the opposite course of the government of South Africa, which is in the throes of race riots resulting from its recently-enacted policy of Apartheid.

Smokey the Bear makes his debut. Charles Schulz's *Peanuts* comic strip is syndicated. Sugar Pops and Minute Rice make bland food faster and more convenient than ever before. And the terminally trendy spend their free time learning to mambo and square dance. Things are looking better already!

The economy begins a turn for the better that foretells good times for all in the coming decade. Harley launches their new models with high hopes of having their best year ever.

1950 Hydra-Glides

For 1950, two basic versions of the Panhead were offered in each displacement size, the 61ci E and EL and 74ci F and FL. In addition, sidecar gearing could be ordered on the E and F, making the ES and FS models. All were fitted with Hydra-Glide forks. Base-model 61s carried a retail price of $735, and the 74s carried a retail price of $750. Both prices were unchanged from 1949. The 1950 Panheads were available in four standard colors and four optional colors. Standard at no extra charge were Brilliant Black, Ruby Red, Riviera Blue, and Police Silver (for police bikes only). Optional for $10 extra were Metallic Green, Flight Red, Azure Blue, and White.

Hydra-Glides for 1950 were little changed from the 1949 models. Returning on the 1950 model were the streamlined tank emblem and sergeant stripes on the rear fender, but there are many small changes that distinguish the 1950 Hydra-Glide from the 1949 model.

Mellow-Tone Muffler

When viewed from the right, the most apparent difference between the 1949 and 1950 Panheads is the new muffler. Gone was the old "rocket-fin" muffler, replaced by a new tubular muffler that tapered to a straight pipe at each end. Harley-Davidson named it the "Mellow-Tone" muffler after its deeper, more mellow exhaust note. Like the 1949 muffler, this muffler was painted silicone-black on standard bikes. Unlike the 1949 muffler, this muffler was available in a chrome-plated finish, for $3.50 extra, or as part of the Deluxe Solo and Sport Solo groups.

Adjustable-Trail Forks

Several important changes were made to the front end. Spring forks were no longer offered for 1950 because new, adjustable-trail Hydra-Glide forks were offered (for $5 extra) that allowed the rake angle to be increased for more stable handling with sidecar and package-truck motorcycles. Externally, there were few clues to distinguish the adjustable forks from the fixed-rake Hydra-Glide forks. The easiest way to spot adjustable forks is to look at the top cover of the forks, by the handlebar risers. If two large, chrome plugs stick up above the cover outboard of the risers, the fork is the fixed-rake model. If the top cover is smooth, without showing the 6 plugs, the fork is most likely the adjustable-rake model (fixed-rake 1958 and 1959 Servi-car forks are also smooth on top and may have been retrofitted to some Panheads).

Adjustability was built into the adjustable fork's lower fork bracket. When two bolts in the lower bracket are loosened, the position of the bracket can be moved in relation to the steering stem. Two positions are possible: solo and raked sidecar.

The fork sliders for 1950 and later forks were die cast for a smoother appearance, and were not painted. For an

A deluxe sidecar attached to the 1949 Hydra-Glide owned by Walt and Joanne Fitzgeralds of Holt, Missouri. As the sticker on the front of the chair implies, Walt and Joanne take their sidecar rig all around, even up to Pike's Peak. Walt says the bike has plenty of power to haul the couple, the chair, and a trailer they tow.

State of the Art, 1949
Harley-Davidson FL vs. Vincent-HRD Series C Black Shadow

Once again in 1949, clocks seemed to be synchronized in Milwaukee and Stevenage, as both Harley-Davidson and Vincent-HRD gave their big twins new suspenders. (In the case of the new Hydra-Glide, I should really say "suspender," no matter how odd it sounds, because that model was left with only the sprung seat for rear suspension. I must also admit that, technically, the Series C Vincents had been formally introduced in mid-1948, but the new forks and rear hydraulic dampers had been only sporadically available until well into 1949.)

When we last compared, each machine was being developed along different lines. The last round of updates gave the Vincent even more power, making it the ultimate choice of speed freaks, whereas the Harley gained a little power and a lot of civility, making it the ultimate touring machine. The changes for 1949 did little to change the course of either machine's development, but let's compare them anyway.

Harley's new Hydra-Glide forks gave the FL a smoother ride, a modern and robust look, and state-of-the-art front suspension technology for the day. Vincent's new Girdraulic forks gave the Black Shadow a controlled, compliant ride, but they were just a late-1940s update of 1920s technology (they were on a technical par with the hydaulically damped spring forks that had become optional on the Harley in 1946) and they upset the gracefully balanced appearance of an otherwise pleasing machine. In combination with the new hydraulic dampers for the sprung rear end, however, the Girdraulic forks gave the Vincent the best suspension in motorcycling and opened another performance gap that H-D would not close until 1958.

As we shall see (and see again in our next installment), what's good for the motorcyclist is not always good for the motorcycle company. Vincent-HRD continued blissfully along their lonely path of engineering-excellence-over-all-other-considerations until a flood of red ink sent the company into receivership in August of 1949, whereas H-D continued to refine their big FL until all their early competitors went out of business.

Rollie Free's 1948 record-shattering run and the photo of Free blasting over the salt flats while lying prone on the rear fender with feet stretched out behind gave Vincent-HRD the kind of publicity that just can't be bought when the photo was reprinted in both motoring magazines and mainstream publications such as Life. The fortunate result for Harley was that many enthusiasts who had been unfamiliar with the British marque before its new-found fame assumed that HRD somehow stood for Harley-Davidson. No one can know for sure how many (if any) eager buyers were sold new Panheads after walking into H-D dealerships and asking after a new Black Shadow, but the potential for confusion worried Vincent-HRD enough that they dropped the HRD portion of their name in 1949.

---

extra $3.50 at the time of order, the factory would polish the sliders and brake backing plate. The polished sliders and backing plate were also included in the Deluxe Solo and Sport Solo groups.

The 1949 fenders with spot-welded brackets had proved so troublesome that the brackets were riveted on (with five rivets on each side) for 1950 and later front fenders. The new fenders proved better able to resist cracking under the V-twin's formidable vibration.

Sometime during the 1949 or 1950 production run (I could find no documentation of exactly when), the factory began stamping the name "Hydra-Glide" in the angled V-panel at the top end of the front fork panel. This new panel with Hydra-Glide and the four horizontal stripes on each side of the headlight was used through 1954.

Internally, the 1950 forks were updated with six baffle plates and a new breather valve. These updates prevented air from being trapped in the forks and the baffle plates prevented oil from being pumped out the breather.

New Oil Filter

For obvious reasons, oil filters had been a popular option since their introduction in 1948. The early oil filters attached directly to the oil-return fitting on the oil tank. In 1950, a revised oil filter was introduced that mounted the chrome-plated filter away from the oil tank to isolate it from vibration. The new filter is supported by a mounting arm to the frame and is connected to the oil tank by a short metal return tube. A mounting stud in the cap of the new filter attaches to the mounting arm. According to *Shop Dope No. 305* (issued on April 4, 1950), a conversion kit was offered to convert the earlier oil-tank-mounted filter to the new frame-mounted filter. The kit was priced at $1.50.

New Cylinder Heads and Valve Guides

New cylinder-head castings were introduced in 1950 with larger intake ports that gave the 1950 Hydra-Glides 10 percent more "zoom and steam," according to *The Enthusiast* of September 1949. Gone was the plugged hole that was near each exhaust port on the 1948–49 heads. Also, new numbers—"119 50 FRONT" or "119 501 REAR"—were cast in relief into the underside of the head between the pushrod holes. These castings were used through 1954.

Bronze exhaust-valve guides (replacing steel guides) were introduced on the new head castings and were fitted to all 1950 and later motors built through January 1957.

New Carburetors

Feeding the new cylinder heads on 1950 models were recalibrated versions of the M-36 (61s) and M-45 (74s) carburetors used in 1949. Updates to these carburetors included a fixed jet, "limited" adjustability of the high-speed needle, and a larger accelerating well. The result was better throttle response and the ability to quickly fine-tune the carburetor. These carburetors worked so well that H-D offered a program to update the earlier carburetors. If the earlier carburetors were returned to H-D by a dealer along with a conversion fee of $5, H-D would return an M-36A or M-61 carburetor (for M-36 carbs that were returned) or an M-45A or M-74 carburetor (for M-45 carbs that were returned).

About mid-year, the 61s were fitted with the new M-61 carburetor with a 1-1/8in venturi. The M-61 carburetor was used on the 61s through 1952 and on FLE motors for 1953-54. Late in 1950, the 74s were fitted with the M-74 carburetor with 1-5/16in venturi, and this carburetor was standard until it was superseded by the M-74B carburetor during the 1951 season.

Detail Changes

For restorers and others interested in such minutia, the gear-cover screws were changed to Phillips-head type for 1950 and 1951. They were still cadmium plated, however. Beginning in 1950 and continuing through mid-1953, straight-slot and Phillips-head screws were used interchangeably during production to fasten the tappet-blocks to the right crank case (only straight-slot screws had been used in 1948 and 1949). For all 1950–64 Panheads, the screws that fasten the outer primary cover to the inner cover are Parkerized filister-head screws with Phillips slots (they had been straight-slot, filister-head screws).

Another subtle change was made to the outer primary cover, to the mounting area for the primary-chain inspection cover. The mounting screws for the inspection cover were drilled at 6 o'clock and at 12 o'clock (they had been at 3 o'clock and 9 o'clock on 1949 and earlier covers). The standard chain and clutch inspection covers were still painted black to match the finish of the outer primary cover, but the optional inspection covers were now chrome-plated steel, rather than polished stainless steel. Stainless steel was also discontinued for the generator end cover. Panhead generator end covers were all painted black for 1950–54.

Even more subtle, the seam style on the Deluxe Solo Seat were new for 1950. The cut ends of the leather were no longer visible where the leather seat cover is stitched to the leather piece that was riveted to the seat pan because the edge of the seat cover wrapped around and underneath the cut end of the bottom leather, and the stitching went through all three layers of leather. The Deluxe Solo Seat was a very popular option and cost an additional $7.50 at the time of order.

The 1950 front safety guard was the same as the 1948–49 type, except that for the first time it was offered in chrome-plated finish from the factory on a new Panhead. The plated guard was available at the time of order for an additional $3.60 or as part of the Deluxe Solo and Sport Solo groups. Standard front safety guards were painted black.

The larger-diameter (1/8in) inner front-brake cable introduced in 1949 often rubbed inside the 5/16in upper cable tube, so a new upper tube of 3/8in diameter was

A gorgeous 1950 Hydra-Glide owned by D.R. Schwantz. This beauty was restored by Elmer Ehnes. Note the new-style Mellow-Tone muffler, which was used through 1951, and the unpainted fork sliders. Standard mufflers were painted black and had Parkerized hangers. Optional mufflers were chrome plated and had stainless steel hangers. This is a beautiful restoration, but a few non-stock items are worth pointing out (sorry, Elmer): the Deluxe Solo Seat shown is the 1955 and later style, the exhaust pipes are chromed when they should be silver painted, D-rings are fitted to the rocker covers (these weren't introduced until 1951), the rocker covers should be secured by twelve round-head Phillips screws each (hex-head screws were first used to fasten the rocker covers in 1950, but only three were used per head in place of three of the round-head screws) and whitewall tires are fitted (H-D didn't offer whitewalls on new bikes until 1958). Even so, I'd be proud to call it my own!

introduced in 1950. The adjusting screw on the new cable was increased to 5/16in.

Finally, the gas lines were given rubber mounts at the gas tank and carburetor ends to reduce the chance of the gas line developing a crack from vibration.

New Saddlebags

The black King Size leather saddlebags for 1950 were the same as the 1948–49 bags except that the piping was available in red or white (instead of orange; the white piping was a running change made during the 1950 production year) and the buckles were plain-style (buckle frames are uniform in thickness on all edges, unlike the oblong "western" buckles used on previous bags). Another running change was the addition of fringed King Size saddlebags with white leather fringe around the bottom edge of the cover and side.

New, smaller bags were introduced during the 1950 model year for the 45ci models, but they were also available for installation on the Big Twins. The Streamliner saddlebags were a more compact bag with orange plastic piping and a complex pattern of decoration, including nickel dots on the top of the cover, three Z-shaped designs of ten nickel dots each on the side of the cover, a single row of nickel dots along the lower edge of the sides of the bag, three leather straps with nickel buckles, and an oval nickel piece to each side of the center buckle. Nickel dots are arranged around the nickel ovals and in three single rows sweeping down and back from the ovals. This bag was offered in 1950 and 1951 (in 1952, the color of the piping was changed to red).

1950 Production

For 1950, H-D sold 10,265 Panheads: 7,407 FL, 544 FS, 2,046 EL, and 268 ES. The sales lead for the 74 model over the 61 model was growing wider. This should have surprised no one, as the price difference between the two models had shrunk to just $15.

Panhead sales were down by more than 20 percent compared to 1949, and many factors contributed to the decline. Indian had introduced a new Chief with hydraulic forks and a motor that was stroked to 80ci, and Indian dealers' floors were well stocked with the Norton, Matchless, Royal Enfield, Vincent, and other popular British bikes distributed in America by the Indian Sales Corporation. Triumph was experiencing such great success with its larger, U.S.-targeted models that it was gearing up to open an East Coast warehouse and distribution center to augment the West Coast-based Johnson Motors. As a final stroke of bad luck, some of H-D's best customers had been recalled to service and sent off to the Korean War.

The most important *immediate* reason for the decline, however, was that pent-up demand from the war and postwar years had finally been satisfied. All the *traditional* H-D customers who could afford one, had replaced their earlier machines. The most important reason for the long-term decline to come was that H-D was unable to, or didn't want to, serve the needs of the only segments of the motorcycle market that were experiencing rapid growth—the so-called outlaw riders and sport riders.

Uniformed riding clubs and fully dressed bikes were going the way of the dinosaurs while the "chopper" and "biker" cults were rapidly growing. Harley actively discouraged their dealers from serving these new rebels, so a lively underground of unfranchised shops and aftermarket parts manufacturers began to grow. Harley's future was being shaped even though they chose not to participate.

Second, H-D really wasn't adapting their Big Twin to make it appeal to customers for more refined or sporting machines, as Triumph and the other foreign makers were doing. Harley *had* made the Panhead a more civilized machine, but they had not yet gone far enough. So, despite Harley's best marketing efforts, sales would continue to decline until the next big change was made (the high-performance FLH of 1955). Problem was, H-D took so long to get there that even that next stage was only far enough to get some of their traditional clientele to upgrade to the new model—not nearly enough to win new converts. So it went for more than another decade.

But change was in the wind. In the final days of 1950, the last of the company founders, Arthur Davidson (secretary and general sales manager), and his wife were killed in an automobile accident. The second generation of Harleys and Davidsons now controlled all top management positions.

Model Year 1951

As the 1951 models begin rolling off the production line, the war in Korea escalates dramatically. Chinese troops pour across the Yalu River and push the United Nations forces back, taking the South Korean capital of Seoul for the second time. General Douglas MacArthur rallies the UN forces to push the Communists back to the Yalu River and argues for crossing the Yalu into China. Truman disagrees and relieves MacArthur of his command. The general returns to a ticker-tape parade in New York City and delivers his "Old soldiers never die; they just fade away" speech. The draft age is lowered to eighteen, and more than 250,000 U.S. troops are sent to Korea. Cease-fire talks begin at Panmunjon. The first of many cease-fires begins and quickly ends.

The 1949 and 1950 rear fender was fitted with the "sergeant" stripes on each side of the taillight. Note that the chain recess at the front of the fender is cutaway at its rear edge. This is not the correct fender for a 1950 Panhead (the cutaway chain recess was introduced in 1952). The correct fender would have an intact chain recess with three vertical ribs stamped into the metal.

D.R. Schwantz's 1950 EL Panhead. The cutaway in the chain recess is more noticeable in this photograph. This bike is fitted with several optional items apparent in this view: front and rear safety guards, chrome primary-chain and clutch inspection covers, polished front-brake backing plate, and rubber-mounted bars with the center link for the handlebar riser (chrome-plated bars are rubber mounted; black bars are solid mounted). The riser link was added in mid-1949 to reinforce the rubber-mounted bars (it was not used on solid-mounted bars).

Back home, Jack LaLanne spawns a whole new industry by bringing the cult of physical fitness to the television screen. The first commercial color-TV broadcast is made. Humphrey Bogart and Katherine Hepburne burn up the silver screen in *The African Queen*. The best-seller *Washington Confidential* stirs the Communist-under-every-rock hysteria with statements such as "When you find an intellectual, you will probably find a Red." Holden Caulfield, in J.D. Salinger's *Catcher in the Rye*, raises adolescent angst to an art form at the same time as William F. Buckley does the same for smarminess, with his influential *God and Man at Yale*. Willie Mays and Mickey Mantle make their Big League debuts, and Joe DiMaggio retires.

Despite the war, increasing mobilization of military might, and calls for wage and price freezes, the economy grows by 15 percent while inflation and unemployment drop to 0.7 percent and 3.3 percent, respectively.

In a surprise move, Triumph began to set up a new distribution facility in 1950 in the town of Towson, Maryland, a suburb of Baltimore. No longer would Johnson Motors of Los Angeles, California, be the sole Triumph distributor in the U.S. Johnson's territory was split, the eastern states now being serviced by the new Triumph Corporation—nicknamed TriCor. The new facility is fully ready for business by January 1951 and Triumph sales immediately skyrocket. During 1951, sales of Triumph motorcycles nearly triple, from about 1,000 machines to over 2,700—and the other imports experience similar sales growth.

That is why, in June 1951, The Motor Company felt justified in petitioning the U.S. Tariff Commission for relief from what they saw as unfair foreign competition. The hearings that followed resulted in embarrassment and failure for The Motor Company when the Tariff Commission ruled against Harley-Davidson in 1952.

This sparkling 1950 Hydra-Glide is owned by Gary Nelson. This machine is fairly stock, but it does show a few incorrect bits, including the 1954–64 Jubilee horn. Shown is the correct Deluxe Buddy Seat and King Size saddlebags with plain-style buckles (the one nit I might pick about these accessories is that the piping on the bags should be red for 1950–53 bags; orange piping was used for 1948–49).

1951 Hydra-Glides

For 1951, only the high-compression EL and FL were listed on the H-D order blanks. Sidecar gearing could be ordered on the EL and FL, making the ELS and FLS models. (Note: the low-compression 51E and 51F models are listed in the Model Descriptions section of *The Legend Begins*. Either *Legend* is is in error, or these low-compression machines were special-order or export-only items.) All were fitted with Hydra-Glide forks.

Compensating, perhaps, for the lack of a price increase the previous year, prices for 1951 jump by 20 percent to $885 (EL) and $900 (FL).

Four standard and four optional colors were offered for 1951. Standard at no extra charge were Brilliant Black, Persian Red, Rio Blue, and Police Silver (for police bikes only). Optional for $10 extra were Metallic Green, Metallic Blue, and White. Lots of small changes were made for 1951, both inside and out. The most prominent of these was the new, two-piece gas-tank emblems. Gone was the Brooks Stevens–designed emblem that was used from 1947–50, replaced by a chrome-plated-brass emblem that featured the H-D name in script with a separate underline bar, each piece fastened to the tank by three Phillips-head, countersunk screws. This two-piece emblem is used through 1953, and the top, script portion was also retained for 1954 (the underline bar was deleted).

Chrome-plated front-fender emblems with the name "Hydra-Glide" were offered as a $1.50 option for 1951. This nameplate was optional for 1951–54.

Rear fender trim was also changed. The three sergeant stripes astride the taillight were replaced by a single, wider stainless stripe on each side of the taillight that continues the line started by the side trim pieces that flow back from the front-fender tip. This rear fender was also a one-year-only item, having both the three vertical channels pressed into the flat of the chain recess and the holes for mounting the new single-stripe trim pieces.

Chrome plating was used on the S and Y exhaust pipes for the first time (rather than silver paint). Plated S- and Y-pipes are correct from 1951 on. The front and rear header pipes, however, were still painted with the aluminized silver-silicone paint.

The adjustable-rake forks received a minor change for 1951. The two rake-adjustment bolts on the lower fork triple tree used in 1950 were replaced by a single longer bolt and nut, simplifying adjustment.

The long rod from the shifter lever to the transmission was updated with the addition of a rod end at the transmission end (the old rod had a right-angle bend that engaged the transmission shifter lever). This rod end provided more positive shifting and a more durable connection than did the hooked end.

A minor change to the frame was introduced in mid-1951. The horn-mount blocks were given rounded edges (rather than square edges). This frame was used only for 1951 (the frame for 1952 still had the rounded blocks, but had a new-style tool-box mount).

Early Hydra-Glide handlebars have a large slot on the bottom of the tube's center. The wires and control coils route through the handlebar tube and exit through the center slot. The bars often crack at this point—especially on the solid-mounted bars because solid bars are exposed to greater vibration and are not equipped with the top riser link to reinforce the riser. Cracking would remain a problem until 1951, when new bars were introduced with a thick center sleeve reinforcement. The optional rubber-mounted bars are chrome-plated and the standard solid-mounted bars are black-painted. These bars were used through the 1953 season.

The front safety guard was strengthened for 1951. The new guard was formed of one long tube with mounting brackets in the center and on each end. The lower mounting brackets mount to the frame by a single bolt each. The welded-on center bracket is fastened to the frame's upper front-safety-guard bracket by two bolts.

For restorers of 1951 Pans, several changes to mounting hardware are worth noting: transmission-cover screws were changed to Phillips-head types and in mid-1951 the generator-mounting screws were changed to Phillips-head types (early-1951 and previous used straight-slot screws).

Motor Updates

"Believe it or not, there's chrome inside the OHVs," boasted *The Enthusiast* of September 1950, referring to the new chrome-plated compression rings in the 1951 motors. These new rings were designed to reduce scuffing and wear during the critical break-in miles, helping to ensure that the cylinder walls remained smooth for a better ring seal.

Note that the fork caps are absent to the outside of the handlebar riser, which indicates that this bike is fitted with the adjustable-rake forks that were new for 1950. By loosening a couple bolts and pulling the forks forward, the forks could be raked out to increase stability when the bike is used with a sidecar. Because of this feature, the spring forks were no longer offered as an option. The chromed knob atop the steering stem operates the steering damper. Standard damper knobs were black.

A new camshaft was also fitted that incorporated ramps on the opening and closing sides of the lobe to smooth out valve action. These ramps worked in conjunction with new hydraulic lifters (designed for slower leak-down of oil) to make the valvetrain even quieter. The new cam was changed to a two-piece design with a separate gear pressed onto the cam shaft.

Pushrod ball sockets frequently worked themselves loose, sometimes falling out, and sometimes causing oil starvation to the hydraulic lifters. The problem was fixed for good in 1951 when new rocker arms were introduced that had the ball sockets machined right into the rocker arm.

Right-side view of Gary Nelson's 1950 shows the relatively smooth, die-cast gear cover that was fitted to 1948–50 motors (1951–53 motors were fitted with a rougher, sand-cast version of this cover). This cover features the number 97-403 cast in the inside. The ridge angling up and to the front is for the breather pipe from the gear case to the breather sump. The circular area near it is for the pinion-shaft bushing. Both these features were no longer visible on the sand-cast cover introduced in 1951. Note that the gear cover is secured by Phillips-head screws which are correct for 1950 and 1951. However, the generator mounting screws at the front of the cover should be straight-slot screws (1948–mid-1951). Note also the premature use of rocker cover D-rings (not introduced until 1951) and hex-head screws (should be round-head Phillips screws).

For 1951, the eight-rib-style of gear cover was retained, but the surface of the casting was noticeably "rougher" in appearance because it was sand-cast, rather than die-cast. Its appearance further differed in that the ridge for the breather tunnel (stretches diagonally from the lower rear corner to the upper center of the cover) and the outline of the pinion bushing were no longer visible. This cover bears the casting number 97-401 on the inside

The screws that fasten the primary-chain inspection cover are at 6 and 12 o'clock. This positioning was new for 1950 (the screws had been at 3 and 9) and was used through 1954, the last year for the "diamond" style primary cover. Also note the rivets that fasten the fender brackets and the thin, stainless trim strip at the lower rear edge of the fender. This strip was standard from 1949 to 1957.

and has a cast-in breather baffle plate. This sand-cast, eight-rib cover is correct for 1951–53 Pans. The gear cover is fastened by Phillips-head screws, but the generator mounting screws at the front of the cover are straight-slot screws for early 1951 bikes and Phillips head for later bikes. Phillips generator screws are correct on late 1951–57 Panheads.

About midway through the 1951 production run, 74ci machines were fitted with an updated carburetor, the Linkert M-74B. This carburetor was used on the 74s through 1965.

Another mid-season change was the substitution of a new pinion shaft that is slightly larger in diameter than the old shaft so that the pinion gear is a tighter press fit over the shaft. This change was implemented at the factory on engine numbers higher than 51FL6137 and 51EL6976. The new shaft is identified by the 5/16in, left-hand-threaded hole in the shaft end that is plugged with a screw.

Very late in the season, the factory began installing new, stronger piston pins with thicker wall diameters.

To cure chronic problems with oil leakage from the pushrod tubes, H-D engineers introduced new push-rod-tube seals made of a "Neoprene-cork composition." The new seals weren't perfect, but they went a long way toward keeping the oil in the tubes and the dirt out.

Radio-equipped police bikes for 1951 were fitted with a two-brush version of the Model 48 radio generator and a separate voltage regulator. The third brush of the original Model 48 was discarded, and the remaining pair of brushes and the commutator were made 12-1/2 percent wider for longer life and greater current output. This is the only year the two-brush Model 48 was used.

With the addition of "D-ring" reinforcements to the rocker covers, there was new chrome on the outside of the engine, too. The D-rings were named for their D shape (which matched the shape of the rocker cover's flanged edge). Each ring was made of three 1/16in layers of sheet steel, spot-welded together, chrome plated, and drilled for twelve mounting screws. D-rings were made to evenly distribute the pressure applied by the mounting screws over the entire surface of the rocker-cover flange, preventing over-tightened mounting screws from distorting the edge of the cover, causing an oil leak. Each D-ring and rocker cover was secured by twelve mounting screws: nine Phillips screws and three Allen-head cap screws, each with a lock washer. The Allen-head screws were used on the three holes on the front side of the front cylinder and the rear side of the rear cylinder (the low points of the head) where oil sometimes pooled above the gasket surface. The seal had to be especially tight on these edges, so Allen-head screws were used because they could be tightened to a higher torque figure without stripping than could the Phillips-head screws.

The new D-rings and screw combination sealed the rocker covers well and looked good, so many owners of earlier Panheads have updated their rocker covers with these D-rings. However, the steel D-rings were original only on Panheads built from 1951–54.

The final change to the engine was a new exhaust-port clamp. The old clamp was a plain strap clamp made of stainless steel. The new clamp was formed with a shoulder on one edge of the clamp. The shouldered edge is installed toward the head.

First Foot-shift Panheads

Some of the last Panheads produced in 1951 featured a long-overdue update that would be officially announced for the 1952 models: foot shift and hand clutch. If you see a 1951 bike with a high serial number that has foot shift, it may indeed have had foot shift installed at the factory. This would be very difficult to document, however, because the "F" that denotes that the bike is a foot-shift model was never stamped on the motor as part of the serial number.

1951 Production

Sales of H-D Big Twins continued their long slide for 1951; only 76 ES, 1,532 EL, 135 FS, and 6,560 FL Hydra-Glides were sold, a total of 8,303. Compare this figure to the 8,014 FL machines that had been sold in 1948, and you can see why H-D executives' level of panic over the flood of foreign machines really peaked in early 1951. (Note: The above figures list sales for Models ES and FS. According to the order blanks, all sidecar models should be Models ELS or FLS. It is unclear whether the sales figures are really meant to be for the latter.)

Model Year 1952

I Like Ike. That about sums up 1952. Fatherly former-general Dwight D. Eisenhower is drafted by the Republican Party and wins a land-slide victory over Democratic nominee Adlai Stevenson in the November election. Let the fabulous 1950s begin.

Not so fast, Ike's inauguration is not until January 1953. Meanwhile, the war in Korea drags on through the year. China's Chou En-Lai and Russia's "Uncle Joe" Stalin meet in Moscow to discuss how they can make the most of the Korean War. Our own "Uncle Joe"—McCarthy, that is—continues to rant and bask in the attention it brings. And the United States shows the Reds who's boss when it touches off its new H-Bomb at Eniwetok Atoll.

Around the world, technology marches on. The poliomielitis epidemic continues, but hope rises as Jonas Salk tests his new polio vaccine. RCA corporation develops small transistors to replace the vacuum tube. And the first sex-change operation is performed.

On June 16, the U.S. Tariff Commission rules against Harley-Davidson's request for increased tariffs on imported motorcycles, and the glory days really begin for the British. Harley's Big Twins fall on hard times.

Hearts throb with increased vigor as our smiling friend points out each new feature of his 1951 Hydra-Glide. The ladies are almost overcome as he points to the handsome new tank emblems, the most visible change for 1951. The script part of the emblem was standard for 1951–54, but the underline bar was only used through 1953. This machine must be a pre-production model because it is not fitted with the D-ring rocker-cover reinforcements that were introduced for 1951. The proud rider outfitted the bike handsomely with optional equipment, but my guess is that he's feeling pretty stupid at this point for not having spent the extra $21 for the optional Buddy Seat. *Photo copyright Harley-Davidson*

1952 Hydra-Glides

For the second year, only the high-compression EL and FL were listed on the H-D order blanks. When ordered with the optional foot shift, they were designated ELF and FLF. When ordered with sidecar gearing, they were designated ELS and FLS. Note: the low-compression E and F models are listed in the Model Descriptions section of *The Legend Begins* as being available for 1952. Either *Legend* is in error, or these low-compression machines were special-order or export-only items.

Base-model 61s carried a retail price of $955, and base-model 74s carried a retail price of $970.

Only two solo option groups were offered for 1952: the Deluxe Solo Group for $73.50 and the Utility Solo Group for $28.45. Worth noting is that the Deluxe Solo Group is nearly $50 cheaper than in 1951, mostly because the saddlebags were deleted from the group. For police bikes, the Standard Police Group was offered for $85.50.

The Panheads were available in five standard colors and three optional colors for 1952. Standard at no extra charge were Brilliant Black, Persian Red, Rio Blue, Tropical Green, and Police Silver (for police bikes only). Optional for $10.30 extra were Metallic Bronco Bronze, Metallic Marine Blue, and White.

A cutaway view of an early-1951 Panhead engine. Note the D-ring reinforcements fitted around the rocker cover rims. The 1951 to late-1954-style D-rings shown are constructed of three steel layers spot-welded together and fastened to each head with nine Phillips-head screws and three Allen-head screws. The Allen-head screws were fitted into the front three holes of the front head and the rear three holes on the rear head (the low points of each head) because they could be tightened to a higher torque than could the Phillips-head screws to more positively seal these leak-prone areas. Note the hydraulic lifters atop the pushrods (correct for 1948–52 motors), the spigot to drip oil on the intake valve and spring (used for 1949–65), the Phillips-head gear cover screws (correct for 1951–52), and the straight-slot generator mounting screws (correct for 1948-mid-51). *Photo copyright Harley-Davidson*

Foot Shift

Even today, many Harley riders still profess to prefer their motorcycles with the traditional hand shift. That view was even more prevalent in the early 1950s, but the new foreign machines all had foot shifters, and the feature was seen as essential to a motorcycle's sporting image. Even Indian had beaten Harley when they fitted a few Chiefs with foot shift in late 1949 and early 1950. Harley finally realized they had been swimming against the flow for too long, and introduced a few foot-shift models in very late 1951, but the feature was not formally introduced until the 1952 season.

Harley's management was too canny to make such a radical change *mandatory*, so the Models ELF and FLF were listed as no-extra-cost options for 1952; hand shift was still available for those who *The Enthusiast* of September 1951 called "[d]yed-in-the-wool hand shift riders." No reliable figures exist to tell us whether the new foot-shift models outsold the hand-shift models. But the figures listed in *The Legend Begins* show that by 1954, the foot-shift models were outselling the hand-shift models by a margin of nearly two to one. The margin continued to widen every year, and by 1965, only a few hand-shift models were produced.

Harley's new system used a hand lever on the left bar to operate the clutch and a foot lever at the front of the left footboard to change gears. The shift pattern is the familiar "one down, three up," with neutral between first and second. The hand lever for the front brake was moved to the right handlebar.

Many new components were added to the transmission on foot-shift models, including a redesigned shifter drum, an indexing cam, and a spring-loaded plunger to keep the transmission in the gear selected.

To help the weak human hand in performing a task formerly performed by the weight and strength of the leg, a spring-operated clutch "booster" was added; it mounted alongside the frame's left, front downtube. Even with the booster, a four-finger squeeze is still required to pull in the clutch lever, but that's OK. If you have trouble pulling in the clutch, you probably couldn't kick-start the thing either. The clutch-booster cover was painted black from 1952 to 1954, and cad plated thereafter. Chrome-plated covers were optional on new machines from 1959 on, although they were available through the accessory catalogs at an earlier date.

New left gas tanks were fitted to foot-shift machines. Gone were the shifter-pivot lug and shifter gate on the left side of the tank. The new left tank was as smooth and streamlined as the right tank.

The final F in "ELF" or "FLF" was not stamped into the left crankcase as part of the engine number, so hand-shift and foot-shift engines were all stamped 52EL or 52FL, followed in each case by the engine number. Thus, there is no way to tell whether a 1952 and later Panhead was originally hand-shift or foot-shift. Some of the parts provide strong clues—a left-hand gas tank without the shifter-pivot lug, for example—but these parts may have been altered or retrofitted since the bike was built. Providing that the parts are available, the bike can be restored to either shift configuration and still be correct. That is, unless the bike is equipped with the optional three-speed transmission with reverse, which was only offered in hand-shift form. For 1952, the optional transmission was available for $8.60 at the time of order.

Motor Updates

Harley-Davidson introduced a seemingly bizarre change to the exhaust valves in 1952—they Parkerized

Previous page: This 1954 FL is owned by Eugene Schrier. The 1954 tank emblem consists of a metal Harley-Davidson nameplate. This nameplate was also used on 1951–53 gas tanks, along with a separate chrome underline piece. For 1951, the three sergeant stripes on each side of the taillight were replaced by a single, wider stainless steel stripe on each side of the taillight, and the single stripe was fitted through 1954. Note also the new gear cover with four cooling fins, rather than eight, that was introduced in 1954 and was standard through 1962. This machine is fitted with the wishbone-style frame, of which there were two versions for 1954. Early-1954 frames had flattened dowtubes where the mounting blocks had been for the 1949–53 frame-mounted horn. Downtubes on mid-1954 frames were not flattened for the mounting blocks. In late-1954, a new straight-leg frame was introduced that was used through 1955.

The classic Jubilee Trumpet horn was introduced in 1954. The horn's power pack is mounted on the left side of the motor, and the long trumpet threads between the cylinders and bends forward toward the front of the bike. New control spirals were introduced in 1954 and were once again fastened to the handlebars by a large end nut. The D-rings on this machine are secured by nonstandard cap screws. The correct screws for 1951–54 are three Allen-head screws (at the front of the front head and at the rear of the rear head—the low points of the heads) and nine round-head Phillips screws per head, each with a lock washer. Late-1954–55 bikes were fitted with new-style thick aluminum D-rings with only six mounting-screw holes in each D-ring, thus only six hex-head screws were used to secure each rocker cover to its cylinder head. The six-screw arrangement did not seal well, so twelve-hole D-rings were used on 1956 and later Panheads.

them! The Parkerizing process uses chemicals to apply a phosphate coating to metal surfaces, making them highly resistant to rust and corrosion. Dozens of exterior parts are Parkerized, but why would internal parts that are continually showered with oil need such protection? They don't, but the coating is provided for another good reason: The coating left by the Parkerizing process absorbs oil and holds it to the parts, keeping them well lubricated during the critical first miles of break-in. Harley's pet name for the new valves is "Parko-Lubrized."

About midway through the 1952 season, starting with engine number "about 52FL3529" (according to Shop Dope No. 330), a new right crankcase was introduced that was the same as the 1948 to early-'52 cases except that a boss for a screen and check valve was added to the case, just to the right of the rear tappet block. Oil to the cylinder-head feed passages is routed into the boss and filtered through the screen, ensuring that the oil to the heads and hydraulic lifters is free of dirt and foreign particles. The check ball prevents the oil in the passage from draining back into the case after the motor is shut off so that any lifters that collapse under spring pressure will quickly refill when the motor is started. The screen and ball assembly are held in place by a straight-slotted cap screw that threads into the boss.

The screen proved useful in keeping dirt out of the lifters, but the screen could become clogged, restricting oil flow to the rockers and lifters, if it wasn't cleaned occasionally. The check ball was less effective, and was soon eliminated from production. In any case, the check ball was not needed after 1952 because the hydraulic lifters were relocated to a new position, below the pushrods, in 1953.

A later change made during the 1952 production run was the "rotating" exhaust valve. Engine number 52FL3910 was the first to have these valves, which were fitted with a new valve-stem cap that keeps the rocker arm from bearing on the top of the exhaust-valve stem, allowing the valve to rotate when it is open. When the engine is running, the rocker arm pushes down on the top of the valve-stem cap, the valve is pushed off its seat, and the valve is rotated by the swirling exhaust gasses that are forced out the exhaust port. Because the valve seated in a slightly different position each time, the tendency to "burn" exhaust valves was reduced. The rotating valves were used on FL models through 1960 and on FLH models through early 1958. Rotating exhaust valves were also available as a kit that could be retrofitted to earlier Panheads. The kit listed at $4.50 in May 1952.

Over time, the check balls in the oil pumps would develop ridges from hundreds of cycles of seating and unseating. Balls being balls, sometimes they would roll slightly while open, so the worn-in ridge would not seat evenly against the stop. The result is that oil from the tank would drain into the crankcase when the bike was shut off. To remedy this problem, Harley engineers designed a new pump with stemmed

This 1954 Panhead is an FLF model—the last F meaning that it was built with foot shift, a feature first fitted to a few very late 1951 Big Twins but officially introduced for 1952. Foot-shift twins were fitted with new left tanks that no longer had the lug for the shifter pivot or the mounting holes for the shifter gate. The change to foot shift required a clutch hand lever on the left handlebar (the brake moved to the right handlebar), a spring-assisted clutch booster (mounted vertically along the left front downtube), and a foot-shift lever. The clutch booster cover shown is chrome plated. Standard booster covers were actually painted black for 1952–54; for 1955–65, they were cad plated, but chrome-plated covers were available through the accessory catalogs. Chrome booster covers were first offered on new Panheads in 1959 as part of the Chrome Finish Group. The round chrome or stainless cover on the left side hides the horn's power pack. The Deluxe Solo Saddle shown on this bike is correct for 1955 and later Panheads. The 1948–54 style Deluxe Solo Seat has a three-piece leather skirt with rosettes and nickel dots.

A very rare, unrestored 1955 FL in the Hollywood Green optional paint scheme. Along with the tanks and fenders, the oil tank, primary cover, and tool box were painted in the one-year-only pastel green color. This paint scheme was a $10 option. Color matched bridge extra. The bike is outfitted with the correct 1954–56-style Deluxe Buddy Seat and Speed King saddlebags, each with the nickel "comet" trim pieces. Shown with the bike is Tony Andreason. The bike is owned by the Planes of Fame East air museum, but the bike is Tony's to ride whenever the sun is shining.

check balls that would ensure more consistent seating of the ball, and the pump was another of the running changes introduced during the 1952 production year. The oil pressure was no longer adjustable on the new pump, and the new check valves proved to be only marginally more reliable than the old round check balls, so the pump was used only on late 1952 to early 1954 Panheads. However, this pump was sold as the replacement pump for all parts orders during this period, so this pump may have been retrofitted to earlier bikes.

As it had been for the 1948 and 1949 Panheads, the gear cover on the 1952 machines was once again fastened by straight-slot screws. Straight-slot gear cover screws are correct for 1952–65 Panheads.

New Generators

Early in the production year, the Model 32 three-brush generator (which had been used on all non-police Harley twins since 1932) was replaced by the Model 52 generator. The new generator is also a three-brush design that is used in conjunction with a cut-out relay (still mounted just forward of the ignition timer), but without a voltage regulator. The Model 52 generator was fitted to civilian Panheads through 1957.

Radio-equipped police bikes also got a new generator. In place of the two-brush Model 48 radio generator, the 1952 police bikes were fitted with the Model 51 radio generator. Like the generator it replaced, the Model 52 is a two-brush, 6V generator with an attached cooling fan and a separate voltage regulator. The new radio generator had a redesigned field coil and wider brushes, allowing it to produce more current (20amp versus 18amp) at a lower rpm than the older generator. This generator could be ordered on non-police bikes for an extra charge of $37.25.

Frame

The frame fitted to 1952 Panheads was a wishbone-style, similar to the one introduced during the production run in 1951 (with rounded corners on the horn-block mounts), but it carried several new features: an inverted-U-shaped toolbox bracket with both legs of the U welded to the lower rear frame tube on the right side; a wider top motor mount (the mount is no longer L-shaped); a wider combination rear-tank mount and seat T-bracket; a sturdier lower front engine mount; and the frame build date stamped on the right side of the top motor-mount bracket, just below where the bracket is welded to the frame. This is a one-year-only frame; in 1953 the lower front motor mount was made even beefier.

Fenders

For the third year in a row, a new rear fender was fitted. The 1952 rear fender still had the single stainless steel stripe on each side of the taillight, but it had only one vertical channel stamped into the metal flat of the chain recess because the rest of the recess was now cut away. This style of fender was fitted through 1954.

If the Deluxe Solo Group was ordered, a 2in "Deluxe OHV" nameplate was fitted to each side of the front fender. Deluxe OHV nameplates are correct for all 1952–54 Hydra-Glides ordered with the Deluxe group. However, these nameplates were not offered for sale separately from the group, so if a restored bike has these name plates, it should also have all the other items in the group. Hydra-Glide name plates were offered separately, for $1.50 a pair.

Low-Tone Muffler

Externally, the muffler on the 1952 Panhead looked the same as the Mellow-Tone muffler that had been intro-

New for 1955 was the tank emblem shown, the 3/4in thick aluminum D-rings, the oval taillight, and adjustable license-plate holder. The taillight was painted the same color as the fender for 1955-65 Panheads, but was fitted with the chrome lens door shown. Also shown is the correct Deluxe Solo Seat for 1955 and later, and the straight-leg frame and front safety guard that had been introduced in late 1954. Again, this is a very nice restoration, but there are a couple of minor flaws. First, the aluminum D-rings for 1955 were only fitted with six holes for mounting screws and were retained by six hex-head screws. Second, whitewall tires are not correct on 1957 and earlier Panheads. Third, the stainless steel cover shown on the steering lock was not introduced until 1956. This motorcycle is owned by Rob Carlson of Kokesh Motorcycles and was restored by Elmer Ehnes.

From the left, the most prominent new feature for 1955 is the "smooth" style outer primary cover that was fitted to 1955–64 Panheads. This primary cover has three removable covers. The front-most and smallest only appears on bikes fitted with the new, optional compensating sprocket (an engine shock absorber). The center cover is the primary inspection cover, and the rearmost is the clutch inspection cover. Both rear covers were painted black unless the optional chrome-plated covers were ordered. Two other 1955 changes are not readily apparent: the front fork covers have three diagonal stripes on each side of the headlight (older covers had four horizontal stripes), and the plumber-nut style manifold that had been used since the 1930s was replaced by a new O-ring manifold. Not to criticize, just to set the record straight, the instrument cover should be painted the color of the gas tank, the cylinders should be painted silver, and the rear fender should have the cutout in the chain recess on the rear fender and only one vertical channel stamped into the recess. The three-channel type shown is correct only for 1949–51. Motorcycle owned by Rob Carlson of Kokesh Motorcycles.

duced in 1950, but it received extensive internal revision to give it an even mellower tone. The new design eschewed baffle plates for a resonating chamber and an expansion chamber, resulting in a muffler that was quieter and had less back pressure than the previous muffler. Harley dubbed it the "Low-Tone" muffler. This muffler was supplied as the standard muffler on single-muffler systems through 1965.

Accessories

Among the dozens of options and accessories that could be specified at the time a bike was ordered, a couple stand out as new and significant for 1952. For the first time, front and rear turn signals were listed on the order blank in 1952. The lamps were essentially the same chromed, bullet-shaped lamps that were introduced as parking lights in 1949. The front signal lamps mount to the sides of the fork and have clear lenses. Rear signal lamps mount beneath the seat and also have clear lenses. Factory turn signal installations included a switch on the handlebar and an indicator light mounted to a plate attached to the handlebar riser link. Turn signals cost $16.75 when ordered on a new bike in 1952 or $15.75 when ordered separately from the accessory catalog. Turn signals had been offered for the first time in the 1951 accessory catalog.

For the ultimate in color coordination, the popular King Size saddlebags were offered with leather dyed Rio Blue, Persian Red, or Tropical Green for bikes ordered in these colors—and the cost for these leather beauties was only $1 more than for the plain black ones. They must not have been a popular option, because these bizzarely dyed bags were again offered in 1953—even though one couldn't order a 1953 bike painted to match the bags (Rio Blue, Persian Red, and Tropical Green had been dropped from the color selection). To further boggle the bag-buyer's mind, the black bags could be ordered with red or white trim, and even with white fringe.

1952 Production

Harley-Davidson experienced another drop in sales of nearly 20 percent for 1952 Big Twins. Only 6,700 Panheads went out the factory door, consisting of 5,554 FL, 186 FS, 918 EL, and 42 ES. Sales of the venerable 61ci models had dropped to less than one in five, so H-D dropped the model at the end of 1952.

Model Year 1953

Ike is inaugurated, and he works hard to deliver on his promises of peace, prosperity, and the middle road. The Dow-Jones index begins to rise, peace negotiations begin in earnest in Panmunjon, and Ike reinstates the tradition of Easter-egg rolling at the White House. In July, world, Ethel and Julius Rosenberg are electrocuted at Sing-Sing Prison.

On the lighter side, Norman Vincent Peale lavishes *The Power of Positive Thinking* on an American populace intent on grabbing the good life. Americans don dorky, disposable glasses and thrill to the new 3-D color movies, newspaper ads, and cartoons that sprout up across the country.

Records topple and the impossible begins to seem commonplace. Edmund Hillary and Tenzing Norkay top Mount Everest. Salk's polio vaccine is ready for mass inoculations against the most dreaded disease in America. And for the first time, a patient survives open-heart surgery.

Conformity is epidemic, but ominous signs of rebellion encroach from the fringe. Elvis Presley cuts the song

A happy looking bunch poses with a pair of 1955 H-D twins, a KH and an FL in the optional Hollywood Green paint scheme. Each bike carries its own version of the V-medallion, a 1955-only item. *via Jerry Hatfield*

Ike delivers peace when an armistice is signed with North Korea and China.

Arch-enemy Joseph Stalin dies, and the menace of Communism overseas seems less threatening, but grows at home. "Subversives" are barred from teaching in public schools, and the Screen Actors Guild bans Communists from membership. Charley Chaplin is driven out of the country by slander. Even classic tales such as Robin Hood are criticized as being Communist. Librarians are ordered to remove books by authors who are suspected of Communist sympathies. There is even serious talk of branding such books with a red star. Finally, despite pleas of clemency from all over the country and around the

My Happiness for $4. William S. Burroughs' book *Junkie* is published to critical acclaim. And *Playboy* hits the newsstands. Most ominous of all for H-D and the other motorcycle manufacturers, the film *The Wild One* is released in December 1953 (more on this later).

1953 Hydra-Glides

For 1953, the only Big Twin offered was the 74, but it was offered with the choice of two motors—the high-compression FL motor and the new FLE. Each motor was available with hand-shift (FL or FLE) or foot-shift (FLF or FLEF) and with optional sidecar gearing (FLS, FLES, or FLFS). Per usual H-D practice, only FL or FLE is stamped

THE HYDRA-GLIDE

into the case as part of the serial number. Base-model machines carried a retail price of $1,000, a modest $30 increase over the previous year's prices.

Hydra-Glides were again available in five standard and three optional colors for 1953. Standard at no extra charge were Brilliant Black, Pepper Red, Glacier Blue, Forest Green, and Police Silver (for police bikes only). Optional for $10.30 extra were Cavalier Brown, Glamour Green, and White.

Traffic Combination Motor

The 61ci bikes had been discontinued at the end of the 1953 season. In 1952, the larger 74s had cost only $15 more than the 61s, so it was natural that most riders opted for the greater power and torque of 1200cc over 1000cc. Sales figures for 1952 show that the 74s out-sold the 61s by a margin of more than five to one. Such figures made the decision to discontinue production of the smaller bike seem logical. Why make and stock parts for the smaller bike when that smaller bike is such a minute part of total sales?

But the 61 had qualities that endeared it to police departments and commercial users. Its smaller carb and milder cam shaft made it ideal for escort work and use in heavy traffic. To compensate these users for the loss of their beloved 61, H-D introduced a special FLE "Traffic Combination" version of the 74 that was fitted with the cam and M-61 Linkert carburetor from the 61 to give the Traffic Combination 74 the excellent low-speed performance of the 61. The Traffic Combination motor was fitted with the 61 cam and carburetor for model years 1953 and 1954. For model years 1955 and 1956, Traffic Combination motors were still fitted with the 61's cam shaft, but were fitted with the standard 74's M-74B carburetor.

Relocated Hydraulic Lifters

Despite the many updates to the oil pumps, lifters, and rocker arms implemented from 1948 to 1952, H-D engineers never really solved the Panhead motor's chronic problems with ticking lifters until the lifters were relocated from their former position atop the pushrods to their new location at the top of the tappets, below the pushrods, on the 1953 motor. The new lifters were far closer to the oil pump, so the oil pressure to them was more constant and reliable.

To implement the new system, many new parts were required: right crankcase, tappet blocks, tappets, lifters, adjusters, and pushrods. To supply oil to the new lifter location, the new case had an oil passage to feed oil to the tappet blocks, the new tappet blocks (now made of cast iron) had a passage to carry oil from the case to a hole in the tappet, and the new tappets had a hole in the flat on their sides to pick up oil from the tappet block and feed it to the lifter, which is slip-fit into a hole in the top of the tappet. The new hydraulic lifter consisted of a cylinder (with a pressed-in check-ball assembly) and a plunger that fit into the cylinder. The new pushrod had the ball end at

The speedometer on a 1956 FLE restored by Elmer Ehnes. This is the style of speedometer introduced in 1956. Changes for that year included the light gold center (replacing the gray center that had been in use since 1953), and the numerals, hash marks, and the company name are all painted in "green Day-Glo" (they had been painted in yellow for 1953–55) on the underside of the glass. This basic design (not withstanding small changes such as different colored tenth-mile numerals) was used for 1956–61 non-police Panheads. Note that this bike has hand shift, which by 1956 was becoming rare.

the top rather than at the bottom, a pressed-in bottom fitting that was threaded for the screw-in adjuster. The new lifter system worked so well that it was used through the end of the Panhead line with only a few minor changes to the pushrods and adjusters. Indeed, this same basic design is still in use on Harley Big Twins today.

Like all tappet blocks from 1950 to 1952, early 1953 tappet blocks were secured with eight straight-slot or Phillips-head screws (there was no real pattern of which motors were fitted with which type). Later 1953 tappet blocks were secured by eight hex-head screws without lock washers, and these hex screws were used through 1965.

New Return Oiling System

In pre-1953 motors, oil from the heads was returned through a passage in the left side of each cylinder to passages in the left and right crankcases, where it drained into the cases. In the new motor, oil from the heads drains down a passage in the left side of the cylinder and through a hole in the cylinder wall, where it helps lubricate the cylinders and contributes to the splash lubrication of the other bottom-end components. To help keep the extra oil out of the combustion chamber, new oil-control rings were introduced. The new oil return used redesigned left and right crankcases and new cylinders. The new left case is the same as the 1952 case, except the oil channel on the rear cylinder base and the oil passage on the front cylinder base have been omitted. The new right case is the same as the late 1952 case, except the oil channel on the rear cylinder base has been omitted. The new cylinders each have a smaller rocker-feed passage on the right side and a new-style oil return passage that goes to a hole in the cylinder wall. These new crankcases were used on 1953 and 1954 models, and the new cylinders were used through 1962.

New Speedometer

After five years of production, the Panhead speedometer was due for a face lift. The 1953-style Stewart-Warner speedometer differs from the 1948–52 speedometer in many small details: the raised ring that forms the background for the numbers is now painted black; the lower face is painted dark gray; the numbers go one through twelve in a larger block type, and the 2mph division marks, with longer and wider marks denoting the tens, are painted on the underside of the glass; the bar-and-shield emblem on the glass is replaced by "Harley-Davidson" in yellow-silver; the 1953 odometer and trip meter mile numerals are white on a black background and the tenth numerals are black on a white background; the pointer is white (instead of red); and the color of the painted numbers, mph divisions, and words on the glass is now yellow-silver (instead of cream-ivory). This speedometer was used only for 1953 (the pointer was changed to red and the tenth numerals are red painted on a black background for 1954).

Small Changes

In late 1953, a new pinion-shaft bearing was introduced that had twenty-four 1/4x0.270in rollers instead of twelve 1/4x0.600in rollers. The new bearing uses the same spacers as the old bearing.

The frame for 1953 was basically the same as for 1953, except that the lower front motor mount was beefed up. This frame was the last frame fitted with horn-mount blocks because a new horn would be introduced in 1954.

The covering on the optional Deluxe Buddy Seat is vinyl (instead of leather) for 1953 and later.

1953 Production

The foot-shift option introduced the previous year was proving very popular, outselling the hand shift by nearly two to one. Unfortunately, the new feature wasn't bringing in the new customers that H-D had hoped it would, and sales eroded by another 20 percent. Total sales of 5,337 Big Twins (1,986 FL and 3,351 FLF) were less than the number of FL models sold the previous year. This was also the year that Harley's long-time rival, Indian, closed their factory doors forever. As H-D approached its official 50th anniversary, prospects for America's last motorcycle manufacturer looked very grim.

Model Year 1954

In December 1953, as the 1954s are rolling off the production line in earnest, H-D's image takes a real drubbing in the sensationalist biker flick *The Wild One*. The movie begins with the warning: "This is a shocking story. It could never take place in most American towns—but it did in this one. It is a public challenge not to let it happen again." And it only gets more shlocky from there. Though the "bikers" in the movie seem almost wholesome by today's standards and their antics in taking over Bleeker's Cafe in the town of Carbonville probably wouldn't rate a disorderly conduct charge in most towns today, the movie really shocked audiences in 1953 and 1954. No longer did the American public think of a motorcycle club as a group of uniformed Shriners riding full-dress Harleys in the Fourth of July parade. A club was now seen as a bunch of unshaven, drunken rowdies, as typified by the "Black Rebels" MC featured in the movie. Worse yet, the worst of the worst—"Chino" (played by Lee Marvin) and his club—rode Harleys in the movie, while the anti-hero "Johnny" (played by Marlon Brando) and his group rode Triumphs. After this movie and a whole slew of imitators, America had a whole new idea of what kind of people they'd meet on a Harley.

Meanwhile, Joe McCarthy stubs his toe when he starts a probe of the *Army* for harboring Commie symps. The Army fires back, accusing McCarthy of seeking favors for Private David Schine. McCarthy's long decline begins in earnest when he shows his stripes in televised Senate hearings, culminating in a Senate condemnation for contempt of Senate.

Even the McCarthy sideshow cannot detract from the shock in some quarters and jubilation in others that the Supreme Court rules that racial segregation in American public schools is unconstitutional.

In an embattled country previously called French Indochina, the Communist Viet Minh rebels under leader Ho Chi Minh capture the French fortress at Dien Bien Phu, breaking the will of the French to continue their occupation of Vietnam. Shortly thereafter, Vietnam is divided at the 17th Parallel, creating a Communist north and a non-Communist south. America is courted as Vietnam's new "Sugar Daddy."

Alan Freed brings rock-n-roll to the radio, and Bill Haley's *Rock Around the Clock* becomes the best-selling single to that point in history. Girls begin wearing poodle skirts. Boys begin wearing faded Levi's. "Squares" wear crew cuts and "flattops." "Greasers" wear "ducktail" haircuts. Tranquilizer sales to stressed-out moms skyrocket.

Near the end of the year the TV series "Davy Crockett, Indian Fighter" hits the air waves making stars of Fess Parker as Davy and Buddy Ebsen, as Davy's sidekick. Kids—and some politicians—across America don coonskin caps, repeat Davy's mantra of "Be sure you're

This 1956 FLH is one of the many Panheads owned by Canadian collector Robin Gauthier, owner of Southside Cycles in Nanaimo, British Columbia. The FLH is a high-performance version of the 74 that was first introduced in mid-1955. The 1955 FLHs had higher compression pistons (8:1 versus 7.25:1) and polished and flowed intake ports to give about 10 percent more horsepower. Later FLHs were also fitted with the higher-lift Victory cam introduced in 1956. FLHs for 1956–60 were fitted with the V decal shown, on both sides of the oil tank (1955 FLHs were not fitted with this decal). This deluxe FLH is fitted with the optional black Royalite plastic bags with two nickel "comets" on each that are the correct style for 1954–56 Panheads, the solo windshield with red lower panels (red and blue panels were first available in 1956), the "bologna slicer" front bumper (used from late 1955–57), the Bumper King rear bumper with slicer grille (both optional for 1954–57), and the Super Soft Deluxe Buddy seat (this type and skirt trim is correct for 1954–57; the regular buddy seat received this style of trim in 1957). The two-tone paint scheme shown differs slightly from stock, but is attractive nonetheless.

right, and then go ahead," and sing the famous theme song: "Davy, Davy Crockett, king of the wild frontier . . ."

For reasons unknown outside The Motor Company's boardroom, H-D chooses 1954 as the year to release its 50th anniversary models. (Counting 1903 as year one, 1953 would be year fifty. And didn't H-D celebrate their ninetieth anniversary in 1993? Hmmm.)

In celebration of their golden anniversary, all 1954 Panheads are fitted with the 50th Anniversary Medallion on the top of the front fender. The medallion is a gold satin finished, stamped badge consisting of a 2-1/2in disc background with a large V superimposed over the disc and a bar and shield superimposed on the V. "Harley-Davidson" appears in script on the bar, "50 Years" on the top part of the shield, and "American Made" on the lower part of the shield. This lovely medallion is hard to find today, but no restoration of a 1954 Panhead is complete without it.

1954 Hydra-Glides

For 1954, the 74 was again offered in standard FL form and in FLE Traffic Combination form, with regular, police, or sidecar gearing, and with hand shift or foot shift. Base-model machines carried a retail price of $1015, a modest $15 increase over the previous year's prices.

The Panheads were offered in eight standard, solid-color paint schemes and seven optional two-tone schemes (no extra charge) for 1954: Pepper Red, Glacier Blue, Forest Green, Daytona Ivory, Anniversary Yellow, Black, Silver (Police Group only), White (Police Group only), Pepper Red tanks with Daytona Ivory fenders, Glacier Blue tanks with Daytona Ivory fenders, Forest Green tanks with Daytona Ivory fenders, Daytona Ivory tanks with Pepper Red fenders, Daytona Ivory tanks with Glacier Blue fenders, Daytona Ivory tanks with Forest Green fenders, and for Motor Maids members only, Cadillac Grey tanks and Azure Blue fenders.

The gas-tank emblem for 1954 Panheads was the H-D emblem used from 1951–53, but without the chrome underline strip.

Jubilee Trumpet Horn

The lovely new Jubilee trumpet horn was introduced in 1954. The new horn body mounted on the left side of the motor and the long trumpet tube wound between the cylinders, to the right side of the motor, then bent 90deg toward the front, where it flute out into a graceful trumpet. The carburetor mount bracket was redesigned to allow clearance for the horn. An instant classic, the Jubilee horn was fitted to Panheads through the 1964 season. The trumpet is cadmium- or chrome-plated steel (sometimes listed as "polished" on the order blanks). The horn cover is listed as chrome-plated for 1954 and 1955, but is listed as polished for later years. All horn covers that I have examined are made of stainless steel, but it is possible that they were chrome-plated for some years. The horn bodies are painted black.

Frames for 1954

With the introduction of the Jubilee horn, the horn-mount blocks were no longer welded to the frame downtubes. The very first 1954 frames still had downtubes flattened in the area where the horn mounts would have been welded. Mid-production 1954 frames were still of the wishbone design, but the downtubes were no longer flattened.

Late in 1954 a new frame was introduced—in a sense, reintroduced. The wishbone style of frame that had been introduced on the first Panheads in 1948 was replaced by a new straight-leg style of frame, similar to the one used on the last of the Knuckleheads in 1947. The frame change is most discernible when the bike is viewed from the front. The downtubes of the wishbone frame dog-leg out noticeably to each side; the downtubes of the straight-leg frame are straight tubes. This new frame was also used for 1955.

Safety guards for the 1954 wishbone frames were the same as the guards used since 1951. Late-1954 straight-leg frames once again used the guard that was used from 1941 to 1947. This was a one-piece tubular guard with an inverted-T-shaped mounting bracket (with four holes) held to the frame by two U-bolts. It was used from late 1954 through 1957. Standard guards were painted black, but chrome-plated guards were optional for $6 at the time of order or as part of the Deluxe Solo Group.

Handlebars And Controls

New, "faster-acting" throttle and spark-control spirals were introduced. These were held to the handlebars by a 3/8in end screw that threaded onto the end of the handlebar, much like the 1948 spirals had. To accommodate the new spirals, revised handlebars with threaded ends were introduced. These handlebars were otherwise the same as the 1951–53 bars, and were offered in Buckhorn or Speedster lengths. Solid-mounted bars

For 1956, Panheads were painted in one of the best two-tone paint schemes H-D ever applied. This one is painted in black with Champion Yellow tank stripes. This particular bike is an FLE, meaning it was fitted with the Traffic Combination motor that was optional for 1953–56 Panheads and was intended to provide the excellent low-speed performance of the 61ci models that had been dropped after the 1952 season; 1953–54 Traffic Combination motors were fitted with the cam and carb from the 61, whereas 1955–56 FLEs were only fitted with the 61's cam and the M-74B carburetor that was standard on the FL and FLH. The frame for 1956 was similar to the straight-leg frame introduced in late 1954, with the addition of a stainless steel cover for the steering lock and larger holes for the coil-mounting blocks. This frame was used through 1957.

Sex machine, 1956. He thinks she's jazzed by his neat haircut and gleaming white socks, but she's really swooning over the bike's optional Pepper Red or Atomic Blue hard saddlebags and new dual exhaust. These optional-color bags were available only for 1956. Black bags were standard until 1959, when white bags were first offered. The dual exhaust system was first offered on new machines in 1956, although they had been offered through the accessory catalogs since 1954. On the 1954 to early-1961 dual exhausts, the front cylinder's exhaust fed only the right muffler, and the rear cylinder's exhaust fed only the left muffler. *Photo copyright Harley-Davidson*

were black; optional rubber-mounted bars were chromed.

Motor Updates

The pinion shaft, oil-pump worm gear, and pinion gear were redesigned for 1954 to reduce gear case noise. Gone were the splines for the pinion gear, replaced by a taper and key. A key was also used to hold the worm gear in place. This new pinion shaft was used only for 1954. A new oil pump was fitted that contained many internal revisions, including a change back to round check balls, replacing the stemmed check balls used since late 1952. This new oil pump was used through 1955.

A new style of gear cover made its debut in 1954. Previous Panhead gear covers (and most of the Knucklehead covers too) had eight horizontal ribs on the cover, but the new cover had only four ribs. The gear cover was still sand cast, but now had the number 25217-40 cast in relief on the inner side and was fitted with a new bushing for the new pinion-shaft. This style of four-rib gear cover is correct for 1954–57 motors.

During the 1954 production run (starting with motor number 54FLE2077), two lock screws were added to prevent the race for the pinion-shaft bearing from turning in the case. A new race, having two seating notches for the lock screws, was introduced, and the holes were drilled and tapped in the cases to the notch positions. Subsequent orders for replacement races to be installed in earlier motors were supplied with notched races, and *Shop Dope No. 348A* recommends that these earlier cases be drilled for the lock screws with a new H-D drilling jig.

Later in 1954, a new bearing was introduced (starting with engine number 54FL5010). This bearing was wider overall, so the bearing spacer previously used on the flywheel side was no longer used. The new bearing still used twenty-four rollers, but the rollers were longer (0.360in vs. 0.270) to increase the bearing area.

Very late in 1954, new-style D-rings were introduced. These rings were cast of aluminum, and were made much thicker than the old-style welded-steel D-rings to help seal the rocker covers more efficiently. Instead of twelve mounting-screw holes, only six were drilled in each new D-ring. The new ring is much more rigid than the old D-ring, so H-D engineers thought that six hex-head cap screws would be enough to seal the rocker cover. Unfortunately, they were wrong. The covers often leaked, so revised D-rings with twelve mounting holes were issued for 1956.

Detail Changes

For the second year in a row, the speedometer was given a facelift. The 1954 Stewart-Warner speedometer is the same as the 1953 speedo, except that the pointer is red and the tenth-mile numerals are painted red on a black background. This speedometer, too, is a one-year-only item.

A good squeeze to the brake hand lever or boot to the rear brake pedal often resulted in a loud squeal and chatter. In an attempt to prevent the squeal, the brake linings were shortened for 1954, which resulted in smoother, quieter, more powerful brakes. These shoes and linings were still being fitted to the last Panheads in 1965.

A new-style shifter shaft was fitted in 1954. It was no longer splined, so a new foot lever and optional heel lever were also introduced to mount on the new, smooth shaft.

Dual Exhaust

Though not listed on the order blanks until 1956, and thus not really "correct" for a restoration of a 1954 Panhead, a dual exhaust system was first offered for the Big Twins in the 1954 accessory catalog. The dual exhaust system used the same front header pipe and S-pipe as the single system and two of the mufflers used on the single system, but the other pipes were unique to the dual system. The front cylinder was connected exclusively to the right muffler through the front header, the S-pipe, and a new, straight pipe. The rear cylinder connected exclusively to the left cylinder through a new pipe that snakes back and to the left from the exhaust port. The new left and right pipes were chrome-plated.

New Saddlebags

"Stunning, new, streamlined saddlebags, replete with advancements and features, will add still further class and distinction to the renowned 74," claimed *The Enthusiast* for September 1953. Plastic saddlebags were first offered as an option for the Big Twins in 1954. The correct bags are black Royalite (hard plastic) bags trimmed with two silver "comet" pieces and seven silver dots arranged in a reverse-L-shape in front of the comets. These hard bags are correct for 1954–56 Panheads. (White bags were not offered on the order sheets until 1959, but white Royalite bags were later offered as a retrofit kit. For 1956 only, these bags were also offered in Pepper Red or Atomic Blue.)

The plastic bags are far more weatherproof than their leather counterparts and much easier to remove, too. Pull two pins and each bag lifts free of its frame. Opinion varies on the plastic bags' styling. Some riders think they look great. Others prefer the classic look of leather bags. Once again, however, H-D was smart enough to accommodate both points of view on its order blanks.

Two sizes of leather bags were still offered in 1954 and both were restyled. The large leather bags were called "Speed King" bags and cost $37.75 at the time of order. Speed King saddlebags for 1954–56 are decorated with white piping (around the edge of the top, along the lower edge of the cover, and along the edge of the side), nine rectangular nickel pieces arranged in three rows of three (angling toward the rear) on the top of the cover, two nickel comet pieces on the sides of the cover, three leather straps angling toward the back with angled chrome speed buckles, and three round nickel dots near the lower edge of the side (one just to the front of each buckle). A fringed version of the Speed King was also offered, for $39.95.

Buddy Seats and Bumpers

Harley-Davidson must have gotten a hell of a deal on winged comets in 1954 because they put them everywhere they would fit. The Deluxe Buddy seat featured 2in foam padding, plastic covering, and a new skirt with—you guessed it—comets, one on each side. It could be ordered for $23.75 on a new bike. For those of really tender tush, a Super Deluxe Buddy Seat was offered. It featured 4in foam padding, leather covering, and, of course, the comets. It could be ordered for $35 on a new bike.

Two styles of optional rear bumper were offered for 1954 and 1955. The old-style bumper (available since late 1948) featured a chromed, tubular bumper that gently curved in at the ends. The new bumper features a larger, chrome bumper piece and can be ordered with the "bologna-slicer" grille. Either bumper could be ordered for $9.75, and the grille costs an additional $6.90. Neither of these bumpers are sturdy enough to offer any real protection. They are just another means of hanging more chrome on a Panhead.

1954 Production

Crushing hopes that the anniversary models would excite customers, Panhead sales finally bottomed out (temporarily) in 1954, at 4,757 units, just over one-fourth of what they had been in 1948. The incremental changes that had been the rule since 1949 were no longer enough to induce the Harley faithful to buy. The FL's power and performance had not improved appreciably since 1948, while the competing British bikes were getting bigger and faster each year. Customers wanted more horsepower, and Harley decided to give it to them.

Model Year 1955

The good times continue to roll in 1955, but some disturbing developments tone down the glad-fest. The evils of Communism are given a new face as Nikita Krushchev becomes the Soviet Communist Party's Secretary. A chink appears in the armor of U.S. confidence as Ike suffers a heart attack, and the stock market immediately plummets. The seeds of a new war take root as the United States begins backing South Vietnam.

James Dean's star rises with strong performances in *Rebel without a Cause* and *East of Eden*, but then his "immortality" is assured when he dies in a car crash.

Davy Crockett mania grows into a full-blown marketing phenomenon. Setting the example for the many spin-off marketing bonanzas that would follow, opportunists cash in to the tune of $300 million (in 1955 dollars!) selling Davy Crockett coonskin caps, plastic muskets, powder horns, and knives, not to mention trading cards, lunch boxes, and pajamas. Youngsters George Lucas and Steven Spielberg put down their plastic muskets long enough to note the future possibilities.

Many long-running TV shows debut, including *The Lawrence Welk Show*, *Gunsmoke*, *Captain Kangaroo*, and *The Mickey Mouse Club*. The game show *The $64,000 Question* rises to the top of the ratings. And Disneyland opens in Anaheim, California.

Rosa Parks refuses to give up her seat on the bus and through her courage, focuses America's attention on the apartheid at home.

For 1957, a new two-tone scheme, tank emblems, and front-fender tip were standard. The tank emblem and fender tip were both made of plastic for the first time. The fender tip is correct for 1957 and 1958. The tank badge is correct for 1957 only (the 1958 emblem is very similar, but it has black lettering and a gold background). The chrome-plated oil tank is not correct for 1957 (they were first offered in 1963). Also out of place is the 1958-and-later-style twin-tube seat hand rail. This lovely 1957 FLH is one of many fine machines owned by Dan Olberg.

The rock-n-roll hits just keep on coming, including Fats Domino's *Ain't It a Shame* and Chuck Berry's *Maybelline*. Youth culture rises to even greater prominence. Movie and music stars increasingly embrace motorcycling, but H-D lets a golden opportunity go by when they let other companies lead. Rather than images of wholesome stars having good clean fun on America's only motorcycle, the public sees only thugs on Harleys in biker flicks.

1955 Hydra-Glides

Nineteen fifty-five was a year of big changes for the venerable Panhead. Engine power had grown steadily since the lower end had been designed for the Knucklehead motors of the early 1940s, so steps were taken to beef it up to withstand further power increases. The first of these power increases was the mid-year introduction of the hot rod FLH Super Sport Big Twin with a higher-compression (8:1) motor. The new motor was offered along with the FL and FLE (which now had only the cam from the old 61, but not the carburetor from the 61). These motors were available in bikes with regular, sidecar, or police gearing and with hand shift or foot shift. Unlike the "F" for foot shift and the "S" for sidecar gearing, the "H" in "FLH" is proudly stamped onto the motor as part of the serial number.

Base-model FLs and FLEs retailed for $1,015 (the same as the previous year's prices), but base-model FLHs retailed for $1,083.

Seven standard colors and one optional color were offered. Standard were: Pepper Red, Atomic Blue, Anniversary Yellow, Aztec Brown, Black, Silver (Police Group only), and White (Police Group only). Hollywood Green was available for $10 extra (the outer chain guard, tool box, battery cover, and oil tank were also painted in Hollywood Green). The order blank also lists, at no extra charge "any combination of tanks in one color and fenders in another using our standard colors, except Hollywood Green."

The FLH Super Sport

The 1955 production year, a new Super Sport version of the 74 was introduced, the FLH. This machine featured a special motor with polished and flowed intake tracts that increased horsepower by about 10 percent. Nineteen fifty-five FLHs were not fitted with FLH decals (they are only distinguishable from FL models by the "FLH" stamped into the motor as part of the serial number). Later FLHs (possibly including very late 1955 FLHs) were fitted with a special FLH decal on both sides of the oil tank.

Small Changes

From the front, the new upper fork cover and new, chrome-plated V-shaped medallion on the top of the fender jump right out. The four horizontal stripes on each side of the headlight were replaced by three diagonal stripes on each side, cradling the headlight in a V shape. Like the previous cover, this cover is black-painted steel unless the optional stainless steel fork trim ($10.65 additional) or Deluxe Solo Group was specified at the time of order. The headlight is rubber-mounted to reduce breakage of headlight mounts and mounting bolts, as well as to insulate the lamp filaments from engine and road vibration. The new front fork cover and rubber-mounted headlight are fitted to Panheads through 1959.

New FLs and FLHs ordered with the Deluxe Solo or Standard Police groups had stamped V-medallions at the top forward part of the front fender. The medallion is a large V with a bar and shield superimposed. "Harley-Davidson" is stamped in relief out of the bar. "1955" is stamped in relief out of the top part of the shield, and "FL" or "FLH" is stamped out of the bottom part of the shield. These medallions are fitted only to 1955 bikes. (FL medallions should only be fitted to bikes with motors stamped FL, and FLH medallions should only be fitted to bikes with motors stamped FLH.)

The new tank emblem is a large piece with "Harley-Davidson" in script, superimposed on a large V. A new

Dan Olberg is lucky enough to own a matched pair of 1957 H-D twins, an FLH Hydra-Glide and a Sportster, both painted in correct-style Pepper Red and black two-tone schemes. Note that the two-tone line wraps around the tank emblem on the Hydra-Glide but bisects the emblem on the Sportster. Nineteen fifty-seven was the first year for the Sportster and the last year for the Hydra-Glide.

wing-bolt closure (in place of a lock) was fitted to the tool box. Tool boxes are still painted black (chrome covers were first offered on order blanks in 1959).

From the rear, the new taillight is apparent. Also, the single stainless steel stripe that was fitted on each side of the light is no longer used. The die-cast, tombstone-shaped taillight with integral license-plate bracket used since 1948 was replaced by an oval-shaped, stamped-steel taillight and a separate license-plate bracket mounted ahead of the light. In *The Enthusiast* of September 1954, H-D claims a weight reduction of 15oz for the new light. Just think. If they'd've used titanium, they probably could have shaved another four or five ounces off this 600lb machine.

The taillight body is painted the color of the fender, but the rim piece that frames the lens is chrome. This style of taillight is correct through 1972. The license-plate bracket is adjustable and painted black (standard) or chrome-plated. The new taillight and license bracket required a new rear fender with the necessary mounting holes. The fender and bracket were used through 1957.

Smooth Primary Cover

From the left side, the outer primary-chain cover looks decidedly different from the "diamond" cover used in previous years, and the clutch-booster cover is cadmium plated (it had been painted black). Standard clutch-booster covers were cad plated through the end of the

Panhead line, but chrome covers were available through the accessory catalogs. Chrome booster covers were first offered on new Panheads in 1959, as part of the Chrome Finish Group.

The new primary cover is rounded, smooth, and painted gloss black. It's fitted with a small primary-chain inspection cover and a larger clutch inspection cover, and features a raised strip running from the front edge to the clutch "bulge." The inspection covers are also painted black, but chrome-plated covers are optional. In addition, the new primary cover may have a third cover, smaller and farther forward than the other two. I say "may have" because the hole that the cover plugs is present only if the motorcycle was ordered with the new, optional compensating sprocket (which acts as an engine shock absorber and sold for $15, exchange). This new cover allows access to lubricate the compensating sprocket, is about the size of a quarter, and is chrome-plated. The smooth primary cover was used through 1964.

The inner primary-chain cover was new, as well, and was made in separate designs for foot- and hand-shift bikes. The main change is that the new cover has a larger sprocket-shaft hole and revised mounting perch to bolt up to the revised left crankcase (see below). The inner chain guard is mounted to the crankcase by three bolts with spring washers, and a gasket is fitted between the chain cover and crankcase. Spring washers and gaskets work together to reduce rattling and vibration. These new inner primary covers are used through 1957.

Timken Bearings

The left crankcase and sprocket shaft were redesigned to use tapered Timken bearings in place of the former roller bearings. The shaft is keyed only at the flywheel end, has ten splines at the sprocket end, and is made of harder, 4620 nickel-moly steel. At 4-15/16in long and 1-1/4in in diameter, the new shaft is longer and larger in diameter than the previous sprocket shaft (which had been used in all Harley Big Twins since 1930). This new sprocket shaft is used for 1955 only.

The left case featured a smooth surface inside the primary-chain mounting ring (previously, there had been a raised mounting boss and three radial ribs) and the number "24599-55" cast in relief on the inside of the case. The redesigned case is used through 1957.

Timken bearings are designed to take thrust and radial loads, so the flywheels are redesigned for use without thrust washers. The left flywheel is a one-year-only part that has a thick shoulder for the Timken bearing to seat against.

The pinion-shaft bearing was also replaced with one of larger area, so the right crankcase and pinion shaft were redesigned to accommodate the new bearing. The new shaft is "crowned" to reduce end pressure on the bearing

An older restoration of a 1957 Big Twin that was originally a police bike, as evidenced by the square oil tank on the right side. This bike is fitted with the correct Speed King leather saddlebags that were used from 1954–57. The bike is owned by Gary Nelson.

rollers. Like the new left case, the new right case and gear shaft are used through 1957.

O-ring Manifolds and Heads

Plumber-nut manifolds had been used even before the first Knucklehead in 1936. These manifolds were simple, and sealed fairly well when new, but the solid joint they created between the heads and the carburetor transmitted and amplified the effects of the engine's vibration, foaming gas in the carburetor. Over time, vibration also caused the manifold bushings to wear against the manifold and create air leaks. Even when they sealed well, the plumber nuts were a pain to properly loosen or tighten in the cramped V of the motor.

In 1955, H-D released a completely new manifold design (and new cylinder heads to match) that eliminated all these problems: the O-ring manifold. No longer is the intake manifold fastened to the inlet nipple with the large plumber nuts. Instead, a large O-ring is sandwiched between the end of each nipple and the end of each manifold tube, and each nipple–O-ring–manifold junction is covered and sealed by a large strap clamp. A lip on each cylinder end of the T-shaped manifold helps hold the O-ring in place, and the carburetor still mounts to the manifold with four bolts. The manifold is made of cast iron, bears the number "27027-55," and is painted silver. This manifold was used through 1957. (In 1958, yet another manifold was released; it is identical to the 1955–57 manifold, but is cast aluminum and is not painted.)

The new cylinder heads have a cast-in inlet nipple (previous nipples were separate steel pieces that threaded into the intake ports) that is designed to connect with the new O-ring intake manifold. Each head has the mark "16704 55 FRONT" or "16705 55 REAR" cast in relief on the underside of the head between the pushrod holes. Cylinder heads for the FLH motors have polished and flowed intake ports.

Heads for 1955 were drilled for only six valve-cover mounting holes (rather than twelve) because the 3/4in aluminum D-rings with six holes (which had been introduced on very-late-1954 Panheads) were again used. (Note: Because the six-hole D-rings did not seal well, most 1955 Panheads were retrofitted with the later twelve-hole D-rings and had the additional holes drilled for the mounting screws. Nevertheless, to be stock and original, 1955 Panheads should have the six-hole D-rings.)

Speedometer

The 1955 Stewart-Warner speedometer was slightly changed from the 1954 speedometer: the tenth-mile numerals were painted black on a white background (instead of red numerals on a black background). This speedometer is used only for 1955.

State of the Art, 1955

Harley-Davidson FLH vs. Vincent Series D Black Prince

In a final bout of synchronicity, both Vincent and Harley took their next bold steps in 1955. Curiously, Harley-Davidson's step was in Vincent's direction, and vice versa. Harley's step was, of course, to offer a hot-rodded version of its Big Twin, the FLH, with its specially ported and flowed intake ports. Vincent's step was to offer more civilized versions of their Rapide and Black Shadow—the Black Knight and Black Prince—but in typical Vincent fashion, these updates were carried to a bizarre extreme that would not be equaled until Honda reintroduced the scooter-on-steroids look with its Pacific Coast models of the late 1980s. So, with that cryptic introduction, let's once again compare the world's premier V-twins.

Since little had changed on the Harley since 1949, let's not compare every feature. Rather, let's go through the many changes to the Vincent to see how the balance was changed.

To make the world's premier musclebike into a more practical road bike, Vincent fitted the Black Prince with coil ignition for easier starting, full-coverage body work to reduce engine noise and protect the rider, a new rear suspension that isolated the rider from the rise and fall of the rear wheel, and softer spring rates for the front and rear suspension.

In function, the two bikes were still miles apart. The Vincent was faster, smoother, and had better suspension and rider protection, while the Harley was basically the same big American touring machine that it had been since 1949, with about 10 percent more horsepower to give it a bit more spunk and availability of foot shift to make gear shifts easier. Impossible as it may seem in light of their respective reputations, the FLH was now rated as the more powerful machine at 60hp, versus Vincent's rating of 55hp for the Black Prince.

Did this mean the FLH was new king of speed? Unfortunately not, because the Harley still outweighed the Vincent by more than 150lb and the new body work made the Black Prince far slipperier than the unfaired FLH. Even so, the FLH was an exciting new step for H-D. Better yet, it was successful, for the higher performance FLH gave a much-needed boost in sales after the worst postwar sales year for Big Twins yet. And FLH sales continued to grow every year after, until the FLH became the best-selling Big Twin model.

Did it mean the Black Prince was the new the king of the road and that Vincent would grow and prosper? Again, no. As capable as it was, the Black Prince's functionality came at the cost of the one attribute on which no motorcycle manufacturer can afford to compromise: style. The new fairing and bodywork covered the entire engine, giving the machine a futuristic, but slab-sided appearance that was totally at odds with the muscular grace of previous Vincents. Vincent had succeeded admirably in making its Black Prince a supreme real-world road-burner, but it went too far too fast and alienated its traditional customers while producing a bike that was still too expensive to win them a new customer base. The result (when combined with losses from other ventures) was that Vincent was once again driven into bankruptcy, while Harley's sales rose, albeit temporarily.

Which brings us to the ultimate point of the comparisons in these sidebars: they allow honest criticism of Harley's products to be combined with a perfect cautionary tale of why one must not judge The Motor Company too harshly. Face it, the Harleys and the Davidsons were canny at the business of making motorcycles. If all a company had to do was make the best and fastest, Vincent would be bigger than Honda today. But, as many motorcyclists the world over lament, Vincent did not even survive the 1950s, when British motorcycles were dominant. Harley-Davidson didn't always produce the world's best motorcycles, but it has survived more than ninety years by knowing what its customers want and how to make a profit by doing so. As Jerry Hatfield so succinctly put it in his superb book *Inside Harley-Davidson*, "The Milwaukee brand was—and ever remains—a tough outfit."

Seats

Starting in 1955, H-D standard solo seats were stitched with the same type of rolled seam that was used on 1950 and later Deluxe Solo Seats. This style of seat is standard through 1965.

The optional Deluxe Solo Seat (which could be ordered in place of the standard saddle for $7.40) was restyled for 1955. Instead of a three-piece leather skirt with plastic rosettes, the new saddle has a one-piece Royalite rubber skirt with a wing-shaped lobe at each side, and each lobe is decorated with a nickel piece that is shaped like an elongated diamond. The shorter rear part of the skirt is decorated with seven nickel rectangles. As promised in *The Enthusiast* of September 1954, the new seat was a "big hit with pleasure riders and police officers." This flashy, new saddle is a correct option for 1955–65 Panheads.

Sidecar

With the introduction of the new taillight and license-plate bracket, the taillight and license-plate bracket on the sidecar's fender were eliminated.

Front-Fender Bumper

A new-style, optional front bumper was introduced in late 1955. This bumper is called, depending on who is asked, the "bologna slicer," "antenna," or "Venetian blind" bumper because it has three chrome "blades" with their edges pointed forward (the blades are similar to those included in the optional grille for the rear bumper). The blades bridge the gap between two chromed, J-shaped tubes that mount to the fender and reach forward and up, each topped off with a chromed ball. This bumper offered little in the way of protection, but gives a very 1950s look to the front end. The bumper was an $8.75 option in 1955. This bumper is a correct option for 1955–57 Panheads.

1955 Production

Sales improved somewhat for 1955, but not enough to make a huge difference. A total of 5,142 were sold: 953 FL, 853 FLE, 63 FLH, 2,013 FLF, 220 FLEF, and 1,040 FLHF. No one really knows for sure why the sales increased, but my guess is that it's due largely to the introduction of the new factory hot-rod, the Super Sport FLH. Even though it was introduced in the middle of the production run and was a bit more expensive, the FLH accounted for 1,103 sales, more than 20 percent of the total.

Model Year 1956

America's love affair with Ike continues in 1956. Ike trounces Adlai Stevenson again, but after the election, Ike must deal with a House and Senate controlled by the Democrats.

Krushchev declares, "We will bury you!" and that the Russians will build intercontinental ballistic missiles (ICBMs). The Hungarians try to kick out the Soviets, but Soviet troops invade and brutally crush the revolt.

Desegregation picks up steam, despite rioting and set-backs. Blacks boycott the buses in Montgomery, Alabama, and many demonstraters are arrested before bus segregation ends. Martin Luther King, Jr. preaches nonviolent protest, arguing that "Unearned suffering is redemptive."

The Cult of Elvis begins. With such hits as *Hound Dog* and *Love Me Tender*, Elvis won over everyone, including Ed Sullivan, who had vowed never to allow Elvis on his show. Sullivan eventually pays Elvis $50,000 for three appearances on the show. The world is Elvis' oyster, and "The King" develops a burnin' love for Milwaukee iron. So, what did he buy? A tarted up, red and white 1956 KH that *The Enthusiast* of May 1956 says cost $3,000. List price for a 1956 KH was only $935. To get the bill up to $3,000, he must have ordered every option *and* a matching Big Twin with every option.

1956 Hydra-Glides

For 1956, the Big Twin was again offered in FL, FLE, and FLH trim, with choice of standard, side-car, and police gearing and hand shift or foot shift. Base-model FLs and FLEs retailed for $1,055, and base-model FLHs retailed for $1,123, each just $40 more than the previous year's prices.

For 1956, the items that had been part of the extra-cost Standard Solo Group (and Utility Solo Group before that) were included in the base price. These items included a black front safety guard, an air cleaner, a jiffy stand, and black 5.00x16in wheels and tires. Three new civilian solo option groups were offered to dress up the basic bike. The Chrome Finish Group included all the most popular dress-up accessories (chrome front safety guard, muffler, handlebars, rims, and other bits) for $54. The Road Cruiser Group included the basic touring accessories (Deluxe Buddy Seat, leather saddlebags, windshield, and others) for $106 (with Super Deluxe Buddy Seat substituted for Deluxe Buddy Seat add $13). The King of the Highway Group included all the basic touring accessories plus much more (cigarette lighter, dual exhaust, buddy seat rail, plastic saddlebags, turn signals, and others) for $191.50.

The two-tone paint scheme for 1956 is one of the most handsome ever used on a Harley. Tanks were given graceful, side stripes that arc up and forward from the lower rear edge of the tank, around and past the V tank emblem used in 1955. This scheme was offered in seven standard colors and one optional color. Standard were: Pepper Red with white tank stripes and red fenders, Atomic Blue with Champion Yellow tank stripes and blue fenders, Champion Yellow with black tank stripe and yellow fenders, Black with Champion Yellow tank stripes and

Dan Olberg's 1957 FLH. This beautiful Panhead has several chrome-plated items that were not offered in 1957, including the oil tanks and tool box (plated tool boxes were first offered on new bikes in 1959).

black fenders, Silver (Police Group only), and White (Police Group only). Available for $5 extra are Flamboyant Metallic Green with white tank stripes and green fenders. Though not listed on the order blanks, gas tanks could be ordered in standard colors without tank stripes, at no extra cost, according to *The Enthusiast* of September 1955.

New Air Cleaner

A new-style air cleaner was fitted to the 1956s. The new stainless steel cover is still 7in in diameter but is now fastened by a chromed center screw, rather than by J-slots on the cover's edge. The data plate that had been riveted to earlier air-cleaner covers is no longer fitted. Instead, the information from the data plate is stamped into the cover. Inside the cover is a new, replaceable filter element made of corrugated paper (rather than oiled copper) backed with wire mesh. Harley claims the new filter has an area of 182sq-in. This new style of air cleaner was used through 1965.

Victory Cam and other Motor Mods

H-D engineers built "more 'Z-O-O-M' in the FLH for 1956," according to September 1956 *The Enthusiast*. The 1956 FLH motors are fitted with the hot, new "Victory" cam shaft. The new cam has higher lift (1.342in versus 1.334in) and narrower lobes (1.075in versus 1.10in). In combination with the polished and flowed ports and higher-compression pistons that are also included in the FLH package, the new cam gives the FLH 12 percent more power than the FL. This cam is used in 1956–69 FLH motors. Ever enthusiastic, the writers of *The Enthusiast* boasted that the FLH "takes off like a guided missile."

The Timken sprocket-shaft bearings and new sprocket shaft that were introduced in 1955 were indeed stronger than the older parts, but the design made the inner bearing difficult to remove for servicing. The inner bearing seated against a shoulder on the left flywheel, so the shaft had to be removed from the flywheel before the bearing could be pressed off the shaft. To correct the problem, H-D engineers released a new set of left lower-end components. The new left flywheel lacked the bearing shoulder that had been used on the 1955 flywheel. Instead, the bearing shoulder is added to the new sprocket shaft, spacing the bearing away from the flywheel just enough to allow a bearing puller to get a grip on the bearing. The sprocket-shaft's key slot is also made deeper. This sprocket shaft is used through 1964. The new left flywheel is used through 1960.

Many top-end parts that had been introduced in 1955 were also replaced in 1956. The 1956 cylinder heads were entirely new castings with nine fins on the pushrod side (instead of six), twelve valve-cover mounting holes, and the casting mark "16700 56 FRONT" or "16701 56 REAR" cast into the head between the pushrod holes, but now the casting mark was on the top of the head in the area covered by the valve cover. These new heads were also used for 1957.

New versions of the 3/4in, cast-aluminum D-rings were fitted for 1956. These new D-rings had twelve mounting holes for a better valve-cover oil seal. Each cover was fastened by twelve hex-head cap screws. These D-rings and screws are correct for 1956–65 Panheads.

Problems with oil draining from the oil tank through the lifters, into the crankcase, were finally solved by fitting a new check-valve spring in the oil pump. This new oil pump was used through mid-1962.

The frame was slightly modified for 1956. The coil-mounting-block holes are 3/8in (rather than 5/16in), and a stainless steel cover was added to the steering-head lock. This frame is used in 1956 and 1957.

The H-D patent decal was no longer placed on the left side of the oil tank. For 1956 and later, it was on the front of the oil tank, hidden from view by the seat-post tube. On FLH models, a new FLH decal was used on both sides of the oil tank. The FLH decal consists of a large, red V on a silver shield with the black letters "FLH" over both. This decal was used on all 1956–60 FLHs.

New Speedometer

The Stewart-Warner speedometer was given another facelift for 1956. The lower face is painted a "light gold" and the numerals, 2mph division marks, and the words "Harley-Davidson" are painted in "green Day-Glo" on the underside of the glass.

1956 Production

Sales increased again for 1956, to 5,806. Included in this total are 856 FL, 671 FLE, 224 FLH, 1,578 FLF, 162 FLEF, and 2,315 FLHF. In its first full year of production, the FLH had risen to be the new star of the line-up, accounting for almost half of total sales.

Model Year 1957

The space race dominates the world news for 1957. The Russians take an early lead when they boast of the first successful ICBM launch. A short while later, they twist the knife again when they successfully launch their *Sputnik* satellite into orbit. Then they do it again, launching *Sputnik II* with the dog Laika aboard. Meanwhile America successfully launches the Thor ICBM, but the first attempt at launching a satellite, the Viking, blows up on the launching pad. Ever eager to rub America's nose in it, Krushchev taunts that the Soviet satellites are lonesome "waiting for American satellites to join them in space."

Integration struggles again dominate the domestic news. Sen. Strom Thurmond (then a Democrat) performs a record filibuster of 24hr 18min, but still fails to block passage of civil-rights legislation. The Arkansas National Guard is called in to *prevent* black students from entering white high schools. Ike sends in federal troops to straighten out the ARNG.

Evangelism reaches the big time as the Rev. Billy Graham draws a crowd of 92,000 to Yankee stadium in New York City. Drive-in churches gain in popularity.

Many of the most enduring icons of the 1950s make their first appearances. *Leave It to Beaver* and *American Bandstand* debut on national TV. The Hula Hoop and Frisbee become fads.

Elvis' hot streak continues with the hit songs *All Shook Up* and *Jailhouse Rock*, not to mention the inimitable *Elvis' Christmas Album*. What does he do with his new-found wealth? He puts aside his red and white 1956 KH and buys a 1957 Hydra-Glide. Finally, The King rides the King of the Highway.

1957 Hydra-Glides

For 1957, only the FL and FLH were offered, with the rider's choice of standard, police, or sidecar gearing and with foot shift or gear shift. FLHs retailed for $1243, and the FLs retailed for $1167, both about 10 percent higher than the previous year's prices.

A new two-tone paint style was standard for 1957. Instead of 1956's side stripes, 1957 tank tops were painted with a contrasting panel on the top of the tank. Four standard color combinations were offered: Pepper Red with Black tank panels and red fenders, Skyline Blue with Birch White tank panels and blue fenders, Birch White with Black tank panels and white fenders, and Black with Pepper Red tank panels and Black fenders. Optional at no extra charge: Police Silver (Police Group only), Birch White (solid or with black tank panels), any standard color without tank panels, fenders painted to match the tank panel. And optional for a $5 extra charge was Metallic Midnight Blue with Birch White tank panels and blue fenders

For 1957 the Panhead rode in the shadow of its new little brother, the first Sportster. Harley engineers had been busy getting the Sportster ready for production and were hard at work on the next big round of changes to the Panhead, scheduled for 1958, so few changes were made to the Big Twin for 1957.

For the first time on the Big Twins, H-D experimented with plastic tank emblems and front-fender tip. The emblems were round, plastic discs with a silver-colored rim and a background divided in quadrants (two of which are silver; the other two are red). The name "Harley-Davidson" is printed over the top of the disc in red, block letters, in two lines. This emblem was used for 1957 only. The plastic front-fender tip is decorated with the bar-and-shield logo in red and a silver or gold V (both colors are present on NOS parts). Stainless steel trim strips sweep back from the fender tip to the fork sliders. This fender tip is correct only for 1957 and 1958. The side trim strips continued to be used with the new fender tip introduced in 1959 and both pieces are used through 1965.

The stainless steel rocker covers that had been used since 1949 were replaced for 1957 with stamped aluminum covers that are otherwise the same as earlier covers. Aluminum covers are correct for 1957–65 Panheads.

Several small changes refined the engine. New pushrods were fitted that are shorter overall so they can be adjusted down and removed easier. Since 1950, Panhead motors had been built with steel intake valve guides and bronze exhaust-valve guides. Starting February 1, 1957, new steel alloy exhaust-valve guides were introduced to replace the bronze guides. The new exhaust-valve guides are "threaded" inside to trap oil and improve lubrication. The intake guides are not threaded because threaded guides would allow too much oil to leak into the combustion chamber. Starting with motor number 57FLH4444, new, stronger valve springs are fitted to all FLH motors.

Small changes were made to the speedometer, as well. The 1957 style Stewart-Warner speedometer is the same as the 1956 speedo, except that the tenth-mile numerals are painted red on a black background. In addi-

The last of the spring-fork Panheads with the last of the Hydra-Glides. Shown are Dave Monahan's rare 1949 springer and Dan Olberg's 1957 FLH.

tion, a new, thinner speedometer cable was fitted from the transmission to the speedometer.

The optional leather King Size and Fringed King, and Streamliner saddlebags were equipped with bag hangers that had two studs and a U-shaped padlock fitting to secure the bag to the hanger, allowing the bags to be detached quickly from the bike or to be locked to the bike. These bags are also equipped with "never sag" expanders.

Extra-large Big Bertha saddlebags were optional for 1957 only. Like the other 1957 leather bags, these bags use the quick-disconnect leather bag mounts and "never sag" expanders.

Harley inventory must finally have run out of nickel comets, so the optional black Royalite hard plastic saddlebags got a facelift in 1957. The new bags were trimmed with a red "shark" or "jet" overlaid on a silver, slanted oval.

Further evidence that the comets were finally out of stock: The Deluxe Buddy seat was restyled with a tooled-leather skirt with large, nickel dots on each side replacing the comets.

1957 Production

Sales dropped once again for 1957, to 5,616. This total includes 1,579 FL, 164 FLH, 1,259 FLF, and 2,614 FLHF. Once again, the FLH is almost half of the total. More interesting, over half of the FLs sold were hand-shift bikes, whereas hand-shift bikes were just a minuscule portion of the FLHs sold.

So ended the Hydra-Glide line. During eight years of production, the King of Bikes—or at least the bike of The King—gained weight, power, better lifters, and a stronger bottom end. What it really needed was rear suspension. And that's the headline feature of the Hydra-Glide's successor, the Duo-Glide of 1958.

CHAPTER THREE

1958-1964
The Duo-Glide

As early as the pre-teens, motorcycle manufacturers had begun fitting production motorcycles with rear suspension. The first of these were simple sprung-frame systems without hydraulic damping such as those on the Brough SS 80s of the late 1920s and the Vincent-HRDs beginning in 1928. A bit later, plunger rear ends came into fashion, being fitted to the BMW R51 of 1938, the Indian Chief of 1940, and many others. The next step in the evolutionary chain was a swingarm rear suspension with hydraulic dampers such as that on the 1948 Series C Vincents, the 1949 AJS and Matchless, the 1954 BSA and Triumph, and the 1955 BMW.

By the early 1950s, the Panhead's hardtail rear end was clearly old-fashioned, and out-sized saddlebags and crash bars could no longer hide that fact. Primitive early roads had kept vehicle speeds

The 1960 speedometer was identical to the speedometer that had been introduced in 1956. For 1957, the tenth-mile numerals on the trip meter were red on a black background. For 1958–61, the trip-meter tenth-mile numerals were changed back to black on a white background. Also shown in this view is the green neutral-light indicator that was added to the instrument panels of 1959–61 foot-shift bikes. Before 1960, the optional, adjustable-trail forks for sidecar use were easily spotted because the top fork covers on non-adjustable forks were smooth (the vent caps extended through the cover on standard forks). Top covers are smooth for all 1960 and later forks, as shown here.

Right: This 1960 Duo-Glide is owned by Rob Carlson of Kokesh Motorcycles and was restored by Elmer Ehnes. It was restored as a trim sports model, with narrow Speedster-style bars and an aftermarket solo seat. As is usual on Elmer's restorations, it is not over-restored, and attention to correct finish and every detail are astonishing. Non-stock items are few: the seat shown is not the Deluxe Solo seat that was available on new machines, and the rear chain guard should be painted black.

low, so H-D engineers were reluctant to add the weight and complexity of rear suspension when their time-proven "suspension" of fat 5.00x16in tires and sprung seat cushioned the blows well enough for most riders. But in the 1950s, America's vast network of roads was quickly evolving toward the freeway system we enjoy today. As speeds rose, so did the call for a real rear suspension. This call was answered in 1958 with the introduction of the Duo-Glide.

Not being among the pioneers of rear suspension, H-D had the luxury of examining the best of their competitors' designs, thus H-D skipped the spring frame and plunger frame and introduced a swingarm frame with a hydraulically-damped shock absorber on each side.

Continuing the tradition started with the Hydra-Glide, the new model was named the Duo-Glide. The Hydra-Glide was developed gradually over the next seven years to become the classic American touring bike.

Model Year 1958

The space race continues in 1958. The U.S. makes its first successful satellite launch when *Explorer I* launches from Cape Canaveral. A short time later, the Soviets launch *Sputnik III*. NASA is formed and announces Project Mercury, with the stated goal of putting a man in space within two years.

Minor skirmishes escalate around the world. Riots break out in Beirut, and Ike sends in the Marines. A coup overthrows the Algerian government. Communist Chinese aircraft bomb islands held by Nationalist Chinese, and Ike orders the Navy to resupply Nationalist troops on the islands. Communist rebels led by Fidel Castro capture a Cuban provincial capital, and the U.S. begins to take the threat seriously. Vice President Richard Nixon is stoned by an angry crowd in Caracas, Venezuela.

The prosperous 1950s slow somewhat as the U.S. economy sinks into a slight recession. Politicians point fingers. Alaska is admitted as the forty-ninth state.

On one societal extreme, the Beatniks gain prominence, and Jack Kerouac's *Dharma Bums* is published to critical acclaim. On the other extreme, the John Birch Society is formed. The last Federal troops leave Arkansas after restoring the appearance of order following the desegregation riots.

The TV show *77 Sunset Strip* debuts, and one of its stars, Edd "Kookie" Byrnes later rides an H-D Topper scooter on the show and appears in H-D ads. Elvis scores another hit single with *Hard-Headed Woman* before being inducted into the Army. Unfortunately, he had to leave his Harleys at home.

1958 Duo-Glide

Duo-Glides were sold with FL and FLH motors, with the rider's choice of standard, police, or sidecar gearing and with foot shift or gear shift. FLHs retailed for $1,320, and the FLs retailed for $1,255, both about 10 percent higher than the previous year's prices.

A new paint style with two-tone tanks and fenders was standard for 1958. The tanks were fitted with round plastic tank badges, similar to those that had been fitted in 1957 (1958 badges are gold and black though). The top of the tank was painted in a contrasting color that wraps around the top of the emblems to cover the top half of the front part of the tank. The following standard color combinations were available: Skyline Blue tank top and Birch

For 1958, new heads were fitted that have noticeably longer fins. Attached to these heads is a new version of the O-ring manifold made of cast aluminum. This unrestored 1958 Duo-Glide is owned by Jerry Richards and is shown in front of Rochester Harley-Davidson in Rochester, Minnesota. Most of the items in the King of the Highway option group are fitted to this bike, including the Super Deluxe Buddy Seat with the correct twin-tube hand rail that was new for 1958, dual exhaust, plastic saddlebags, and many other items. Several items on this super-nice machine are not correct: correct bags for 1958 are black (white plastic saddlebags were first offered on new bikes in 1959 but were offered as a retrofit kit for the 1958 Duo-Glide), the trim strip on the lower, back edge of this bike's front fender is correct for 1949–57 (however, it is possible that some very early 1958 fenders were so equipped), and the cylinders should be painted silver. Note that the new Duo-Glide frame lacks the sidecar-mounting loops that were fitted to all earlier Panhead frames. This frame style was fitted to all 1958–64 Duo-Glides.

The front-fender tip that had been introduced on the 1957 Hydra-Glide was used again on the new Duo-Glide. The tip was made of plastic, but had stainless steel side trim pieces. This bike is also fitted with the Aristocrat front bumper, which was new for 1958. This fender tip was replaced after the 1958 model year, but the front bumper was optional through 1965. Whitewall tires were first offered as an option on new machines in 1958.

White sides, mudguards with white top and blue sides; Calypso Red tank top with Birch White sides, mudguards with white top and red sides; Sabre Gray Metallic tank top and Birch White sides, mudguards with white top and gray sides; Black tank top and Birch White sides, mudguards with white top and black sides; Police Silver (Police Group only); and Birch White (Police Group only). Any standard color solid (without tank panels) was available at no extra charge.

In 1958, the number of option groups started to spin out of control, with numerous sub groups available to customize the main option group.

Duo-Glide Frame

Like the last of the Hydra-Glide frames, the Duo-

The Duo-Glide taillight was the same oval taillight that had been introduced in 1955. This style of taillight was used through the end of the Panhead line, and was always painted the color of the fender. Correct casting marks on the lens are highlighted with wax.

Glide frame is a straight-leg cradle frame with twin downtubes, large-diameter backbone tube, and vertical seat post behind the motor. However, the Duo-Glide frame is new from the seat post back.

The left and right lower tubes no longer extend all the way back to the axle mount forgings; they each now end at a swingarm-pivot forging. A tube bridges the left and right forgings, and the rear transmission mount is welded to this tube. The conventional, forked swingarm pivots about a long swingarm axle, riding on a roller bearing at each end, and the axle-mount forgings are welded to the end of the swingarm arms. The mount for the teardrop tool box disappeared with the old lower rear tube on the right side, so new mounts were added to the rear vertical tube and lower forging on the right side, to which the tool box attached vertically, with the larger end down. Also, the "loop" sidecar-mount forgings are no longer welded to the front downtubes. On 1958 and later motorcycles, the sidecars mount to forgings that are held to the motorcycle frame by U-bolts.

The left and right top, rear tubes no longer stretch from the seat-post tube to the axle-mount forgings. Instead, they end at the front of the shock-mount forgings, and another tube bridges the gap between the right and left forgings at the top. A vertical tube stretches from the shock-mount forging to the swingarm-pivot forging on each side. Each shock-mount forging has two mounting lugs, a large one for the top shock mount (located just above the vertical tube from the lower forging) and a

Plenty of room for even long legs to stretch out on the new 1958 Duo-glide. This well-appointed machine features the Super Deluxe Buddy Seat and the optional whitewall tires, which first became available on new 1958 Big Twins. *Photo copyright Harley-Davidson*

Jerry Richards' Duo-Glide has all the accessories. Shown here are the optional spot lamps, front running lights, control-coil covers, and rubber-mounted handlebars.

smaller one toward the aft end of the forging for the fender-support arm.

The Duo-Glide frame is known as the "step-down" frame because the upper-shock-mount forging bends down noticeably between the top shock mount and the cross-brace just in front of the mount. Harley-Davidson engineers got it right the first time in designing this frame; it was used without change from 1958 to 1964.

From front to rear, dozens of parts were modified to fit the Duo-Glide frame.

The stem and top triple tree for both the fixed- and adjustable-rake forks are modified to fit the new frame. These new fork assemblies are used only for 1958 and 1959. The forks are otherwise the same as on previous Panheads.

The 1958 Duo-Glide used the same front fender tip and side trim strips as were used in 1957, but a new chromed Duo-Glide emblem was mounted to each side of the fender, and the small stainless steel trim strip that protected the lower rear rim of the fender was no longer fitted. Duo-Glide emblems are standard from 1958 to 1964.

A new, one-piece, tubular front safety guard mounted with a single bolt (rather than with two U-bolts) to a new bracket between the frame downtubes. This new guard is correct for 1958–65 Panheads.

A new oil tank was designed to fit the new frame. This oil tank is similar to the horseshoe oil tanks that had been used on the OHV twins since 1940, except that the new tank has two battery tie-down tabs welded to the tank, at the back of the battery well. (The battery tie-downs on hardtail machines had bolted to the rear fender.) This new oil tank is correct for 1958–64 Panheads. The oil-filter assembly also required modification to fit the Duo-Glide frame. The filter unit is the same as used on previous bikes, but the bracket and oil-return line are new parts to fit the swingarm frame. This new filter assembly was used on 1958–64 Panheads.

Toolboxes on Harley's OHV twins had been teardrop shaped and horizontally mounted since the 1940 Knucklehead, but this tradition was changed for 1958. The right shock absorber cuts diagonally through the space occupied by the old tool box, so the tool box was

The optional chrome rail for the optional Deluxe and Super Deluxe buddy seats was redesigned in mid-1958 to the new "twin-tube" design. The new rail consists of a thicker, chromed main tube that stretches around the back of the seat and a smaller upper tube connected to the main tube at the small tube's ends and in the center by a V-shaped reinforcement. The old-style rail (consisting of a single tube that wraps around behind the seat) was offered in early 1958, so either style is correct for 1958, but only the new style rail is correct for 1959 and later. Also, the Buddy Seat helper springs were revised to fit the new frame.

The optional, bullet-shaped turn signals were given redesigned mounts for 1958. These new turn signals were used through 1962.

The Royalite plastic saddlebags continued to be offered for the Duo-Glide. The bags themselves were the same as the late Hydra-Glide bags, but the mounts were revised for the Duo-Glide frame. Only black bags are correct for 1958, but black and white bags are correct for 1959 and later. (White bags were later offered to retrofit to 1958 and earlier models, but they were not available on the new machines.)

A new optional "Aristocrat" front bumper was introduced in 1958 that matched the style of the "twin-tube" Buddy Seat hand rail. The Aristocrat front bumper is correct for 1958–65. A matching Aristocrat rear bumper was introduced later in the 1958 production year. It is also correct for 1958 and later Panheads.

1958 Production

Despite a minor recession, 1958 Panhead sales were up by about 7-1/2 percent from the previous year. Harley-Davidson built 1,591 FL, 1,299 FLF, 195 FLH, and 2,953 FLHF. As before, about half the FL models were still hand shift, while relatively few of the FLH models were hand shift.

It is prudent to interject a note on "rarity" here. Often you'll see an ad that reads something like this: "Ultra rare 1958 FLH, one of only 195 made!" Are 1958 FLHs rare or not? Yes, if they are original hand-shift models, then only about 195 were made. But nearly 3,000 foot-shift FLHFs were made for 1958, and the "F" for foot shift was not stamped into the motor as part of the serial number. Because there is no way to conclusively document that a given bike was delivered from the factory as a hand-shift bike (unless the owner possesses the original Harley delivery documents), don't get suckered into thinking that such a bike should be worth more than any other 1958 FLH. It is so easy to convert a bike from foot-shift to hand shift that there could easily be more hand-shift 1958 FLHs today than H-D originally built.

Model Year 1959

Several new heats of the space race are run in 1959. The "Mercury Seven" become national heroes. The Soviets reach the moon first with *Lunik II*. America's *Pioneer IV* passes the moon and heads toward the sun.

The new style of chrome-plated rear-fender tip shown on Seber's Duo-Glide was optional on 1959 and later Panheads.

Those pesky Communists are in the news again. Fidel Castro's rebels take Havana. Nikita Krushchev claims the Soviets have attained military superiority. Krushchev meets with Ike at Camp David and then tours the United States. On sampling the food in Des Moines, Iowa, the ever-gracious Krushchev comments, "We have beaten you to the moon, but you have beaten us in sausage making." He is denied entrance to Disneyland because of security concerns.

Buddy Holly, Ritchie Valens, and the Big Bopper become rock-and-roll's first casualties when they die in a plane crash. New stars such as Dion, Ray Charles, and Bobby Darin rise to take their places.

When not encumbered with bags and a lot of touring accessories, the Duo-Glide was still a fairly trim machine, at least when compared to the Electra-Glide. A few non-correct items are worth noting on this otherwise beautiful machine: the kick-starter pedal is the 1963 and later style, and the valve-cover D-rings should be the natural silver color of the aluminum.

But the most sensational news stories are the "payola" scandal and the investigations into the rigging of quiz-shows. Later in the year, a famed winner of $129,000 on the quiz show *Twenty-One* admits before a Congressional hearing that the show's producers gave him the answers in advance.

1959 Duo-Glides

For 1959, the 74ci Big Twin was offered in two basic models—FL and FLH—and in foot-shift or hand-shift versions of each. In addition, sidecar or police gearing could be specified at the time of order. The FLH machines carried a retail price of $1,345, and the FL machines retailed for $1,280, each a modest $25 increase in price over the previous year.

A handsome, new two-tone paint scheme and new tank emblems distinguish the 1959 models. The emblems consist of a red disk background, pierced by a large, chrome arrow. The shaft of the arrow has the company name embossed into it, and the letters of Harley-Davidson are painted red. Two-tone tanks feature Birch White side panels that wrap gracefully around the arrow tank badge. In my opinion, the 1949 two-tone tanks are one of the three best applied to the Panhead series. The tank emblem was used again for 1960, but a different two-tone scheme was applied.

Three standard color combinations were offered: Skyline Blue with Birch White tank side panels, Calypso Red with Birch White tank side panels, and Black with Birch White tank side panels. Optional were Hi-Fi Turquoise with Birch White tank side panels, Hi-Fi Red with Birch White tank side panels, Police Silver (Police Group only), Birch White (Police Group only), and any standard color solid (without tank panels).

Detail Changes

Perched atop the tanks is a revised instrument cover for foot-shift bikes, but the speedometer is the same design used the previous year. The new dash is identical to the one that had been in use since 1947, except that it features a neutral-indicator light covered by a green, domed lens. This new indicator is positioned to the left and slightly forward of the center mounting bolt on the dash. This dash style is correct for all foot-shift Panheads from 1959–61. The instrument panel was painted the same color as the tank unless the Chrome Finish Group was ordered, in which case the panel was chrome plated.

Rather than the plastic front fender tip used from 1957 to 1958, the 1959 Panhead was given a new, chrome-plated fender tip. Viewed from straight on, the new tip looks like a large V with a mountain peak rising above it. This style of front fender tip is correct for 1959 to 1965 Panheads. A matching chromed rear fender tip was also released in 1959 and was optional for all 1959–65 Panheads.

Starting in 1959, the footboards were painted black. Earlier footboards had been Parkerized but were unpainted. For all 1959–64 Panheads, the footboards were Parkerized (Bonderized) and then painted gloss black.

Standard clutch-booster-spring covers were cadmium plated, but a chrome-plated cover was optional for the first time as part of the Chrome Finish Group. Chrome-plated covers were optional for 1959–65. It is possible that some late 1958 bikes were fitted with chrome covers.

The 1959 tool box was the same vertically-mounted, teardrop-shaped, smooth-covered tool box introduced in 1958, but chrome-plated covers were optional on new machines for the first time in 1959, as part of the Chrome Finish Group or separately from the accessories list (they may have been available earlier from the accessory catalogs or aftermarket sources). Standard covers were painted black.

For 1959, the Royalite plastic saddlebags decorated with the rocket emblems were first offered in white (they had been offered in black since 1957). Both black and white versions of these bags were offered on new 1959–62 Panheads and are correct for these years. These bags were also offered in the accessory catalogs for later Panheads, but the bags had a winged rocket design, rather than the "jet" or "shark."

To replace the rear stand that was deleted when the swingarm frame was introduced and simplify tire changes, a new center stand was introduced as an option in 1959.

The smooth-style primary cover was carried over onto the Duo-Glide models. Correct finish on the cover is black. Nineteen fifty-nine was the first year that chrome-plated clutch-booster covers were offered as an option on new Panheads. Correct finish for 1952–54 covers is black. Correct finish for 1955–65 standard covers is cadmium plated. However, chrome-plated covers were offered through the accessory catalogs prior to 1959.

Above: This view shows the late-1958–61 swingarm and 1958–62 rear chain guard. The bolts joining the rear-fender braces and fender should have Phillips heads.

Right: Chrome-plated Duo-Glide front-fender emblems were standard from 1958–64.

THE DUO-GLIDE 223

Sporting machines from the past for the person who truly does have everything: Rob Carlson's 1960 Duo-Glide and a P-51 Mustang.

Finally, the straight-slot screws that fastened the rear fender to the support for 1958 were replaced for 1959 and subsequent years with Phillips-slot screws.

1959 Production

Production for 1959 was down by about 4 percent from the previous year. Harley-Davidson built 1,201 FL, 1,222 FLF, 121 FLH, and 3,223 FLHF. For the first time, the high-performance FLH models resoundingly outsold the more sedate FL models. As before, about half the FL models were still hand shift, while relatively few of the FLH models were hand shift.

The stiff competition from Triumph and the rest of the imports heated up even more in 1959. Triumph released their ultimate Harley slayer in the twin-carb T120 Bonneville model. More ominously, Honda motorcycles went on sale in the United States.

Model Year 1960

Fitting for an election year, politics dominated the news. The debate between presidential contenders Richard Nixon and John F. Kennedy draws 75 million viewers. Kennedy narrowly defeats Richard Nixon, and the Democrats sweep the House and Senate.

The battle of "my missile's bigger than your missile" continues as Ike boasts that the Atlas ICBM has a range of 5,000mi and Krushchev spits back that the Soviet ICBMs have a range of almost 8,000mi. So there. The pissing match heats up again when the U-2 spyplane flown by Francis Gary Powers is shot down over Soviet territory. Ike tries to deny that anything happened, and Krushchev embarrasses Ike before the whole world by producing the captured pilot and big chunks of the plane. Krushchev cancels the upcoming U.S.-Soviet summit. Later, he shows his stripes by pounding his shoe on the table at the United Nations.

In pop culture, the first prime-time cartoon, *The Flintstones*, makes its debut. Chubby Checker's song *The Twist* starts a dance craze that sweeps the nation, and Elvis returns to the charts with the single *It's Now or Never*. Ray Charles' *Georgia on My Mind* becomes an instant classic. And Berry Gordy starts Motown Records.

The car culture that had been such a big part of the 1950s continues into the new decade, while the scooter craze is on the wane. Harley-Davidson introduces the Topper, a boxy new scooter endorsed and ridden by Edd "Kookie" Byrnes of the television show *77 Sunset Strip*.

1960 Duo-Glides

For 1960, the 74ci Big Twin was again offered in two basic models—FL and FLH—and in foot-shift or hand-shift versions of each. In addition, standard, sidecar, or police gearing could be specified at the time of order. The FLH machines carried a retail price of $1,375, and the FL machines retailed for $1,310, each a $30 increase in price over the previous year.

A new two-tone gas tank scheme with a colored top and white side panels with a colored stripe curving from front to back, underneath the arrow-and-ball tank emblem was standard for 1960, in Skyline Blue with Birch White tank side panels or Black with Birch White tank side panels. Optional were Hi-Fi Blue with Birch White tank side panels, Hi-Fi Red with Birch White tank side panels, Hi-Fi Green with Birch White tank side panels, Police Silver (Police Group only), Birch White (Police Group only), or any standard color without tank panels.

Shrouded Headlight

The Hydra-Glide forks were given a face-lift for 1960. Gone were the front fork cover with the three V stripes and the separate headlight, replaced by a two-piece shroud that covered the front of the fork and enclosed the headlight. The shroud pieces are stamped aluminum, either polished or painted black. Shrouded headlights are correct for 1960–65 Panheads.

Harley would say they borrowed the styling from the XLH Sportster of 1959, but (it may be sacrilege to point out) the shroud on both Harley-Davidson models looks suspiciously like the shroud that had been introduced on Triumph twins in 1949 and abandoned on its top-of-the-line Bonneville for 1960.

The forks were fitted with new top fork brackets, handlebars, handlebar risers, and riser covers. Two types of top fork brackets were introduced, one for adjustable-rake forks and another for non-adjustable forks. The new brackets were necessary to accommodate the new bars and risers and were used through 1964.

The new handlebars were two-piece bars with a separate bar for each side. As in previous years, Buckhorn or Speedster handlebars were offered, and all had threaded outside ends for the 3/8in end screws that retained the control spirals (these are the same spirals that had been used since 1954). Solid-mounted bars were black; optional rubber-mounted bars were chromed. The separate bars are clamped in the center by the handlebar clamp, and the handlebar clamp is then bolted to the fork top bracket. This clamp takes the place of the risers that had been used since 1949. On rubber-mounted

Rob Carlson's 1960 Duo-Glide is fitted with a lot of optional chrome-finished parts, including wheel rims, toolbox cover, shock-absorber caps, and muffler. When chrome-plated mufflers were fitted, the Parkerized muffler hangers were replaced by stainless steel hangers, as shown.

bars, the clamps featured rubber bushings to isolate the bars from engine vibration. These two-piece bars are correct for 1960–64 Panheads.

Handlebar clamps are covered by a large, metal cover. Standard covers were unpolished aluminum, but polished covers were optional. This style of handlebar cover is correct for 1960–65. If a steering damper was fitted

THE DUO-GLIDE 225

(H-D recommended the steering damper *only* for use with a sidecar), the handlebar cover was drilled with a large hole for the steering damper shaft knob.

Brackets and lower panels for the optional windshields were redesigned to fit the new headlight nacelle. The new windshield assembly was used through 1965. The mounts for the optional spot lamps were also redesigned to work with the new nacelle (the lamps themselves are the same). The new lamp assemblies were also used through 1965.

Detail Changes

In mid-1960, the stellite-faced exhaust valves that had been fitted to the FLH since mid-1958 were finally fitted to FL models, as well. These valves were fitted to all FL and FLH models through 1965.

A new rear brake drum was fitted for 1960. The main difference between this and the drum it replaced was that the drive sprocket was riveted to the new hub with 3/16in rivets (rather than 1/8in rivets). This new hub featured the number "41409-48A" cast in relief on the hub side. This hub was used through 1962.

New Buddy Seats

The optional Super Deluxe Buddy Seat was completely redesigned to give a more modern look. The new seat featured a vinyl top covering, vinyl side covering, and leather skirt. The seat was offered in all white; red top, white side, and white skirt; or black top, white side, and white skirt. This seat is correct for 1960–64 Panheads.

For a really modern look, a frame-mounted buddy seat was available in 1960 for the Panhead. The new seat was offered in all white, black and white, and red and white. These frame-mounted seats were offered through 1965.

1960 Production

Sales for 1960 were slightly higher, at 5,967 Panheads. Harley-Davidson documents do not show how many of each model were sold. Even though it was by far the most expensive bike in the line-up, the Duo-Glide was Harley's best seller by far, outselling even the new Topper scooter.

The stylish way to travel America's highways and airways. Rob Carlson's Duo-Glide and a restored B-25 Mitchell at the Anoka County, Minnesota, airport.

A 1960 Duo-Glide all decked out for the freeways with the King of the Highway Group. This top-of-the-line trim package included a windshield (clear, red, or blue lower panels), compensating sprocket, dual exhaust, chrome front and rear safety guards, white or black saddlebags, and choice of Frame-Mounted Buddy Seat (black and white, red and white, or all white), Deluxe Solo Saddle, or Super Deluxe Buddy Seat (black and white or red and white). Although frame-mounted seats were first offered on new Duo-Glides in 1960, this bike is fitted with the correct style of post-mounted Super Deluxe Buddy Seat, which was offered in all white, red and white, and in black and white. This unrestored FL is owned by Wayne and Liz Baye. When the Bayes bought it in 1993, it hadn't been run in twenty years. Even so, Wayne says it "purrs like a kitty in a creamery."

Model Year 1961

JFK is inaugurated as president, and he urges Americans, "Ask not what your country can do for you; ask what you can do for your country." He creates the Peace Corps, but stubs his toe at the Bay of Pigs.

Once again, the Russians take the lead in the space race when they launch Yuri Gagarin into space for a 1hr, 48min orbit. Soon after, NASA launches Alan Shephard into space for 15min in *Freedom 7*. JFK commits America to the goal of landing a man on the moon before the decade's end.

Cold War tensions continue. East Germany erects the Berlin Wall. Russia resumes nuclear testing. America responds in kind. JFK advises families to build bomb shelters, and the Civil Defense Department circulates 22 million copies of *Family Fallout Shelter*.

The 1960s really begin as Timothy Leary and Richard Alpert publish *Psychedelic Review* and JFK sends 4,000 military "advisers" to South Vietnam. Diana Ross and the Supremes sign with Motown, and Bob Dylan begins his singing career in Greenwich Village.

1961 Duo-Glides

For 1961, the 74ci Big Twin was again offered in two basic models—FL and FLH—and in foot-shift or hand-shift versions of each. Standard, sidecar, or police gearing could be specified at the time of order. The FLH machines carried a retail price of $1,400, and the FL machines retailed for $1,335, each a modest $25 increase in price over the previous year.

Gas tanks were given new "star" tank emblems and two-tone paint schemes for 1961. Standard color combi-

THE DUO-GLIDE

nations were Pepper Red with Birch White tank side stripes, and Black with Birch White tank side stripes.

Optional were Hi-Fi Blue with Birch White tank side stripes, Hi-Fi Red with Birch White tank side stripes, Hi-Fi Green with Birch White tank side stripes, Police Silver (Police Group only), Birch White (Police Group only), and any standard color solid (without tank panels).

Dual-Point Ignition

The big change for 1961 was the switch to what is known today as a "single-fire" ignition. Since before the days of the Knucklehead, Harley Big Twins had been fitted with a single-point timer and a twin-lead coil that fired both spark plugs every time the points opened—the wasted-spark system. For 1961, the entire ignition system—timer, points, condenser, and coil—was changed to use separate primary and secondary ignition circuits for each cylinder.

Instead of one set of contact points and a two-lobed points cam, the new timer used two sets of contact points and a new single-lobe cam. It also carried a separate condenser for each set of points. As on the earlier timer, ignition advance was controlled manually by twisting the spiral on the left handlebar. The timer body and cover were cadmium plated (chrome-plated covers were optional), and the timer was driven at half-speed by a gear in the gear case. The dual-point timer was fitted from 1961 to 1964.

Instead of a single square-section coil with twin leads, the new system uses twin round-section, single-lead coils. The new coils have no integral mounting lugs, so the two coils are fastened together at the bottom by a connector and then are bolted to a bracket by a mounting plate and bolt, and the bracket mounts to the frame on the left side, just forward of the oil tank. The coils are usually covered by the optional chrome-plated cover.

Early 1961 Panheads (prior to 61FLH7987) were assembled with the same left flywheels that had been used on motors with the earlier, single-point timers. These flywheels only have a timing mark for the front cylinder, since this was all that was necessary to time the single-point ignition. To properly time these motors, a mechanic must use a special Harley-Davidson timing gauge that is screwed into the rear cylinder's spark-plug hole to sense the piston position. Motors numbered 61FLH7987 and higher have a new left flywheel with a timing mark for the rear cylinder.

Detail Changes

A new style of FLH decal made its debut on 1961 FLH models. The new decal consists of a large, red, stylized H (its shape suggests that of a lightning bolt) on a white field, framed by checkered stripes above and below. This decal should be applied to both sides of the oil tank on all 1961–64 FLHs.

Inside the motor, new pushrods were fitted that differed slightly in design from the old rods. The main body

A 1960 Duo-Glide in the optional Hi-Fi Blue and white two-tone scheme. With the exception of some small spots that have been repainted, this Duo-Glide is unrestored. It wears California Highway Patrol rear safety guards, nonstandard leather bags, and the 1963 and later "popsickle" starter pedal, but is otherwise in very original condition. This bike is owned by Jerry Richards.

section of the new rod is longer than the body of the old rod, but the pressed-in bottom piece on the new rod is much shorter, so the overall length of the two rods is the same: 8-13/16in. This new rod is correct for 1961–65 motors.

In the never-ending quest to make their Big Twins more maintenance-free, Harley-Davidson fitted an updated generator with bearings that did not require frequent greasing. Like the Model 58 generator it replaced, the new Model 61 generator was a two-brush, 6V generator used with an external voltage regulator mounted alongside the rear cylinder, on the left side. This generator is fitted to 1961–64 civilian Big Twins. Radio-equipped

Panheads for these years were equipped with the same Model 51 radio generator that had been used since 1952.

The optional dual exhaust systems fitted to Panheads through early 1961, were in effect, twin single-exhaust systems. On these systems, the left muffler was connected by a combination left-rear/rear-header pipe to the rear cylinder only, and the right muffler was connected via the front header pipe, S-pipe, and right dual-exhaust pipe to the front cylinder only.

On the new system, introduced during the 1961 sales season, a new rear header pipe and left rear pipe connected the exhaust from the front and rear cylinders together to feed both mufflers. The new system used the front header, S-pipe, and Y-pipe used on the single-exhaust system plus a new rear header pipe that connected to the Y-pipe and had an integral connection for a new left rear pipe. This new left rear pipe snaked around behind the engine and back to the left muffler. S-pipe, Y-pipe, rear header, and left rear pipes were chrome plated. Standard mufflers were the short, tubular mufflers that had been fitted since 1958 (optional "fishtail" mufflers were introduced in late 1961). The new interconnected dual exhaust is correct for mid-1961–64 Panheads. Also optional for late 1961 and later exhaust systems was a new chromed exhaust pipe guard that clamped to the bend of the front header pipe.

1961 Production

Panhead production bottomed out once again during 1961, to 4,927 units, 17 percent fewer than the previous year. Hondas were being sold by the tens of thousands, and Harley-Davidson's sales were suffering.

Model Year 1962

Tiny little Cuba is the center of a frightening showdown between the U.S. and USSR. JFK cuts off trade to Cuba, and pays a ransom of $2.5 million for the prisoners from the Bay of Pigs operation. Spyplane photos reveal the presence of Soviet missiles on Cuba, and JFK sets up an air and sea blockade of the island. Krushchev and JFK stare each other down. Krushchev blinks first, and the Russians remove the missiles.

John Glenn becomes a national hero when he is launched in *Friendship 7* to become the first American to orbit the earth. Marilyn Monroe crashes to earth, dead from an apparent drug overdose.

Desegregation struggles continue with demonstrations and counter demonstrations tearing the south apart. The governor of Mississippi bars a black student from the state's university. JFK sends Federal troops to keep order. The poignant film *To Kill a Mockingbird* is released.

1962 Duo-Glide

For 1962, Duo-Glides were again offered in FL and FLH form, in foot-shift or hand-shift versions. Standard, sidecar, or police gearing could be specified at the time of order. The FLHs retailed for $1,400, and the FLs retailed for $1,335, each the same price as the previous year.

The 1962 Duo-Glides were offered in two standard color combinations: Tango Red with Birch White tank side stripes and Black with Birch White tank side stripes. Optional were Hi-Fi Blue with Birch White tank side stripes, Hi-Fi Red with Birch White tank side stripes, Hi-Fi Purple with Birch White tank side stripes, Police Silver (Police Group only), and Birch White (Police Group only).

As sales for the Big Twin languished, Harley-Davidson seemed less inclined to spend any money updating them. With the exception of an internally-revised oil pump introduced in mid-1962, only cosmetic changes were made for 1962. The most prominent of these is the new paint job for the gas tanks. The tanks are given new, racing stripes that sweep back and taper from the instrument cover to the rear end of the tank. The star tank emblem that had been introduced in 1961 is used, again, on these tanks.

The Stewart-Warner speedometer was given yet another facelift for 1962. This speedometer features a flat, single-level face that has a bare aluminum center panel shaped like a tombstone. The name "Harley-Davidson" is painted in black on the aluminum, just to the rear of the trip meter. Mile-per-hour numbers (one through twelve), hash marks for the tens, and dots for the intermediate 2mph increments are bare, brushed aluminum out of the black painted outer face of the speedometer. The odometer and trip-meter miles numerals are white on a black background, and the trip meter 1/10-mile numerals are black on a white background. This style of speedometer is correct for 1962–65 Panheads.

The new speedometer is housed in a new instrument cover. The new instrument cover is similar to the previous dash. The main difference is that the rectangular center GEN/OIL lens is omitted and replaced by three (two, on hand-shift bikes) separate, round indicator-lens covers. The left (red) lens covers the generator light, the center (green) lens covers the neutral light, and the right (also red) lens covers the oil-pressure light. On hand-shift bikes, the center indicator (neutral) light is omitted. As was true for the previous instrument covers, standard covers were painted the color of the tank. Chrome-plated covers were optional. This instrument cover is correct for 1962–65 Panheads.

The optional front spot lights were given new housings with shallower, more rounded backs, and new brackets were introduced to mount these new lamps to the forks. These new lamps are correct for 1962–65.

1962 Production

Harley-Davidson production was up slightly in 1962, to 10,497 units, of which 5,184 were Duo-Glides.

Nineteen sixty Duo-Glides were given a new style of two-tone paint scheme but used the same tank emblem used in 1959.

Meanwhile, business was booming for the foreign competition. Triumph's sales were up over 2,000 units, but the biggest competitor was Honda, which was selling as many motorcycles as all other makers combined. Honda was gradually introducing larger models, and other Japanese makers—including Kawasaki, Suzuki, and Yamaha were making their mark.

Model Year 1963

Rising star Bob Dylan sang *The Times They Are A-Changin'*—and was he ever right. Folk, the "Motown Sound," and "surf" music take over the airwaves. *I Want to Hold Your Hand* is released, and "Beatlemania" begins to spread across the globe.

JFK visits the Berlin Wall and boldly reaffirms America's commitment to a free West Berlin by declaring, "Ich bin ein Berliner." Soviet cosmonaut Valentina

New, two-piece handlebars were introduced in 1960. The bars mount together and to the fork by a center clamp that replaces the riser. The center clamp is covered by a new cover, shown here. This bike is fitted with the optional steering damper, which was normally fitted only to sidecar-equipped bikes. Note that it also has the optional cigarette lighter mounted to the front of the riser cover.

Tereshkova becomes the first woman in space. Alexander Solzhenitsyn provides the first real look at life behind the Iron Curtain in his book *One Day in the Life of Ivan Denisovich*.

In the South, civil strife explodes. Desegregationists march in Birmingham, Alabama, and are met by riot police, electric cattle prods, police dogs, and fire hoses; more than 1,000 are arrested. Led by Martin Luther King, Jr., over 250,000 civil-rights marchers descend on the nation's capital, and King delivers his famous, "I have a dream . . ."speech. Public schools in Louisiana and South Carolina are integrated. A bomb explodes in one of Birmingham's Black churches, and four young girls are killed. A University of Mississippi professor is arrested for desecrating a Confederate flag in a painting.

As the year draws toward a close, JFK is assassinated in Dallas, Texas. Lyndon Baines Johnson is sworn in as president. The whole nation mourns, and sales of the new tranquilizer Valium take off.

1963 Duo-Glide

For 1963, the Duo-Glide was again offered in two basic models—FL and FLH—and in foot-shift or hand-shift versions of each, with sidecar or police gearing optional. The FLHs retailed for $1,425, and the FL machines retailed for $1,360, each $25 more than the previous year.

The two-tone paint scheme on the tank was changed once again for 1963. As it did in 1962, the tank had racing stripes, but for 1963 the stripes swept back along the top of the tank rather than down along the sides of the tank. Three standard color combinations were offered: Tango Red with white tank stripes, Horizon Metallic Blue with white tank stripes, and Black with white tank stripes. Optional were Hi-Fi Turquoise with white tank stripes, Hi-Fi Red with white tank stripes, Hi-Fi Purple with white tank stripes, Police Silver (Police Group only), and Birch White (Police Group only).

The tanks were also given a new bar-and-shield tank emblem made of stamped aluminum. The elongated bar has the company name stamped into the bar. This emblem is correct for 1963–65 gas tanks.

Outside-Oiler Heads

For 1963, Harley-Davidson engineers extensively modified the Panhead engine so that oil to the heads is routed through external oil lines, a system used on all Knucklehead motors, but abandoned for the first Panhead motor. Why the change back? I don't really know, but two possible explanations come to mind. First, oil routed through an external line would arrive at the head at a cooler temperature than oil routed through a passage in the hot cylinder casting. Second, an oil line with two fittings is easier to seal than are the two gasket surfaces—above and below the cylinder—that each internal oil passage must go through.

This view of the front of Jerry Richards' 1960 Duo-Glide shows the polished aluminum headlight shroud that was new for 1960. The chrome-plated front hub cap was available in the King of the Highway Group or for order separately. Note the removable cover on the hub cap. This allowed access to the grease fitting for the wheel bearings.

A boss for the external oil line was added to the right crankcase, placed to the right of the "peak" created in the case at the point where the tappet blocks meet. Oil is routed to the boss through a hollow bolt from oil passages in the redesigned gear case. This right crankcase and gear cover were used in 1963 and 1964. The left case was not revised.

This Duo-Glide poses on its optional center stand while an enormous storm sweeps in from the Black Hills. This bike is fitted with the correct early style of dual exhaust, on which the front cylinder is connected to the right muffler, and the rear cylinder is connected to the left muffler, with no interconnection between the two. This system uses the same front header pipe and S-pipe as the single system, but all the other pipes are new. Shown here is the new straight pipe that connects the S-pipe to the muffler, replacing the Y-pipe. Not shown is the new rear header pipe that curves around to the left side of the bike and back to the muffler. The mufflers are shorter versions of the single muffler.

New cylinders were introduced that no longer had the oil passages on the right side of the casting. However, the cylinder castings still had the oil-return passage in the left side of the casting and were still painted silver. These new cylinders were used from 1963 to 65.

Perched atop the new cylinders were new cylinder heads that had a drilled and threaded boss between the lowest two fins on the right side, near the intake port. The oil line from the crankcase branched off and attached to the boss on each head, and a passage from the boss led to the rocker-feed passages in the head. The new heads still used an O-ring intake manifold, and FLH heads still had polished and flowed intake ports. Outside-oiler heads were used from 1963 to 65.

Detail Changes

The bicycle-pedal style of kick-starter pedal was replaced with the one-piece "fudge-sickle" style starter pedal for 1963. Standard pedals were molded of black rubber, but white pedals were available as an option. The one-piece pedal is correct for 1963–65 kick starters.

The drive-chain guard was revised slightly for 1963. The new guard is much more deeply valanced than its predecessor and the rear tip flares out. The guard also features an embossed oval to provide clearance for the brake line swivel fitting that protrudes from the brake backing plate.

More powerful rear brakes were fitted for 1963. The new brake hub looks just like previous hubs, except that it is deeper (2-1/8in instead of 1-7/8in) to use wider brake shoes (1-13/16in instead of 1-5/16in) and lacks the dust lip that had been cast into previous hubs. This hub is correct for 1963–65 Panheads. A new backing plate was introduced to go with the new hub and shoes. The new backing plate is 8-5/8in in diameter (the old plate was 8-1/8in) and has a rolled lip around the edge to replace the dust lip

For 1961, the Duo-Glide was given a new style of two-tone paint scheme and a new tank emblem, as shown. The star tank emblem was carried over into 1962, but the two-tone scheme was changed yet again. Also new for 1961 was the Model 61 two-brush generator and the dual-point timer. The new timer had a separate set of points for each cylinder, and these points triggered separate coils for each cylinder. This new "single-fire" ignition was stock from 1961–64. Inside the pushrod covers are new pushrods. If you look real close, you can see how tightly the rear header has to bend to wind its way to the left side of the bike. The sharp bends in the pipe were overly restrictive, so in late 1961 H-D introduced a new dual-exhaust system with new pipes to interconnect the left and right systems. The new dual system includes a new Y-pipe through which exhaust from the rear header pipe and S-pipe from the front header is routed to the right muffler. The new rear header pipe has a connection on the left where a separate pipe to the left muffler attaches. The new system was used from late 1961 through 1964.

that was deleted on the new hub. It also features a reinforcement plate attached by four rivets to the outside of the brake backing plate, covering the wheel-cylinder mounting area to below the mounting stud. The hub and backing plate are painted black. These rear brake hubs, shoes, and backing plates are used on 1963–65 Panheads.

Accessories

New fiberglass saddlebags replaced the optional Royalite plastic bags in 1963. These bags mount to the carriers with two latches and a spring clip and have a rubber molding stapled to the top rim of the bags to seal the cover. These new bags were available in black or white and are the correct bags for 1963 Panheads.

The venerable bullet-shaped lamps that had been used for the front and rear parking lights and for the turn signals were replaced with round-back lamps and new mounts for 1963. The front lamps have amber lenses and mount to the sides of the forks, and the rear lamps have red or amber lenses and mount to a chromed bracket that wraps around the taillight. These lamps are correct for 1963–65.

Next pages: Two torchbearers of the Panhead movement with two of their bikes—Gary Strom (left) and Rob Carlson of Kokesh Motorcycles in Spring Lake Park, Minnesota. Both Pans were restored by Elmer Ehnes.

THE DUO-GLIDE

A pair of big American twins for 1961. The 1961 FLH shown features the 1961–64-style of FLH decal which was attached to both sides of the oil tank of all FLHs, and the optional Super Deluxe Buddy Seat and white plastic saddlebags. The admiring twins are equipped with optional H-D sweatshirts. *Photo copyright Harley-Davidson*

1963 Production

Panhead sales reached an all-time low of 4,300 during 1963. Overall sales were just as poor, off by over 11 percent. Harley-Davidson sold just 9,873 motorcycles, the smallest total sales since 1940.

Model Year 1964

LBJ and Barry "Extremism in the Defense of Liberty is No Vice" Goldwater slug it out in the presidential race. LBJ wins in a landslide. He promises not "to send American boys 9 or 10,000 miles away from home to do what Asian boys should do for themselves." He lies. A short time later, the Gulf of Tonkin Resolution passes and American boys *are* sent to fight a war that Asian boys should be fighting for themselves.

The Beatles come to America, and 10,000 screaming fans greet them at John F. Kennedy Airport. The singles, *She Loves You* and *A Hard Day's Night* sell at record pace. The movie *A Hard Day's Night* brings Beatlemania to the big screen.

Also on the big screen, Peter Sellers stars in two of the most memorable movies of all time, the comedy *The Pink Panther* and the Cold War parody *Dr. Strangelove, or How I Learned to Stop Worrying and Love the Bomb.*

On the small screen, baby-boomer favorites *Flipper*, *Gilligan's Island*, *The Munsters*, and *The Adams Family* debut.

Back in the USSR, Krushchev's out; Leonid Brezhnev's in. China explodes its first nuclear bomb.

The poetic and powerful Cassius Clay beats up on Sonny Liston, winning the heavyweight title in seven rounds.

For 1962, the tank was given a tapering racing stripe on each side of the instrument cover. Note the mounting hardware for the saddlebags, visible here because one bag is removed. This 1962 Duo-Glide is owned by Dr. Paul Anderson. The turn signals on this bike are the 1963 and later type.

The Hell's Angels beat up on California. The publicity gives the Bay Area bad boys national infamy, and give's Harley's image a black eye that does not fully heal until the late 1980s.

1964 Duo-Glide

For 1964, the 74ci Big Twin was again offered in two basic models—FL and FLH—and in foot-shift or hand-shift versions of each. In addition, standard, side-

The unrestored 1962 Duo-Glide owned by Robert Berquist displays the correct style of front parking/turn-signal lights, attached to an aftermarket light bar for the non-stock spot lamps. New round-back spot lamps with sealed-beam bulbs were the optional lights from the factory.

Below: This is the two-tone scheme introduced for 1963. On the tank is the 1963–65 bar-and-shield tank emblems. In addition to these cosmetic changes, the motor was updated with external lines to deliver oil from the gear cover to the cylinder heads.

The style of speedometer shown was new for 1962. This speedometer has a single-level face with a "tombstone"-shaped, brushed-aluminum center and three miles digits on the trip meter. This speedo was fitted to all civilian Panheads from 1962 to 1965 and was surrounded by a new instrument cover. The new cover had three separate indicator lights—generator, neutral, and oil—in line between the cover's mounting bolt and the ignition switch, and was used through 1965. At top left, the aluminum handlebar cover has been removed to show the handlebar "riser" (in reality, it is just a center clamp that joins the left and right handlebar halves).

The sun's last rays highlight all the chrome on the Duo-Glide owned by Dale Overfelt of Kansas City, Missouri.

This bike is not all that correct, but sparkles nonetheless. The two-tone paint scheme shown is correct for 1965.

An unrestored, but repainted, 1963 Duo-Glide owned by Richard Eberhardt. Two-tone paint schemes were standard, but single-tone paint schemes were available by special order. The chrome-plated oil tank was optional from the factory for 1963 and 1964 Duo-Glides only. Just ahead of the oil tank is the chrome-plated coil cover, which covers the two separate coils that became standard in 1961 with the introduction of the two-point ignition timer. New for 1963 were the round-back turn signals and fiberglass saddlebags. This bike is also fitted with the optional spot lamps, which are the round-back style with 6V sealed beam bulbs that are correct for 1962–64. A look underneath the saddlebags reveals the two-piece, chrome-plated rear chain guard that became optional the following year, in 1964.

The beautiful 1964 Duo-Glide owned and restored by Gene Schrier of Everett, Washington. Gene restores his machines to the standard of, "How Harley would build them today." That means no Parkerized or cad-plated parts—chrome instead. This bike might do poorly in an official judging, but most people would concede that it shines in a way the stock bikes never did. Non-stock chrome bits shown here include the rear-brake pedal (should be cad-plated), chrome footboards (should be painted black), and chrome-plated rocker covers (should be brushed aluminum).

Gene Schrier went to great pains to correctly recreate the two-tone paint scheme. He traced the pattern off an original set of tanks for his painter to use as a pattern and had him spray the tanks and fenders in the optional Hi-Fi Red and white combination. He had the cylinders painted black to help them shed heat better. Stock cylinders were painted with an aluminized silver-silicone paint.

car, or police gearing could be specified at the time of order. The FLH retailed for $1,450, and the FL machines retailed for $1,385, each just $25 more than the previous year.

The two-tone paint scheme on the tank was changed once again for 1964, but little else was changed. Instead of racing stripes, the 1964 tanks have broad white side panels. The Panheads were offered in two standard color combinations: Fiesta Red with white tank panels and Black with white tank panels. Optional were Hi-Fi Blue with white tank. Hi-Fi Red with white tank panels, Police Silver (Police Group only), and Birch White (Police Group only).

The tanks again used the bar and shield emblem.

The inner primary-chain housing was slightly revised, with a new position for the breather-pipe hole. This inner guard was used for 1964 only.

In late 1964, an optional two-part (upper and lower) rear chain guard was introduced. This chrome-plated guard was optional for 1964 and 1965.

The optional fiberglass saddlebags were also slightly redesigned in 1964. The rubber sealing strip that had been stapled on the upper rim of the earlier bags was replaced by weather stripping glued around the cover's edge.

The left side of Gene Schrier's 1964 Duo-Glide looks just as good, but has just as much extra chrome. The rear chain guard is the valanced type that had been introduced in 1963. Stock guards were painted black.

1964 Production

Harley-Davidson's sales surged by 34 percent for 1964, and most of the increase was from sales of Duo-Glides and Sportsters. Big Twin sales rose from 4,300 in 1963 to 5,500, while sales of Sprints and other small bikes were flat.

Why the sudden change in Harley's fortunes? Possibly, because the war babies and baby boomers reached early adulthood. Possibly, because the economy was strong. Possibly, because leisure time was increasing for Americans at all social levels, and many Americans had more disposable income to spend on their leisure. Most likely, it was the cumulative impact of all. Whatever the reason, Harley-Davidson and all the other motorcycle makers experienced record sales for the next several years.

CHAPTER FOUR

1965
The Electra-Glide

A new era dawned for Harley-Davidson at the start of model year 1965. The flagship model for that year was the first major upgrade to the Panhead line since the Duo-Glide of 1958. Outwardly, the new bike looked a little pudgier, but not all that different from the last Duo-Glide of 1964. The good stuff was hidden from view behind new covers and cases, but chrome script on each side of the front fender gave name to the new era in a dialect all H-D fans were sure to understand.

Electra-Glide.

For the first time, the big-inch Harley motor could be brought to life at the touch of a button.

If you haven't guessed by now, the big change was electric start. Sure, other bikes—mostly Japanese tiddlers and the 1964 H-D Servi-Car—had been fitted with electric start before 1965, but electric

The new front fender badge announces the most revolutionary feature of the new Harley Big Twin—electric start. Several other motorcycles had been fitted with this feature before the E-Glide, but they were all little tiddlers that were so easy to kick over that electric start was little more than a gee-whiz gimmick. On a high-compression, 1200cc V-twin, electric start was—even in 1965—much more than a gimmick. The fender tip shown here was introduced in 1959, and the Aristocrat bumper shown was introduced in 1958. This machine is owned by Jan Berghoff.

Right: This machine shows uncommon attention to correct finishes on all parts. Cadmium-plated spokes, axle, axle-adjusting screw, shock-absorber adjusting ring, transmission filler plug, and brake pedal are all correct. However, the trim strip at the rear of the front fender is not correct for the 1965 Electra-Glide. Restoration by Elmer Ehnes.

start was just a token feature on little 50–250cc bikes that could be kicked over by the average five-year-old. To the owner of a high-compression 1200cc FLH, electric start means a whole lot more. More than anything Harley-Davidson had ever done, this change had a *cultural* impact.

Kick starting had always been an honored rite of passage among H-D riders. The standard answer to a son's/little brother's/nephew's/neighborhood pest's longing pleas of "When can I ride it?" were answered (in condescending tones) with, "Maybe some day—*if* you can kick start it." How do I know? That's the answer I got. And I can tell you that it sure looked like a man-sized job to me, then. Now, many years later, it doesn't seem like such a big deal, but to those who are not spurred on by a very strong desire to take the beast for a ride, the task of starting the Big Twin seems like more trouble than it is worth. Even in the early days, when people were still accustomed to seeing cars started by hand cranks, the Harley starting ritual had impressed the uninitiated as an arcane ritual that required equal parts grunting, cursing, and praying. Choke on one or two clicks. Retard the spark. Open the throttle all the way. Leap up and give a couple priming kicks. Turn on the ignition. Push slowly down on the kick starter until you feel the compression build. Gather your strength. Then leap up and come down on the lever with all the force you can muster, while still keeping your demeanor as nonchalant as possible. If all is well, the mighty beast springs to life and you feel like a hero. If not, you kick some more and swear to the gods of V-twin thunder that you'll give the bike a *complete* tune-up this Sunday, right *after* you go to church.

Die-hard traditionalists were seriously unhappy. Not only had Harley taken away their central initiation rite, but the starter and huge new battery necessary to start the bike had added over 75lb more to a bike that had already put on nearly 100lb since the "light," nimble, springer Panhead of 1948.

Everyone else was thrilled. The Electra-Glide was a big bike for the motorcycling equivalent of "the masses." Here was a Big Twin that was not just for the young and strong. Anyone who could swing a leg over it and reach the ground with at least one toe could start and ride it. Older riders, smaller riders, and those with weak knees could join the sport and cruise America on the ultimate long-haul touring bike of the day. In one brilliant bout of refinement, Harley-Davidson had reached the next rest stop on the long highway to making their Big Twin more civilized.

Model Year 1965

Electric starting on the Electra-Glide isn't the only thing to have cultural implications in 1965. By any standard, this is a year of momentous events.

Harley-Davidson's flagship for 1965 was the new Electra-Glide. The extra-large, 12V battery necessary to power the new electric starter was much too large to fit in the former location in the "U" of the oil tank, so the oil tank was redesigned. The new square tank mounts to the left side of the bike, the battery to its right. To allow clearance for these components, a new frame was introduced that lacks the "step down" in front of the top shock mounts. The result was a chunkier look that really shows the weight the Panhead put on in the eighteen years since it was introduced. This Electra-Glide is owned by Eugene Schrier. He restored it to his how-Harley-would-build-them-today standard, with lots of extra chrome. Though this bike has one, tool boxes were not fitted to Electra-Glides.

The war in Vietnam heats up, and LBJ makes clear his intention to support the government of South Vietnam. One of his first steps is to offer North Vietnam $1 billion if they'll just take their guns and go home. Ho Chi Minh thumbs his nose at the offer. His generous bribe spurned, LBJ orders more bombing of North Vietnam. When he thinks Uncle Ho has learned a lesson, LBJ grounds the bombers and asks Ho if he's now ready to be friendly. "Nuts" (or something to that effect), says Ho. The war escalates, and by year's end 190,000 U.S. troops are in Vietnam, and 1,350 have been killed.

War protests begin in earnest. Draft cards are burned, and a law is passed making it a crime to mutilate or destroy them. Thousands follow Timothy Leary's advice to "Drop out, turn on, and tune in," and "Flower Power" becomes part of the antiwar cry. Mimicking the Buddhist monks who immolated themselves in the streets of Vietnam, a Quaker, Norman Morrison, immolates himself on the steps of the Pentagon.

Malcolm X is assassinated by Muslim militants at a speech in Harlem. In classic 1960s irony, the number-one enemy of White racists is murdered by Black racists.

Martin Luther King leads a fifty-four-mile Freedom March from Selma, Alabama, to Montgomery, Alabama. At the city outskirts the marchers are attacked with tear gas and billy clubs. King's stature among non-racists in America approaches that attained by Gandhi in India.

On the other side of the country, the Los Angeles ghetto called Watts erupts in a fiery riot, and more than a thousand National Guardsmen are sent to restore order.

Cesar Chavez fasts for twenty-five days to convince militant migrant workers to eschew violence and join his peaceful strike against grape growers. American consumers boycott grapes.

Cassius Clay proves he *is* the greatest in the world when he knocks out Sonny Liston in the first round of their rematch.

Amphetamine "diet pills" are prescribed to anyone who wants them, for every ailment from everyday fatigue to depression. As youth turns to LSD and marijuana, their parents turn to prescription amphetamines and tranquilizers.

Unsuccessful against the Communists, LBJ brings "Socialism" closer to home in the form of his "Great Society." He secures $1.4 billion to bring Appalachia into the twentieth century. The bill creating Medicare passes, as does the Voting Rights Act of 1965, which eliminates literacy tests as a prerequisite to voting and authorizes federal supervision of elections. The Higher Education Pact passes, authorizing the spending of $2.3 billion on education. The Department of Housing and Urban Development is created.

Before jetting off to Hanoi, Jane Fonda stars with the inimitable Lee Marvin in the classic Western melodrama/musical *Cat Ballou*. Marvin wins an Oscar for Best Actor.

Musical legends—old and new—top the charts, with Elvis, the Beatles, and newcomers the Rolling Stones all going Gold. Sonny and Cher also make ripples with the schmaltzy *I Got You Babe*.

Safety Nazis get their manifesto in Ralph Nader's book *Unsafe at Any Speed*. Fortunately, Nader and his ilk have bigger fish to fry for many years to come than Harley-Davidson and the other motorcycle makers.

Electra-Glides for 1965

The Electra-Glide was offered in two basic models—FL and FLH—and in foot-shift or hand-shift versions of each. Foot-shift machines were designated FLHFB and FLFB. The hand-shift machines were FLHB and FLB. Why the letter "B" to denote electric start? Your guess is as good as mine, but I think I know why they didn't use the letter "E," which would seem to have been the logical choice. That letter had been used to denote the Traffic Combination motors sold from 1953 to 1956, so Harley-Davidson wanted to avoid any chance of confusion. Order any of the models with sidecar gearing, and the letter "S" is added to the designation. Harley-Davidson likes consis-

The Electra-Glide was still powered by the Panhead motor, but much of the rest of the bike was new. This view shows the new, cast-aluminum primary cases that rigidly connect the motor to the transmission and provide a flex-free mount to handle the torque of the electric starter. These cases are shown in their correct, unpolished form. Also shown is the optional one-piece heel-and-toe shifter that was new for 1965. Toe shifters were standard on all foot-shift Panheads, but a separate, add-on heel shifter could be ordered on 1952-64 foot-shift Panheads. This E-Glide was restored by Elmer Ehnes.

tency, so neither the "B" nor the "S" nor the second "F" is stamped onto the case as part of the motor number.

As we shall see, the Electra-Glide was substantially updated, and all the updates carried a pretty substantial price. The FLH machines carried a retail price of $1,595, and the FL machines retailed for $1,530, each a $145 increase in price over the previous year. Standard for that price were an electric starter, black front safety guard, 5.00x16in black wheels and tires, air cleaner, Jiffy Stand, and 5gal gas tanks (foot-shift models only; hand-shift models have the old 3-3/4gal tanks). The rider tool kit was no longer included, but could be ordered separately. Police or sidecar gearing was available for no extra charge.

As had been the case since 1963, only two major option groups were offered—the Chrome Finish Group and the King of the Highway Group—but numerous subgroups were offered. The Chrome Finish Group was a way to really dress up one's Electra-Glide with most of the polished and chromed accessories anyone could want, all for one package price. One new item is included in the group: chrome oil-tank strips for the new, square oil tank. The King of the Highway Group contained even more dress-up accessories and all the equipment to make what was then the only *real* touring bike in the world. Decked out with all the bright bits from the Chrome Finish Group (which you had to order along with the King of the

Could it really be Ollie North and Tammy Wynette out for a cruise in 1965? Only the maker of this super-secret spy photo knows for sure. The smiles on their faces prove that even super-spooks and country-western stars were enamored with the new Electra-Glide. *Photo copyright Harley-Davidson*

Highway Group),–a frame-mounted buddy seat, fiberglass bags, windshield, dual exhaust with extra-quiet fishtail mufflers, turn signals, and all the rest,–the Electra-Glide was one impressive beast. Compared to the effete Triumphs, Nortons, and BMWs of the mid-1960s, the robust Electra-Glide truly was the King of the Highway.

Contributing to the substantial look of the Electra-Glide were the new 5gal gas tanks. These tanks are shaped much like the 3-3/4gal tanks used on previous Panheads, but the new tanks are wider. The two-tone paint scheme on the tank was changed once again for 1965. Instead of broad white tank panels, the 1965 tanks had white bottom panels with a pinstripe along the panel edge. Two standard color combinations were offered: Holiday Red with white tank bottoms and Black with white tank bottoms. Optional were Hi-Fi Blue with white tank bottoms, Hi-Fi Red with white tank bottoms, Police Silver (Police Group only), and Birch White (Police Group only). The bar and shield emblem was used on the tanks again for 1965.

Chrome-plated fishtail mufflers were the standard on dual exhaust systems, and these mufflers were offered in regular and super-quiet versions. Chrome-plated "straight-type" mufflers were optional on dual systems. A black-painted Low-Tone "straight-type" mufflers was standard on single system; a chrome-plated Low Tone muffler was optional. Among the extra chrome bits on this bike is the front header pipe. Stock front header pipes were silver painted, but a chrome cover was optional.

Electric Leg

On the left, massive, new primary covers immediately catch the eye. The solenoid for the starter juts forward from the clutch bulge of the inner cover, and the electric starter attaches to the motor side of the inner cover just above the clutch assembly and lays transversely across between the transmission and oil tank. As we shall see, these new primary covers are the backbone of the new electric start system.

Prior to the Electra-Glide, the motor and transmission had each been mounted separately to the frame, and the only connection between the two had been the primary chain. The stamped-steel inner primary-chain cover had attached to the left crankcase of the motor but wasn't fastened to the transmission because the tranny had to be adjustable fore and aft in its mounts to tension the primary chain. This arrangement had worked fine for kick-start Panheads, but the stamped-steel inner primary cover used on these bikes was far too flimsy to hold the high-torque starter motor in precise alignment with the starter gear on the clutch, especially since the cover was not even attached to the transmission.

The solution was to design new inner and outer primary covers that would rigidly link the motor and transmission and would provide a rigid mount for the new starter. The transmission could no longer be moved in its mounts to adjust the primary chain, so an adjustable chain tensioner was mounted to the inner primary cover. Access to this tensioner was provided by a removable plate in the center of the outer cover. This plate is shaped like an elongated oval and attaches to the cover with four screws, and it is to this plate that the new-style buddy-seat foot pegs attach. Both inner and outer primary covers were unpolished and unpainted.

Also inside the new primary cover was a new clutch assembly. This new clutch used the same plates and springs as the 1964 clutch, but almost everything else was new, including the clutch hub, clutch push rod, main-shaft nut, clutch rod, and clutch release lever. Most importantly, the clutch shell was fitted with a ring gear to mate with the starter-shaft gear that is driven by the electric starter. On hand-shift bikes, the clutch is operated by a revised foot lever, and on foot-shift bikes the clutch is operated by a new, die-cast aluminum hand-lever assembly.

Never ones to cut their own throat by forcing change and its customers, Harley-Davidson left the kick starter in place on the Electra-Glide. For those who refused to compromise their manliness, H-D made special plates to cover the starter and solenoid holes after the contemptible new devices were removed. It is also possible that new machines could be special ordered from the factory without the electric starter.

More Volts

By the early 1960s, most automobiles, and a few motorcycles, had made the switch from 6V electrical systems to 12V electrical systems. In 1964, Harley-Davidson followed suit on their Servi-Cars. Twelve-volt systems have overwhelming advantages over 6V systems for motorcycle use. Since the 12V system operates at twice the voltage, the generator only needs to supply half the amperage to generate the same amount of power. And because the components only have to carry half the amperage, all components in the system—generator, starter, wire gauge, and others—can be made much smaller and lighter. A byproduct of the reduction in wire gauge is that more loops of wire can then be wrapped around the armature and field coils of the generator, resulting in greater current output than would be possible in a 6V generator of the same size. So for 1965, Harley-Davidson gave their Big Twins and Sportsters a 12V system.

Did this make the Electra-Glide a lighter Hog? Get serious. Ever since 1948, the Panhead had slowly been refined into the great American touring bike. With each step, it became more powerful, more comfortable, and easier to live with, but it also became more complex and gained weight.

In the Electra-Glide, Harley-Davidson was intent on making a two-wheeled Cadillac, not a lightweight sports machine. The 12V system was not an effort to make the bike lighter, but was mostly to modernize the electrical system so it could power an electric starter that would make the new Big Twin—here it comes again—more civilized. It could also power newer and more expensive accessories.

The new generator was a two-brush design that made use of a separate voltage regulator. It mounted across the front of the motor and was driven by a gear in the gear case, just like the 6V generator it replaced, and was attached by hex-head screws. The new generator put out enough power that it was also used on radio-equipped police bikes.

To accommodate the Electra-Glide's new electrical system, 12V bulbs were used in the headlight, taillight, and in the optional spot lights, parking lights, and turn signals.

Chassis

Starting at the front, the wheels are the same 16in wheels that had been standard since 1941 (18in wheels were no longer optional, having been dropped after 1963). Black wheels were still standard, but chrome wheels were included in the Chrome Finish Group, or were available from the Supplementary Equipment list. Whitewall tires were also available from the list.

The front fender is the same Air Flow front fender with riveted brackets that had been used since 1950, with the front fender tip that had been introduced in 1959, but—starting a tradition that would endure for more than thirty years—the fender proudly carried a chromed Electra-Glide emblem on each side.

The forks were largely the same as those of 1964, except that new fork top brackets were fitted to both the adjustable and non-adjustable forks. Trim and headlight nacelle were unchanged, but, of course, a 12V, sealed-beam headlight was fitted.

Most of the Electra-Glide's front-end accessories were also the same or were minimally changed. The optional solo windshield was the same as the one that had been introduced in 1960 and was offered with clear, red, or blue lower panels. The optional spot lamps were the same round-back design that had been introduced in 1962, but for 1965 they were fitted with 12V, sealed-beam bulbs. The front turn signal lamps were the larger, rounded design that had been introduced in 1963, but they were fitted with 12V bulbs. These lamps were fitted with amber lenses and were also used as parking lamps. The older, bullet-shaped lamps that had been introduced in 1949 were also available as parking lamps, fitted with 12V bulbs and clear lenses.

Two-piece handlebars were fitted to the new E-Glide, as they had been to Duo-Glides since 1960, but left and right bars were slightly revised. The left bar no longer was fitted with a control spiral (because the timer is now automatically advanced), and the right bar was fitted with a starter button. These bars were still available in Speedster or Buckhorn style for no extra charge, and could also be ordered in rubber-mounted form. Rubber-mounted bars were chrome-plated; solid-mounted bars were painted black. An all-new frame was designed for the Electra-Glide. It was a straight-leg, swingarm frame with a steering-head lock, but it had been significantly revised for the electric-start motor. The most noticeable difference is that the frame no longer "steps down" from the shock-mount forgings to the upper frame rails.

Bolted to the front of the frame was the same front safety guard that had been used since 1958; it could be had in black-painted or chrome-plated form.

The rear safety guard was still a two-piece unit (as it had been since 1958), but its top mount no longer fastened to the frame in front of the top shock mount. Instead, the guard seemed to sprout from the center of the top shock mount. Tops of the shock absorbers were no longer covered with the dome caps. New chromed caps were fitted that encircle the shock-absorber stud but have an open center so that the new safety guard can be fastened to the stud. The rear safety guard was included in the King of the Highway package, but could also be ordered separately. It was available painted black or chrome plated. Besides the new caps, the only change to the shock absorbers is to the adjusting ring at the bottom of the shock, which has twelve holes (previous shocks had only four).

Hand-shift Electra-Glides were fitted with the old 3-3/4gal tanks because no 5gal tanks were built with the necessary lug for the shift-lever pivot. There is some evidence to suggest that the 3-3/4gal tanks were also available on special order for foot-shift bikes.

The Electra-Glide used the "tombstone" speedometer that had first been used in 1962, and the speedometer was housed in the same instrument cover (fitted with the green neutral indicator light) that had been fitted to foot-shift Panheads since 1962. The speedo and cover were both used on the new Shovelhead Big Twins for 1966 and 1967.

Motor

Inside the Electra-Glide beats the heart of the Duo-Glide, with a new, automatic-advance pacemaker that

This Electra-Glide is decked out with just about all the options save the windshield. This view highlights the new helper springs for the red-and-white Super Deluxe Buddy Seat. This Electra-Glide is owned by Robin Gauthier of Southside Cycles in Nanaimo, British Columbia.

worked with its electric starter to make the whole bike more user friendly. No longer was a complicated CPR ritual required to restart that heart. No more manually retarding the timing and kicking over the motor two or three times with the ignition off to prime the motor. All that was necessary on the E-Glide was a notch or two of choke and a gentle touch to the starter button. Then, when it's time to ride off, no more worrying about advancing the timing.

The motor itself was largely unchanged from the outside-oiler motor that had first been introduced in 1963, but it was given new cases and was connected rigidly to the transmission by the radically new primary-chain housing described earlier. The left crankcase was redesigned to bolt up to the new inner primary cover, and the right case was redesigned to eliminate the boss on which the spark-control cable mounted (this boss originally held the generator cut-out relay). Also, the breather tube no longer extended through a tunnel in both cases to the primary-chain housing. Instead, the breather pipe extended across behind the case.

On the right, the most visible change was the new, smooth gear cover. Like the cover used in 1963–64, the new cover has oil passages that route oil through a hollow mounting bolt to the boss that feeds the oil lines to the heads, but the new cover lacks the four horizontal cooling fins. Instead, the cover is flat, with a fairly rough, sand-cast texture and is left in bare aluminum finish. It is secured with straight-slot screws.

Sadly, the polished trumpet of the Jubilee horn is no longer present. The Jubilee horn was replaced by a small-

For 1965 only, the rear safety guard attaches to the upper shock-mount stud. Gone are the optional, chrome-plated, dome caps to cover the top of the shock absorbers, replaced by the new shock caps shown.

er, 12V horn that mounted inside the fork shrouds. The new horn lacked the long, graceful trumpet that crossed through the V of the cylinders and curved forward on the right side.

Exhaust Pipes and Mufflers

Standard on the Electra-Glide was a single exhaust consisting of a front header pipe, an S-pipe, a rear header pipe, a Y-pipe, and a muffler. The front header and rear pipes were the same as those that had been used since 1948, and were painted silver. Each header pipe was fastened to the exhaust nipple by a new-for-1965 ferrule-style

The Electra-Glide's speedometer and instrument cover were unchanged from those introduced in 1962. The speedo and cover were perched atop new, larger, 5gal gas tanks. These tanks contributed to the more massive look of the new Electra-Glide and gave America's new ultra-tourer a range of 200–250mi. Also new for 1965 were the hand-lever assemblies, with cast aluminum levers and mounts and ball ends on the levers. This bike is fitted with the optional steering damper (operated by the knob that sprouts from the handlebar cover). The new, black push button on the right bar is the starter button.

Underneath the optional Deluxe Solo Seat are the cap and oil lines to the new oil tank. Instead of the metal lines used with the old oil tank, rubber lines were used. Just below the filler cap is the new, internal oil filter that was optional for 1965. The old-style external oil filter was no longer used.

clamp made of stainless steel. Optional chrome header-pipe covers were still available, as was a chrome plated, clamp-on pipe guard for the front header. The S-pipe and Y-pipe were new for 1965, and on some later Electra-Glides, the two pipes were combined into an elongated Y-pipe. These pipes were chrome plated. The standard muffler was the same style of black-painted, tubular muffler that had first been introduced in 1950 as the Mellow-Tone muffler and updated in 1952 as the Low-Tone muffler. A chrome-plated muffler was optional, as was the "finned and extension" chrome fishtail muffler.

Three optional dual exhausts could be ordered, differing only in the choice of mufflers. Available were dual exhausts with the chromed short "straight-type" (short versions of the Low-Tone muffler that had been introduced in 1958), normal-tone fishtail mufflers, and the extra-quiet fishtail mufflers. In addition to the mufflers, each of these systems used five pipes: a front header pipe (the same as used on the single exhaust), an S-pipe (the same as used on the single exhaust), a Y-pipe (chrome plated, but a different pipe from the one used on the single exhaust), a rear header pipe that connects to the Y-pipe and has a connection for the left muffler pipe (chrome plated), and a left muffler pipe (chrome plated).

Oil Tank, Filter, and Lines

With the electric starter came the need for a large battery. The 32amp, 12V battery needed to reliably crank the 1200cc Panhead motor was far too large to fit the traditional battery recess at the rear of the U-shaped oil tank. And even on a frame as large as the Electra-Glide's there was no other place left that was big enough for the battery. So the oil tank received its first drastic redesign in nearly three decades. Gone was the lovely horseshoe-shaped tank that had been such a big part of the Harley look since 1936, replaced by a squat, rectangular tank offset to the left side so the battery could sit on the right. Also gone were the metal oil lines and chromed filter, replaced by rubber lines and a filter that fit inside the filler hole of the oil tank.

Functional? Yes. Stylish? Definitely not.

Where the horseshoe oil tank had given the earlier Big Twins a wasp-waisted look, the Electra-Glide's blocky battery and oil tank were prominent love handles, contributing more than any other feature to the undeniable impression that the Big Twin had truly reached middle age and was losing the battle of the bulge.

Given the right mindset, however, a bulge becomes just another place to hang more chrome. If the Chrome Finish Group was ordered, a special chrome strip was attached to the oil tank. On FLH models, a new-style FLH decal consisting of an H and a checkered flag on a rectangular background was affixed to the left side of the tank. The King of the Highway Group included a chrome cover to at least put the battery out of sight.

The Electra-Glide's oil tank is black, but an optional chrome strip was available to dress it up. If the bike is an FLH, the new-style FLH decal shown in the photo was attached to the chrome strip. Eugene Schrier's 1965 FLH is painted in Hi-Fi Turquoise and white, which was an optional color combination in 1963. The horn shown is not the correct style for 1965. Stock horns were behind the fork shrouds. It also has many parts chrome plated that were not chromed on stock bikes.

The 1965 Electra-Glide was fitted with the same bar-and-shield tank emblems that had been used since 1963, but was given a new two-tone paint scheme. This Electra-Glide in the optional Hi-Fi Blue and white combination and is owned by Jerry Richardson.

Seats

Standard Electra-Glides were fitted with the post-mounted Standard Solo Seat. Optional post-mounted seats were the Deluxe Solo Seat and the Super Deluxe Buddy Seat. The Super Deluxe was available in all white, red top with white sides and skirts, and black top with white sides and skirts. A padded back rest was also available to make the Super Deluxe Seat even more plush. For those who preferred the more modern look of a frame-mounted seat, the Frame Mounted Buddy Seat was available in all white and in black and white.

Rear End

The swingarm for the new frame was the same as the one that had been introduced in 1963. Attached to the swingarm was the 16in rim and tire that had been standard on H-D Big Twins since 1941. As on the Duo-Glides, black rims and 5.00x16in blackwall tires were standard, but chrome rims and whitewall tires were optional. The brakes attached to the rear wheel were the wider type that had been introduced in 1963.

Two rear chain guards were available on the Electra-Glide. The standard was the valanced rear guard that had been introduced in 1963. This gloss black painted guard covers the top length of drive chain and the top of the rear sprocket. Optional was the two-piece chromed chain enclosure that covers the upper and lower lengths of chain and wraps all the way around the back of the rear sprocket. This rear chain guard had been introduced about midway through the 1964 model year.

Rear Fender

The rear fender was also revised to accommodate the new, non-"step-down" frame. Like the Duo-Glide fender it replaced, the new fender has front and rear halves that join together at a hinge so the rear half may be swung upwards for easier tire changes. In fact, the new fender differs only in minor detail from the Duo-Glide rear fender it replaced.

Attached to the rear of the fender was the same oval-shaped, stamped-steel taillight that had been used since 1955, except, of course, that a 12V bulb was fitted inside. The taillight body was painted the same color as the fender, and a chrome-plated lens door covered the rim of the red taillight lens. The license-plate bracket mounted above the taillight. This bracket is the same that had been used on the Duo-Glide.

If the optional round-back parking lights or turn signals were ordered, they were fitted with red lenses and mounted to a broad, chrome-plated stalk that attached to the underside of the taillight body. If the older-style, bullet-shaped parking lamps were ordered, they were also fitted with red lenses, but they mounted to the license-plate bracket.

Jan Berghoff's full-dress 1965 FLH Electra-Glide is painted in the standard Holiday Red and white paint scheme.

If the King of the Highway Group was ordered, the chrome "peaked" rear fender tip and Aristocrat rear bumper were supplied. Both of these were the same as those that had been introduced in 1958 and 1959, respectively. These items could also be ordered from the accessories list.

Electra-Glide Production

The motorcycle market was on the rise during 1965, and Harley-Davidson sales rose along with all the other motorcycle manufacturers' sales. Electra-Glide sales were 2,130 FLB and 4,800 FLHB, for a total of 6,930 Electra-Glides (about 26 percent higher than sales of the 1964 Duo-Glide). For perspective, this is the highest sales year for Harley's Big Twin since 1951.

Past and Future

In the eighteen years it was in production, the Panhead saw the whole American motorcycle business transformed. In 1948, Harley-Davidson was the world's largest motorcycle company and Indian was still a viable concern, but the British motorcycle manufacturers were coming on strong and a man named Soichiro had just founded Honda Motors. By 1965, Harley-Davidson was the *only* American motorcycle manufacturer left, the British bike craze was already on the wane, but Honda alone was selling more motorcycles in the United States than all other manufacturers combined.

And the Panhead was itself transformed in many ways. The first Panheads were trim and elemental large-bore sporting machines that even with saddlebags and a windshield were still relatively light at under 600lb. By 1958, the Panhead had suspension at both ends but weighed closer to 700lb and gave away all sporting pretense to its smaller brother, the Sportster. By 1965, the Panhead Electra-Glide was a behemoth, a two-wheeled land yacht that weighed more than 700lb in stripped form, but started at the touch of a button. Add fiberglass saddlebags, a windshield, dual exhaust, chrome bits, and a cigarette lighter and the Electra-Glide could top 800lb. The classic American touring bike was born.

The following year, the Big Twin motor was given yet another top end, and a new Harley moniker was coined: the Shovelhead, and it, too, would stay in production for eighteen years. The Shovelhead-powered Electra-Glide would go through its own evolution, getting disc brakes, alternating-current electrics, and a full fairing. Before long, the Electra-Glide would also devolve into more elemental machines such as the Super Glide, Low Rider, and eventually the sporting FXRS–bikes that helped Harley-Davidson through some tough times.

In the early 1980s, the trend toward a kinder, gentler Big Twin that started on the first Panhead in 1948 resulted in the Evolution Big Twins that put Harley-Davidson back on the road to prosperity. And the loop was finally closed in the 1990s with the outstanding success of a whole range of models that mimic the styles set on the Panhead springers and Hydra-Glides.

APPENDIX

1948-65
Harley-Davidson Big Twin Options Group

1948 Equipment Groups

Equipment Group	Equipment	Retail Price
DeLuxe Solo Group	Includes Steering Damper, Front Safety Guard, Jiffy Stand, 5.00x16in Tires, Hydraulic Shock Absorber, Colored Shifter Knob, Deluxe Solo Saddle, Set Deluxe Saddle Bags, Rear Safety Guard, Chrome Air Cleaner, Chrome Headlamp, Chrome Fender Tips, Chrome Exhaust Pipe Covers, Chrome Rims, Chrome Front Fender Lamp, Chrome Tail Lamp, Chrome Generator End Cover, Chrome Relay Cover, Chrome Timer Cover, Chrome Foot Lever Bearing Cover, Chrome Chain Inspection Plate, Chrome Clutch Cover	$92
Sport Solo Group	Includes Steering Damper, Front Safety Guard, Jiffy Stand, 5.00x16in Tires, Hydraulic Shock Absorber, Colored Shifter Knob, Deluxe Solo Saddle, Chrome Air Cleaner, Chrome Headlamp, Chrome Fender Tips, Chrome Exhaust Pipe Covers, Chrome Front Fender Lamp, Chrome Rims, Chrome Tail Lamp, Chrome Generator End Cover, Chrome Relay Cover, Chrome Timer Cover, Chrome Foot Lever Bearing Cover	$59.25
Utility Solo Group	Includes Steering Damper, Front Safety Guard, Jiffy Stand, 5.00x16in Tires, Chrome Front Fender Lamp, Chrome Air Cleaner	$24
Standard Police Group	Includes Utility Solo Group (see above), Hydraulic Shock Absorber, Rear Wheel Siren, Speedometer Hand Control, Deluxe Solo Saddle (Police plate optional in place of fender lamp)	$73
Utility Group— Sidecar or Package Truck Motorcycle	Includes Steering Damper, Front Safety Guard, 5.00x16in Tires, Hydraulic Shock Absorber, Chrome Fender Lamp and Chrome Air Cleaner	$33.50
Deluxe Sport Sidecar Group	Includes Windshield and Apron, Spare Wheel Carrier, Spare Wheel with 5.00x16in Tire Attached, Fender Lamp and Wiring, Chrome Tail Lamp, Chrome Fender Tip, Chrome Rims	$90.50

1949 Equipment Groups

Equipment Group	Equipment	Retail Price
DeLuxe Solo Group	Includes Front Safety Guard, Jiffy Stand, 5.00x16in Wheels and Tires, Stainless Steel Air Cleaner, Chrome Relay Cover, Stainless Steel Timer Cover, Stainless Generator End Cover, Colored Shift Ball, Chrome Head Light, Chrome taillight, Chrome Rear Fender Tip, Chrome Exhaust Pipe Covers, Chrome Rims, DeLuxe Solo Saddle, Chrome Front Parking Lamps, Stainless Steel Chain Inspection Cover, Stainless Steel Clutch Cover, Stainless Fork Trim (five pieces), Stainless Foot Lever Bearing Cover, Pair King Size Saddle Bags, Rear Safety Guard, Chrome Hub Caps, Chrome Rear Bumper, Stainless Steel Muffler Shield	$115
Sport Solo Group	Includes Front Safety Guard, Jiffy Stand, 5.00x16in Wheels and Tires, Stainless Steel Air Cleaner, Chrome Relay Cover, Stainless Steel Timer Cover, Stainless Generator End Cover, Colored Shift Ball, Chrome Head Light, Chrome taillight, Chrome Rear Fender Tip, Chrome Exhaust Pipe Covers, Chrome Rims, DeLuxe Solo Saddle, Chrome Front Parking Lamps, Chrome Mirror, Stainless Steel Chain Inspection Cover, Stainless Steel Clutch Cover, Stainless Fork Trim (five pieces), Stainless Foot Lever Bearing Cover, Stainless Steel Muffler Shield	$67.75
Utility Solo Group	Includes Front Safety Guard (Black), Jiffy Stand, 5.00x16in Wheels and Tires, Stainless Steel Air Cleaner Chrome Relay Cover, Stainless Steel Timer Cover, Stainless Generator End Cover	$21.15
Standard Police Group	Includes Front Safety Guard, Jiffy Stand, 5.00x16in Wheels and Tires, Stainless Steel Air Cleaner, Chrome Relay Cover, Stainless Steel Timer Cover, Stainless Generator End Cover, Rear Wheel Siren, Speedometer Hand Control, DeLuxe Solo Saddle (Police Special)	$87
Utility Group for Sidecar or Package Truck Motorcycle	Includes Front Safety Guard, Steering Damper, Hydraulic Shock Absorber, 5.00x16in Wheels and Tires, Stainless Steel Air Cleaner, Chrome Relay Cover, Stainless Steel Timer Cover, Stainless Generator End Cover, Front Fender Lamp	$38.50
DeLuxe Sidecar Group	Includes Windshield and Apron, Spare Wheel Carrier, Spare Wheel and 5.00x16in Tire, 5.00x16in Wheels and Tires (Both Wheels), Chrome Sidecar Fender Light and Wiring, Chrome taillight, Rear Fender Tip, Chrome Rims (Both Wheels), Chrome Hub Cap (new style)	$102

1950 Equipment Groups

Equipment Group	Equipment	Retail Price
DeLuxe Solo Group	Includes Front Safety Guard (Chrome), Air Cleaner, 5.00x16in Wheels and Tires, Jiffy Stand, Colored Shift Ball, Chrome Head Light, Chrome taillight, Chrome Rims, Stainless Fork Trim, Chrome Exhaust Pipe Covers, Chrome Muffler, Chrome Clutch Inspection Cover, Chrome Timer Cover, Chrome Primary Chain Inspection Cover, Polished Fork Sliders and Brake Side Cover, Pair King Size Saddle Bags, Rear Safety Guard (Chrome)	$95.50
Sport Solo Group	Includes Front Safety Guard (Chrome), Air Cleaner, 5.00x16in Wheels and Tires, Jiffy Stand, Colored Shift Ball, Chrome Head Light, Chrome taillight, Chrome Rims, Stainless Fork Trim, Chrome Exhaust Pipe Covers, Chrome Muffler, Chrome Clutch Cover, Chrome Timer Cover, Chrome Primary Chain Inspection Cover, Polished Fork Sliders and Brake Side Cover	$53.70
Utility Solo Group	Includes Front Safety Guard (Black), Air Cleaner, 5.00x16in Wheels and Tires, Jiffy Stand	$19.95
Standard Police Group	Includes Front Safety Guard (Black), Jiffy Stand, 5.00x16in Wheels and Tires, Air Cleaner, Rear Wheel Siren, Speedometer Hand Control, DeLuxe Solo Saddle (Police)	$67.90
Utility Group for Sidecar or Package Truck Motorcycle	Includes Front Safety Guard (Black), Air Cleaner, 5.00x16in Wheels and Tires	$15.60
DeLuxe Sidecar Group	Includes Windshield and Apron, Spare Wheel and Carrier, 5.00x16in Wheels and Tires, Sidecar Lamp and Wiring, Chrome Tail Lamp on Fender, Rear Fender Tip, Chrome Rims (two wheels), Chrome Hub Cap	$102.45

1951 EQUIPMENT GROUPS

Equipment Group	Equipment	Retail Price
DeLuxe Solo Group	Includes Front Safety Guard (Chrome), Air Cleaner, 5.00x16in Wheels and Tires, Jiffy Stand, Colored Shift Ball, Chrome Head Light, Chrome taillight, Chrome Rims, Stainless Fork Trim, Chrome Exhaust Pipe Covers, Chrome Muffler, Chrome Clutch Cover, Chrome Timer Cover, Chrome Chain Inspection Cover, Polished Fork Sliders and Brake Side Cover, Pair King Size Saddle Bags, Rear Safety Guard (Chrome)	$115
Sport Solo Group	Includes Front Safety Guard (Chrome), Air Cleaner, 5.00x16in Wheels and Tires, Jiffy Stand, Colored Shift Ball, Chrome Head Light, Chrome taillight, Chrome Rims, Stainless Fork Trim, Chrome Exhaust Pipe Covers, Chrome Muffler, Chrome Clutch Cover, Chrome Timer Cover, Chrome Chain Inspection Cover, Polished Fork Sliders and Brake Side Cover	$66.50

APPENDIX 253

Equipment Group	Equipment	Retail Price
Utility Solo Group	Includes Front Safety Guard (Black), Air Cleaner, 5.00x16in Wheels and Tires, Jiffy Stand	$25.50
Standard Police Group	Includes Front Safety Guard (Black), Jiffy Stand, 5.00x16in Wheels and Tires, Air Cleaner, Rear Wheel Siren, Speedometer Hand Control, DeLuxe Solo Saddle (Police)	$78.75
DeLuxe Sidecar Group	Includes Windshield and Apron, Spare Wheel and Carrier, 5.00x16in Wheels and Tires, Sidecar Lamp and Wiring, Chrome Tail Lamp on Fender, Chrome Rims (two wheels)	$122

1952 Equipment Groups

Equipment Group	Equipment	Retail Price
DeLuxe Solo Group	Includes Front Safety Guard (Chrome), Air Cleaner, 5.00x16in Wheels and Tires, Jiffy Stand, Chrome Rubber Mounted Handlebars (either Speedster or Buckhorn), Chrome Rims, Chrome Headlight, Chrome taillight, Stainless Fork Trim, Chrome Clutch Cover, Chrome Timer Cover, Chrome Primary Chain Inspection Cover, Chrome Muffler, two "DeLuxe OHV" Name Plates on Fender, Polished Fork Sliders and Brake Side Cover, and Chrome Exhaust Pipe Covers	$73.50
Utility Solo Group	Includes Front Safety Guard (Black), Air Cleaner, 5.00x16in Wheels and Tires, Jiffy Stand	$28.45
Standard Police Group	Includes Front Safety Guard (Black), Jiffy Stand, 5.00x16in Wheels and Tires, Air Cleaner, Rear Wheel Siren, Speedometer Hand Control, DeLuxe Solo Saddle (Police)	$85.50
DeLuxe Sidecar Group	Includes Windshield and Apron, Spare Wheel and Carrier, 5.00x16in Wheels and Tires, Sidecar Lamp and Wiring, Chrome Tail Lamp on Fender, Chrome Rims (two Wheels)	$136.60

1953 Equipment Groups

Equipment Group	Equipment	Retail Price
DeLuxe Solo Group	Includes Front Safety Guard (Chrome), Air Cleaner, 5.00x16in Wheels and Tires, Jiffy Stand, Chrome Rubber Mounted Handlebars (Specify Speedster or Buckhorn), Chrome Rims, Chrome Headlight, Chrome taillight, Oil Filter Assembly, Stainless Fork Trim, Chrome Clutch Inspection Cover, Chrome Timer Cover, Chrome Primary-Chain Inspection Cover, Chrome Muffler, 2in DeLuxe OHV Name Plates on Fender, Polished Fork Sliders and Brake Side Cover, and Chrome Exhaust Pipe Cover	$83.30
Standard Solo Group	Includes Front Safety Guard (Black), Air Cleaner, 5.00x16in Wheels and Tires, Jiffy Stand (Specify Speedster or Buckhorn Handlebar)	$28.45
Standard Police Group	Includes Front Safety Guard (Black), Jiffy Stand, 5.00x16in Wheels and Tires, Air Cleaner, Rear Wheel Siren, Speedometer Hand Control, DeLuxe Solo Saddle (Police). (Specify Speedster or Buckhorn Handlebar)	$85.50
DeLuxe Sidecar Group	Includes Windshield and Apron, Spare Wheel and Carrier, 5.00x16in Wheels and Tires, Sidecar Lamp and Wiring, Chrome Tail Lamp on Fender, Chrome Rims (two wheels)	136.60

1954 Equipment Groups

Equipment Group	Equipment	Retail Price
DeLuxe Solo Group	Includes Front Safety Guard (Chrome), Air Cleaner, 5.00x16in Wheels and Tires, Jiffy Stand, Chrome Rubber Mounted Handlebars (Specify Speedster or Buckhorn), Chrome Rims, Chrome Headlight, Chrome taillight, Oil Filter Assembly, Stainless Fork Trim, Chrome Clutch Inspection Cover, Chrome Timer Cover, Chrome Primary-Chain Inspection Cover, Chrome Muffler, 2in DeLuxe OHV Name Plates on Fender, Polished Fork Sliders and Brake Side Cover, Chrome Exhaust Pipe Covers, and Chrome Plated Horn and Cover	
Standard Solo Group	Includes Front Safety Guard (Black), Air Cleaner, 5.00x16in Wheels and Tires, Jiffy Stand. (Specify Speedster or Buckhorn Handlebar)	
Standard Police Group	Includes Front Safety Guard (Black), Jiffy Stand, 5.00x16in Wheels and Tires, Air Cleaner, Rear Wheel Siren, Speedometer Hand Control, DeLuxe Solo Saddle (Police). (Specify Speedster or Buckhorn Handlebar)	
DeLuxe Sidecar Group	Includes Windshield and Apron, Spare Wheel and Carrier, 5.00x16in Wheels and Tires, Sidecar Lamp and Wiring, Chrome Tail Lamp on Fender, Chrome Rims (two wheels)	

1955 Equipment Groups

Equipment Group	Equipment	Retail Price
DeLuxe Solo Group	Includes Front Safety Guard (Chrome), Air Cleaner, 5.00x16in Wheels and Tires, Jiffy Stand, Chrome Rubber Mounted Handle Bars (Specify Speedster or Buckhorn Handlebars), Chrome Rims, Chrome Headlight, Oil Filter Assembly, Stainless Fork Trim, Chrome Clutch Inspection Cover, Chrome Timer Cover, Chrome Primary-Chain Inspection Cover, Chrome Muffler, Polished Fork Sliders and Brake Side Cover, Chrome Exhaust Pipe Covers, Chrome Plated Horn and Cover, and Front Fender Medallion	$88
Standard Solo Group	Includes Front Safety Guard (Black), Air Cleaner, 5.00x16in Wheels and Tires, Jiffy Stand. (Specify Speedster or Buckhorn Handlebars)	$31.50
Standard Police Group	Front Safety Guard (Black), Jiffy Stand, 5.00x16in Wheels and Tires, Air Cleaner, Rear Wheel Siren, Speedometer Hand Control, DeLuxe Solo Saddle and Front Fender Medallion	$90.00
DeLuxe Sidecar Group	Includes Windshield and Apron, Spare Wheel and Carrier, 5.00x16in Wheels and Tires, Sidecar Lamp and Wiring, Chrome Rims (two wheels)	$129

1956 Equipment Groups

Notes when ordering. "On all 74ci OHV models the following are now regular equipment items: -Front Safety Guard (Black), Air Cleaner, Jiffy Stand, and 5.00x16in Black Wheels and Tires. Trip Odometer is standard equipment on OHV"

Equipment Group	Equipment	Retail Price
Chrome Finish Group	Includes Chrome Front Safety Guard, Chrome Rubber Mounted Handlebars, Chrome Rims, Chrome Headlight, Stainless Fork Trim (five pieces), Chrome Clutch Inspection Cover, Timer Cover, Primary Chain Inspection Cover, Chrome Muffler, Polished Fork Sliders, Polished Brake Side Cover, Polished Horn Body and Cover, Chrome Exhaust Pipe Covers, Colored Plastic Grips, Chrome Instrument Panel Cover	$54
Road Cruiser Group	Includes DeLuxe Buddy Seat #52503-36 (exchange), King Saddle Bags #90994-53, Compensating Sprocket (exchange), Oil Filter Assembly, Rear Bumper, Rear Bumper Grille and Solo Windshield (all clear, clear and red or clear and blue)	$108
Road Cruiser Group	With Super DeLuxe Buddy Seat instead	$119
King of the Highway Group	Includes Super DeLuxe Buddy Seat 52503-54 (exchange), Rear Bumper, Rear Bumper Grille, Oil Filter Assembly, Compensating Sprocket (exchange), Chrome Cross Over and Dual Mufflers, Front Hub Cap, Directional Signals, Front Bumper 91075-55, Cigarette Lighter, Buddy Seat Rail, Chrome Luggage Carrier, Chrome Boot Guard, Plastic Saddle Bags (Pepper Red, Atomic Blue or Black), and Solo Windshield (all clear, clear and red, clear and blue)	$191.50
Standard Police Group	Includes Rear Wheel Siren, Speedometer Hand Control, DeLuxe Solo Saddle (exchange). (Specify Speedster or Buckhorn handlebars)	$65
DeLuxe Sidecar Group	Includes Windshield and Apron, Spare Wheel and Carrier, 5.00x16in Wheels and Tires, and Chrome Rims (two wheels)	$127

1957 Equipment Groups

Equipment Group	Equipment	Retail Price
Chrome Finish Group	Includes Chrome Front Safety Guard, Chrome Rubber Mounted Handlebars, Chrome Rims, Chrome Headlight, Stainless Fork Trim (5 pieces), Chrome Clutch Inspection Cover,	$64.90

Road Cruiser Group	DeLuxe Buddy Seat (in place of standard saddle), leather white welt King Saddle Bags 90994-53A (attached), Hydra-Glide Windshield (blue, red, or clear) Compensating Sprocket (in place of rigid), 91007-52 Rear Bumper, 91023-52 Rear Bumper Grille, 49153-36 Chrome Rear Safety Guard (With Super DeLuxe Buddy Seat instead of DeLuxe, add $11; with DeLuxe Solo Seat in place of DeLuxe Buddy Seat, deduct $13.50; with Plastic Saddle Bags 90851-54 in place of 90994-53, add $2)	$117.35
King of the Highway Group	52503-54 Super DeLuxe Buddy Seat (in place of Standard Saddle), 90651-54 Plastic Saddle Bags and Carrier, Hydra-Glide Windshield (blue, red, or clear), 91007-52 Rear Bumper, 91023-52 Rear Bumper Grille, Compensating Sprocket (in place of rigid), Dual Muffler with Crossover, 43303-49 Front Hub Cap, 68550-50 Directional Signals, 91575-49A Buddy Seat Rail, 53403-52 Chrome Luggage Carrier, 65700-38 Chrome Boot Guard, 49153-36 Chrome Rear Safety Guard (With DeLuxe Solo Seat in place of Super DeLuxe Buddy Seat, deduct $23; with DeLuxe Buddy Seat in place of Super DeLuxe Buddy Seat, deduct $9.50)	$192
Standard Police Group	Includes Rear Wheel Siren, Speedometer Hand Control, DeLuxe Solo Saddle (exchange) Specify Speedster or Buckhorn handlebars	$65
DeLuxe Sidecar Group	Includes Windshield and Apron, Spare Wheel and Tire and Spare Wheel Carrier, Chrome Rims	$119

1958 Equipment Groups

Equipment Group	Equipment	Retail Price
Chrome Finish Group #F-1	Includes Front Safety Guard, Rubber-Mounted Chrome Handle Bars (Speedster Or Buckhorn), Chrome Rims, Chrome Headlight, Stainless Steel Fork Trim (Five Pieces), Chrome Clutch Inspection Cover, Chrome Timer Cover, Chrome Primary-Chain Inspection Cover, Chrome Muffler, Polished Fork Sliders, Polished Brake Side Cover, Polished Horn Body and Cover, Chrome Exhaust-Pipe Covers, Colored Plastic Handlebar Grips, Chrome Instrument-Panel Cover, Oil Filter (Attached), Chrome Caps For Rear Shock Absorber and Two Clamps With Screws, Nuts and Washers	
Road Cruiser Group #F-2	Includes 52503-58 Deluxe Buddy Seat (in place of standard saddle), Chrome Front Bumper, 90851-58 Pair Plastic Saddle Bags and Carrier, Windshield (Blue, Red, Or Clear), Compensating Sprocket (In Place Of Rigid), Chrome Rear Safety Guard, Chrome Front Parking Lamps (White)	
Road Cruiser Group #F-3	Same as #F-2 with Deluxe Solo Saddle 52006-47A in place of 52503-58 Deluxe Buddy Seat	
Road Cruiser Group #F-4	Same as #F-2 with Super Deluxe Buddy Seat 52504-58 in place of 52503-58	
King of the Highway Group #F-5	Includes 52504-58 Super Deluxe Buddy Seat, 66373-54 Chrome Battery Cover, 90851-58 Pair Plastic Saddle Bags and Carrier, Windshield (57998-56 Blue, 57999-56 Red, 58002-49 Clear), 59885-48 Chrome Rear-Fender Tip, 59235-48 Rear-Fender Flap, 40277-55a Compensating Sprocket (Exchange), 65425-58 Dual Mufflers With Crossover, 43303-49 Front Hub Cap (Attached), 68550-58 Directional Signals, 91575-49a Buddy Seat Rail, 65700-38 Chrome Boot Guard, 49150-58 Chrome Rear Safety Guard, 53403-58 Chrome Luggage Carrier (Not Attached), 91075-58 Front Bumper (Not Attached), 43895-56 Chrome Axle and Fork Stud Caps (Attached)	
King of the Highway Group #F-6	Same as #F-5 with 52006-47A Deluxe Solo Saddle in place of 52504-58 Super Deluxe Buddy Seat	
King of the Highway Group #F-7	Same as #F-5 with Deluxe Buddy Seat 52503-58 in place of 52504-58 Super Deluxe Buddy Seat	
Standard Police Group #FP-1	Includes 91129-58 Hand-Controlled Front-Wheel Siren, 67301-38 Speedometer Hand Control (Attached), 52006-47a Deluxe Solo Saddle (Exchange)	
Standard Police Group #FP-2	Same as FP-1 with 91131-58 Foot-Controlled Front-Wheel Siren	
Sport Sidecar DeLuxe Group #SC-1	Includes 88850-36 Windshield and Apron (Attached), Spare Wheel and Tire, Two Chrome Rims, and 89150-36 Spare-Wheel Carrier	

1959 Equipment Groups

Equipment Group	Equipment	Retail Price
Chrome Finish Group #F-1	Includes 49038-58 Chrome Front Safety Guard, Rubber-Mounted Chrome Handle Bars (Speedster Or Buckhorn), Chrome Rims (Two), Chrome Headlight, Stainless Steel Fork Trim (Five Pieces), Chrome Clutch Inspection Cover, Chrome Timer Cover, Chrome Primary-Chain Inspection Cover, Chrome Muffler, Polished Fork Sliders, Polished Brake Side Cover, Polished Chrome Horn Cover and Trumpet, Chrome Exhaust-Pipe Covers, Colored Plastic Handlebar Grips, Chrome Instrument-Panel Cover, Oil Filter (Attached), Chrome Caps For Rear Shock Absorber and Clamps With Screws Nuts and Washers, Chrome Clutch-Booster-Spring Cover, Chrome Tool-Box Cover	
Road Cruiser Group #F-2	Includes Deluxe Buddy Seat (In Place Of Standard Saddle), Chrome Front Bumper, Pair White Plastic Saddle Bags and Carrier, Windshield (57998-56 Blue, 57999-56 Red, 58002-49 Clear), Compensating Sprocket (In Place Of Rigid), Chrome Rear Safety Guard, Rear Bumper, and Rear Chain Oiler	
Road Cruiser Group #F-2a	Same As #F-2 But With Pair Black Plastic Saddle Bags Instead Of White	
Road Cruiser Group #F-3	Same As #F-2 With Deluxe Solo Saddle In Place Of Deluxe Buddy Seat	
Road Cruiser Group #F-3a	Same As #F-3 But With Pair Black Saddle Bags Instead Of White	
Road Cruiser Group #F-4	Same As #F-2 With Super Deluxe Buddy Seat 52504-58 In Place Of 52503-58	
Road Cruiser Group #F-4a	Same As #F-4 But With 90851-58a Pair Black Plastic Saddle Bags Instead Of White	
King Of The Highway Group #F-5	Includes Super Deluxe Buddy Seat, Chrome Battery Cover, Pair White Plastic Saddle Bags and Carrier, Windshield (57998-56 Blue, 57999-56 Red, Or 58002-49 Clear), Compensating Sprocket (Exchange), Dual Mufflers With Crossover, Directional Signals, New-Style Buddy Seat Rail, Chrome Boot Guard, Chrome Rear Safety Guard, Chrome Luggage Carrier (Not Attached), Front Bumper (Not Attached), Chrome Axle and Fork Stud Caps (Attached), Rear Chain Oiler, and Rear Bumper (Not Attached)	
King Of The Highway Group #F-5a	Same As #F-5 But With Pair Black Plastic Saddle Bags Instead Of White	
King Of The Highway Group #F-6	Same As #F-5 With Deluxe Solo Saddle In Place Of Super Deluxe Buddy Seat	
King Of The Highway Group #F-6a	Same As #F-6 But With Pair Black Plastic Saddle Bags Instead Of White	
King Of The Highway Group #F-7	Same As #F-5 With Deluxe Buddy Seat In Place Of Super Deluxe Buddy Seat	
King Of The Highway Group #F-7a	Same As Group #F-7 But With Pair Black Plastic Saddle Bags Instead Of White	
Standard Police Group #Fp-1	Includes Hand Controlled Front-Wheel Siren, Speedometer Hand Control (Attached), Deluxe Solo Saddle (Exchange) and Oil Filter (Attached)	
Standard Police	Same As Fp-1 With Foot-Controlled Front-Wheel Siren Sport Sidecar Deluxe Group #Sc-1 Includes Windshield and Apron (Attached), Spare Wheel and Tire, Two Chrome Rims, and Spare-Wheel Carrier	

1960 Equipment Groups

Equipment Group	Equipment
Chrome Finish Group #F-1	Includes 49038-58 Chrome Front Safety Guard, Chrome Rubber Mounted Handle Bars (Speedster Or Buckhorn), 43007-40 Chrome Rims, 45964-49 Stainless Steel Fork Covers (Two), 60557-36 Chrome Clutch Inspection Cover, 32589-36 Chrome Timer Cover, 60573-36 Chrome Primary-Chain Inspection Cover, 65203-58 Chrome Muffler, Polished Fork Sliders, 44141-50 Polished Brake Side Cover, 69022-54 Chrome Horn Cover and 69140-54 Chrome Horn Trumpet, 65550-58 Chrome Exhaust-Pipe Covers, Colored Plastic Handle Bar Grips, 71271-56 Chrome Instrument-Panel Cover, 63800-58 Oil Filter, Chrome Caps For Rear Shock Absorbers, 38495-58 Chrome Clutch Booster-Spring Cover, Polished Headlamp Nacelle and Polished Handlebar Cover
Road Cruiser Group #F-2	Includes 91007-58 Rear Bumper, 91075-58A Front Bumper, 90849-59 White Plastic Saddle Bags and Carrier, Windshield (57996-60 Clear, 57998-60 Blue, 57999-60 Red), 40277-55A Compensating Sprocket (In Place Of Rigid), 63587-58 Rear Chain Oiler, 49150-58 Chrome Rear Safety Guard, Frame-Mounted Buddy Seat (Indicate Choice 52485-60 Black and White, 52481-60 Red and White and 52489-60 All White)
Road Cruiser Group #F-2A	Same As #F-2 But With 90851-58A Black Plastic Saddle Bags Instead Of White
Road Cruiser Group #F-3	Same As #F-2 With 52006-47A Deluxe Solo Saddle In Place Of Frame-Mounted Buddy Seat
Road Cruiser Group #F-3A	Same As Group #F-3 But With 90851-58A Black Saddle Bags Instead Of White
Road Cruiser Group #F-4	Same As F-2 With Super Deluxe Buddy Seat In Place Of Frame-Mounted Buddy Seat (Indicate Color Choice 52504-58A Black and White Or 52505-58 Red and White)
Road Cruiser Group #F-4A	Same As #F-4 But With 90851-58A Black Plastic Saddle Bags Instead Of White
King of the Highway Group #F-5	Includes 66373-54 Chrome Battery Cover, 90849-58 Pair White Plastic Saddle Bags and Carrier, Windshield (57996-60 Clear, 57998-60 Blue, 57999-60 Red), 63587-58 Rear Chain Oiler, 40277-55A Compensating Sprocket (In Place Of Rigid), 65425-58 Dual Mufflers With Crossover, 68550-58 Directional Signals (Partially Attached), 65700-38 Chrome Boot Guard, 49150-58 Chrome Rear Safety Guard, 53403-58 Chrome Luggage Carrier (Not Attached), 91075-58a Front Bumper (Not Attached), 91007-58 Rear Bumper (Not Attached), 43895-56 Chrome Axle and Fork Studs (Attached), 43303-49 Front Hub Cap Attached, 59887-59 Rear Fender Tip, and Frame-Mounted Buddy Seat (52485-60 Black and White, 52487-60 Red and White, 52489-60 All White)
King of the Highway Group #F-5A	Same As #F-5 But With 90851-58A Black Plastic Saddle Bags Instead Of White
King of the Highway Group #F-6	Same As #F-5 With 52006-47A Deluxe Solo Saddle In Place Of Frame Mounted Buddy Seat
King of the Highway Group #F-6A	Same As #F-6 But With 90851-58A Black Plastic Saddle Bags Instead Of White
King of the Highway Group #F-7	Same As #F-5 With Super Deluxe Buddy Seat In Place Of Frame-Mounted Buddy Seat (52504-58a Black and White Or 52505-58 Red and White)
King of the Highway Group #F-7A	Same As Group #F-7 But With 90851-58A Black Plastic Saddle Bags Instead Of White
Standard Police Group #FP-1	Includes 91130-58 Hand-Controlled Front-Wheel Siren (Attached), 67301-38 Speedometer Sand Control (Attached), 52006-47A Deluxe Solo Saddle (Exchange) and 63800-58 Oil Filter (Attached)
Standard Police Group #FP-2	Same As #FP-1 With 91131-58 Foot-Controlled Front-Wheel Siren
Standard Police Group #FP-3	Same As Group #FP-1 But With 91126-59 Foot-Controlled Rear-Wheel Siren In Place Of 91130-58 Hand-Controlled Front-Wheel Siren
Sport Sidecare DeLux Group #SC-1	Includes 88850-36 Windshield and Apron (Attached), Spare Wheel With Chrome Rims (Two) and Tire, and 89150-36 Spare Wheel Carrier

1961 Equipment Groups

Equipment Group	Equipment
Chrome Finish Group #F-1	Includes 49038-58 Chrome Front Safety Guard, Chrome Rubber-Mounted Handlebars (Specify Style), 43007-40 Chrome Rims, 45964-49 Stainless Steel Fork Covers, 60557-36 Chrome Clutch Inspection Cover, 32589-36 Chrome Timer Cover, 60573-36 Chrome Primary-Chain Inspection Cover, 65203-58 Chrome Muffler, Polished Fork Sliders, 44141-50 Polished Brake Side Cover, 69022-54 Chrome Horn Cover, 69140-54 Chrome Horn Trumpet, 65550-58 Chrome Exhaust-Pipe Covers, Colored Plastic Handlebar Grips, 71271-56 Chrome Instrument-Panel Cover, 63800-58 Oil Filter, 54704-60 Chrome Caps For Rear Shock Absorber, 38495-58 Chrome Clutch Booster-Spring Cover, Polished Headlamp Nacelle, Polished Handlebar-Clamp Cover, and 31800-61 Chrome Spark-Coil Cover
Road Cruiser Group #F-2	Includes 91007-58 Chrome Rear Bumper, 91075-58A Chrome Front Bumper, 90849-59 White Plastic Saddle Bags and Carrier, Windshield (57996-60 Clear, 57998-60 Blue, 57999-60 Red), 40277-60 Compensating Sprocket (In Place Of Rigid), 63587-58 Rear-Chain Oiler (Attached), Super Deluxe Buddy Seat (52504-58A Black and White, 52505-58 Red and White)
Road Cruiser Group #F-2A	Same As #F-2 But With 90850-58 Black Plastic Saddle Bags Instead Of White
Road Cruiser Group #F-3	Same As #F-2 With Frame-Mounted Buddy Seat (52485-60 Black and White, 52481-60 Red and White, Or 52489-60 All White) In Place Of Super Deluxe Buddy Seat
Road Cruiser Group #F-4	Same As #F-2 With Deluxe Solo Saddle In Place Of Super Deluxe Buddy Seat
King of the Highway Group #F-5	Includes 66373-54 Chrome Battery Cover, 90849-58 White Plastic Saddle Bags and Carrier, Windshield (57996-60 Clear, 57998-60 Blue, 57999-60 Red), 63587-58 Rear-Chain Oiler, 40277-60 Compensating Sprocket (In Place Of Rigid), 65425-58 Dual Mufflers With Crossover, 68550-58B Directional Signals (Partially Attached), 65700-38 Chrome Boot Guard, 49150-58 Chrome Rear Safety Guard, 53403-58 Chrome Luggage Carrier (Not Attached), 91075-58A Chrome Front Bumper (Not Attached), 91007-58 Chrome Rear Bumper (Not Attached), 43895-56 Chrome Axle and Fork Stud Caps (Attached), 43303-49 Front Hub Cap (Attached), 59887-59 Chrome Rear Fender Tip, and Super Deluxe Buddy Seat (52504-58A Black and White, Or 52505-58 Red and White)
King of the Highway Group #F-5A	Same As #F-5 But With 90851-58 Black Plastic Saddle Bags Instead Of White
King of the Highway Group #F-6	Same As #F-5 With Frame-Mounted Buddy Seat (52485-60 Black and White, 52487-60 Red and White, Or 52489-60 All White) In Place Of Super Deluxe Buddy Seat
King of the Highway Group #F-7	Same as #F-5 with Deluxe Solo Saddle in place of Super Deluxe Buddy Seat
Standard Police Group #FP-1	Includes 91130-58 Hand Controlled Front-Wheel Siren (Attached), 67301-38 Speedometer Hand Control (Attached), 52006-47A Deluxe Solo Saddle (Exchange), and 63800-58 Oil Filter (Attached)
Standard Police Group #FP-2	Same As FP-1 With 91131-58 Foot-Controlled Front-Wheel Siren Instead Of Hand-Controlled
Standard Police Group #FP-3	Same As Group #FP-1 But With 91126-59 Foot-Controlled rear-wheel siren in place of 91130-58 hand-controlled front-wheel siren
Deluxe Sidecar Group #SC-1	Includes 88850-36 windshield and apron (attached), Spare Wheel With Chrome Rims (Two) and Tire, and 89150-36 Spare-Wheel Carrier

1962 Equipment Groups

Equipment Group	Equipment
Chrome Finish Group #F-1	Includes Chrome Clutch Booster-Spring Cover, Chrome Clutch Cover, Chrome Exhaust-Pipe Cover, Chrome Front Safety Guard, Rubber-Mounted Chrome Handlebars (Speedster Or Buckhorn), Chrome Horn Trumpet and Cover, Chrome Primary-Chain Inspection Cover, Chrome Instrument-Panel Cover, Chrome Mirror, Polished Brake Side Cover, Chrome Muffler, Chrome Oil Filter, Chrome Rims, Chrome Shock-Absorber Caps, Chrome Spark-Coil Cover, Chrome Timer Cover, Polished Fork Sliders, Polished Handlebar-Clamp Cover, Polished Headlamp Nacelle, Stainless Steel Fork Covers
Road Cruiser Group #F-2	Includes Chrome Front Bumper, Chrome Rear Bumper, White Plastic Saddle Bags and Carrier, Solo Windshield (Clear, Red, Or Blue), Compensating Sprocket, Rear-Chain Oiler, Super Deluxe Buddy Seat (Black and White, Red and White, Or All White)
Road Cruiser Group #F-3	Same As #F-2 But With Frame-Mounted Buddy Seat In Place Of Super Deluxe Buddy Seat (Red and White, Black and White, Or All White)
Road Cruiser Group #F-4	Same As #F-2 But With Deluxe Solo Seat In Place Of Super Deluxe Buddy Seat (Note: Black Plastic Saddle Bags May Be Substituted For White At No Extra Charge)
King of the Highway Group #F-5	Includes: Chrome Axle and Fork-Stud Cap, Chrome Battery Cover, Chrome Boot Guards, Chrome Front Bumper, Chrome Rear Bumper, Chrome Rear Fender Tip, Chrome Dual Mufflers (Super Quiet; Standard Dual Muffler May Be Substituted For Super Quiet At No Extra Charge), Chrome Luggage Carrier, Chrome Rear Safety Guard, Compensating Sprocket, Front Hub Cap, Directional Signals, White Plastic Saddle Bags, Rear-Chain Oiler, Solo Windshield (Blue, Clear, Or Red), Super Deluxe Buddy Seat (Red and White, Black and White, Or All White)
King of the Highway Group #F-6	Same As #F-5 But With Frame-Mounted Buddy Seat (Black and White, Red and White Or All White) In Place Of Super Deluxe Buddy Seat
King of the Highway Group #F-7	Same As #F-5 But With Deluxe Solo Seat In Place Of Super Deluxe Buddy Seat (Note: Black Plastic Saddle Bags and Carrier May Be Substituted For White; Also, Standard Dual Muffler May Be Substituted For Super Quiet At No Extra Charge)
Standard Police Group #FP-3	Includes Deluxe Solo Seat, Foot-Controlled Rear-Wheel Siren, Oil Filter, Rear-Chain Oiler, Solo Windshield (Clear), Special Police Speedometer, Speedometer Hand Control. (Note: Front Wheel Sirens (Formerly Indicated In Groups FP-1 and FP-2) Are No Longer Available On Solo Models). Specify 50002-58 Special Jiffy Stand When Rear-Wheel Sirens Are Ordered. When Chrome Finish Group #F-1 and Standard Police Group #FP-3 Are Ordered Together, Allow For Oil Filter Charged For In Each Group.

1963 Equipment Groups

Equipment Group	Equipment
Chrome Finish Group #F-1	Includes Chrome Clutch Booster-Spring Cover, Chrome Clutch Inspection Cover, Chrome Exhaust-Pipe Covers, Chrome Front Safety Guard, Chrome Rubber-Mounted Handlebars (Speedster Or Buckhorn), Chrome Horn Trumpet and Cover, Chrome Primary-Chain Inspection Cover, Chrome Instrument Panel, Chrome Mirror, Chrome Muffler, Oil Filter (Attached), Chrome Rims, Chrome Shock-Absorber Covers, Chrome Spark-Coil Cover, Chrome timer Cover, Polished Brake Side Cover, Polished Fork Sliders, Polished Handlebar Cover, Polished Headlamp Nacelle, Stainless Steel Fork Covers
King of the Highway Group #F-5	Includes Chrome Axle and Fork-Stud Caps (Attached), Chrome Battery Cover, Chrome Boot Guard, Chrome Front Bumper, Chrome Rear Bumper, Chrome Rear Fender Tip, Dual Chrome Super-Quiet Mufflers, Chrome Luggage Carrier, Chrome Rear Safety Guard, Compensating Sprocket, Front Hub Cap (Attached), Chrome Oil Tank, Directional Signals, White Fiberglass Saddle Bags and Carrier, Solo Windshield (Blue, Clear Or Red), Super Deluxe Buddy Seat (Red and White, Black and White, Or All White) (Optional For All King Of The Highway Groups: Standard Dual Muffler 65425-61 May Be Substituted For Super Quiet and Black Fiberglass Saddlebags and Carrier May Be Substituted For White At No Extra Charge)
King of the Highway Group #F-6	Same As #F-5 But With Frame-Mounted Buddy Seat (Black and White, Red and White, Or All White) In Place Of Super Deluxe Buddy Seat
King of the Highway Group #F-7	Same As #F-5 But With Deluxe Solo Seat In Place Of Super Deluxe Buddy Seat
Standard Police Group #FP-1	Includes Deluxe Solo Seat, Foot-Controlled Rear-Wheel Siren, Oil Filter (Attached), Clear Solo Windshield, Special Police Speedometer, and Speedometer Hand Control (Attached) (Note: When Chrome Finish Group #F-1 and Standard Police Group #FP-1 Or #FP-2 Are Ordered Together, Allow For Oil Filter Charged For In Each Group)
Standard Police Group #FP-2	Same As #FP-1 But With Foot-Controlled Rear-Wheel Siren

1964 Equipment Group

Equipment Group	Equipment
Chrome Finish Group #F-1	Includes Chrome Clutch Booster Spring Cover, Chrome Clutch Cover, Chrome Exhaust Pipe Covers, Chrome Front Safety Guard, Chrome Handlebars—Rubber Mounted (Specify Choice), Chrome Horn Trumpet and Cover, Chrome Inspection Cover, Chrome Instrument Panel, Chrome Mirror, Chrome Muffler, Oil Filter (Attached), Chrome Rims, Chrome Shock Absorber Covers, Chrome Spark Coil Cover, Chrome Timer Cover, Polished Brake Side Cover, Polished Fork Sliders, Polished Handlebar Cover, Polished Headlamp Nacelle, Stainless Steel Fork Covers (2)
King of the Highway #F-5	Includes Chrome Axle and Fork Stud Cover (Attached), Chrome Battery Cover, Chrome Boot Guard, Chrome Front Bumper, Chrome Rear Bumper, Chrome Rear Fender Tip, Chrome Dual Mufflers—Super Quiet, Chrome Luggage Carrier, Chrome Rear Safety Guard, Compensating Sprocket, Front Hub Cap (Attached), Chrome Oil Tank, Directional Signals, White Fiberglass saddle bags, Solo Windshield (specify color: blue, clear or red), Super DeLuxe Buddy Seat (Specify Color: Red and White, Black and White, Or All White)
King of the Highway #F-6	Same As #F-5 But With Frame-Mounted Buddy Seat (In Place Of Super), Specify Color—Black and White, Red and White, Or All White
King of the Highway #F-7	Same As #F-5 But With Deluxe Solo Seat (In Place Of Super Buddy Seat). Note: Black Fiberglass Saddle Bags and Carrier May Be Substituted For White and Normal Dual Tone Muffler 65427-62 May Be Substituted For Super Quiet At No Extra Charge
Standard Police Group #FP-3	Includes Deluxe Solo Seat, Rear Wheel Siren (Foot Control), Oil Filter, Clear Solo Windshield, Special Police Speedometer, and Speedometer Hand Control. Specify 50002-58 Special Jiffy Stand When Rear Wheel Sirens Are Ordered. When Chrome Finish Group #F-1 and Standard Police Group #FP-3 Are Ordered Together, Allow For Oil Filter Charged For In Each Group

1965 Equipment Group

Equipment Group	Equipment
Chrome Finish Group #F-1	Includes Chrome Clutch Booster Spring Cover, Chrome Exhaust Pipe Covers, Chrome Front Safety Guard, Chrome Handlebars—Rubber Mounted (Speedster or Buckhorn), Chrome Instrument Panel, Chrome Mirror, Chrome Oil-Tank Strip, Rear-Chain Oiler, Chrome Muffler, Oil Filter (Attached), Chrome Rims, Chrome Shock Absorber Covers, Chrome Spark Coil Cover, Chrome Timer Cover, Polished Brake Side Cover, Polished Fork Sliders, Polished Handlebar Cover, Polished Headlamp Nacelle, Stainless Steel Fork Covers (2)
King Of The Highway #F-5	Includes Chrome Axle And Fork Stud Cover (Attached), Chrome Battery Cover, Chrome Boot Guard, Chrome Front Bumper, Chrome Rear Bumper, Chrome Rear Fender Tip, Chrome Dual Mufflers—Extra Quiet, Chrome Luggage Carrier, Chrome Rear Safety Guard, Compensating Sprocket, Front Hub Cap (Attached), Chrome Oil Tank, Directional Signals, White Fiberglass Saddle Bags, Solo Windshield (Specify Color: Blue, Clear Or Red), Super Deluxe Buddy Seat (Specify Color: Red And White, Black And White, Or All White)
King Of The Highway #F-6	Same As #F-5 But With Frame-Mounted Buddy Seat (In Place Of Super), Specify Color—Black And White Or All White
King Of The Highway #F-7	Same As #F-5 But With Deluxe Solo Seat (In Place Of Super Buddy Seat). Note: Black Fiberglass Saddle Bags And Carrier May Be Substituted For White And Normal Dual Tone Muffler 65427-62 May Be Substituted For Extra Quiet At No Extra Charge

SHOVELHEADS

BY TOM MURPHY

Acknowledgments

Without the help of all the Shovelhead riders out there, this book wouldn't have been possible. So many people I met only over the telephone went out of their way to help me that I think their names should be listed as co-authors, if it were possible.

Primarily, thanks to Harley-Davidson, in the persona of Dr. Martin Jack Rosenblum, historian and chief guardian of the faith for H-D and Steve Piehl, H-D's Manager of Public Relations, both of whom spent considerable time insuring I had much-needed aid and assistance when it came to accuracy in this manuscript. Also I owe a lot to my shepherd, Greg Field, who kept me on the proper path through all this, and to my editor, Lee (we need more information) Klancher, without whom, I'd still be writing short stories.

To everybody who stood still while I asked for "one more shot," or sent valuable pictures to a voice on the other end of a telephone line, thank you—it's your bikes that made this book. The only parts I accomplished all by myself are the mistakes.

—*Tom Murphy*
Campbell, California

Introduction

Every Harley owner seems to have his or her individual preference when it comes to a specific year and model of Harley-Davidson. Some of us lean toward the new bikes, figuring the Evo is the best thing to happen to the V-twin since American Machine and Foundry (AMF) went away. Others think H-D quit building motorcycle engines when the valves moved up into the head. My preference has always been the Shovelhead, probably because most of my first years with motorcycles were spent trying to fix one old worn-out Harley after another, and I never owned a bike that would run more than two days in a row until my finances allowed me to be owned by a brand shiny-new 1982 FXRS fitted with the last-generation Shovelhead motor.

Shovels had been around in one guise or another for 16 years prior to my purchase, so I wasn't exactly taking a wild chance by signing up for three years of payments. Actually it was a fairly easy decision to buy a Shovelhead, as the last bike in my garage had been a 1980 Sportster—an instrument of torture to rival anything found in the Tower of London. When the Sporty was new, it ran a whole 300mi before the engine let go, and the bike had to be towed back to Sunnyvale Harley-Davidson, near San Francisco. Four weeks later it was returned to me with the admonition to "Take it easy for the first 500mi; don't run the new engine above 3000rpm." This time it stayed away from the dealer for a whole 400mi—bad countershaft in the transmission, major oil leak. Seems as though there had been a batch of shafts improperly hardened from the supplier, and I had one of them. To the shop it went once more.

Seven days slid by, and my bike was mine again. Needless to say, I wasn't overcome with certitude as far as reliability went. However, this time all the parts seemed to want to stay in their rightful places for a while, so off I went on a tour.

Here's where I learned about engine vibration...wow, did that engine vibrate. Below

You can tell these are factory photos by looking at the paint scheme that flows from the bike over the top of the helmets of the two riders. I'm not sure why the girl on this 1973 Super Glide is smiling, as it looks like her partner has taken up the whole seat, leaving her to straddle the fender.

3000rpm—where I had run it for what seemed like 60 years—it ran fine, not smooth, but OK. Twist the throttle to anything above 3000, and it would vibrate so hard it put various parts of my anatomy (which shall remain nameless, but had to do with fathering children) to sleep. This bike and I were not destined to remain together much longer. When my friendly dealer announced the presence of an 80ci sport bike similar to the Super Glide, but with a rubber-mounted engine, called the FXRS, the Sportster's days were numbered. I think the Sportster was the only Harley-Davidson I ever unloaded with less than 2,000mi on the clock.

The Sporty's rapid replacement was due to a 20mi test ride spent on what was soon to be mine and the bank's new Shovelhead. The guys running Sunnyvale Harley-Davidson figured that letting me ride the new scoot would do the selling job for them. They were right. I wrote another check, signed a contract again, went back into more debt, and rode away happy.

I think I paid the grand total of $7,184, counting all government tariffs and anything else the shop could stack on the contract. One benefit—along with the bike—came a somewhat under-the-table credit for $200 worth of accessories. Also, I got to choose the color and paint scheme on the bike. It was all black originally, but I went for the black and orange that H-D's been using for years on their racing bikes. Took a whole two weeks to get the new fenders and tanks with the right paint. Try doing that today! These days just finding a new bike for sale is hard enough, let alone ordering one in your favorite colors. But in 1982, you could go down to your local dealer with a particular color on a sample chip, and H-D's paint shop would reproduce it on your new bike

Mountain View, California, 1966. Five Traffic Division motor cops get ready to go out and keep the streets safe. Four are on Shovelheads, while bike number six, ridden by the father of the man who gave me the photo, is a Panhead. *Forrest "Trees" Linderman*

within six weeks. As I said, things are a little different today. The factory still says they will custom-paint your bike, but the waiting list is so long that most people just take what rolls off the truck.

I still own the bike—matter of fact it's the only H-D I own—and hope to keep it, along with the new bike I have on order, for quite a few years. It's been stone-ax reliable, runs fine, and is totally housebroken. Matter of fact, the only time it has ever leaked oil was when we swapped the factory oil lines over to the metal braided type, and that was the line's fault, not the bike's. If the new bike shows up anytime soon, I'll just park the FXRS and keep it for hot sunny days.

Harley-Davidson has never been noted for rapid changes, and building the Shovel went right along with this leisurely philosophy. In the fall of 1965 they made what was for them a mighty design leap—they changed the cylinders and heads on the FLH. The Panhead had been soldiering along since shortly after the end of World War II—1948 to be exact—and after only 18 years, its time was up. When H-D engineers designed the Shovelhead, they kept the same basic cases and accessories as on the Pan, just went to the new cylinders and heads. The generator stayed in the same place, most everything else stayed as it was. The Panhead's Linkert carb only made it through the 1966 model year before disappearing off the engine. For 1967, the fuel and air mixed in a Tillotson carb, replete with its own fair share of problems, later to be replaced by a Bendix, equally cursed, and finally by a Keihin with its own set of interesting peccadilloes.

The early Shovel shared so many parts with the Pan that it wasn't uncommon to see Shovel top ends on Pan cases, or once in a while the other way around.

This 1968 FLH shows the optional long seat. As you can see by the H on the oil tank, this is the hotter-engined FLH (as opposed to the FL with 5hp less), drum brakes, white saddlebags, and all. Owned by Ernie Marietta from Northern California.

The early Shovels were actually a little bit slower than the kickstart Panheads, even though the Shovel was advertised as more powerful with 60hp, 5hp more than the Panhead. Most of this was due to added weight on the new bike. A 1952 FL tipped the scales at just under 600lb, while the 1966 Electra Glide pushed down with 780lb. A Pan even held about a 10mph speed advantage over the first Shovels. Things haven't changed much, as a stock 1994 California Evo, showing all of 39hp on the dyno at Custom Chrome's RevTech facility in Morgan Hill, California, won't get close enough to a Shovel to see its taillight in a drag race. The more things change…

The FLH had a sister bike—the FL—rated at 54hp. This engine was aimed at police departments and government agencies where reliability was thought to be more important than speed. Most police departments and government agencies took one ride on an FL and opted out for the FLH. They didn't like slow any more than the rest of us. The sales figures show the FLH outsold the FL by a vast majority.

These days, how fast an old Harley can go is mostly rhetorical, but the motorcycle magazines of the 1960s managed to get the FLH up to a thundering 98mph after a sufficiently long run. In today's world of 178mph Japanese plastic bikes, that top speed looks fairly slow; however, not many of us plan to flog our 20- to 30-year-old bikes up to warp speed any time soon. Besides "go fast" wasn't what these bikes were all about anyway. They were there to give you a ride on a real motorcycle—not one that leaked rice!

Trying to sort out the various and sundry models of the Shovelhead produced during its 19-year run can be quite confusing. Some of the bikes listed in the catalogs only appeared on paper, never on a dealer's floor. For instance, the 1972 model lineup showed an FLHF foot shift along with an FLH hand shift. This was the last year a hand shift was offered, and it's quite possible all of the 8,100 FLH bikes sold were sold as foot-shift only. The factory gamely advertised the bike with a foot clutch and tank-mounted shifter, but demand was nonexistent.

We will cover each model offered every year, even if it's only mentioned by type. For one person to keep track of all the different models produced over time would take a prodigious memory, and a real need to know. As mentioned, in 1972 both hand-shift and foot-shift bikes appeared in the catalog. They were listed as FLHF, FLH, FLPF, and FLP—"P" standing for "police." FLHF designates Electra-Glide with foot shift. In 1973 they eliminated most of the model designations, electing to go with just FL and FLH. The sales records for both years only show the bikes listed as FL and FLH, so the factory didn't differentiate too much when it came to actual accounting, except in 1974–75 where the police bikes were singled out as the FL Police. Sales of both types in 1973 amounted to 1,025 FLs and 7,750 FLHs, with the FX Super Glide selling 7,625 for a total sales of 16,400. Honda probably dropped more bikes off the boat while unloading that year.

Sales of the big bikes really didn't start to pick up substantially until the Evo made its appearance. Most sales figures back in the 1970s show a total of all Harleys sold, including Sportsters and the Italian bikes made by Aermacchi, to run right around 45,000–70,000 units, with the Sportster holding the top sales rung with most models sold. Then came changes.

The AMF Years

The 1970s saw a lot of changes for H-D. After being acquired by AMF in 1969, H-D had to walk the line chalked by a whole different group of suits. Some said joining with AMF was a good deal as H-D badly needed the influx of capital to update antique equipment and increase production. Some said lots of other things about the merger. Either way, the AMF logo appeared on all 1971 gas tanks and was there to stay through all the 1970s and up to the end of the 1981 model year.

During the AMF years, a lot of changes came about—some good, some not so good. Now that AMF Harley-Davidson existed, corporate changes tended to happen at the same rate steel rusts…as opposed to the glacial movement speed before the merger. Quality control went down the tubes while more government rules concerning noise and pollution appeared than ever before. Harley's engineering staff had to fight on two fronts, with most of the effort being applied to conforming to federal regulations. At the same time, the parent company decided to move most of H-D's opera-

Mike Quinn's 1971 FLH is about as stock as a 1971 FLH can be. The exhaust pipes don't even have any blue on them yet. That year, the throttle was changed to a twist grip with a single cable running to the carb but no return spring. Prior years had a spiral throttle with its cable running inside the bars. This was the year of the carb change from the venerable Tillotson to the Bendix/Zenith. *Nick Cedar*

tions from Milwaukee to an unused plant in York, Pennsylvania. This caused a lot of hard feelings among employees who lost jobs, and quality control further eroded.

Two sides exist to every story. AMF was a large business whose chief aim was to make money. Whether that was done by making motorcycles or lawn furniture, they didn't care. AMF really didn't have the slightest idea of how to run a motorcycle company, so it had to go through a learning curve while building Harleys. Unfortunately, sometimes this made the customer the final engineer for the bikes.

The immense boom in motorcycles also put a strain on AMF and H-D. Total sales went from 28,850 in 1970 to 75,403 in 1975 (22,245 being Big Twins, the balance being Sportsters and smaller Italian bikes). As a result, the factory equipment and people running that equipment were sorely taxed to keep quality in pace with production. The build quality dropped and sales suffered.

To give credit to AMF, if they hadn't come along in 1969 and taken H-D in tow, the Motor Company might only be a golf-cart manufacturer today. In 1969, sales revenues of all products were just over $49 million. When the turnover took place in 1981, sales had risen to $300 million. AMF's ownership of H-D wasn't all bad. Still, some of the bikes carry a stigma if an AMF logo appears on the tank.

As an example of some of the problems, most of the 1979 and 1980 bikes had to have the valve seats replaced within the first few thousand miles. Harley handled the problems under warranty, but the situation didn't do much for building customer satisfaction. The Japanese motorcycle manufacturers didn't help things much either when they flooded the market with bikes that were both inexpensive and reliable. For a while, it looked like H-D was going to join Henderson, Indian, and all the other defunct American brands if quality did not improve, and soon.

Note that the seat helper springs on this 1976 FLH are attached to the frame and the center post is disconnected. This gives the bike the two-step feeling when entering a turn. First the bike leans over...then the seat shifts over and falls into the direction of the turn, making the rider feel less than connected to what's going on below.

Here's a later model seat on a 1979 FLH. Not only is it more secure, but also it gives the passenger some semblance of a place to sit.

Things still didn't get much better when the 1981 models arrived. The biggest problem appeared on the 1981 FLHC, which left the factory with totally unbalanced flywheels. At the same time, engine knock due to lowered pump-gas octane got worse and could only be controlled by dropping the compression ratio to 7.4:1, dropping horsepower in the process. However, the owners didn't have to put up with massive vibration problems for long, as the bike usually shook hard enough to break down within a few thousand miles. This lack of quality, coupled with horsepower loss due to tightened emissions, brought H-D ever closer to the brink. Sales of the V-Twins in 1980 were 33,414, and in 1981 they fell to 31,504, a loss of 1,910 units.

Adios AMF

Problems continued with quality control at AMF H-D throughout the late 1970s and into the 1980s. Management and leadership were playing musical chairs without any chairs. Projects in the mill like the five-speed and Tour Glide didn't happen when planned. A recession was eating up the market. For the 1979–80 year sales of $280 million, H-D showed less than a $12 million profit.

Salvation was at hand. AMF decided to restructure its lineup of recreational companies and decided H-D was to go on the chopping block. Thence ensued a mad scramble of some of the upper management at AMF who were died-in-the-wool motorcycle crazies and figured they could buy H-D and turn the company around.

The only item that stood between Vaughn Beals, Richard Teerlink, and the hirsute Willie G. (all of whom should be canonized as far as I'm concerned) was the $75 million AMF wanted for H-D. AMF may have let quality go to hell and run sales to an all-time low, but they weren't going to let H-D go for free.

Beals, along with about 12 other totally aggravated colleagues, tubed AMF and went looking for a way to supplement $10 million of their own money with another $65 million needed to ransom H-D. Boy did they have a job of selling to do! Just about every lending agency rejected their requests. Finally, Citicorp cut a check to AMF for the needed funds, and Beals and company had a motorcycle business. Citicorp also got something out of the deal to the tune of $12 million per year for their generosity. Ever think you're in the wrong business? Move paper, make millions. Move wrenches and be damn glad to get $12 per hour. See, mom was right, you should have stayed in school and got that masters degree in business.

Later on, the company was able to arrange much better financing through the insurance syndicates. The day the AMF banner came down from the shops and off the bikes was celebrated all

Harley-Davidson President Charlie Thompson (left) and Chairman Vaughn Beals completed a 3,806mi transcontinental ride on two 1980 FLT Tour Glides from Vancouver, Canada, to Daytona Beach, Florida, on March 3, 1980. The ride involved 39 riders and took 78 hours to run. Neither bike had any adjustments, and the oil tanks were sealed on both FLTs. Oil mileage averaged 2,578 miles per quart. *Harley-Davidson*

over the country. Harley now only had to pay back the loan, turn around quality, improve the morale of the workers, and make a profit. The last ten years have shown the results. Harley has moved from being a rolling joke to being the most desired vehicle in the world. None of this would have happened without a lot of very hard work on the part of the people of H-D. Everybody from Richard Teerlink and Vaughn Beals, down to the guy who sweeps up the metal shavings, made the company what it is today.

Going Uphill

First though, H-D had to play catch-up with their products. They were headed in the proper direction with the Super Glide and its spin-offs but were still being hounded by government regulations.

In 1982 H-D—minus AMF—came out with an updated model of the FX series, called the FXRS, sporting a rubber-mounted engine, a new oil-control package, and a five-speed transmission. The big touring FLTs already had the benefits of rubber engine mounts, but they used a frame that wouldn't work on the FX bikes, so a new one was designed to take the 80ci motor and five-speed while still retaining the Super Glide look.

The people at the factory got their act together, and quality on the last few years of Shovelheads was much improved. By the time of its replacement by the Evo in mid-1984, the Shovel was quite a reliable motor, capable of running for 50,000–60,000mi without major repair—a big change from engines of the previous decade.

INTRODUCTION 267

All of Harley-Davidson's corporate officers gather for a cross-country ride to celebrate the 75th anniversary in 1978. Vaughn Beals is on the FLH with the "75th Anniversary" sticker on the front fender; Willie G. is to his left. Charlie Thompson is on the Electra Glide behind Willie G. *Harley-Davidson*

Throughout the Shovelhead years, sales of the big bikes stayed consistently around the 7,000-per-year range during the 1960s, only climbing over 10,000 after the FX series began in 1971. In 1981, the FX bikes outsold the FLs 22,708 to 8,796. Clearly, the factory-chopper look was taking over in popularity. Now, anyone could have what appeared as a custom bike without having to spend months tearing down an FLH and investing thousands of dollars in aftermarket parts.

So, years 1966 to 1984 saw the Shovelhead go through many incarnations. It started out as a kickstart with electric backup, four-speed, 74ci Milwaukee vibrator, and ended up a smooth, five-speed, 80ci, reliable machine.

The Bikes in the Book

For the most part, the bikes appearing in this book belong to people who ride them frequently—weather permitting or not. Shovels haven't been new for eleven years, so finding one that hasn't had something changed—even something as small as a turn signal—is hard to do. These are the bikes you ride. These aren't factory-prepared show bikes—they're the ones you, the readers, have owned and put a lot of money, time, and affection into keeping on the road.

Buying a Shovelhead

Be advised that there are a few semi-talented people out in Harley land that might try to pass off something as what it isn't—like a factory hand-shift 1973 FLH. Now this is a fairly rare bike, as the factory didn't build any, but the parts do exist to make one up. You might still buy it, as long as you are aware of what it is. In a few years it might even be worth a couple of bucks more just because it's a Harley, but don't lay money on it. Take the time to look carefully at what you are trying to buy. If possible, take along someone who knows enough about Shovels to recognize a phony and is disinterested enough to keep you from spending money if you catch a case of "gotta-have-its."

If the one item that makes the bike more valuable looks fairly new compared to all the rest of the bike—beware. Try to take the bike to a dealer for a pre-purchase inspection, just as is done with airplanes. Any reputable owner won't object to you having an inspection done by a Harley-authorized shop, providing you pay all expenses. Should he resist an inspection by the pros and you can't live without the bike, be sure to check it carefully and definitely ride it before handing over more than a deposit. If you do buy it, and then find problems after you've owned it for a few weeks, don't feel alone; we've all done the same thing at least once. Hold onto this thought—the old Romans even had the same problem—their motto was *caveat emptor*...buyer beware.

All the mounted motorcycle force of Louisville, Kentucky, join for a picture on their Shovelheads at the finish line of historic Churchill Downs horse track. More horsepower is gathered on the infield than ever saw a race. This picture was taken in the late 1970s, sometime after 1977.

Investment?

Above all, buy what you want and enjoy it. If it's your first Harley, you'll learn more about motorcycles and people than you ever thought possible. And I fully believe that *all* Shovels will appreciate in value as they age and the price of new Harleys goes up, so your money's safe. I just came from my dealer in San Jose, where I spent some time lusting after one of their touring machines again. To give you an idea as to where prices are going, check this: A pre-sold blue 1995 FLHTC sitting on their showroom floor, replete with all the factory chrome, stereo radio, and even catalytic converters, but no dealer-installed options, runs:

Base 1995 FLHTC: $14,518

Freight and prep: $745 (a lotta bucks for a truck ride and a wax job)

California license and registration: $344

Doctor fee (maybe medical?): $35

Sales tax@8.25 percent (eek!): $1,262.09

Grand Total: $16,404.09

Figure a down payment of 10 percent is $1,650, and your $348 payments only run sixty months.

A lot of people have said that the cowboy never vanished, he just turned into the Harley rider. Judging by this picture, that could be quite true.

I asked about a deal—what with being a writer and all; plus I've known these people since I helped build their back shop area nine years ago. Rich, the salesman, said if the guy who laid down the deposit dropped out of the sale he'd knock the $.09 off the price, making it an even $16,404. He said all the bikes except for *one* Ultra Classic Electra Glide ($20,000 plus) are sold up through the first six months of 1996. He just quit taking deposits after that point.

Now you are probably reading this shortly into 1996, so you have in your hand what I'm writing in November of 1995. I doubt seriously things will get any better any time this century as far as availability, and lack of new scooters will do nothing but drive the price of clean older bikes upward. How high can prices go? Remember, the new 1964 FLH Panhead went out the door for the princely sum of $1,673; a 1967 FLH could be had for $2,100. Today, one 1966 FLH that belongs to a Federal Express corporate pilot in Memphis recently changed hands for $12,000. He has a 1971 FLH that can be yours for $10,000. If it's like the 1966, it will go away at the first phone call.

I paid $6,900 base price for my 1982 FXRS in December of 1981, and I hope, if I have to sell it to own the new bike, it goes away for close to $10k, 'cause you can guess why I'm real aware of the exact price of a 1995 FLHTC. Yup, and I'm going to have to wait for a 1996 that won't even be built until mid-May, six months from now, so I'll be paying even more when it arrives. I don't really want to part with the FXRS, and hope to be able to hang on to it, but as I said in my last book on performance Big Twins, I needed a touring bike to get out to the people who do the building and riding. My 1982 FXRS will be retired when the new bike arrives, and only sold if a large profit can be realized. Do I think Shovels are a smart investment? Is a bear Catholic?

To celebrate the Nation's Bicentennial, Harley issued a special edition called the "Liberty Edition" of the FLH-1200. Paint was black metallic, the seat was black also, and decals commemorating the event adorned the fairing, tanks, and top bag. This 1976 Liberty poses at the National Cemetery in Phoenix, Arizona.

PART ONE

The 1966–84 FL Series

The Shovelhead engine powered all big Harleys from 1966 to 1984, in 74ci and 80ci sizes. This is the "generator motor" with the ignition timer mounted on a shaft in front of the number-one cylinder push-rod cover. *Harley-Davidson*

In order to really talk about the first Shovelhead, the 1965 Panhead—from which the new motor was derived—needs to be described. This way the progression from the older engine to the Shovelhead becomes clear.

The last Panhead hit the shops in 1965. By then it had come a long way from the first 61ci and 74ci bikes of the late 1940s and early 1950s. The 1965 Pan sported an electrical starter—the second production Harley to do so, the first being the 1946 Servicar. The electrical system got a bump up from six-volt to 12-volt, and a heftier battery was included to help turn through the engine. Now that it started with a button, a new name was in order. Harley christened the new bike the Electra-Glide in obvious reference to its new capabilities. Later years saw the hyphen between "Electra" and "Glide" disappear. The first photos of a 1965 FLH Electra-Glide show the now-standard left foot shift, hand clutch, and button on the right handlebar that engaged the starter. Optional equipment, which many ordered, included dual mufflers, saddlebags, solo windshield, rear package rack, more

The Shovelhead first appeared in 1966. The head was new, but the cases were basically straight off the Panhead engine. This 1966 FLH is a highly polished stock machine. New for 1966, the six-sided Harley-Davidson emblem replaced the bar-type used on the Panhead. The new emblem would be around through 1971. *Doug Mitchell*

chrome trim on the fender, and case guards. Unfortunately, the larger battery and the existing swingarm rear suspension took up some of the room occupied by the black oblong toolbox, which had been mounted on the right side of the frame in front of the shock. The toolbox left, never to return as a factory installation. Nowadays a similar toolbox, black or chrome, is offered as an option for some of the current models.

The engine was still the same overhead valve (OHV) V-twin of 74ci as the prior year. Power stayed at an advertised 60hp, but now it had the job of pushing almost 790 unladen pounds down the road. This was quite a weight gain from earlier models without all the electrics. The early 1950s

Pan weighed right around 600lb; however, this was before the bike was given rear suspension (1958) and without all the options so dearly loved by owners.

The Electra Glide Panhead stayed around only one year before H-D changed the engine for the 1966 model to what has become known as the Shovelhead.

Motorcycle magazines in the 1960s sometimes didn't exactly report how things really were with products they road-tested. If pressed against the wall, they would admit that vibration in Harleys was a little, ever so tiny, insignificant, small problem. The need to clamp a piece of inner tube between your teeth over 60mph was a totally unfounded rumor (although I have the chipped teeth to prove it).

Now, I'm not sure who built their test bike, but it obviously wasn't the same gnomes who put together the 1963 Panhead I used to own. Mine was box stock, no trick pipes, no black paint with death's heads on the tanks. I worked for Boeing Aircraft in Seattle at the time, and my shift started at six-in-the-dark AM. I wasn't smart enough to drive a car when the weather went bad—rain was considered just a normal day—so every morning at 5:00 AM, I was out in the driveway kicking the bike alive. Just retard the spark, crack the throttle, click on two notches of choke, turn the engine through a couple of times with the ignition off, set the choke fully closed, light the ignition, and kick.

Easy, huh?

Sometimes it took one kick to fire—sometimes the helmet, jacket, shirt, and gloves were on the

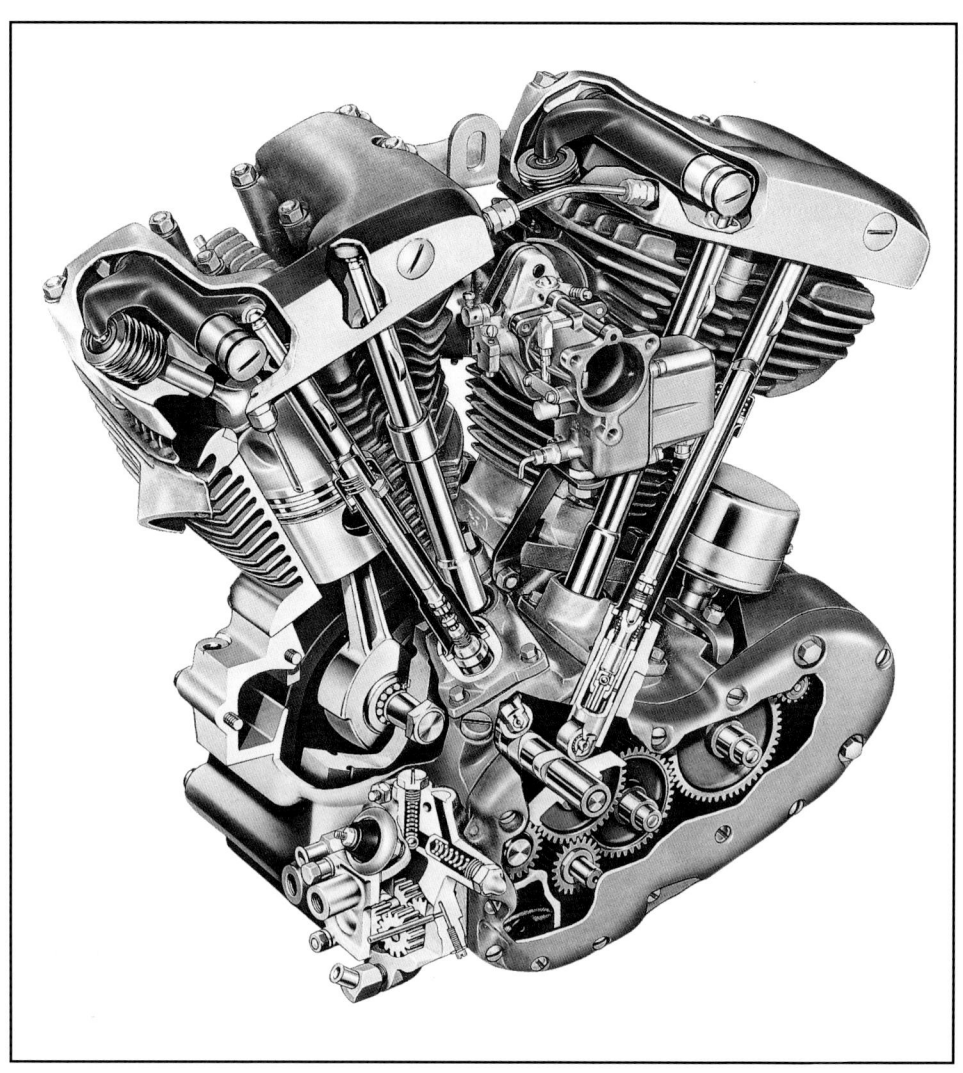

A cutaway of the same motor shows valve operation all the way from the cam, through the roller tappets, via the push rods and through the rockers to the valve. The oil-pump gears also can be clearly seen at the back of the engine. *Harley-Davidson*

ground by the time it lit off. Then it had to warm up, of course, or else it'd die when the clutch first went home—five minutes at the least before it could move under its own power. Being 18 years old (stupid), I usually managed to use a lot more throttle than necessary when leaving to show my appreciation for easy-starting bikes.

Two weeks of this, with my "silent" Harley, and the neighbors dropped by to mention capital punishment, ropes in trees, and other unpleasant outcomes if I didn't cease and desist with the noise. I ended up having to push the bike almost one block away before I could start the engine. Then it was a hurried 70mph ride to Boeing's Renton plant so as not to be late. One of the most welcome updates H-D ever made was adding electric start to their Big Twin.

1966 Electra Glide: The First Shovelhead

Production
    FLH (both models): 5,625
        FLHFB: 74ci foot-shift Super Sport
        FLHB: 74ci hand-shift Super Sport
    FL (both models): 2,130
        FLFB: 74ci foot-shift
        FLB: 74ci hand-shift

Along about 1965, Harley-Davidson decided, in its usual way, to make improvements on the Panhead. Normally, H-D changed a little bit each year, with the frame and suspension getting upgraded one year, and the motor the next. For the 1966 model year, the engine got

Spin the motor around and this is what the drive side looks like. The generator is mounted to the front of the engine, just below the ignition timer and is gear-driven off the engine. *Harley-Davidson*

the upgrades. Instead of putting a cover over the rockers on top of the engine, as on the Panhead, now the Shovel had real rocker boxes with the rockers mounted in them. When viewed from the side, the rocker boxes had the shape of a coal shovel, hence the name Shovelhead. To those of you under 35, coal is a black, greasy rock burned to make heat—kinda like diesel oil in hunks. Coal got from the coal bin in the basement to the furnace with a shovel of a particular shape. Looked at upside down, the coal shovel bore a resemblance to the new top end.

New parts included rocker housings, rockers and shafts, push rods, exhaust valves, and a few other small parts. The rest of the engine—intake valve, valve springs, hydraulic lifters, and all the rest carried forward from the Pan. The right crankcase was modified, the oil-feed port moved from between the lifter guides to behind the rear lifter guide. Cylinders stayed the same, the generator still rode in front, the carb changed to a Linkert model DM for this year only. Other than that, the motor was unchanged. The engines were so similar that Shovel top ends would easily fit a set of Pan cases.

Frames

When Harley-Davidson started producing Electra Glides with new and improved starters and bigger batteries, they found out that the frame would have to be opened up in the center section in order to fit all the bigger electrics within. If you look at an Electra Glide frame, and a Duo-Glide frame. the differences become apparent. Other than that, the frames fitted to the first Shovelheads are similar enough to where a Pan engine will fit into a Shovel frame, and versa visa.

The Shovel used the same rear frame section that the Panheads had in 1965. However, the shocks were still mounted way too far forward to provide adequate control for the rear swingarm, which in turn let the rear wheel wander under high loads. This was done so that law enforcement agencies and touring riders had enough room to mount saddlebags, radio gear, riot batons, shotguns, and all the other necessities of motorcycle riding.

Having the rear dampers set so far down, the swingarm gives the bike some rather unpleasant handling characteristics that show up at the worst possible time. This can be seen when following an early FLH into a turn. The rear wheel seems to take on a life of its own, running and hopping from side to side as the rider stuffs the bike into a turn.

Even though cornering isn't the big bikes' strong suit, if all is right with the suspension it can be bent around at a surprising rate of speed for a bike that weighs more than a sack of anvils. Some of this is due to the bike feeling like its center of gravity is 2ft below ground. The rest is due to the bike's ability to get you through the corner no matter how many parts are grinding off below. Those that hurry an FLH tend to replace floor boards rather frequently.

Today, the handling of the FL series isn't much better or worse than your average Gold Wing, but back in 1967 the only other bikes for comparison were Triumphs—which went around corners well enough to prove England is full of crooked roads—and the occasional Bultaco 250cc or Ducati of the same size, either of which would leave the bigger bikes for dead at the first hint of a wiggle in the road. The Japanese bikes available at the time—Kawasaki 350 Avengers and Suzuki 500s—usually had the advantage of acceleration, even if they handled like a goat on roller-blades.

A small part of the cornering problem was brought on by the original Goodyear 5.10x16in tires mounted front and rear. Goodyear said the tires were designed especially for H-D, and in some respects they were right. The tires were fairly abrupt in transition due to their rather sharp tread-to-sidewall angle. They really wanted to go in a straight-line like a car tire. When called upon to lean over, they hesitated before making the transition from straight line travel to a lean angle. Riding an early Shovel fitted with the stock Goodyears was an extremely steady experience on the California freeways. I can remember clearly setting the throttle to a good cruising speed, then sliding back on the seat to the grab rail and hanging my boots over the passenger pegs. I'd sit tall, with my arms folded tight against my leather jacket, watching people watching me. My friend, whom I felt seriously needed mental care, would sit all the way back on the luggage rack of his bike and wave at passing cars (kids don't try this at home).

And here's the bike with the engine fitted. The 1966 Electra Glide was the first Shovelhead. Some optional equipment is shown on this bike—saddlebags, windshield, crash bars, and seat among the main items. *Harley-Davidson*

The point is that, other than I'm probably very lucky to be able to write this book, the bike was extremely reluctant to move from a straight path. Part of this was due to the weight and frame design, part to the square-section tires.

Later in the year, after one particular frog-strangler of a storm, we took both bikes up a dirt road in the Santa Cruz Mountains and played "fall down." We could only get up to 20mph or so before the street tires slid out in a spray of mud, so no one was hurt when the bike's went over. I fell twice, and he went down three and a half times. The tires would slowly slide out to one side or the other, and the bike would lay down on its crash bars in the glop like a farm pig in a mud wallow. We finally had to give up and turn around when the bikes flat wouldn't go any farther, but were both laughing so hard that we dropped them both again. No damage was done, other than mud everywhere. Guys on Maicos and Husqvarnas sure looked at us funny, though.

Harley suggested 20psi tire pressure in the front and 24psi in the back when riding solo. Actually, 30psi helped a lot more toward making the bike handle in the turns. I'd crank the bike into a particularly nasty, decreasing-radius turn, and no matter how much metal was throwing sparks, the bike would always track through the corner like a motorized anvil. Admittedly, the speed was a lot slower than that of the rice-rockets; however, we traveled stately, nary a wobble in sight. Now all this went out the window should you lean a little too far into the turn to where the muffler became the main source of traction instead of the rear wheel. At that point, life became much more interesting as the rear end stepped out one or two feet in a resounding hop. Once the rear rubber regained touch with the road, everything worked right again—but this made for a few tense moments indeed. As my failing memory tells me, I think the bike would ride up on the muffler easier when turning right than left—might have been me though. I was always more hesitant to go rubbing parts briskly upon the tarmac when turning left at oncoming traffic as opposed to having nothing but the odd lamppost to kiss while turning to the right.

Other changes

Small, but important changes to the rest of the bike included moving the fuel shut-off valve, operated by screwing down to shut off the flow, from its place on the top of the Panhead's left gas tank in front of and to the side of the speedometer. Now a petcock hung from under the left tank. The steel line connecting the two tanks became rubber. The ignition timer featured a new clamp.

The tank emblem changed to a six-sided metal item with the name "Harley-Davidson" embossed down the middle. This emblem stayed on the tanks through 1971. The rounded "half-moon" foot boards, in use since 1940, gave way to a new rectangular design. This was the last year of the round air filter and cover, pointed fender tips, and optional fishtail mufflers. Paint on the tank was two-tone, primary color underneath a white panel down the side. Wide at the front, the white panel tapered down to a rounded point at the bottom rear of the tanks. It had a 1/2in stripe, separate from the main. A similar colored 1/2in stripe, separated by a 1/4in gap, outlined the white panel. Black, Indigo Metallic, Hi-Fi Blue, gold, and Sparkling Burgundy were among the colors offered for 1966. Model designation included the letter "B" to designate electric start.

This 1966 FLH sports the buddy seat with two helper springs attached and a back support rail. Aside from a little too much chrome and polishing of the aluminum, it's close to what they looked like stock. *Doug Mitchell*

Everything from the mousetrap to the cover in front of the rear shock has either been polished, or chromed, except for the primary case cover. The bag mounted above the bars was an option for that year. The Panhead had a fuel shutoff valve in front of the left gas cap; the Shovel has it moved off the tank and down under the left side. *Jeff Hackett*

This is what a box-stock 1967 FLH looked like, fresh off the factory floor or, as in this case, fresh off the restorer's floor. Look closely at the left side and you can see the "mousetrap" clutch spring and mount on the front frame downtube. *Jeff Hackett*

1967 Electra Glide

Production
   FLH (all): 5,600
      FLHFB: 74ci foot-shift Super Sport
      FLHB: 74ci hand-shift Super Sport
      FLH: 74ci hand-shift
   FL (all): 2,150
      FLFB: 74ci foot-shift

In the second year of Shovelhead production, H-D changed the oil ring on the pistons back to a cast-iron model instead of the three-piece and expander they had been using prior to this. Turns out that the oil rings were outlasting the rest of the engine. Also, break-in tended to take too many miles, and too much oil slipped passed while the ring was breaking in. The replacement ring did an adequate job of keeping oil out of the combustion chamber and allowed the friction surfaces between it and the cylinder to mate rapidly, which reduced oil consumption. Somewhat a case of one part being built too well.

The old Linkert Model DC gave way to a Tillotson pumper carb. This had an accelerator pump as part of the carb. When the throttle was twisted, the pump gave a shot of gas right away. Most other carbs of the time relied on air velocity through the carb venturi to create enough vacuum to lift some fuel out of the float bowl. A quick shot of raw fuel ensured easier starts and faster throttle response while underway.

The venerable fishtail mufflers were replaced by a new, optional "turnout" type muffler. The rear brake drum was updated along with its axle and wheel spacer. The only other changes on the bike were cosmetic, like new rectangular fender tips (another optional extra) and a few other small pieces. Paint remained similar to the 1966 bikes, except that the white panel tapered to a point at the rear of the tank. Standard colors were Black and Crystal Blue. Optional colors were Sparkling Burgundy and Hi-Fi Blue.

This two-toned 1967 FLH has a white panel on the tank where the 1968s had the crackle finish.
Jeff Hackett

The "ham can" air cleaner cover is a change from the round cover used in 1966. Note the unpolished gear-cover case below the carburetor. This is correct for restoration, and how the cover came from the factory. *Jeff Hackett*

1968 Electra Glide

Production
    FLH (all models): 5,354
        FLHFB: 74ci foot-shift Super Sport
        FLHB: 74ci hand-shift Super Sport
    FL (all models): 1,718
        FLFB: 74ci foot-shift
        FLB: 74ci hand-shift

This FLH has just about all the options. Whitewall tires to fishtail pipes, it even comes with a centerstand. I think the two-tone seat is a nice touch.

The major internal engine change for 1968 was the replacement of the steel-bodied oil pump with an aluminum-bodied pump featuring new pressure-feed gears. The starter problems were finally rectified by 1968. The starter now came from Homelite and was more than fit for the job of turning over two cylinders of 37ci each. The starter used an automotive-type Bendix spring operating through a pinion to engage the ring gear on the clutch. The 12-volt battery was uprated to 53amp-hr, making for easier cold-morning starts and allowing all the various electrical accessories and lights that some owners were so fond of hanging on the bike.

Outside the engine, the one part conspicuous by its absence was the clutch mousetrap. Previous years' foot-shift bikes had a clutch booster mounted under the left tank on the front down tube. Its purpose was to aid the left hand while pulling in the clutch, which took a bit of muscle as the clutch

Elsewhere in this book you'll see some more of Mike Quinn's bikes. Among others, he owns this immaculate 1967 red FLH with optional turnout mufflers. *Nick Cedar*

About the only thing not stock on the 1967 FLH are the highway pegs mounted on the crash bars. *Nick Cedar*

The front fender of this 1967 FLH sports an emblem and chrome rail, both optional in that year. *Nick Cedar*

Below
In 1967, both hand- and foot-shift versions of the FLH were available. This version is, obviously, one of the more popular foot-shirt varieties. *Nick Cedar*

was the same as the one used when the pedal was operated by a much stronger leg.

Under a cover was an over-center spring that aided in the clutch pull once the handlebar lever was pulled in about one inch. The clutch cable from the handlebar lever went to this mousetrap instead of the actual clutch. From there, a rod operated the clutch release arm. This was of significant help when trying to hold in the clutch at a stoplight, but made for somewhat a strange feeling as the lever was let out. There was a definite feel when the mousetrap went to work pulling the clutch in; coming out, a rider could actually feel the boost of the spring working to push the lever out. A new clutch release arm, cable, and linkage replaced the mousetrap and its operating rod. Now a cable went all the way from the clutch lever on the handlebar to the clutch release arm.

The speedometer housing received the biggest cosmetic change that year. Gone were the three separate round indicator light lenses between the alarm clock speedometer and the rotating ignition switch. The replacement panel sported three rectangular lenses aligned in a strip between the speedometer and the ignition switch. From the left, the indicator lights were for high beam, neutral, and oil pressure. This dash

The paint on the 1968 Electra Glide was two-toned with the center portion being a black crackle finish, as shown on this tank. The engine side cases have been highly polished. This was done by the owner, as H-D was into the "agricultural implement" look at the time and didn't polish anything. Even the wheel spokes were just painted silver.

continued on all FL and FLH (not the five-speed FLHT) up to 1984. It also did duty on the 1971–71 FX models and 1980–84 Wide Glide.

The standard gas tanks were rated at 3.5gal, with 5gal tanks optional.

Paint schemes took a strange turn with the middle white panel being replaced with a black crackle finish. Standard colors included Black and Jet Fire Orange. Optional colors included Sparkling Burgundy and Sparkling Blue. Some very late production bikes had the tank colors divided longitudinally with the base color on top, separate by a white stripe from the crackle finish, the emblem mounted in the white stripe.

From 1967–69, FLHs didn't change very much. This Alabama owner has added some rather interesting ends to the exhaust pipes and a little bit of chrome that wasn't from the factory, but other than that, the bike is stock. *Jeff Hackett*

Previous page
A 1969 Electra Glide in blue. The year 1969 was the last year for the chrome header pipe covers, generator, and external ignition circuit breaker. The rear shocks had to sit far forward on the swingarm to give room for the saddlebags. The battery sits under a chrome cover in front of the shock. *Jeff Hackett*

The Tillotson carb still fed the engine, and owners still bitched about the carb, but it was scheduled for replacement in the next year's model run.

The model designation methods changed in 1970. No longer was "B" used (as in FLHB, for designating electric start). Now a "P" was added

I thought this 1971 FLH deserved to be shown to the public. Not very often do you see a real saddle on a Harley. Tassels on the leather bags, leather thongs hanging from the bar ends, I'd say the owner is western oriented, wouldn't you? *Jeff Hackett*

to designate Police bikes whether they were hand-shifted or foot-shifted. The more powerful bikes were identified FLH and FLHF, depending on where the shifter resided.

The serial numbering convention changed also. Now year of manufacture was spelled out by using a letter for the decade and a number for the year. Hence a 1970 serial number would begin H0, H1 for 1971, H2 for 1972, and so on. This letter digit code is followed by another code for the model and the serial number.

1971 Electra Glide

Production
    FLH (all models): 5,475
        FLHF: 74ci foot-shift Super Sport
        FLH: 74ci hand-shift Super Sport
    FL (all models): 1,200
        FLPF: 74ci foot-shift, low-compression
    FL Police Special
        FLP: 74ci hand-shift, low-compression
    FL Police Special

Now this 1971 FLH is more to my liking. Wide whitewalls for the look, straight pipes for the sound, and a tall sissy bar to rest your favorite lady against while cruising the back roads of summer. *Jeff Hackett*

This is the year that the letters "AMF" first appeared on the tanks. Underneath, the new carb was a Bendix/Zenith to replace the Tillotson. (Actual changeover may have started late in the 1970 production run.)

1972 Electra Glide

Production
    FLH (all models): 8,100
        FLHF: 74ci foot-shift Super Sport
        FLH: 74ci hand-shift Super Sport
    FL (all models): 1,600
        FLPF: 74ci foot-shift, low-compression
    FL Police Special
        FLP: 74ci hand-shift, low-compression
    FL Police Special

Another of Mike Quinn's bikes, a totally stock 1971 FLH. The 1971 FLH had its throttle changed from the old-style "spiral," with control cable inside the right bar, to a more modern single-cable, twist grip with no return spring. This was the last year for the front drum brake and the six-sided tank emblem. *Nick Cedar*

The biggest change for 1972 was the changeover from a mechanically actuated front drum brake to a single hydraulically actuated disc; rear brakes were still drum. On bikes built prior to the disc brake installation, checking the right handlebar we encounter a lever. On some motorcycles, this is commonly referred to as the front brake lever; however, on the early FLH series it could only charitably be called a "speed-reducer" or "hill-holder." The front drum brake was an 8in by 1in drum, connected to the lever by a rather stout cable sufficient enough to secure a Lake Erie ore barge. All this is rather impressive looking, what with the big polished cover on the left side of the wheel and all, but it has one minor drawback—it doesn't work. Once the brake lever is applied, the mechanical bits and pieces all do their job making the front fork bob up and down—that's about all they do, though. After the first hard application, the front lining and drum cease to have much friction between them, making braking action minimal at best. Pulling harder on the lever (be sure and sign up for a class in upper body improvement, concentrating on the arms and hands, prior to attempting this) adds slightly more retardation—usually much too late to be of any good. One should have matters firmly in hand and a good idea of stopping distances prior to rid-

Every front fender needs a bumper. This is what you got in 1971. Methinks the protection was secondary to the looks. *Nick Cedar*

Check the difference between this speedometer and the one on Rick Newman's 1966 a few photos back. This is the new style changed over in 1968. *Nick Cedar*

ing in a crowded city festooned with hills—like San Francisco, for instance.

In times of need, the rear brake can be called into play to aid the front binder. It's operated by a large black pedal attached to a piece of iron that looks like it served as a turn-signal mount on a German pocket battleship. All this connects to a hydraulic cylinder of distinctly automotive antecedents. Great leverage can be applied through the cylinder by the aforementioned lever-cum-pedal assembly, causing some rather interesting howls as the rear tire ceases to rotate. This does little to retard forward motion, however. The FLH is quite content to continue in a straight line with rear wheel rotation completely at a stop and the front end bobbing like a rubber duck in a bathtub on the *Queen Mary* on a stormy night. Thank God the bike tends to be stable no matter what is done while riding.

If authenticity is your ultimate game and you don't wish to spoil the original lines of your pre-1972 Shovel by adding a front disc brake or two, you might consider taking the front brake shoes down to a reputable friction-material shop (listed in the *Yellow Pages* under Friction Material or Brakes) and see if they might have some of that old nasty metallic lining floating around. A particular brand that comes to mind is Velva-Touch, a lining with a lot of metal and a low rag content. At any rate, the gentlemen at the shop should be able to bond on a better quality lining than comes from the average aftermarket or H-D supplier.

One disadvantage to the metallic lining is that it requires a fair amount of heat to work properly. Warming the brakes prior to using them extensively helps a lot.

Just you and your significant other riding on that big white seat on a long summer's eve; enjoying the countryside and listening to the burble of that big, slow-turning engine. *Nick Cedar*

One advantage is that the metal in the lining ensures that the drum will always have a fresh surface, as the linings do tend to turn down the drum a bit after extended use. However, this shouldn't be a problem on a bike used mostly for riding around with one's beloved on the back when the sun is warm and the roads are dry.

In the exhaust department, longer tube mufflers were stuck back behind the rear axle almost to the end of the rear fender. They sat so low that they would drag on any turn taken at more than a gentle lean, and going up driveways the lower part of the muffler would grind.

As for the engine's innards, the oil pump got a new set of drive and driven gears, but other than that the engine stayed the same. Mileage wasn't anything to brag about, 39mpg being the best reported.

Cosmetic changes included the new "AMF Harley-Davidson" long rectangular tank emblem that was to be around until H-D bought itself back in 1981. Now the handlebar switches were encased in one single plastic housing on each handlebar, rather than in the individual metal ones for each switch used prior to this year. Paint continued, to be two-tone with the second color arranged as a split oblong oval starting at the front of the emblem and ending four inches behind.

Next page
The pipes are covered with smooth chrome heat shields to keep the yellow-blue burns from showing. The year 1971 was also the last year for the six-sided tank emblem. *Nick Cedar*

Foot Clutches

Foot clutches and hand shifters were no longer a part of the H-D catalog by 1973, and a good thing that was. By point of illustration, I'd like to relate a small story that took place a number of years ago. The cast is me, a Panhead of uncertain parentage, and the entire city of San Francisco—hills, garbage trucks, and all.

Picture riding a motorcycle with the clutch under your left foot as in a car. It would behoove you to ensure that you get your right foot down for support at stoplights if you roll up in gear, as your left foot has to run the clutch when the light changes. My old Panhead H-D had a foot clutch, without an over-center control to keep it engaged when depressed. That pig was guaranteed to provide the odd thrill now and then. Evidently the bike had served as a sidecar hauler up to the time the owner bought a car, and the clutch had been run as a suicide setup since the old owner didn't have to put his foot down to hold the bike up when riding the side hack. Of course, I got it after the owner had already sold the hack to someone, but it still ran with the suicide clutch, mammoth spring and all. One fine summer's day in my spotted past, when I was young and exploring San Francisco on my prehistoric mount, especially sticks in mind.

I was enjoying the travels up and down the many hills of the city, watching people watch me on my oil-dripping, unmuffled, parts-dropping behemoth, when a light turned red at the top of Franklin Street. And I do mean at the top. Parts of Franklin would rate as a number six ascent in difficulty for free-climbers. Anyway, I found myself up at the top chugging along about 25mph, needing to stop before becoming part of a seafood truck coming from the left. All was fine up to a point. I managed to select first gear before I came to a stop. This saves that little embarrassing moment of indecision while a gear is located when the light goes green and the duck two feet behind you in the sanitation truck drops his clutch with a "clunk" you can hear over your bike's exhaust just before he buries the throttle on his Cummins diesel.

The ol' right foot proudly held up its end on the pavement. Even the front brake was working for a change. If you're keeping track, you see that both feet, and the right hand are fully occupied keeping the bike from rolling back into the garbage scow behind me. The left hand was on light duty, only keeping its side of the bars pointed straight.

One thing I hadn't taken into consideration—Yet! Some of the hills of San Fran are off-cambered for rain runoff. This happened to be one of them. As I sat at what was turning out to be the world's longest light, my bike ever so slowly started to tilt to the left, leaning into the camber of the road. Well, if you've been counting, it was obvious my lower left extremity was fully occupied keeping the clutch in while the right side kept me up. Being the sharp person I was, I quickly realized my options were narrowing at a rapid rate. If I sat there and did nothing, soon I'd be horizontal and a prime candidate to get my neck run over. If I lifted my left foot off the clutch to stabilize the bike, the engine would undoubtedly die, at which time the light would go green and I'd get eaten by 15 tons of garbage on six wheels. If I did what was looking to be my only way out and side-stepped the clutch while punching the throttle, I'd probably end up part of a advertisement on the side of a passing bus.

By this time, I had approached the point of no return as far as lean angle. Figuring it was the least harmful of a number of nasty choices, I wound the throttle to the stop and side-stepped the clutch. All available horsepower thundered to life and the front wheel lofted slightly as the bike launched forward through the red light. The next couple of seconds only took about a month to pass. I know I cleared one car's rear bumper by the thickness of a lottery ticket. I did hear brakes somewhere to my left, but I opted not to look. One housewife type in the crosswalk made a rather rude noise at me in passing. All in all, I figured I got off lucky that time. I also figured it was more than time to part company with that bike, as this wasn't the first time it had enlivened my day with moments of sheer terror. Once it even had the nerve to catch fire, but that was easily dealt with, as there were six of us standing nearby with a good supply of used beer on hand, so to speak.

1973 Electra Glide

Production
  FLH 74ci Super Sport: 7,750
  FL 74ci: 1,025

Not too many changes took place in 1973, but the ones that did were important. A hydraulic disc brake replaced the hydraulic rear drum. The saddle was made slightly longer, giving a little more room for the passenger. Again, the oil pump was changed, this time with new scavenge gears. The cone gear cover was updated from side oiling to end oiling. The tail lamp, in use since 1955, changed.

The bike now weighed 738lb with the King of the Road package, which included windshield, spotlights, front and rear case guards, fiberglass saddlebags (protected with chrome guards around their sides that tied into the rear case guards), the new sprung saddle, and a half tank of fuel. Wheelbase was 61.4in, the seat put you 34in off the ground—quite high compared to a new Electra Glide Standard with 28in of seat height. Harley rated the engine at 66hp, sufficient to haul all that weight and mass down the quarter-mile at 15.42sec and 84mph.

Cycle World magazine managed to get one to run 0 to 60 in 7.6sec, and they succeeded in bring it back to a halt in just under 170ft. All this and it produced 37mpg.

Now there was no tool box, no centerstand, no kick lever, no lock for the steering head. The turn signals worked as long as you held down the button, a feature carried up through the end of Shovelhead production. Paint schemes were solid color with atransfer decal that consisted of a series of oblong bars 6in by 1/2in carried down the tanks through the center of the emblem.

Harley built a series of 70th Anniversary editions in 1973. In effect they were the same FLH with different trim and paint options. Nice to have if you want a special edition, but only the paint and decals make it different.

Right
Jeff Hackett caught this 1975 FLH one day as it rolled by on a sunny day. Not completely stock, it's still a good example of an older Electra Glide. Check all the chrome covers under the seat. This was so none of that ugly "mechanical" stuff showed from either side. This bike also wears another set of those "quiet" fishtails. Even the exhaust pipes have chrome covers over them to hide any discoloration. I count eleven red lights on the back—how 'bout you? *Jeff Hackett*

A 1973 FLH at speed. I don't know what it is, but Harley ad models always have *such* a satisfied look on their faces. *Harley-Davidson*

1974 Electra Glide

Production
- FLH-1200: 5,166
- FLHF: 1,535
- FL-Police: 900

This year saw the demise of the old Bendix carb, replaced by a Keihin, with fewer knobs and levers to adjust. An alarm system became standard. Mounted in a black box behind the license plate, it was key operated. This is one feature H-D should have kept on all their bikes. The Police model had a Stewart-Warner "Police Special" calibrated speedometer that read from 0 to 120mph and was said to be accurate within 1/2mph.

1975 Electra Glide

Production
- FLH-1200: 7,400
- FLHF: 1,535
- FL-Police: 900

The 1975 model year was pretty much a carryover year. The biggest change was that the old style "spiral" with the control cable inside the right handlebar (in use since 1954) throttle was changed to a modern twist grip with a single-cable external cable with spring return. Also, the ends of the bars sported new grips

Most importantly, 1975 was the last year that the FL motor was offered. From here on out, only the higher compression FLH motor was available.

Left
The "AMF Harley-Davidson" emblem shows prominently on the tank. This bike has some optional trim, like the chrome piece running up the back of the front fender and the rail running down its top, and the front bumper that were options in 1975.
Jeff Hackett

Below left
When the FL was ordered as a police bike, it came with a Stewart-Warner speedometer marked "Police Special" and was supposed to be accurate to 2mph. The choke knob mounts right in the top center of the console with the high-beam, neutral, and oil-pressure lights right below.

Below right
The rear fender on this 1976 FL-P is hinged to make tire changing easier. Funny, I thought that's what dealers were for.

1976 Electra Glide

Production
FLH-1200: 11,891

All Big Twin models were powered by the high-compression FLH motor because the FL motor had been discontinued at the end of 1975 production.

Our nation celebrated its 200th anniversary in 1976. In honor, H-D offered a Bicentennial Edition for the year. All the graphics were decals applied over black metallic paint. The fairing sported the H-D eagle over the bar and shield with a stylized red-white-blue 1976 over the eagle's head. The tanks had a similar decal over and under the AMF H-D emblem; eagle on top and "Made in USA" underneath. On top of the Tour-Pak was a "Liberty Edition" decal.

The 1976 Police model had the same calibrated speedometer as in prior years.

To celebrate the Nation's Bicentennial, Harley issued a special edition called the "Liberty Edition" of the FLH-1200. Paint was Black Metallic, the seat was black also, and decals commemorating the event adorned the fairing, tanks, and top bag. *Harley-Davidson*

Most specials and limited editions really don't command a premium price on the used Shovelhead market yet. If I were looking for a Harley to put in the front room and watch appreciate, I'd probably look for a 1976 Liberty Edition in the condition that this one's owner, Robert McCollum, has maintained. The decals on the fairing, tour box, and tanks are just about perfect. He's kept the mileage down to 5,200, with the only changes over almost 20 years being the brake calipers. *Robert McCollum*

This "Liberty Edition" decal on the rear trunk was one of the special paint and decals that differentiate the bike from a stock Electra Glide. *Robert McCollum*

1977 Electra Glide

Production
  FLH-1200: 8,691
  FLHS -1200: 535

The transmission received the bulk of the changes for this year. The new main drive gear got new caged bearings; the countershaft got new caged needle bearings. The oil breather valve was improved for better scavenging from the gear cases and crankcase.

The seat now grew a bit longer and was called a "Dual-Bucket." The seat now had a step to it with grab handles on the passenger end. For once the passenger had a dedicated place to sit.

Sidecars were available in most model years, though not many bikes were ordered as such. This is one of about 300 1978 FL-Ps and FLHs that came stock with a sidecar. Actually, very few FLs came with a hack because the extra power of the FLH was needed to pull the greater weight. *Ken Bradford*

All the sidecar bikes, like this 1978 FL-P owned by Ken Bradford, had a steering damper and adjustable-rake forks installed as standard equipment. Crank down on this knob, and the steering got stiffer, which aided the handling. *Ken Bradford*

Mechanical Ignition

Up until this time, all H-D ignition systems used the mechanical point system to fire the plugs at the proper time. From 1966 to 1977, all the Shovelheads used the same bits and pieces either mounted on an ignition timer sticking up from the right side of the cases, or inside a timing case on the right side of the engine under a cover secured by two screws. Either way, what was inside was pretty much the same: a set of mechanical contact points, a condenser, and a two-lobed cam that is driven off the engine, with lobes that lifted and broke the electrical contact between the movable contact point and the stationary contact point. This break in electrical flow allowed a short pulse of DC voltage to be fed to the ignition coil's low-voltage primary windings. These windings in turn caused a voltage to be generated in the high, or secondary, windings. Just 12 volts went in from the points to the coil, but 6,000 volts came out the other side of the coil through the high-tension leads to the spark plugs. If all was right in the world and the fuel-air mixture was in the cylinders when the spark lit, power was made by the burning gases expanding against the piston, which then transferred the energy down to the crank where it was converted into rotational energy and from there drove the rear wheel by way of a primary chain, gearbox, rear drive chain, and rear sprocket. The whole power transfer to the rear wheels was turned on and off by the clutch.

As the timing cam rotated and lifted the points, two things happened over a period of time causing the timing to shift ever so slightly. The actual contact between the contact point cam follower and the timing cam was a small non-metallic block. As the lobes turned past this block, it slowly wore down, causing the points to close up from their proper .018in gap. If not maintained, the points could close up to where they ceased to break contact and no spark was produced. This was the cause of a lot of hard-starting engines in the past.

Secondly, every time the points opened, a spark was generated between the points. Usually when troubleshooting an engine that refused to start, the mechanic would remove the points cover, turn on the ignition, and break the points contact with a screwdriver. When he said; "Yup, you got spark to the points," this is the spark he was talking about.

Well, every time the spark arced from one point to the other, a small amount of metal was oxidized or burnt. After so many openings and closings of the points, usually around 5,000mi of operation, the points were burned badly enough to hinder electrical contact. This made for a weak spark and poor starting.

Combine the two, points closing up and burnt contacts, and all the bike would do was provide you with a lot of exercise by way of the kickstarter. Or, if you had an electric foot, it would cheerfully turn over until the battery's tongue was hanging out. Back in the 1960s and 1970s a lot of people didn't understand the relative simplicity of the points system and tended to do what most people do when they don't understand something—they left it alone. After a while, the bike slowly started getting harder to fire, especially on those cold mornings when you were a little late to work.

The scenario then sometimes went like this. A call was made to another bike owner who had been riding a few years longer than you, so should presumably know more about what's going on in the electrics department. Just because he only rides a Triumph is no reason to think he doesn't understand what makes a Harley tick. He agrees to come over and bail you out of your quandary—masculine ego won't let him say he doesn't know any more about Harleys than where to put the gas.

Later in the day, he arrives, and the two of you immediately start working on the problem by pulling the float bowl off the carb. Then the float needle falls out of the carb when both of you are playing with the little screw that drains the float bowl—you know, the one you didn't remove before pulling the bowl and spilling gas on your pants. Good thing you left your cigarettes outside.

Then, finding nothing in the float bowl other than some gunk in the bottom, you reinstall it, only stripping one screw in the process. When the gas is turned on and begins to run out the breather onto your already saturated pants leg, you think the float's stuck, so you deliver a healthy blow to the float bowl with the back of a hammer. All this does is spray more gas over the ground. Shut the petcock off, sit and think for a while.

Your guardian angel must be smiling on you today 'cause your buddy rests his hand on the ground, sticking the float needle into his palm. Many hours later, the carb is back to where it was before you started pulling parts. Your buddy says let's check spark. Good idea. You pull one plug lead, insert a screwdriver into the cap and hold it next to the case to see if there's a spark when the engine turns over.

Would have worked better if you had made sure the bike was in neutral before turning the engine over. Oh well, the bleeding will stop eventually and you won't need those fingers on your clutch hand for a few weeks 'cause the bike doesn't run anyway.

This time you ensure the trans is in neutral before trying to turn the engine again. Sure would be easier if you had pulled the spark plugs first, wouldn't it? Now you have it right, plugs out, screwdriver next to the coil, finger touching the metal shaft of the screwdriver. Funny how a spark that makes you jump hard enough to hit your head on the bars isn't enough to light a plug.

Next, the points cover comes off. Now you have a chance to play with all that strange stuff in there.

Anyway, you get the idea. Mechanical devices that rub on each other and wear, coupled with a lack of knowledge about what makes an engine run, will either keep you from riding your bike, or help you obtain an education the hard way. By the way, all the above actually happened over the last 30 years to me, or people I know.

Getting rid of the points for a sealed "black box" ignition system was one of the best things H-D ever did. The basic concept is the same as mechanical ignition, just nothing rubs and wears. The ignition cam now has a trigger in it that causes a signal to be sent when it passes by a sensor. In turn the sensor sends the signal to an amplifier where it's pumped up and sent to the ignition coil where the high voltage is produced in the same way as before.

Even though you hear words like "Hall Effect," transducer, CD Ignition, and others, all the theory is the same; a trigger sends a signal, the signal is boosted, and the coil is triggered. As long as the electronics don't fail, nothing much goes wrong. No arms to break, no wires to short, no points to burn. Usually any electronics failure will happen in the first one or two hours of operation. If you make it through that period, you can be pretty sure everything will work for a long time.

There are a few people going around saying that converting back to mechanical points gives better ignition, hotter spark, finer control of events, or some hooey like that. Mostly they mean they don't understand electronics because they can't see it move, so they want to go back to the old ways. Believe me, if the old mechanical system had any good characteristics, it would be in use today. I don't know about you, but I haven't seen any Indy car mechanics, or the guys who make H-D's VR1000 engine run, with points files or feeler gauges in their hands. Matter of fact, the VR1000 has Weber Electronic Fuel Injection (EFI) tied together with electronic ignition, so both the sparks and fuel mixture are entirely controlled by computer. These days, any tuning or setup requires a lap-top computer as much as a good set of tools.

Don't be surprised to see more of this type of setup appearing on street bikes in the real near future. Harley's new Ultra Classic Electra Glide for 1995 comes with Sequential Port Fuel Injection. Cold starts are no problem, fuel mileage improves, and there's nothing to wear out—at least not in the first 100,000mi.

This seems like a long way to go just to talk about points versus black boxes, but I wouldn't spend the time if I hadn't seen a lot of new (less than 10 years) riders with heads full of old war stories about how "them new 'tronic ignitions ain't worth a pound of used beer. Stick with points, Sonny; at least they can be worked on." Sure can—every 5,000mi, or sooner—whether you want to or not!

Maintenance on the 80ci motor stayed the same as on the earlier engines. Oil changes still covered the pipes with black goo due to the placement of the oil tank drain right above and inboard of the pipes. The usual solution for this is to buy a quick-drain replacement for the oil plug and install it at the first change. It screws into the oil tank just like the drain plug and is set up to be able to fit a plastic hose on the end. Presto—no more spilled oil.

Even back in the 1980s, people were going for the "retro" look. Jeff Hackett caught this 1980 Electra Glide sidecar rig masquerading as a 1950s Panhead. As said before, driving (and you do drive it) a sidecar rig takes a little more work than running a solo rig. First time you try to lean into a corner and nothing happens will definitely make you think. The hard part is getting use to having to point the bars where you want to go. The first few rides are usually quite interesting. *Jeff Hackett*

This year marked the introduction of the FLH 75th Anniversary Edition Electra Glide. Almost all had the 74ci motor. They came with black paint with gold pinstriping on the tanks and fenders and a cast gold eagle on the clutch cover. A leather seat was standard. The front fender had an emblem on its lower rear edge—"Harley-Davidson 75th Anniversary 1200cc Electra Glide."

Seldom mentioned is that eight of the FLH-80 Anniversary bikes were also built in 1978. Other

In 1979, the FLT was born—only 19 were built in that year compared to 4,480 in 1980, so it might be properly said that it came out for real in 1980. Built on a completely new frame, it had a three-point elastomer isolation system for the engine, which drives through a five-speed transmission. The swingarm had repositioned shocks, and the passenger pegs had moved off it onto the frame. An integrated, frame-mounted fairing held two headlights, while a new instrument cluster sat on the tank. The seat was frame mounted and had a large backrest for the passenger. The Tour-Pak and bags came standard. At the time, it was a tour bike second to none. *Ron Hussey*

The 80ci engine in the FLT was free to shake in its mounts. Vibration could be felt up to 2000rpm when the mount's dampening effect came into play. At a stoplight, the engine would shake around while the rest of the bike stood still, but on the road, the vibration was kept to a minimum. This isn't to say the FLT didn't vibrate, just that the vibration that came through let you know there was a motorcycle under you. *Ron Hussey*

than the emblems, the bikes were the same FLH-80s available to everyone in 1978. A total of 2,341 FLH-1200 Anniversary models were built compared to the small number of 80ci Anniversary Editions, so I would think the 80ci Anniversary model might be a little more desirable than its smaller brother. Although, as said before, don't really expect the special editions, differing only in paint or decals, to be worth any more than the regular model of that year.

That's why I advise that if you're looking for an old classic Shovel to ride on sunny Sundays—just you and your significant other enjoying the smog—go for whatever you want. But if you are looking for a scoot that won't require a lot of maintenance in the electrical department, and you like Shovelheads, find one manufactured after 1977, with electronic ignition, and check to see all the stuff in the sparks department is stock.

A new air cleaner grew off the carburetor. In order to help satisfy EPA noise laws, intake noise had to be toned down a bit. The new silencer was approximately the size of a toaster and the nickname stuck. It was also one of the first items to go up on the shelf when the bike rolled into the garage, as the cleaner was too wide for a leg to bend around comfortably. The size of the engine was imprinted on the flat surface of the air cleaner's chrome cover—"1200" or "80" as the case might be. Cast aluminum wheels were also available on the FLH for the first time.

1979 Electra Glide

Production
  FLT Tour Glide 80ci: 19
  FLHC Classic 80ci: 4,368
  FLHC 80ci with sidecar: 353
  FLH-80: 3,429
  FLH-1200: 2,612
  FLH-80 Police: 84
  FLH-1200 Police: 596

Two new models showed up at this time, the FLT Tour Glide (H-D figures list only 19 built in 1979, probably for pre-intro testing, so it is unclear whether the FLT was officially introduced in 1979 or in 1980) and the FLHC Electra Glide Classic, both powered by the bigger engine, although an FLHC with sidecar was offered and one brochure showed it with a 74ci engine—pretty rare beast, though. The only 1979 sidecar rig I

In 1981, H-D built 784 Heritage Edition FLHs. The bike's colors are the same the factory used extensively up to the 1930s. Olive drab and red sound like a strange combination, but it works on the bike. A Heritage wouldn't be a Heritage without fringe on the saddlebags. Harley has continued to ride the nostalgia wave down to the present day with the Heritage Softail Classic, but the 1981 Heritage was the first.

80 Heritage Edition built for"—and there was a space underneath to have a name engraved. Most owners don't put anything permanent there as the next buyer might not have exactly the same name. The clutch "derby" cover had the Heritage Edition logo with a red "80" above and a set of gold wings below. The speedometer was now the federally mandated 85mph in white numerals with an inner km/h (kilometer per hour) scale in blue.

The '81 FLT got a more conventional exhaust system. The front header bends right and sweeps back to the right muffler, while the rear pipe splits, one branch to the left muffler and the other crossing over to the right header and muffler (well, H-D thought it was simpler).

The FLTC Tour Glide Classic—for those who had everything, but needed more—was introduced, carrying a larger Tour-Pak on back and a slightly different two-tone paint scheme with a little more chrome trim for emphasis.

1982 Electra Glide and Tour Glide

Production
    FLT Tour Glide: 1,196
    FLTC Tour Classic: 833
    FLH-80: 1,491
    FLHC Electra Glide Classic: 1,284
    FLHC with sidecar: 95
    FLHF Electra Glide Heritage: 313
    FLHS Electra Glide Sport: 948
    FLHP-80 Police: 317
    FLHP-80: 1,261
    FLHP Deluxe: 270
    FLHP Shrine: 19
    FLHP: 282

Not a whole lot was changed this year. The FLT grew a higher output alternator to handle extras like electric vests, additional lights, trailers with auxiliary lights, electric washer and drier—you get the drift. The foot boards became adjustable, the bars changed, and better seals and locks were introduced for the Tour-Pak and bags. Prior to this change, a good rainstorm and 50mph could fill a saddlebag on a long run; a much better seal eliminated this problem.

Down amongst the machinery, the valves and valve springs were updated. Last, but by no means least, there were new plastic switches riding on the handlebars.

Curiously, H-D production lists show that five FLHP models were available: the FLHP-80 Police, FLHP-80, FLHP Deluxe, FLHP Shrine, and plain FLHP.

1983 Electra Glide and Tour Glide

Production
- FLT Tour Glide: 566
- FLTC Tour Glide Classic: 475
- FLTC with sidecar: 37
- FLH-80 Electra Glide (belt drive): 1,272
- FLHT Electra Glide (rubber-mounted engine): 1,426
- FLHTC Electra Glide Classic (rubber-mounted engine): 1,304
- FLHTC with sidecar: 75
- FLHS Electra Glide Sport: 985
- FLHP Police Standard: 334
- FLHP Deluxe (birch white): 414
- FLHTP (rubber-mounted engine; chain drive): 341
- FLHP Shrine (belt drive): 11
- FLHP (belt drive): 112

Model year 1983 saw the introduction of a new and successful series: the FLHT and FLHTC. Cannily recognizing that many riders wanted the FLT's rubber-mounted engine and five-speed transmission but were put off by the FLT's styling, H-D combined the FLT's frame, five-speed transmission, and saddlebags with the FLH's classic fork-mounted fairing, creating a new ultimate touring bike with classic form and modern function. Now there were two separate and distinct Electra Glide lines: the classic FLH with solid-mounted engine and four-speed transmission and the new FLHT with rubber-mounted engine and five-speed transmission.

If there's a "C" after the model, as in FLHTC and FLTC, that indicates a bigger trunk on back, spiffy paint, and a few chrome touches for the "Classic" look.

To further the never-ending quest for lower seat heights for their advertising copywriters to brag about, H-D gave the FLT and FLTC shorter, stiffer suspension and a cut-down seat. Even the old-fashioned FLH series was given a modern touch: all got the final drive belt as first used on the Sturgis; The FLT and FLHT series retained the enclosed chain.

1984 Electra Glide and Tour Glide

Busy sorting out the last bugs on their new Evolution motor, H-D didn't spend any time updating the Shovelhead motor for its final production run. The last Shovelhead rolled out the factory doors in June 1984, but H-D did see fit to release a few special editions of the Shovelhead FLH and FX models for the 1984 model year. The FLHX last-edition Electra Glide, with full touring gear and fork-mounted fairing, sporting white paint with gold stripes and red pinstriping and wore wire wheels.

The FLHS Electra Glide Sport collected a few Wide Glide parts. Some were built with staggered duals, higher handlebars, forward foot pegs, and controls. Early-production FLHS bikes had the standard setup of dual exhaust and floor boards. Sometime during the middle of the model year, H-D swapped over. Both bikes were wire wheels.

The factory says 467 FLHT bikes were built—232 black and 235 white. A friend of mine in Phoenix has a black one (serial number 1HD1AEK33EY017520—built November 30, 1983) with foot boards and dual turnout mufflers that the factory says was produced halfway through the model run, number 232. His bike has a massive eagle decal on the front of his fairing that he swears came from the factory. The rest of the cosmetics are stock, red and gold striping on the bags and front fender. He thinks, and I tend to agree, this is the last black FLHT Shovelhead built.

Was the 1984 FLT or FLHT ever built with an Evo motor? Two men whose opinions I respect greatly, differ as to the answer; I'll leave it up to

The 1984 FLHS was the last of the FL Shovelheads. By this point, AMF and all the problems with quality were long gone. Now, you could count on the bike actually taking you on a 2,000mi trip without using any oil, or having any of the pieces drop off. This bike has lived in Arizona all its life and spends most of its time inside. The sun would have eaten up the decal on the fairing and faded the paint by now if its owner, Phil Bellini, hadn't kept it under wraps. If you want the bike to stay stock, you pretty much have to give up on the idea of running up lots of miles. *Phil Bellini*

you to find one and send me a picture, care of the publisher.

Harley-Davidson model and production figures do not separate the 1984 production into Shovelhead bikes and Evo bikes. They do, however, list two sets of figures for most models, and one could easily infer that the first set is for production with the Shovelhead motor and that the second for Evolution-powered bikes. I'll go out on that limb and present these figures for what they are worth. These figures show that H-D built in 1984 the following Shovelhead-powered bikes: 446 FLTC, 11 FLTC with sidecars, 974 FLHTC, 14 FLHTC with sidecars, 155 FLH-80 (plus 1,828 Evo-powered FLH-80s, which makes no sense since the FLH supposedly died with the Shovel motor), 791 FLHX (plus 467 Evo-powered FLHX, which again makes no sense), 499 FLHS, 100 FLHTP, and 36 FLHT Shrine. Again, these figures are not exact, but are the best available.

Note that Harley-Davidson figures list several hundred FLH and FLHX models built in 1985, suggesting that Shovels may have been made in 1985. Despite this, the accepted view is that the Shovel, and the FLH, died in 1984.

And so, in 1984, ended almost two decades of Shovelhead touring bikes. What had started out in the mid-1960s as two models—the FL and FLH—that were not all that different from their predecessor, the Panhead, ended up in its last year of production with nine different models ranging in type from the original FLH to the FLHTC.

Many improvements took the 1984 touring bike a long way from the first FLH. Each year from 1966 saw a better bike in the marketplace. Harley was able to improve its bikes and grow as a company even while fighting problems with quality, antiquated equipment, and ownership by a conglomerate only marginally interested in actual motorcycles. If you believe that being "forged in the fires of tribulation" makes for a stronger person, then the same could be said about a motorcycle company owned and operated by extremely dedicated people.

The last full dresser Shovelhead from Harley-Davidson, the FLHTC can only be best appreciated for what it is by spending a few thousand miles traveling across the country on what some say was the last of the "real" Harleys.

PART TWO

The 1971–84 FX Series

As 1970 rolled around, H-D found itself with two products heading in two entirely different directions. The FL series had grown into 800lb road behemoths, suitable for eating miles on the superslab, but not the most maneuverable vehicle once the city streets were reached. The other end of the scale, the Sportster, was trying to be all things to all people. The XLCH version of the Sportster was trying to run in the same performance league as the Universal Japanese Motorcycle (UJM)—usually an in-line four-cylinder with a lot more performance than the Sportster—and the XLH Sportster was being promoted as a small version of a touring bike with its larger tank and optional windshield and saddlebags. This really wasn't where it belonged, but H-D was trying to fill all the niches.

Customs, or "Choppers"

The name "chopper" actually connoted a full dresser that had all the extraneous parts removed down to a light, single-seat, fenderless bike. The old method of how to build a chopper was to start the engine and begin removing parts 'till the bike quit running, then bolt that last part back on.

In later years, the name became synonymous with extended forks, tall "ape-hanger" bars, loud pipes, peanut tanks, and the rest of the modifications that resulted in a bike similar to what was appearing in the wave of 1960s biker movies, produced with casts of tens and costs of hundreds. In reality, all "chopper" originally meant was a clean, fast bike built to run.

Toward the end of the 1960s, choppers began to be popular. Used Big Twins were being stripped of all the extraneous parts unnecessary for function—no case guards, chopped-off rear fender, bobbed or no front fender, and lose the big seat. A healthy coat of some basic color—black being predominate—and a set of loud pipes (punched-out factory mufflers would do if the wallet wouldn't handle any custom work) completed the bike.

Ensuring the rider could be seen, a set of high bars raised him up enough to have to lean back in the saddle and hang his feet on highway pegs, mounted in front of where the foot boards used to be. Now he was set to profile down main street.

Just to prove that not everyone was sleeping at H-D during the AMF years, the stylists at H-D, typified by Willie G. Davidson, grandson of one of the founders and now head of design and styling, went to work to build a factory version of the chopper that anyone could, and hopefully would, walk into the dealership and buy.

Reaching into the parts bin, they picked out the front fork assembly of the Sportster, along with its front wheel and brake. This was mated to a stripped FLH frame and 74ci engine. The whole collection of parts weighed in at 559lb, about 50lb over a Sporty.

The 1971 Super Glide had a massive taillight parked in the middle of the white fiberglass seat. From some angles, this being one of them, the bike had a fairly strange look.

1971 FX-1200

Production
 FX Super Glide: 4,700

Thus was born the FX Super Glide. The "F" came from the FLH, whose motor and frame were used; the "X" from the XL Sportster that contributed the front end. The FL frame sprouted a few new tabs to mount the new equipment, such as those for the new brake pedal and linkage. The FLH's foot boards were replaced on the Super Glide by conventional foot pegs. The left peg mounted to a lug on the chain inspection cover on the primary case (where the FLH's passenger peg mounted), and the right peg mounted through a bar that extended forward from a clamp on the engine-trans locating plate to put the peg in line with the left one.

Instead of designing a new shifter linkage to accommodate the new, more rearward left foot position, H-D engineers merely reversed the shift

Here's where all the factory custom Harleys started. In 1971, H-D grafted the front end of a Sportster to the frame of an FLH. A lot of unnecessary weight was pared off, like the electric starter, dual exhaust, and saddlebags. The only controls on the buckhorn bars are the two turn-signal buttons and the high-beam switch. No electric foot, no stereo—just basic bike. Harley planted a large "1" decal on the tank, so no one would have any trouble with model identification, or where the bike fit in the scheme of things. Red, white, and blue were the only colors for America's "#1 Freedom Machine." The English went slightly potty over this bike. It was written up in every British bike rag available, and everyone who even got to sit on it wanted one worse than breathing. The plastic rear fender/seat combo was only around for one year and is now quite a collector's item. *Marty Greersen—Harley Davidson*

lever on its shaft so that it was reachable by the toes of the left foot on the new peg. Of course, reversing the lever also meant reversing the shift pattern: On the first FXs, first was up and the other three gears were down. This could really screw you up if you owned an FLH and an FX. Or it could prove to be real interesting if you were used to a different bike like a Honda with the standard shift pattern. Fortunately, after a few years, the factory designed a linkage just for the FX, on which the shifter shaft inserted through a hole in the primary case, putting the shift lever behind the peg and giving the bike a standard shift pattern.

Finding neutral in most of the Shovel gearboxes can be a bit of a problem. With the engine off, the bike will have to be rolled slightly while

The emblem on the 1971 Super Glide tank stood out from a red and blue border. The AMF decal has drifted down towards the bottom of the 3.5gal twin tanks (optional on the FLH). *Ron Hussey*

The gearshift lever on the 1971 Super Glide had been turned around to put it closer to the pedal, resulting in a reversed shift pattern: one up and three down. This owner has spun his shifter 180deg so the pattern is back to the standard one down and the rest up. The bolt head should be on top of the lever where it attaches to the shaft, not the nut. *Ron Hussey*

stirring the lever. If the engine's running, it's near impossible to go from second gear to neutral. My standard procedure is to drop into first while still rolling up to a stop, then lift the lever halfway up and hope the trans pops into neutral. This is somewhat of an art and needs to be practiced for a while before you become proficient at hitting neutral instead of second gear.

The brake master cylinder stayed where it had always been on the FLH, but H-D engineers designed a new linkage to connect it to the rear-mounted rear brake cylinder. The pedal attached to the same mounting point as the right foot peg, then swung under the front exhaust pipe and up to put the pedal in front of the peg and slightly higher, where it was easily reached.

No electric starter was fitted, allowing the smaller battery off the Sportster to be installed on the right side, up high, almost under the seat. The kick lever was fitted with a slim, rounded pedal instead of the wide, flat one on the FLH. Passenger foot pegs mounted on the lower shock mounts because the normal mounts now had the rider's pegs.

The optional 3.5gal twin tanks for the FLH were mounted, and the speedometer, warning lights, choke, and ignition switch were located in the same chrome center console used on the FLH. A black insert behind the console filled in the space between the tanks and in front of the seat; a large red-white-blue "1" was prominently displayed in its center. The top of the "1" was blue with seven stars in two rows, the vertical riser had vertical red and white stripes, and the bottom had the company's name on a white background. The horn and its chrome cover—two additional parts borrowed from the Sportster—mounted on the left front downtube.

The FX's exhaust system was all new because the FX's right foot peg position prevented H-D from reusing the standard FLH two-into-one system. The new exhaust consisted of two individual pipes sweeping back from the cylinders welded together in a "Y" just before the single muffler. The rear pipe was routed behind the kickstarter. The muffler was a chrome-plated version of the old tube-type muffler that had been the standard muffler on most 1950s and 1960s Pans and Shovels.

The most striking difference was the seat. Harley had a golf-cart business that was good at making fiberglass bodies and parts for their carts and fairings and sidecar bodies for their bikes. They designed a boat-tailed fiberglass fender/seat combination unlike anything anyone had seen on a Harley before. The taillight tunneled back into the fender almost to the back of the seat. The front of the fender swept down to swingarm level to provide splash protection. This all was attached to the familiar rear fender rails used on the rest of the big bikes.

Fenders and tanks got basic white paint with blue accents above the tank emblem and red below. A small AMF decal rode in the bottom tank accent (many of these must not have had a very good quality of glue as a lot of them seem to have fallen off rather rapidly). Two red stripes ran down the side of the rear fender, and a blue flash tapered from the back of the seat to the top curve of the rear fender. A red center stripe with two blue accent stripes ran the length of the front fender. The air cleaner cover was plain chrome with no adornments.

Stopping power was by full-width drum brake actuated by a lever on the right side of the front wire wheel and the standard rear cast-iron drum on the left with the sprocket mounted on it. The chain guard was chrome plated unlike the black-painted one on the FLH.

This FX has the shifter mounted in the proper position. *Marty Greerson*

The white basic color, with red and blue panels and striping, really made the first Super Glide stand out; even with a factory in the background. *Ron Hussey*

Harley hit upon a good idea with the FX-1200. In its first year of production, over 4,700 were sold. The FLH only outsold it by 775 units. But by 1974, the FX and FXE outsold the FLH by a wide margin.

Now that H-D had regressed back to a kickstarter on the FX Super Glide, the old drill of fuel, choke, throttle, ignition, and kick had to be learned all over. A lot of different methods were put forth by the bike magazines of the day. I think some of them had a lot of fun going through the litany of kickstarting just to prove a Harley is still a Harley.

Most methods went something along the lines of this: turn on the fuel, kick once or twice with the ignition off and the choke on, then turn off the choke, on with the ignition, and try it for serious. When that didn't work, the *Cycle World* method of three kicks with full choke and then ignition on when cold, or one kick—no choke—when hot, seemed to bring the motor to life with fair regularity. If none of these methods worked, it still looked good in your front room, didn't it?

When the bike was finally urged to life, and if your right foot would still support you enough to climb on the bike, you could count on performance significantly better than that of the standard FLH. Zero to sixty times were down to 5.6sec—a vast improvement. The quarter-mile

This blue Super Glide shows its Sportster front end quite clearly, right down to the drum brake. The two-into-one pipe actually worked better than the factory duals, producing a bit more power. The engine was still advertised with the same 66hp as the FLH. *Jeff Hackett*

passed by in 14.43sec, close enough to give a Sportster a good go.

A few very brave magazine crazies from *Road Rider* said the bike was very stable at 120mph, but how they urged it to that velocity is beyond me. The only way I know to get an FX up to 120 per, is to make a sharp right turn in the middle of the Golden Gate Bridge and check the speedometer just prior to hitting the water. Top end was more like 105mph—reached after a long run with a small rider. That's OK, though. Most of us were content just to get the bloody thing started from cold and go enjoy a ride on a much lighter big Harley.

1972 FX Super Glide

Production
FX Super Glide: 6,500

Except for cosmetic details, the second-year FX was the same as the first. The boat-tailed rear fender on the 1971 FX wasn't popular, so for 1972 the FX went to an XL-style fender with a different seat, and the boat-tails went to the trash can—much to restorers' dismay because they are quite valuable today.

For the new FX fender, a set of new alloy rear frame rails had to be fabricated to fit. A standard banana seat sat on top. The six-sided emblem went away, to be replaced by a rectangular version with "AMF" proceeding "Harley-Davidson." Other than that, the FX stayed the same. The motor was still rated at 66hp, and torque—what really made the bike pull—still was 70lb-ft at 4000rpm. The red, white, and blue paint scheme gave way to H-D's standard single color with accents around the tank emblem.

The rear master brake cylinder was repositioned below and behind the right foot peg so that it was actuated through a shorter linkage. The pedal no longer had to snake underneath and around the outside of the front exhaust pipe because the pivot was now above the foot peg instead of below.

The restyled FX was an even bigger hit than the original had been. Production increased to 6,500 units, exactly 1,800 more than for the previous year.

1973 FX Super Glide

Production
FX Super Glide: 7,625

The 1973 Super Glide received many changes. Starting at the front, Japanese Kayaba forks with orange reflectors on the lower tubes and a single disc brake replaced the straight legs and drum of old. The rear brake was also changed to a disc. The tank was completely different; now a single 3.5gal unit mounted up on the frame with more space between the bottom of the tank and the top of the engine. Personal opinion of the author: this has to be the ugliest, dorkiest tank ever built by H-D. The new tank looked very similar to the ones on H-D's Italian-built 350cc Sprint (the tank looked ugly there too). The tank was painted in a solid color with narrow rectangular bars circumnavigating it with the gas cap and emblem interrupting their passage. Willie G.

Normally, the kickstarter lever return spring has a cover over it, as shown here. That way, if it breaks, it won't do any damage should it depart in little pieces. If this does happen without a cover installed, don't worry; your leg will keep all the chunks of spring from falling on the ground.

The 1971 FX came with a plastic rear fender over the FL frame. Harley only used it for one year, then went to a conventional type. The one on this bike sports a trick paint job, but otherwise is the same shape as when it came from the factory. Due to their rarity, these fenders are becoming quite valuable.

must've let this one slip by. Just to prove this was no aberration, the same paint scheme found its way to the FLH with similar resulting appearance. Because the new tank lacked the former tank's center console, on which the speedometer was mounted, the 1973 FX's speedometer was mounted to the handlebars behind the triple clamps where it was driven off the front wheel; still no tach yet.

The ignition switch changed to a small round housing below the left side of the tank. The choke sat right below. The fuel on-off lever was 2in behind the ignition. New plastic switch housings (same as those introduced on the 1972 FL) replaced the individual metal switches formerly used. A hydraulic master brake cylinder sat on the right bar and actuated the front brake through a new lever.

One positive styling change was the switch from the two-into-one exhaust to a set of classic staggered shorty dual exhaust pipes with no crossover pipe—similar to those on the XLCH.

Several other minor changes were also evident, such as that the passenger pegs were repositioned from the lower shock mount to the forward part of the swingarm.

Despite the new tank, Super Glide sales increased again in 1973, to 7,625, a mere 125 bikes fewer than FLH sales that year—maybe because many Super Glide buyers looked on their new mounts as raw material for their own custom machine, so they were not put off by the "bread-loaf" between the seat and the bars.

1974 FX and FXE Super Glides

Production
  FX Super Glide: 3,034
  FXE Super Glide: 6,199

FXE Super Glide

A new Super Glide model was introduced for 1974, the electric-start FXE. The FXE was identical to the FX, except that it had an electric starter and the slightly larger battery from the electric-start XLH Sportster. The new electric foot made it easier for those who didn't have the forbearance and strength of a Ugandan mountain gorilla. Now, getting the Big Twin to life was a simple matter of a little choke and a little button. Sales also showed that a lot of people wanted the chopper image, but didn't want to have to work at it.

Harley was slowly making the Super Glide its own machine with its own parts and linkages distinct from those used on the FLH. In 1972, the FX had gotten its own master cylinder; in 1974, it got its own new shifter mechanism. As part of the new mechanism, both Super Glide models got a new chain inspection cover with a revised left foot peg mount and hole for a new shifter shaft that operated through a new linkage. The shifter now pivoted behind the peg, passed up and over, and operated in the conventional "one-down, three-up" manner. The inner primary cover had to be changed to accommodate the shifter shaft passing through to the shifter linkage.

Carburetion now was controlled by a conventional twist-grip throttle and a single sheathed cable routed outside the tube of the handlebar, instead of by the 1954-style "spiral" with its control wire hidden inside the handlebar tube. The free turning throttle of old was gone, a victim of federal regulations that insisted the throttle be self-closing. A return spring enabled the throttle plate to snap shut if the throttle was released. In order to provide the cruise control similar to the older style throttle, a jam screw was fitted underneath the throttle grip housing. By screwing in the tensioning screw, enough pressure could be exerted

The first 1971 FX Super Glide came with Sportster front forks and triple clamps, mounting a drum brake, an Electra Glide frame, and a fiberglass rear seat. It was painted in patriotic colors and in England was called the "Sparkling America." The British really took to it, and it was featured in Warr's, the oldest motorcycle shop in Britain. The English riders wanted it bad, but it cost the equivalent of a year's salary for most. It was the first of all the Harley semi-customs.

against the twist grip to keep the throttle from closing. The FLH series got the new throttle in 1975.

The transmission got a higher first gear on both bikes, requiring a new mainshaft and countershaft.

The tank stayed the same as in 1973—this time with a set of stripes running under the emblem from its front edge to the rear of the tank and over the emblem in a different color, running from the rear of the emblem to the front of the tank. More factory options like trident-forked sissy bars appear. The list of optional semi-chopper parts grew. Turn signals appeared on the bars for the first time. And a tach joined the speedometer in a new nacelle.

Judging by the number of sales—electric start made the Super Glide attractive to a much wider audience, and for the first time, Super Glide sales outpaced Electra Glide sales.

1975 FX and FXE Super Glides

Production
FX Super Glide: 3,060
FXE Super Glide: 9,350

The 1975 FX and FXE models were essentially unchanged from the 1974 models.

Super Glide sales continued to rise, to 3,060 for the FX and 9,350 for the FXE. In fact, FXE sales alone for 1975 were higher than combined sales for the 1974 FX and FXE. Super Glide sales rose higher every year, and sales of the FXE accounted for all the increase.

1976 FX and FXE Super Glides

Production
FX Super Glide: 3,034
FXE Super Glide: 13,838

The 1976 FX and FXE were similar to the 1975 and 1974. Only small changes appeared during these years. Exhaust systems varied from staggered duals to Siamese headers joined below the cylinders and rolling back to one muffler; then staggered duals again, this time with a balance tube between them.

Liberty Edition

The United States' Bicentennial was being celebrated in a big way, and not to be left out, H-D

In 1972, the fiberglass rear fender gave way to an XL style supporting a frame-mounted seat. Minus the sissy bar (a dealer option), Larry Orton's 1974 FX could pass for stock. Most owners lost the AMF decal about as fast as they got the bike home and in the garage. This one looks just about perfect; the whole bike shows like new. In 1974, the Super Glide was available for the first time with an electric foot. This FX came kick-only. *Larry Orton*

came out with a Liberty Edition of the Super Glide. Basic color was Black Metal Flake. The tank had a decal—well it was almost all decal on the top—starting with a gold-and-white scroll around the filler neck. A gold H-D eagle with upswept wings framed the scrollwork. Below the bird was the "Harley-Davidson Motor Cycles" bar and shield in gold, and the balance of the tank carried another scroll with "1776" on one wing and "1976" on the other. "America" was prominently displayed at the base of the scroll. All in all a lot of decal. Unfortunately it was also prone to fade and crack like all other decals, and if you find one in good condition, try to keep it out of the sun as much as possible. The side emblem got the gold-scroll-and-flag treatment also. The coil cover acquired a gold cast eagle, joined by another one on the headlight mounting nut chrome button cover.

If I owned a Liberty Edition—be it FX or FLH—I'd spend some time looking through *Hemmings* or touring flea markets trying to acquire another set of decals, at least for the tank, and fairing in the case of the FLH. Gas tanks for these years aren't real expensive, so I would probably keep the original tucked away and run the spare. Black Metalflake paint is easy to do, but trying to hand paint those decals, if a replacement set is unavailable, would be a major undertaking.

Super Glide sales accelerated to 3,857 for the FX and 13,838 FXE. The sales dominance of the Super Glide models had reached the point where 1976 FXE models alone outsold FLH models.

1977 Super Glides and Low Riders

Production
FX Super Glide: 2,049
FXE Super Glide: 9,460
FXS Low Rider: 3,742

FXS Low Rider

Late in 1977, the FXS Low Rider appeared. I consider it one of the best looking of the Super Glide series, and wouldn't mind one in my garage. I don't know what I'd use to pay for it, but I'd still like one.

It only came with Gunmetal Gray paint with large red "Harley-Davidson" transfer in two lines of block letters. The dual, 3.5gal tanks (from the

In 1973, Harley hung on the frame probably the ugliest fuel tank ever made. This 1974 FX still carried the tank. The fuel on-off petcock attached to the bottom left, behind the ignition, of the FX's "breadloaf" tank. *Larry Orton*

original FX Super Glide) reappeared with speedometer and tach mounted in the middle on a new console, subsequently used on all Low Riders and later Fat Bobs and Sturgis models. Cast-aluminum wheels built by Morris replaced spoked wheels—19in in the front, 16in in the rear; the edges of the rims were polished. Dual discs rode up front, and a single disc mounted on the right side in the rear.

A new Showa fork replaced the Kayaba. The frame was raked (steering head kicked out to a shallower angle) to stretch the wheelbase and drop the front of the bike. Shorter, stiffer, rear shocks lowered the rear. All this coupled with a thinner stepped seat lowered the seat height to 27.4 in; hence the name.

Flat drag bars on rolled-back risers crowned the forks. Below, the engine cases, barrels, and heads had a black crackle treatment with polished cooling fins, although the cone gear cover and primary cover stayed bare aluminum.

Highway pegs sat in front of the main pegs. An oil cooler rode between and above them, standard for the first time. The exhaust system went to two separate pipes running back to separate attachments on a rather large single muffler with a slight flare and semi-slash at its opening.

The Low Rider was stable in a straight line, but the ride became rough and unsettling when pressed into a corner. Mileage ran near 47mpg, and with sufficient room it could be urged to at

The shifter had been brought through the primary case and the pattern had changed to give the standard one-down, three-up shifting, but the tank wouldn't change up through the end of Shovelhead production. Production figures show 3,034 FXs and 6,199 FXEs built in 1974; by 1983, only 1,215 FXEs were built. *Larry Orton*

least a screaming, mind-blowing, speed-of-light 98mph. This was complemented by a blistering 15sec quarter-mile. Perhaps the 625lb running weight had something to do with its lackadaisical performance. The crouched, low, muscular profile of the Low Rider projected a new image.

FX and FXE Super Glides

Meanwhile, the FXE came with staggered duals, minus the crossover pipe, and shared a new tucked-in kickstarter (the pivot to swing out the pedal was moved to the bottom) with the FXS. From 1977 on, the Super Glide was the budget Big Twin, plainer and cheaper than the Low Rider; this would continue until its discontinuation. It still carried the ugliest tank in motorcycledom, and as the newer, fancier models appeared, the Super Glide began to look even more plain. It could be had with an optional cast rear wheel, though.

The new FXS Low Rider sold 3,742 copies despite its late introduction. These sales came at the expense of some FX and FXE sales, which dropped to 2,049 and 9,400, respectively.

1978 Super Glides and Low Riders

Production
  FX Super Glide: 1,774
  FXE Super Glide: 8,314
  FXS Low Rider: 9,787

Changes were minimal for the FX series in 1978. The Low Rider lost its drag bars for a set of pull-backs. It was also available with optional silver paint with black tank panels and red decal. The "AMF" shrunk, and the factory's logo grew. Both fenders received a black stripe with red pin-striping.

Due to noise regulations, the air cleaner grew to the point where clearance and room for your right leg on the peg was a problem. Usually, when the bike arrived at its new home, the air can was the first thing to go, with the stock pipes following closely behind. The 80ci motor appeared in mid-year, identified by a large "80" on the air cleaner (74s got a "1200"), but weren't available for the FX series until the next year.

In only its second year of production, the FXS outsold the FXE by over 1,400 units, 9,787 for the FXS and 8,314 for the FXE. The plain, kickstart-only FX languished even further in sales, at only 1,774 units sold, so it was discontinued at the end of 1978.

1979 Super Glides, Low Riders, and Fat Bobs

Production
    FXE Super Glide: 3,117
    FXS-1200 Low Rider: 3,827
    FXS-80 Low Rider: 9,433
    FXEF-1200 Fat Bob: 4,678
    FXEF-80 Fat Bob: 5,264

Once H-D found out that factory customs sell faster than beer at a baseball game, there was no stopping them. In 1979 the FX line was the best selling of all H-D's production. Lots of new things happened in that year. The FX series grew to include the Fat Bob, a Low Rider with different paint, buckhorn bars, one-piece king-and-queen seat, and optional wire wheels.

The Fat Bob and Low Rider could be ordered in 74ci or 80ci persuasion. The FXE (the FX was discontinued) came only with the 74ci motor.

The FXE picked up another front disc and a Siamesed exhaust system. The Low Rider gained a sissy bar and a stash pouch. The meaning of the word "stash" back in 1979 may have had a different meaning than it does today. The connotation was that all FXS riders were bad dudes and carried their drugs, drug paraphernalia, and other "stash" of questionable legality in a small pouch perched under the headlight where it would be the first place searched by an officer of the law—another case of trying for the "look" without really walking the walk. Sure sold bikes, though.

Riders wanted the new 80ci motor. The 80ci Low Riders and Fat Bobs outsold their 1200cc brethren by large margins: 9,433 FXS-80s compared to 3,827 FXS-1200s, and 5,264 FXEF-80s compared to 4,678 FXEF-1200s. With its wire wheels, ugly tank, and unraked frame, the increasingly plain-looking FXE Super Glides suffered on the showroom when parked near its fancy siblings, and FXE sales dropped to 3,117, less than half the previous year's total.

1980 FX Series

Production
    FXE-1200 Super Glide: 3,169
    FXWG Wide Glide: 6,045
    FXS-1200 Low Rider: 3
    FXS-80 Low Rider: 5,922
    FXB Sturgis: 1,470
    FXEF Fat Bob: 4,773

FXWG Wide Glide

The introduction of the 1980 FXWG heralded another year of big changes for H-D's FX line. The Wide Glide was a factory chopper taken to its limits. Start at the front forks—a set of stripped and stretched forks set wide apart (like those on the FLH) and the 21in spoked front wheel. A smaller headlight fit between the stanchions and sat above a very abbreviated front fender.

Black 5gal dual tanks held a set of red-to-yellow flames igniting at the front of the tank, curling around the gold bar-and-shield logo and burning to fine points halfway down the tanks. The rest of the paint came in any color requested (black, real black). The black was carried onto the engine and cases with fins polished, but the rocker boxes were polished, and the standard chrome air cleaner cover was used. A speedometer from the FLH now resided in the middle of the tanks; no tach was offered.

The seat now split into two sections, the rear rolling up onto a sissy bar. New, forward controls unique to the Wide Glide (at least for 1980) set the rider's feet way out front—standard position foot pegs were gone. In the 1980 sales brochure, H-D called them "highway pegs," but seeing as how there were no other rider's pegs, the term "forward controls" is more appropriate.

Back at the rear, the fender was bobbed and valanced. The stop light was carried under the rear valance, up out of sight. The staggered dual pipes carried a blacked-out crossover pipe running beneath the massive air cleaner.

All these modifications were a culmination of ideas that started right after World War II and were given a massive boost in 1969 by Peter Fonda as Captain America in the movie *Easy Rider*. He rode a Panhead built on a custom frame with a peanut gas tank of about 6oz capacity, painted up like an American flag. The front end was out so far it was almost in the next frame, and it mounted a 21in wheel on a spool. This bike probably did more for the custom chopper scene than any other bike built before or since. Today, the bike comes across ludicrous, with its rigid frame and zero front brakes, but believe me, after this movie made its run through the drive-in theaters of middle America, everybody who ever thought he wanted to ride a bike and be an imitation hard guy, wanted a bike like Peter's. In less than a year, its clones and copies sprung up all over, and to a great extent, they're still selling—witness the 1980 H-D Wide Glide.

For 1980, you could get all the looks of Fonda's bike without all the discomfort that came with riding it. The FXWG was a factory purpose-built chopper aimed at the crowd who wanted the lean, mean look without having to build it from scratch, or endure the thumps and bounces that came with riding a hardtail (no rear suspension) frame. The Harley "Softail" is a design that tucks the rear suspension underneath and looks

The 1977 FX came with staggered duals (not the ones in the picture, but similar, without crossover pipe.), and all models of the FX got a new kickstarter lever with the pivot at the bottom instead of the top. The Super Glide would remain the entry-level big bike, plainer and cheaper than the new-for-1977 Low Rider. This bike's seen a tank and wheel change, and the rear disc has been drilled. It shows how far an owner will go to change his bike to what he wants, not what the factory builds.

Probably one of the most beautiful Shovelheads, the 1977 Low Rider projected an image of the hard-core biker. It was built for looks rather than performance, and it succeeded; 3,742 built in 1977; 9,787 in 1978, and a total of 13,260 of both engine size, 74ci and 80ci, in 1979. In 1980, the preference for the 80ci motor was shown with three FXSs with the 74ci motors built compared to 5,922 FXS-80s. *Ron Hussey*

like a hardtail. The Softail frame came along in 1984).

The Wide Glide came by that name from its fork tubes being spaced wider apart than those on the other Super Glides. Early choppers would sometimes leave the stock FLH wide steering head on the front when they mounted the 21in wheel. Spacers took up the extra room on the front axle left over from removing the wide 16in wheel and brake assembly and adding a skinny wheel. This gave the effect of the front wheel sitting all by itself way out there on the end of the forks.

In the Wide Glide, H-D built its own version of the same thing, only with twin disc brakes to aid in hauling the thing down to a stop. The boys who built the original spool front ends found they needed to leave a lot of space between their front wheel and whatever was going down the road in front of them because, although the rear brake did in fact stop the rear wheel from turning, it had little effect on forward motion. This led to a few nasty incidents of bent front ends, sometimes with extensive repairs required to the rider as well.

The Wide Glide fulfilled its purpose of looking good; it wasn't, however, the most comfortable place to be on a 200mi ride. The combination of the high bars making your arms fly like the sails on an America's Cup contender and the reclined seating position setting all your weight on your lower spine, ensured that you were more than ready to get off the thing after an hour or so of looking good. For a cruiser rolling to the local watering hole, it couldn't be beat. Going on a trip—take something else, unless you're under 25 and have a very high tolerance for pain. Ride one for 10 years, and I guarantee you'll be on first-name basis with a chiropractor.

All of the bad points mentioned above didn't do much to retard sales of the bike. A total of 6,045 Wide Glides went out the doors in 1980—5,166 in 1981. Willie G. and his design partner Lou Netz had hit upon a winner. With its staggered duals and "high-in-the-front" stance, partly brought about by installing shorter rear shocks to complement the longer front end, it announced that the owner was a little different from the average rider. Ironically, the desire to be a little different from the average led Wide Glide riders to be part of a large crowd, for in its first year of production, the Wide Glide became H-D's best-selling model.

The first-year production Low Rider came, in 1977, with separate pipes into a common muffler, low flat bars, and a seat height 2.5in lower than a Super Glide's. The Low Rider was 70lb heavier than the kickstart-only FX model of the Super Glide. The tach and speedo were mounted on a new console between the 3.5gal tanks. A 19in front and 16in rear Morris cast-aluminum wheel came standard. The frame was raked to stretch the wheelbase and lower the front new Showa forks. The back dropped down courtesy of shorter shocks. Paint was a gunmetal silver with red H-D decals on the tanks. The crankcases, barrels, and cylinder heads were black, although the cone cover and primary cover were left aluminum.

FXB Sturgis

In 1980, H-D was in the chopper/custom bike business in an even bigger way. If you had a bad desire for a set of flames on the tank of your scoot, H-D was there to oblige. Just belly up to the bar at your local dealership and order an FXWG to go—hold the pickles. You got a bike that the factory had built with all the bits and pieces hung on it that you were going to do just as soon as you rode the thing home and got next week's paycheck. This was the epitome of factory participation in building customs, and it showed H-D knew which way to go to reach its customer base.

Next up on H-D's list of factory customs was the FXB Sturgis. It was named after a motorcycle rally called "The Black Hills Classic" held in Sturgis, South Dakota, every August. Sturgis is the rally for Harley-Davidson riders, so it was only natural for H-D to build the Sturgis. It's not a touring bike to ride halfway across the country to South Dakota, but a bike to take to the rally, perhaps behind a motor home, and cruise the scene. Were I to ride to Sturgis on the Sturgis, I might drop the bike off a trailer at some near town, like Bear Butte—eight miles out of Sturgis (really), and ride on in from there.

Spring 1980 saw its introduction. The Sturgis was based on the 80ci Low Rider with lots of blacked-out parts and with primary and rear drive provided by toothed rubber belts, rather than by chains. The trans had to be worked around so the wide (compared to chain) rear belt would fit. Internally, the gear ratios were raised. The same 3.5 gal tanks from the Low Rider appeared with a tach and speedo mounted in the center console. Thanks to the feds again, the speedometer, mounted forward on the tank, read from 0 to 85; the rear-mounted tach covered 0 to 8,000rpm—a figure not many H-D engines were likely to see.

The wheels were cast aluminum with a red pinstripe around the flat part of the rim. Riders got a king-and-queen seat with sissy bar, all similar to those on the Wide Glide. The primary cases, crank cases, cylinders, heads, gear-case cover, rocker boxes, air cleaner, coil cover, transmission, handlebars, and other small parts were either black or blacked-out.

Spark was provided by the new V-Fire electronic ignition giving better starting and overall performance. The kickstarter still remained, though—just in case all the electrics went dead, or the owner wanted to look bad while kicking it to

On the Low Rider, the tach read to 8000rpm and the speedo went to 150mph, but the bike would pull maybe 106mph after a long run, and spinning the engine above 5500rpm was an exercise in noise. The bike sure looked good, though—especially when it was your eyes watching the gauges. *Ron Hussey*

The 1979 Low Rider came with a kickstarter along with the electric foot. It could be had with either the 74ci or 80ci engine up through 1980. If you are looking for something a little different and rather rare, a 1980 FXS-1200 (74ci) would be a good way to go. This 1979 FXS has forward controls, solo seat, and an S&S carb, but is otherwise factory stock. The owner, Richard Meyer, keeps all the stock parts carefully put away.

The kick lever was still there in 1979, but for most it was for appearances only. It added to the look of the FXS Low Rider—helped the image of the sunburned rider with the thousand-mile stare and well-worn right boot.

Harley sold 9,942 FXEF Fat Bobs in 1979—4,678 as 1200s and the rest as 80-inchers. The Fat Bob was a Low Rider with buckhorn bars, different paint, a different seat, and with the option of wire wheels. Most owners opted for cast wheels, making this black bike owned by Steve Liebenau fairly rare. About the only changes to the bike were some extra chrome, yellow plug wires, and mounts for saddlebags.

life. I actually knew a dude who would make a large production out of getting up on the lever and whomping it a good one, all the time while his right thumb depressed the starter button; what can you say?

One thing that will really get you noticed on a Sturgis is the blackness of the bike. Most of the engine, all of the fenders and tank, and the frame is all black. Some red, mainly around the wheel rims, outlines the black enough to draw your attention to just how black the bike is. This is the style and look that Willie G. and H-D were trying to achieve. The bike *will* get you noticed.

With the Sturgis, H-D really came out with a Shovelhead featuring ideas for the future Evolutions. Its major claims to fame were the two drive belts replacing the primary and final drive chains. Harley had sat down with Gates Industries and redesigned the drive system on their bikes to take cogged belts. This turned out to be more than a bolt-on affair, and for a while almost didn't happen. For equal strength, belts have to be wider than chains. The transmission had to be redesigned for belt clearance, and the starter had to be moved out of the way. Belts don't have master links, making removal a somewhat complicated affair. Service on the primary belt turned out to be a major task. Harley later dropped the primary belt partly for this reason, but was still able to provide a sealed primary case, even with a double-row chain that needed oil, and this went a long way toward eliminating leaks.

This Low Rider is probably one of the very few with the stock air cleaner. If you look hard, you can see the numbers "1200" on the cleaner. Liebenau said the only reason the muffler was changed was that the original had rusted out.

The Fat Bob came with two individual fuel tanks with a tach and speedometer in the middle, just like on the Low Rider. Trying to read these gauges at any rate of speed is somewhat difficult as your eyes have to shift and refocus down low. Also the 150mph speedometer has the numerals so close together, they are hard to read at a glance. This is one case where a 0–120mph speedo would make more sense, as not too many Harleys will ever see the needle over on the far right side.

The belts first met with a lot of resistance, riders being the traditionalists they are. Lots of owners were concerned with belts breaking while on a trip. Motorcycle magazines of the time advocated changing the belt when the rear tire was changed, as new tires usually required different tools than the average rider had at home. Also, a method of lifting the back of the bike far enough to clear the rear tire was necessary, and why not swap the old belt for new at the same time the rear tire got changed? We've learned a lot since then about belts and longevity, but someone had to pioneer the changes.

Harley came out with numerous ads at the time, extolling the virtues of belts over chains. Among them, lack of oiling made for a cleaner bike and not having to adjust the belt after the first 500 miles made for less maintenance. When compared to a drive-shaft system, H-D said in effect, drive shafts are great, they last forever—hand them down to your kids. Belts took less power to drive and should last at least 20,000mi.

Actual operation shows a life span more like 30,000 to 40,000mi, depending on how the bike is ridden. For the first few years, H-D included a spare "get-home" belt that could be clipped on if the drive belt broke. This proved more a sop to customer worries than an actual necessity and was soon dropped.

The 1980 FXEF Fat Bob let you sit down in the seat and plant both feet firmly on Mother Earth.
Henry Agundez

The Sturgis took advantage of H-D's desire to build custom motorcycles. To follow the chopper look, H-D stretched the front end 2in. The steering head had a 31.4deg rake angle. What that means is that the front forks have more kickout than the standard offering. Draw a line straight up from the ground to the center of the front fork triple clamps. For our purposes, this will be a perpendicular line relative to the ground. The angle made between the front forks and this imaginary line is the steering rake. Most Harleys get by with an angle closer to 28deg. Stepping the front end out to the Sturgis' rake does two things. First, it gives the bike the "look." Second, it makes the bike want to run in a straight line—*really* want to run in a straight line. As a matter of fact, the increased rake of the Sturgis caused the bike to run the straight and narrow unless a lot of effort on the bars was made to change direction.

The increased rake, coupled with the bike's 64in wheelbase, made it about as stable as a Chevy Suburban. The mildly tuned engine made it just about as fast, too. Nail the throttle, power shift the transmission, hold the throttle to the stop—just a little under 15sec and the quarter-mile flashes by. Well, maybe the word "flashes" isn't quite appropriate. The Sturgis will beat the traffic if pushed, but that's not its real intent.

For down-and-dirty touring, the FXB-80 Sturgis could be set up with a tent and sleeping

This bright red 1980 FXEF Fat Bob shows what most owners do as fairly standard changes. The seat's different, lower to the ground. The engine wears an S&S carb and breathes out through aftermarket pipes, in this case fairly quiet ones.

bag strapped to a sissy bar, or maybe even a set of leather saddlebags hung over the rear seat, and taken out for long tours. Sit back in the breeze, hang your feet on the highway pegs, and enjoy the scenery as the engine spins along at a slow 2700rpm and 60mph. I did it one summer for two months, my wife and I riding individual Harleys—her on her first bike; and my friend Brian riding his just-purchased Sturgis. That time will always live in my mind as the best ride of my life. Three people, three bikes, 200mi per day, and when we stopped in campgrounds, we drew people out of their motor homes to sit and talk with us.

Most were surprised that one of the riders had her own Harley—a 1978 FLH, if my failing memory serves me right, and all the retirees were amazed at how we rode in, pushed down the sidestand, and in 15min had tents up, a campfire painting us, and something cold in our hands. If you think life gets much better than sitting 'round a fire watching the flames reflect off your brand-new bike while you listened to the river run by—

Either cast wheels or spokes were available on the Fat Bob. Only the 80ci engine was available; the 74ci saw its last in 1979 on the FXEF; 1980 saw 4,773 built. This one belongs to Hank Ortega and has already been down to the frame and back up in restoration. He says it goes every day (remember, this is California, some of these shots were taken in November—it was 77 degrees).

The Fat Bob, with the 80ci engine, continued to be a popular bike. It was straight-forward and clean. Plus it carried enough fuel to really go somewhere and look good when you got there. This 1981 has the cast wheels instead of wires. *Chuck Gerwig*

The 1980 Wide Glide was one of the first factory customs, inspired by the countless modified Harley-Davidsons put together in shops and garages. The factory custom and retro bikes became the rock Harley-Davidson founded its phenomenal success of the late 1980s and 1990s.

The Super Glide and Fat Bob were dubbed as street machines with a touring bike's soul in this brochure. Both featured V-Fire II electronic ignition, 8:1 compression ratios, and single 38mm carburetors. The Superglide had the 74ci engine, while the Fat Bob sported the 80ci version. *Harley-Davidson*

you are reading the wrong book. The three of us rode four states, two national parks, and a multitude of KOAs while America grew older and the leaves began their journey from green to brown. Three Shovels, 3,100mi of mostly empty roads, and not so much as a broken fingernail. I still have the bike, I don't have the wife, but the memories of those days dodging falling leaves will stay with me forever. That's why my bike sits on a rug in a warm garage. It's given more to me than a lot of people…

The FXB Sturgis was a limited-edition bike, of which H-D records show 1,470 having been built.

The Name Game

For those of you trying to keep up with all the FX bike names, here we go. A Super Glide is a sorta stripped down Electra Glide with the XLH Sportster front end, the 3.5gal single tank, and the .07-candlepower Sportster headlight, guaranteed to make riding after dark an interesting experiment in how much you can't see. This includes that large animal 100ft in front of your 60mph bike. Yes, some things have to suffer for style. The FXS Low Rider is an FXE Super Glide with more goodies hung on it and a better suit of clothes (twin tanks). The FXEF Fat Bob is a Low Rider with slightly different bits. The FXB Sturgis is a Low Rider with belt drive and lots of black. And the Wide Glide is a Low Rider with bigger tanks, the FLH speedo in the center console (no tach), wide and tall front end, 21in front wheel, and forward controls.

All these motorcycles share a few things in common. The same 80ci Shovelhead engine powers them, except on the FXE, which all had the 74ci motor, and on the FXS-1200 models. The same basic frame (although some differ in rake), shocks, brakes, and lights grace all the bikes. Differences are in cosmetics and items like wheels, pipes, seats, and tanks. The Wide Glide probably departs more from the FX mold than does any of the other bikes.

FXE Super Glide, Fat Bob, and Low Rider

Just 10 full years after the first FX was introduced, the FX line had five distinct models and totally dominated H-D's sales. Total FX sales were 21,422 versus 11,992 for the FLH/FLT. The Super Glide remained the entry-level, low-dollar bike in the FX series. All Super Glides for 1980 were built with the 74ci engine. Sales for the model were up slightly, to 3,169. The FXS Low Rider was available with either motor, but the larger motor was the overwhelming choice of buyers: 5,922 FXS-80s were sold compared to just three FX-1200s. The FXEF Fat Bob was only offered with an 80ci motor. Most of the increase in sales for the other models came at the expense of Fat Bob sales. Just 4,773 were sold, down from 9,962 in 1979.

1981 FX Series

Production
  FXE Super Glide: 3,085
  FXWG Wide Glide: 5,166
  FXB Sturgis: 3,543
  FXS Low Rider: 7,223
  FXEF Fat Boy: 3,691

In 1981, H-D decided to quit competing with itself in the engine department. Most of the big bikes had been offered in 1979 and 1980 with both the 74ci and 80ci motors. Real performance differences, and that between the two engines were minimal; the 80-incher had a skosh more

The Low Rider was another factory custom, with the same basic dimensions and 80ci engine as the Fat Bob but were a lower, leaner look; highway pegs; and some additional pinstriping. Harley-Davidson complemented the Low Rider with a tarted-up Sportster dubbed the Roadster. *Harley-Davidson*

By the 1980s, Harley-Davidson had really pushed the edge on paint schemes. These are just two of the factory custom ideas for bikes. *Harley-Davidson*

Below
You even could find a bike already set up with flames on the tank, if that was your desire. In 1980, Harley-Davidson introduced the FXWG Wide Glide. What helped set it apart were the wide, extended forks holding a 21in spoked wheel, black tank with red and yellow flames, and a 16in rear spoked wheel under a bobbed fender that swoops up at the rear and carries the taillight mounted under the valence. Forward-placed controls (not highway pegs) came standard. This lets you ride in the wind with your arms in the air and butt firmly planted in the low seat. Image? You want image? This bike had it in spades (and flames). *Harley-Davidson*

torque to flog the iron down the road was about all. Even so, the 80-incher was priced slightly higher than the 74—must've cost more to make bigger holes in the cylinders?

Come 1981—no more problem—no more 74. From then until now, the only engine size available in the FX- and FL-series bikes was the 80ci, be it Shovelhead or Evolution. And yes, I've heard, you know a guy who has a friend who knows a dude with a 1981 FLH resting in his well-locked garage in another state with a 74ci engine in it. It's a leftover that H-D put together in the few first 1981 bikes. Well, perhaps, but don't try to win much money at the bar over it. Late 1980 with a 74—sure. Leftover 1980 with 74—OK (H-D didn't always sell everything it made each year, believe it or not!). But a 1981 with a 74, well...

FXE Super Glide

For the first time, the FXE came with an 80ci motor (probably only because the 74ci was no longer made). The kickstarter disappeared. Still, the entry-level big bike, its sales decreased slightly, to 3,085.

FXWG Wide Glide

For 1981, the Wide Glide was little changed, except that the flame paint job was joined by a metallic black scheme with gold pinstripes. Sales declined by about 900 units, to 5,166.

FXB Sturgis

The Sturgis was also updated only slightly. The most important change was from belt primary back to double-roller chain. The most visible change was from flat drag bars to chrome Buckhorn bars. For 1981, the Sturgis was no longer a limited edition, and sales more than doubled, to 3,543.

FXS Low Rider and FXEF Fat Bob

Along with all the others, these models got the new V-Fire II electronic ignition. The Low Rider was the sales star of 1981; sales increased by more than 1,200 units, to 7,223. Fat Bob sales continued their decline, to 3,691 for 1981, so the model was dropped at the end of the year.

1982 FX Series

Production
  FXE Super Glide: 1,617
  FXS Low Rider: 1,816
  FXB Sturgis: 1,833
  FXWG Wide Glide: 2,348

The FX-series lineup was pared to four for 1982 because the FXEF Fat Bob had been dropped. Changes to all rigid-mounted-engine FX bikes were nominal, but the new rubber-mounted FXR series made its debut (see next chapter). The FXB Sturgis got gold cast wheels and black paint with gold pinstripes on the fenders and tank. New plastic switch housings appeared on all FX bikes this year.

Sales for the whole rigid-mounted-engine FX series declined alarmingly because of recession, increased competition from the Japanese, and introduction of the rubber-mounted FXR and FXRS: 1,617 FXE Super Glides, 1,816 FXS Low Riders, 1,833 FXB Sturgises, and 2,348 FXWG Wide Glides were sold, a minor fraction of what

The FXB Sturgis was the first production bike with twin belt drive—primary and rear. The transmission case had to be altered to clear the wider rear belt, and the gear ratios were higher. The primary belt reverted to chain in the 1981 model year. Staggered dual pipes let through the Harley sound. And boy, was it black! Tanks, cases, cylinders, heads, rocker boxes, air cleaner, primary—even the horn was black. It sold 1,470 in 1980; 3,543 in 1981; and 1,833 in 1982, its last year of production. *Harley-Davidson*

The tachometer on this 1980 Sturgis is red-lined at 5300rpm. The speedometer reads to 150mph. The bike would just break the century mark with a stiff tail wind; the top third of the speedometer was only for show.

Tariff to the Rescue

Something else happened along about the start of the 1980s—bike sales went down the toilet. Motorcycle sales for bikes over 650cc dropped by 35,000 unit, between 1981 and 1982. Harley definitely felt the squeeze when that transpired. People had to be laid off, production backed down, and on-hand inventories were reduced. The Japanese, however, still continued to fill the pipeline with low-cost big bikes until they ran out of warehouse space. Big Japanese motorcycle dealers were selling bikes for $40 over cost, paying their salesmen $15 per bike (salesmen were standing in line for the job: $15 per bike x 5 bikes per day = almost enough money to support a 23-year-old man) and hoping to make their money on dealer holdbacks and rebates. A 1982 Suzuki could be bought for less than $3,500, while H-D had their FXRS priced almost double that figure.

In September 1982, H-D petitioned the International Trade Commission for protection in the way of a tariff on Japanese manufacturers, who H-D accused of dumping bikes here for prices not only less than they could be purchased in other countries, but also less than they cost to build. Thousands of unsold Japanese bikes had built up in dealers' inventories. This accounted for the strange practice of selling hoards of new 1982–85 bikes alongside the identical 1986 models in a lot of Honda, Suzuki, Kawasaki, and Yamaha shops. This also contributed to the sudden death of a lot of dealers during 1986 and 1987 when the market became saturated with Japanese bikes, and garages all over this country were full of 1000cc, 100hp bikes with less than 2,000mi on them. At one point large dealers were selling bikes cheaper than the smaller dealers could buy them from the factory. That most of those dealers are but a dim memory today doesn't do much for the people put out of business when the market collapsed and sales of new units dropped over 50 percent.

On April 1, 1983, President Reagan signed into law a tariff on all Japanese motorcycles above 700cc. The tariff was for five years, slowly declining from 45 percent to 10 percent and ending in April 1988. The Japanese protested, but there was nothing they could do about it other than cut back on their production of large bikes. This gave H-D the breathing room to build back up. Now the only American motorcycle company left sits at the top of the heap, totally dominating all sales for bikes above 750cc. When you see a big bike coming down the road, the odds are it's a Harley.

---

each model had sold at its peak. At the end of the year, the FXS Low Rider and FXB Sturgis were discontinued.

1983 FX Series

Production
FXE Super Glide: 1,215
FXWG Wide Glide: 2,873
FXSB Low Rider: 3,277
FXDG Disc Glide: 810

FXSB Low Rider

A new Low Rider was cataloged for 1983: the FXSB Low Rider. Not much was really new on the FXSB, however. It was really just the old FXB Low Rider with the rear belt drive of the FXB Sturgis and replaced both those models for 1983. Proving that many riders thought the belt drive a desirable feature, the new model was the top seller of the FX lineup, at 3,277 units.

FXDG Disc Glide

The Disc Glide was also new for 1983, but it was just a limited-edition Wide Glide with a solid aluminum disc wheel at the rear, a set of black shorty duals, and the belt final drive from the Sturgis. Only 810 Disc Glides were built.

FXE Super Glide and FXWG Wide Glide

Harley engineers were hard at work developing the next-generation engine and new models, so the FXE Super Glide and FXWG Wide Glide models were essentially carryovers from 1982. Sales of the Wide Glide rose by about 500, to 2,873, while sales for the FXE Super Glide fell by about the same amount, to 1,215.

The 1982 FXRS was introduced at York, Pennsylvania, in June of 1981. It had a totally new frame with FLT-type elastomer motor mounts. The seat flipped up to show the battery and oil tank within easy reach. The 80ci motor fed from a new 4.2gal tank with filler hole and fuel gauge in the center. The tach and speedo were borrowed from the Sportster and rode on the bars. Wheels on the FXRS were cast; a cheaper version, the FXR, had wires and came without the padded sissy bar or highway pegs of the upscale bike. This picture shows a pre-production FXRS wearing wire wheels, but all the production models had cast, ten-spoke wheels.
Harley-Davidson

1984 FX Series

Harley-Davidson does not separate models and production between Shovelhead bikes and Evolution bikes in their published production figures. As noted in chapter one, they do, however, list two separate sets of figures for most models (and sometimes more), so I'll go out on the proverbial limb of speculation again and assume that the first set is for Shovelhead-powered bikes, and the second set is for Evo-powered machines. If so, then H-D built 942 Shovelhead FXSB Low Riders (versus 1,935 Evo) and two Shovelhead FXWG Wide Glides (versus 2,225 Evo) in 1984. Figures for the FXE Super Glide are too confusing to decipher because they include listings for both single-tank and twin-tank models—with two sets of figures for each! Finally, two figures are shown for the completely new model, the FXST Softail, suggesting that 3,303 Softails were built with the Shovelhead motor before the final 2,110 were built with the Evolution motor (some sources insist that all 1984 Softails were powered by Evo motors, but sightings at the time and these figures hint that some were built with Shovelhead motors). The FXST Softail is basically a Wide Glide with a new frame incorporating a new suspension that hid the shock absorbers underneath the engine, giving the bike the look of a hardtail bike.

Having progressed from the kickstart-only 1971 FX to the electric-start, rubber-mounted engine FXRS, the stage was set for the future—a new, state-of-the-art, V2 engine and new models taking advantage of the Softail, culminating in the FXSTSB Bad Boy, ultimate in the "retro" look—springer front end, a rigid-appearing frame, and a cloisonné tank emblem, all hinting at the past, while the ultra-reliable Evo motor insures a trouble-free future.

Park a 1995 Dyna Low Rider next to a 1972 FX Super Glide and the similarities become readily apparent. Chart the changes over the years and see how Harley-Davidson, the company, grew with Harley-Davidson, the motorcycle. The Evolution truly evolved from the Shovelhead.

1982—84 FXR Series

Production
  FXR: 3,065
  FXRS: 3,190

Now that Harley-Davidson had successfully mounted the FLT's engine in rubber and mated it to a five-speed transmission, the company decided to bring out FX-series machines with the same type of mounts and the five-speed. The FLT frame without fairing looked too strange to be used on the FX, so an entirely new frame had to be designed. Harley fired up the computer (no, H-D engineers didn't still use beads sliding on strings) and came up with a frame that both looked good when exposed and enabled the engine to be mounted in isolastic mounts. A Sportster-type front fork and headlight assembly was fitted to the new frame, and the bike was called the FXR and accompanied by the more upscale FXRS.

More than just the frame was new, however. The oil tank was mounted in front of the battery under a flip-up seat. The new 4.2gal fuel tank filled through a single hole in the console on the tank's top, and a fuel gauge mounted forward of the filler.

Originally, the name Super Glide II was hung on the bike, but that lasted only a short time. Other names were tried for a while, among them Sport Glide, Low Glide, and the nickname "Rubber Glide." None of them seemed to take hold, and I mostly just called mine an FXRS.

The only similarities between this bike and all the FXs that had gone before it was the name on the tank. It came with a five-speed transmission hooked up to a Shovelhead engine with many new internal changes. The oil piping system was updated with a new oil-control package. New lines helped return oil from the heads to the crankcase instead of it building up in the heads and being forced past the valve guides. Also, a new valve guide and seal package was part of the improvements. Compression dropped to the 7.4:1 level, making the bike much happier on pump gas. Performance didn't seem to suffer much, if at all, with the 0.6 reduction in the compression ratio, as it was as fast as all the other FX series.

The FXR's frame was a great deal stiffer in torsion than the older tubes used on the FX. This meant that the bike resisted flex much better than the others, making for improved handling in the twisties. The shocks were moved back on the frame, and their lower attachment point was at the end of the swingarm instead of in the middle as before. This gave the swingarm more support and less flex out at the end where the rear axle was mounted. In turn this made for less movement of the rear wheel around the swingarm. If you look at the two in a comparison shot, you can see how the old swingarm was able to apply more force to the mid-mounted shock than the new FXR swingarm with the shock right above the centerline of the wheel.

The FXR and FLT series were H-D's first serious attempts at vibration control. The engines still shook all the time, only the vibration didn't pass to the rider. Well, that's not quite true either. Below

By suspending the engine in rubber mounts, vibration wasn't allowed to pass through to the rider. The engine in the rigid-mount bikes would try to slide your feet off the pegs or boards above 3500rpm, while the rubber-mount FXRS and FLT smoothed out enough to make long distance a pleasure. If you remove the engine from a Rubber Glide, be careful with the mounting system. Go by the book as far as setup, or the mounts may not function correctly.

On my bike, the exhaust manifold bolts gave me so much trouble that when the unleaded gas conversion was done, I had the exhaust ports re-contoured to take three bolt flanges, as shown in this picture.

2000rpm, the mounts didn't come into effect, so the bike would shake clean out to the end of the bars, and the front wheel would bounce in time with the engine while you were stopped at lights. Brakes on, it vibrated one way. Brakes off, another. It was amusing to watch, and my brother, mounted on a Japanese V-twin, got a kick out of it. He couldn't see how anything built in the late twentieth century could run so rough. He figured that my H-D would be worn out and worthless after about 10,000mi. Fifteen years later, his 1981 Japanese twin is worth maybe $600, while the FXRS will bring over $8,500.

Once the clutch engages and the tach passes 2000rpm, the rubber mounts come into play. They are tuned to absorb almost all of the vibration above this point. Some still reaches your hands, but only enough to let you know you're on a motorcycle, without putting your arms to sleep.

My 1982 FXRS had somewhat of an interesting event connected with the new oil-control sys-

Just to show how far an owner will take a bike, this is a 1982 FXR with a few modifications. *Jeff Hackett*

This customized 1982 FXR is far from stock, but a better representation of the Shovelhead-powered Harley-Davidson models seen on the streets. Very few of these models remained in factory condition for long. Exhaust pipes, air-cleaner covers, carburetors, and intake manifolds are all likely candidates to be replaced with aftermarket parts. *Jeff Hackett*

tem. In October 1993 I took it into the local dealer to have the heads pulled and the exhaust ports updated with the three-bolt modification, along with having the unleaded gas conversion done at the same time. The lead mechanic noticed something strange about the front head once it was in his hands. One of the oil-return passages hadn't been drilled when the bike was built. Evidently, whoever had been responsible for punching holes either couldn't count or was asleep when my heads came by.

The shop told me about the problem and also mentioned they had called H-D and informed them about the missing hole. This was in 1993 and the bike was built in November of 1981.

Harley said, "Yeah, go ahead and take care of the problem and submit a warranty form." The shop repeated to them the year of the bike, thinking they hadn't heard right the first time and thought the shop said 1992 instead of 1982. Long pause on the other end, until the factory rep came back and said do it anyway.

"It wasn't right from the factory, so we'll stand behind our product and fix it for the customer."

You might think because I write Harley books that this was a favor, but rest assured, the shop didn't know I was a writer, and the factory didn't know my name, which wouldn't have made any difference at all, as I can well attest. They were just standing behind their product. Wonder if any other company, motorcycle or other, would do that. It went a long way toward making believers out of myself and people I've told about it.

Performance benefited from all the improvements. The bike would never be accused of being a canyon terror, but it held its own with anything other than the plastic rockets, and would leave all the other Harleys for dead on a winding road. It wasn't exactly a stone in a straight line, either. Again I have the road rats at *Cycle World* to thank for the figures. They definitely will wring more performance out of a bike than 99.999 percent of the rest of us. They thrashed an FXRS through the quarter-mile in December 1981. Speed was 91mph, elapsed time was 14.26sec. It ran out of oomph at 105mph, as I can testify. There was more left on the tach; the engine just didn't want to pull any harder.

FXRS

The FXRS came with a few more goodies than the FXR. The engine was painted black, and the fins were polished. It had a sissy bar with back pad factory installed and a couple of other minor cosmetic changes, including two-tone paint and highway pegs. The crankcases (cone case left bare aluminum), cylinders, heads, air box, and exhaust crossover were blacked-out. The wheels were cast, as opposed to wires on the FXR. The seat lifted up to reveal the oil tank and battery as on the FXR. Now adding water to the battery or checking oil became a minor chore, so it got done more often, adding to the bike's reliability.

Due to my job taking me all over the world (literally) during the first few years I owned the bike, I didn't get a chance to put more than 5,000mi on it before 1989. It still had the original battery up till then, and it always lit off on the first compression stroke. However, after it sat unattended for six months in 1990, it finally wouldn't start, and I had to buy a new battery. Poor quality if you ask me. Only eight years of neglect, and the damned battery wouldn't hold a charge. The replacement battery lasted until 1993, and now I'm on my third—none of which were H-D parts.

Touring on the FXRS is a pleasant experience for a bike not intended as a real long-distance hauler. It is comfortable running down the road between 75 and 85mph, though, and 400mi days are actually not bad. I did cheat a bit and install a windshield, which aids immeasurably as my body approaches the 50-year mark. The "wind in the face for hours" stuff is beginning to tell on me. Years back, I rode 1,000mi rallies without a care—now a little six-hour chug from San Jose to Los Angeles has me looking for the Tanqueray and a soft bed.

The bike's definitely up to long hauls, even if I'm not. It consistently returns over 45mpg and uses little oil between changes. Having a set of highway pegs along with the standard ones makes moving around on the bike much easier.

One problem I've encountered of late has to do with the instruments, particularly the tach. About 90 percent of my riding is done with the engine turning below 3000rpm. Now that the bike has a few years on it, the tach has grown so accustomed to running below 3,000 that the needle sticks briefly when I run the engine past that point. The tach drive is totally electrical, eliminating a possible dry cable. I think the lubricant in the bushings inside the gauge has become sticky with age and lack of use, perhaps a cleanup and re-oiling would take care of the problem. I'm a little reluctant to open them up for fear of finding a broken something, because parts for these Japanese gauges are totally unavailable. The speedometer is also beginning to show a slight bit of the same thing. I pulled and cleaned the cable, oiled it with a good cable lube and checked for kinks, but it still sticks—same bushings inside?

I wasn't the only one who jumped on one of the new FXRs. Harley sold 3,065 of the FXR model and 3,190 of the FXRS model, meaning that each of the new models outsold any of the solid-mounted FX models.

1983 FXR Series

Production
 FXR: 1,129
 FXRS: 1,413
 FXRT Sport Glide: 1,485

FXRT

The FXRT Sport Glide was introduced in late 1982 as a 1983 model. It was really just an FXRS with the addition of a frame-mounted fairing, hard saddlebags, and a few other goodies. It had a hard time gaining acceptance with the tradition-

oriented Harley buyers due to its nontraditional look. It had all the usual H-D fixtures, but it was covered with a different-appearing fairing. Called the Sport Glide, it was aimed at the sport-touring market shared by BMW and others.

Rolling down the road on the FXRT was actually quite comfortable. The FXRT's frame-mounted fairing, which showed some wind-tunnel influence, is quite similar to the one on the 1980 Tour Glide. The FXRT was a touring Harley for those who spent most of their time running on two-lane roads. The 1984 FXRP police bike, beloved steed of the California Highway Patrol (CHP), drew a lot of its styling from the FXRT. The one CHP I did see on a FXRP said it was a lot more comfortable than the four-cylinder 1000cc Kawasaki police bikes, but didn't have quite the point and squirt of the Japanese bike. Harley made a good deal with the CHP, and they continued riding Harleys until the price difference got too great and they went back to the Japanese bikes.

The Tour Glide will make a good touring bike for those of you who are looking for something lighter than an Electra Glide for long, state-crossing rides. It also shouldn't set you back as much as some of the other FXR series, due to its different styling and general lack of acceptance on the market. Still, it's a Harley, with rubber engine mounts and, in addition, sports a fairly simple pressurized anti-dive front fork. When the front brakes are applied, an electric valve closes between an air tank and the fork tubes, lessening the total volume of air in the system. When the front end tries to dive, it has to work against the increased pressure in the tubes and that slows down the rate of travel, or dive. Release the brake lever, the valve opens and the front end goes back to a soft ride—neat and simple. The rear shocks were also air-assisted.

The FXRT also came with an enclosed chain, just like the larger FLT series, so that'll help keep the gunk off you on long rides. The hard saddlebags have removable liners, semi-waterproof and easily carried into a motel room. Good way to pack ice and liquid refreshment, too.

A solo rider, looking for a Harley to go places, probably could make a pretty decent deal on a

The all-black 1981 FXB Sturgis shows its low, lean look. *Doug Mitchel*

THE 1982—84 FX SERIES 375

low mileage FXRT and not lose a penny in depreciation for as long as he, or she, kept the bike. I'd probably buy one for my wife, but since the only way I can communicate with her is through her divorce attorney, I'll skip it for now.

FXR and FXRS

In only their second year of production, sales of the FXR and FXRS each fell by 50 percent or more, to 1,129 for the FXR and to 1,413 for the FXRS. At the end of the year, the plain FXR was dropped from the lineup. The new FXRT did not generate the interest on the showroom floor that H-D had hoped for. By the end of the year, only 1,485 had been sold. Considering that the sales of the Low Rider improved and the Wide Glide climbed 525 units over the year before, it was clear that the customer was voting with his dollars for the chopper look. Overall sales of the FX series for 1983 were down 13 percent, possibly accounting for some of the decline in FXR sales.

1984 FXR Series

The FXR lineup for 1984 included only the FXRS and the FXRT, both of which may have been built in limited numbers with the Shovelhead motor for 1984, before production switched entirely to bikes with the new Evolution motor.

The major change to the series, besides the new motor, was the lowering of the FXRS and naming it the Low Glide. In an effort to reduce the cost of production and lower seat height, H-D gave the FXRS shorter shocks and forks with stiffer springs and eliminated the right front brake disc. While these mods made the FXRS more like a conventional Harley, and saved the company some money, they also ruined the bike's excellent ride and completely changed its sporting nature. Did most Harley riders care? Probably not, because the bike stayed that way in following years, and sales increased, but it is interesting to note that the longer suspenders and extra disc were again available starting in 1985 on the FXRS-Sport. Maybe some riders did care after all.

Harley-Davidson does not separate models and production between Shovelhead bikes and Evolution bikes in their published production figures. As said before, they do, however, list two separate sets of figures for each model, so I'll go out on that limb one final time and assume that the first set is for Shovelhead-powered bikes, and the second set is for Evo-powered machines. If so, then H-D built 1,079 of the Shovelhead FXRS (versus 1,731 Evo) and 834 of the Shovelhead FXRT (versus 1,196 Evo) in 1984. In addition, a limited edition FXRDG and FXRSDG Disc Glides were built, and all are thought to be Evo-powered, but a few may have been assembled with the Evo motor.

Cross-Country Riding

From 1966 to the advent of the Honda Gold Wing, nothing existed other than the big Harleys when it came to cross-country touring. A lot of other bikes could be set up for long-distance riding by the addition of saddlebags, fairings, and the like. Some could haul two people in relative comfort, but none could equal the feeling of a big Harley. Motorcycling in this country always has been much more than a way to cover distance. Americans never have had to face extremely high gas prices and prohibitive taxes on engine size that most of the rest of the world has seen. In other countries, the motorcycle is a cheap necessary mode of transportation for a lot of families.

I was in China in the 1980s, and I got to learn a little about the people during a one-month vacation throughout the country along with seven other riders on large motorcycles. The amount of attention we garnered taught me what it must be like to be a movie star or political leader. People would gather around at every stop and just stare at us. My wife had long blond hair—very unknown in the Guangdong Province on the South China Sea. Women would come up to her and run their fingers across her hair to see if the color was painted on or real.

Bicycles are the main mode of transportation for millions upon millions of people. Riding a motorcycle is a real improvement in social status. It was not uncommon to see a father, his wife, two kids, and of course a cargo weighing over 50kg traveling down the streets of Shanghai on a 90cc bike. Sometimes even a pig or two got tucked in baskets tied to the front forks. Things are improving in China to the point where automakers will be introducing a 1300cc car in the near future, and more and more Toyotas and Nissans can be found fighting for space with the diesel taxis, but a family of four on a 125cc motorcycle will be very

For 1983, Harley came out with the FXRT Sport Glide. It was the FXR with a new frame-mounted fairing and hard saddlebags. The chain ran fully enclosed for extended life, and it had an anti-dive system incorporated in the front forks. The rear shocks had air assist. This bike was intended to compete with other sport tourers of the day from Europe and Japan. It met a lot of sales resistance from traditionalists but proved to be a good touring machine with a sporting bent. Good bike or no, it only lasted until 1987. *Harley-Davidson*

common for the foreseeable future.

In America, if we want to cover distances, we take a car. Nowhere else has cheap four-wheeled transportation been so readily available. Some sociologists state that the car was instrumental in freeing American youth and starting the migration from farms to urban life. Motorcycles have always been perceived as a statement, as opposed to necessary transportation, in this country. From the earliest board-track racing eighty years ago to the current retro bikes, Harley has been the maximum macho statement. Not many other types of hobbies are tattooed on peoples arms like Harley-Davidson. What's the possibility of a golf pro with "Tru-Flite" adorning a bicep?

People who ride Harleys, ride Harleys. If they could have a faster, smoother, cheaper bike, they'd still buy a Harley. A lot of people want the big bad image but use a Japanese cruiser to do it. The 20-year Harley owners would rather have an H-D in a box than a Honda Shadow in the garage. The past few years' reduced sales of Honda Gold Wings and Yamaha Ventures have left H-D virtually owning the big-bike market. Sales of BMW big bikes have increased tremendously, but the two manufacturers sell to different markets.

But people don't want a bike that's cantankerous, leaks, or breaks. The image of bikers with their cigarettes rolled up in T-shirt sleeves has given way to people of both sexes in designer clothes riding

The Shovelhead Years

Dave St. Onge is the sales manager for San Jose, Harley-Davidson in San Jose California. He started getting his hands greasy back in 1977 during the Shovelhead heyday. He worked everywhere from parts nugget up to service manager for two shops and was part owner of a Harley repair shop in Santa Cruz, California, for a number of years.

"When I first became interested in Harleys, 1977 and '78, they didn't have the screaming demand that they have enjoyed for the past decade. The new 1978 models came out in September and we hung through winter selling a few bikes to die-hard owners and other people with no better sense than to ride off on a new bike when the thermometer read below 30deg.

"Come the spring and we could be assured of a goodly stock of bikes sitting on the showroom floor. The rush to buy hit us around April 1, cleaning out 50 to 70 bikes in a hurry, but prior to spring, a potential customer had his pick of anything in just about any color. Our allotment never varied much from 80 bikes per year. The big shops, like Dudley Perkins, in San Francisco, usually saw anywhere from 150 to 175 per year; however, the smaller shops were pretty much in the same league as us.

"The way dealers qualified for bikes was, and is, kind of strange. If you're not in the new-vehicle business, you might not know that current year's allocations were based on the number of bikes sold the years before. Harley has a dealer's show once a year, around January, usually, where all the dealers from the U.S. and other countries get together for a few days of new-model introductions, renewing old acquaintances, spending money at the bar, and, most importantly, sitting down with the district rep and figuring out what bikes would be ordered for the following year.

"These days, it's pretty much take what you get, in the way of a standardized package—so many FLs, so many Dyna Glides, so many Sportys—all based on past sales performance. If the factory-can build a few extra bikes, you might get the option of picking up two or three more during the year, but that's all. Say the factory builds what they call a "Police Officer's Special," not a police bike, but a bike that they prefer be owned by a current or retired peace officer. It will have a different color combination, and that's about all. The dealership might get lucky and see three—all pre-sold.

"This isn't quite how it worked in the Shovelhead era. Sometimes, the next year's model bikes arrived in their crates while you were still trying to sell the current models sitting on the showroom floor. Just like everything else on earth, H-D responds to the law of supply and demand. New models sitting in your back room? Time to drop the price on the showroom units and move them out.

"Most of the dealers didn't own all their bikes, but purchased them through a "flooring" plan. Harley built the bikes and sent them to the dealers as they rolled off the assembly lines throughout the year. A finance company, like ITT Financial, actually owned the paper on the bikes and charged something in the neighborhood of one percent per month on the unpaid balance. The payback price to the flooring company sometimes dropped as the new model year approached. So a bike that had a sticker price of $6,995 in 1981 might have a flooring cost of $5,456 when it first hits your dealership. As the bike ages, you pay the flooring per month to keep it, making for a large motivation for the dealer to sell what's on the floor, rather than special order something almost identical to an existing bike.

"When the time nears for new-model intro, usually H-D would send you a modified flooring sheet. For instance, using the dealer cost figure of $5,456, after the bike has sat on the rug from November of the preceding year, H-D might send out a modified price of $5,195. This allowed you to reduce the price of your 1982 FXRS by $300 before the 1983 models came out, priced $250 higher. From 1978 to 1986, when the Evo really started taking off, it wasn't unusual at all to see 30 or more bikes sitting on the showroom floor, identical paint and options, only difference being model year. I saw times when two identical bikes, one year apart, sat on the floor, separated by $500.

"The Shovel usually could be counted on to return for at least two or three warranty problems. Sometimes in the late 1970s and early 1980s when AMF was pushing product out the door and letting the customer do the final engineering, it was not unusual to see an FXE return in 450mi with engine problems. At one point, I heard H-D was spending more money on bring-backs than they were making on the new bikes.

"Back when all the bikes came with kickstarters, most of the buyers were die-hard, bugs in the teeth, squashed 50-mission-cap-type riders; they were willing to put up with the Shovel's problems because everything on the road had problems. Triumphs had weird electrics, BSAs shook themselves to death, and Honda had just moved up from 250 and 305cc bikes to a big black 450 in 1966, but the Japanese weren't to be worried about, because all they knew was how to build little bikes. So an FLH vibrated—so what; they all vibrated. If you wanted smooth—take the train. You rode a motorcycle—particularly a Harley—you better be ready to put up with a little discomfort.

"Also, you better be able to put up with working on your bike all the time. A lot of early riders thought nothing of riding through the summer with nothing more than an oil change, a set of plugs, a flat tire, and maybe a clutch cable snapping, or pulling the chain and boiling it in oil (true!), and then putting the bike up in the winter months for a rebuild. Sometimes the rebuild went all the way down to splitting the cases, sometimes it was just a clean-up pass through the cylinders with a hone and a set of new rings, but it was always something.

"Things got better when H-D bought itself out. I saw a lot of the late-production Shovels—say early 1980s—come through my shop with high mileage on them, 40,000 wasn't unusual, without ever having the heads off. Although when the country went to unleaded gas, it raised hell with the valves in the Shovels, as they relied on the lead to help lubricate the valve stem. Most of the Shovels on the road today have had the unleaded conversion, or the owner has resorted to some pretty trick things like aviation gas, aniline oil, or other additives to keep the valves from wearing prematurely.

"The last years of the Shovel, it actually quit going through oil so rapidly. Today an owner would hit the roof if an engine went through a quart of oil every 600mi (plus the EPA wouldn't let the vehicle be sold). In 1966, it wasn't unusual to "lose" a quart every 450–500mi. Even in 1979, getting 670mi to a quart was considered OK.

"In 1981, an oil-control package cleaned up the bikes considerably. Better seals, closer tolerances, and an oil-return line from the heads help double oil mileage.

"Today, not many Shovelheads come through the dealership. After all, it's been 11 years since the last one went out a dealer's door. The ones we do see run in two very distinct categories. Either they are as close to stock and perfect as the owners and their wallets can make them, or they are on their sixth through fifteenth owners and look like they have been thoroughly used and abused. Luckily some owners have caught on to the fact that a Harley doesn't get worth less as it ages, so long as it is kept in reasonable shape. A good Shovel might not make you money, but it's the only bike that you can ride and enjoy for 10 years and still sell it for at least what you paid.

"In some cases, you will actually make money if you sit on the bike for a while. I just wish I had the money to buy some of the bikes that rolled through the shop over the past 15 years. There was actually times when a 1970s Shovel could be picked up for less than $4,000 with under 5,000mi on the clock. What do they call that—20-20 hindsight?"

The Harley Owner's Group

At about the same time H-D filed for the tariff against its Japanese competitors, it also instituted a number of programs aimed at improving their product and changing the company's image from outlaw bikers to wholesome sport riders. One of the greatest ideas to bring customers closer to the company was the formation of the Harley Owner's Group (HOG). More mileage has been made with the use of this one word than any other in H-D's inventory of trademarked logos.

If you are a member of HOG, you know what's available through the largest factory supported club in the world. If you aren't a member, join. My last *Hog Tales*, the club magazine, has more rallies and events going on than you could attend if you had twice as much money and only worked half the year. This year, alone, there are events in places like Australia, where the sixth annual Australian HOG rally is taking place in Queensland, to the fifth annual European rally in Spain. These rallies and the ones in the United States have become so popular that they are usually sold out well in advance and crowds can easily run to 50,000.

Also, if you want a chance to ride a particular model without having to buy it first, HOG holds demo rides all around the States, usually tied in with bike shows or races. A riding schedule can be found in their magazine. Be prepared for lots of people, though. The Laughlin Run, in Laughlin, Nevada, has grown to such a size that all hotel rooms and campsites are reserved at least six months in advance. The town, situated on the Colorado River where it splits Arizona and Nevada, turns into a motorcycle town for the three days of the run. For almost a week on either side of the run dates, motorcycles fill the surrounding areas to capacity. Last I heard, 1995 saw 55,000 people attending.

---

reliable, clean bikes. No one wants to have to heave on a kickstarter for 5min on a warm day in order to ride a bike. If the Shovelhead, with all its amenities, hadn't come along and paved the way for even better scooters, H-D might still be selling 6,000 FLHs per year to the same group of die-hard riders. In a very major way, the Shovelhead was instrumental in opening the sport of touring and big bikes to the world. Bikes had to change if motorcycling was to become widely accepted as a recreational sport.

People wanted an image, but they weren't willing to put up with what it took in the past to maintain that image. The old one-percenters (the one percent of riders who created 99 percent of the problems) became a thing of the past. We've been able to beat down the image of a big, dirty dude on a Harley scaring unmitigated hell out of citizens and causing daughters to be locked inside when he rolls into town.

The movie *The Wild One*, released in December 1953 and starring Marlon Brando and an actor, relatively unknown at the time, named Lee Marvin created an image that took decades to live down. Brando actually rode a Triumph throughout the whole movie—never a Harley. Lee Marvin and his boys rode the Harleys. Most of the cycle scenes were at the beginning of the movie. The balance of it was Brando wandering around in confusion trying to find himself. The movie was banned in England for years because of the image it portrayed.

The Wild One was somewhat based in fact. A gang, known as "The Booze Fighters," not the Hells Angels, rode into a sleepy Northern California town, Hollister, back on July 4, 1947, got drunk, fell off bikes, rode on the sidewalk, fell down some more, got their picture in *Life* magazine, and generally scared the hell out of the locals. No one died, got raped, got shot, or anything major, but it did set a precedent for years to come.

In the 1960s, I rode over a lot of the West Coast on my Panhead. After riding it stock for a few years, I changed over to the long-forks-and-black-paint chopper look. One day riding into Virginia City, Nevada, I was met by two shotgun-toting sheriffs at the city limits who told me I wasn't welcome in their town. I couldn't even ride through. I had to turn around and go back "where your kind of trash belongs." This was just me, nobody else; I had left all my napalm and machine guns at home, opting for a tent and sleeping bag instead. I had said exactly zero to the cops when they stopped me. I had short hair, a helmet, and was sober as a judge (wrong simile?); they just didn't like motorcycles, especially big, black Harley motorcycles. Perhaps if I'd been riding a Honda 250, painted light yellow, they wouldn't have been so scared of me.

Point being, we've come a long way on bikes, and it took a good one like the Shovelhead to begin the process.

The FXRS didn't change much in 1983. It still was the best-handling bike produced by Harley. Sales for the FXRS dropped to 1,413; the FXR sold 1,129. The rubber-mounted engine, high-speed handling capabilities, and superb brakes helped it keep up with the canyon runners, but buyers that wanted the Low Rider look and function came a distant second. *Harley-Davidson*

INDEX

AMF, 266, 268
Aunapa, Al, 62
Baruch, Bernard, 121
BMW, 170
British OHV models, 31
Chamberlain, Neville, 62
Child, Alfred Rich, 51
Chopper, 338
Chrome Group, 105
Chrome Plate Group, 24, 55
Chrome Plate Special, 67, 75
Churchill, Winston, 62, 87
Competition, 50, 62
Corrigan, Douglas "Wrong Way," 66
Crocker motorcycle, 30
Davidson, Sir Walter C., 104, 107
Davidson, William A., 55
Davidson, William G., 168
Davidson, William H., 55, 104
Deluxe Solo Group, 24, 67, 75, 89, 105
Eisenhower, Dwight D., 104
Experimental serial numbers, 17
Farm boys, 126
Ford, Henry, 14
Frame cracking, 45
Franco, Francisco, 21
Free, Rollie, 164, 180
Fukui, Genijiro, 51
Goering, Hermann, 115
Great Depression, 16, 20
Ham, Fred, 62, 87
Harley, William S., 13, 17, 30, 34, 107
Harley-Davidson Topper, 225
Harley Owner's Group, 383
Haynes, Chris, 35
Hindenburg, 53
Hitler, Adolph, 21, 62
Hughes, Howard, 66
Indian, 168
Iwo Jima, 113

Jameson, "Hap," 13
Knucklehead models
   1936, 24–51
   1937, 42–61
   1938, 67–73
   1939, 75–85
   1940, 89–98
   1941, 100–104
   1942, 107
   1943, 109
   1944, 111
   1945, 114
   1946, 116, 117
   1947, 122–128
   74-cubic inch Series, 101
Lewis, John L., 55
Lightning camshaft, 38
Line-boring numbers, 39
Linkert, 34, 94, 102, 103, 105, 293
Lyons, Gerry, 51
Panhead, 119, 128, 129, 253–257, 266, 274, 276
Panhead models
   1948, 143, 154–165
   1949, 168–178
   1950, 179–182
   1951, 147–151
   1952, 188–195
   1953, 195–197
   1954, 197–202
   1955, 202, 203
   1956, 206–208
   1957, 208, 209
   1958, 212–221
   1959, 222–224
   1960, 225, 226
   1961, 227–229
   1962, 229, 230
   1963, 231–236
   1964, 237–241
   1965, 244–252

Petrali, Joe, 64, 65, 164
Pilot production machines, 20
Preproduction machines, 17
Presley, Elvis, 206, 208, 212
Quirk, "Butch," 21, 50
Rikuo motorcycle, 26, 51
Roosevelt, Franklin D., 99, 100, 104, 107, 109
Ryan, Joe, 17
Sankyo, 15, 16, 51
Shovelhead, 254, 256, 271, 273, 277, 279, 337
   1966 engine, 287
   80ci engine, 320
   Buddy seat, 280
   Clutch mousetrap, 295
   Cone motor, 301
   Disc brake, 309
   Drive belts, 358
   External ignition timer, 300
   Fishtail mufflers, 293, 321
   Flex-pipe header covers, 300
   Foot clutches, 313
   Front drum brake, 309
   Generator, 300
   Kickstarter, 301
   King of the Road Package, 314
   Mechanical ignition, 324
   Metallic lining, 310
   Mousetrap, 291, 292
   Rear drum, 314
   Smog motors, 329
   Starter, 295
   Steel valve guides, 322
   Steel-bodied oil pump, 295
   Vibration control, 371
Shovelhead models
   70th Anniversary editions, 314
   75th Anniversary Edition Electra Glide, 322, 327

1965 FLH Electra Glide, 274
1966 Electra Glide, 277, 279, 290
1966 FL, 289
1966 FLH, 274, 280, 286, 290
1967 Electra Glide, 292
1967 FLH, 285, 292, 293, 296, 297
1968 Electra Glide, 294, 298
1968 FLH, 265, 299
1969 Electra Glide, 299, 306
1969 FLH, 301, 302
1970 Electra Glide, 300
1971 Electra Glide, 307
1971 FLH, 267, 307–309
1971 FX Super Glide, 346, 347
1971 FX-1200, 340
1971 Super Glide, 338, 341
1972 Electra Glide, 308
1972 FX Super Glide, 345
1973 Electra Glide, 314
1973 FX Super Glide, 345
1974 Electra Glide, 315
1974 FX, 348, 349
1975 Electra Glide, 315
1975 FLH, 314
1975 FX and FXE Super Glides, 348
1976 Electra Glide, 318
1976 FL-P, 316
1976 FLH, 268
1976 FX and FXE Super Glides, 348
1977 Electra Glide, 318
1977 FLH, 320, 321
1977 FX, 352
1977 Low Rider, 353
1977 Super Glides and Low Riders, 349
1978 Electra Glide, 320
1978 FL-P, 323
1978 Super Glides and Low Riders, 350
1979 Electra Glide, 328
1979 FLH, 268
1979 Low Rider, 357
1979 Super Glides, Low Riders, and Fat Bobs, 351
1980 Electra Glide and Tour Glide, 330
1980 Electra Glide sidecar, 326
1980 FLT Tour Glides, 269
1980 FXEF Fat Bob, 360, 361
1980 Sturgis, 368
1980 Wide Glide, 363
1981 Electra Glide and Tour Glide, 333
1981 FLHC, 268
1981 FX Series, 365
1981 Heritage, 333, 335
1982 Electra Glide and Tour Glide, 335
1982 FX Series, 367
1982 FXR, 374
1982 FXRS, 370
1982–84 FX Series, 370
1983 Electra Glide and Tour Guide, 336
1983 FX Series, 369
1983 FXR Series, 375
1984 Electra Glide and Tour Glide, 336
1984 FLHS, 337
1984 FX Series, 370
1984 FXR Series, 378
Fat Bob, 351, 359, 367
FLT Tour Glide, 328
FXB Sturgis, 356, 367, 368
FXDG Disc Glide, 369
FXE Super Glide, 346, 367, 369
FXRS, 375
FXRT Sport Glide, 375, 379
FXS Low Rider, 367
FXSB Low Rider, 369
FXWG Wide Glide, 351, 367, 369
Liberty Edition, 273, 317, 318, 348
Low Rider, 354, 365
Shriners, 181
Special Solo Group, 114, 122
Spirals, 105
Sport Solo Group, 89, 105
Sportster, 225
Standard Solo Group, 24, 55, 56, 75, 89
Stevens, Brooks, 142, 176
Sturgis, South Dakota, 230
Sucher, Harry, 51
Tappets, 30
Tariff, 183, 187, 369
Tillotson, 293
Tinoco, Robert, 75
Tojo, General Hideki, 100
Touring package, 299
Tour-Pak, 283, 327
Triumph, 170, 183, 225
Truman, Harry S., 109, 113, 121
Utility Group, 89
Utility Solo Group, 89, 114, 122
Vincent, 144, 155, 164, 170, 180, 205
Wild One, The, 121, 197
Yeager, Capt. Charles E., 121

Other MBI Publishing Company titles of interest:

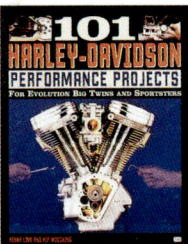

101 Harley-Davidson Performance Projects
ISBN: 0-7603-0370-3

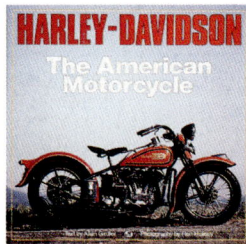

Harley-Davidson: The American Motorcycle
ISBN: 0-87938-603-7

The Harley-Davidson and Indian Wars
ISBN: 0-7603-1353-9

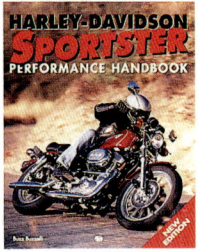

Harley-Davidson Sportster Performance Handbook
ISBN: 0-7603-0307-X

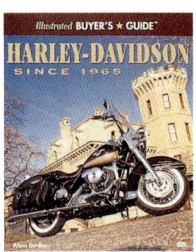

Illustrated Buyer's Guide: Harley-Davidson Since 1965
ISBN: 0-7603-0383-5

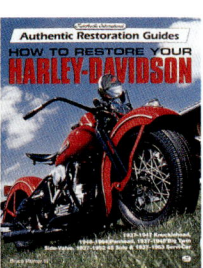

How to Restore Your Harley-Davidson
ISBN: 0-87938-934-6

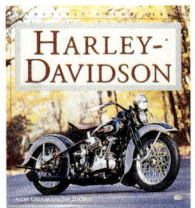

Harley-Davidson
ISBN: 0-7603-0799-7

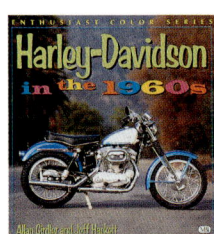

Harley-Davidson in the 1960s
ISBN: 0-7603-1058-0

Classic Harley-Davidson 1903-1941
ISBN: 0-7603-0557-9

Find us on the internet at www.motorbooks.com   1-800-826-6600